Professor Elizabeth Macpherson's Endorsement

Cristy Clark's groundbreaking book *Legal Geographies of Water* is a long-awaited and much-needed treatise on the relationship between law, people, and place, in the context of what is arguably the Earth's most precious resource, water. It is impossible to thoughtfully approach critical concerns or opportunities arising from the growing global water crisis without paying careful attention to the closely entangled and locally embedded relationships of communities and territories. Yet the fields, methods, and approaches of law and geography have rarely been consciously brought together in water research. Clark's new book confidently fills this gap, and I am equally confident that it will become the seminal analysis of legal geographies of water. This book is essential reading for teachers, scholars and practitioners of environmental and resources law, and the growing cohort of interdisciplinary and critical thinkers interested in the hydro-social world.

Legal Geographies of Water is sophisticated in its conceptual depth, exploring the 'pluriverse' of water realities to uncover more radical, more just, and more diverse, alternative water realities. In doing so, the book deepens our understanding of humanity's diverse relationships with water and the law and argues that addressing the water crisis requires a fundamental reconceptualisation of human-water relationships through legal frameworks that recognise water's material agency and relational nature. But this is not just 'pie in the sky' musing about an unreachable watery utopia. Clark uses several carefully constructed and materially distinct empirical case studies to explore her thoughts 'on the ground', which transcend space and time across four continents, and draw on her situated knowledge and reflexive positionality. This is difficult and determined research work, made possible by Clark's obviously strong, reciprocal, research collaborations throughout the globe, allowing her to so skilfully cross the staunch yet unnecessary boundaries of disciplines, jurisdictions, and ontologies. Through Clark's fluid research method, *Legal Geographies of Water* is a book that quenches the intellectual thirst, reflecting the very materiality of water, as something that flows, connects, and sustains us.

Dr Elizabeth Macpherson
Professor of Law
Rutherford Discovery Fellow
University of Canterbury, Aotearoa New Zealand

LEGAL GEOGRAPHIES OF WATER

This book deepens our understanding of humanity's diverse relationships with water and the law, providing a critical assessment of this relationship, and charting the course towards a more sustainable and just water future.

By using legal geography, this book pays particular attention to the place-based inter-relationships between water, people, and law (both formal and informal) and to the ways that law both constitutes and is constituted by the relationship between people and place. Starting in the 1980s, Chapter 2 investigates the early commodification of water through the liberalisation of rural water markets in Chile and the urban water supply and sanitation systems of England and Wales. Chapter 3 then examines the global expansion of neoliberal water governance in the 1990s, starting with donor-driven reforms in the global south and particularly Manila in the Philippines. Chapters 4 and 5 document both the grassroots response to these neoliberal water reforms and the inherent tensions in the attempts of the early 2000s to reconcile the recognition of a human right to water with the ongoing roll-out of market mechanisms, both in the domestic context of South Africa and within the United Nations human rights system. Moving forward again, Chapter 6 examines the recent intensification of neoliberal water governance through financialisation and considers its specific impacts in Detroit and Flint, Michigan. Chapter 7 then considers the renewed global emphasis on living waters and Indigenous ontologies of water by examining the new legislative arrangements for the Whanganui River in Aotearoa New Zealand. The book concludes in Chapter 8 by highlighting the stories of hope that can be found in many of the case studies explored in the book and in emerging examples from around the world.

This book is essential reading for students and scholars interested in water law, security, and justice from across a wide range of disciplines, including environmental studies, law, geography, human rights, and political ecology.

Cristy Clark is an Associate Professor in the Faculty of Business, Government and Law at the University of Canberra, Australia. Her research focuses on legal geography, the commons, and the intersection of human rights and the environment – particularly including water and climate justice. She is the co-author of *The Lawful Forest: A Critical History of Property, Protest and Spatial Justice* (2022).

Earthscan Water Text series

Flood Risk Management
Global Case Studies of Governance, Policy and Communities
Edited by Edmund Penning-Rowsell and Matilda Becker

Water Ethics
A Values Approach to Solving the Water Crisis
David Groenfeldt

The Water Footprint of Modern Consumer Society
Arjen Y. Hoekstra

Water Governance, Justice and the Right to Water
Edited by Farhana Sultana and Alex Loftus

Digital Water
Enabling a More Resilient, Secure and Equitable Water Future
William Sarni

Legal Geographies of Water
The Spaces, Places and Narratives of Human-Water Relations
Cristy Clark

For more information about this series, please visit: www.routledge.com/Earthscan-Water-Text/book-series/ECEWT

LEGAL GEOGRAPHIES OF WATER

The Spaces, Places and Narratives of Human-Water Relations

Cristy Clark

Routledge
Taylor & Francis Group
LONDON AND NEW YORK

earthscan
from Routledge

Designed cover image: iStock

First published 2025
by Routledge
4 Park Square, Milton Park, Abingdon, Oxon OX14 4RN

and by Routledge
605 Third Avenue, New York, NY 10158

Routledge is an imprint of the Taylor & Francis Group, an informa business

British Library Cataloguing-in-Publication Data
A catalogue record for this book is available from the British Library

ISBN: 978-1-032-22597-5 (hbk)
ISBN: 978-1-032-22596-8 (pbk)
ISBN: 978-1-003-27321-9 (ebk)

DOI: 10.4324/9781003273219

Typeset in Sabon
by codeMantra

CONTENTS

ACKNOWLEDGEMENTS

The research that informs this book spans two decades, and so I must acknowledge the assistance, contribution, and support of a long list of people. Alas, the length of this time span also means that I am guaranteed to accidentally leave someone out of this list – a horror that keeps me up at night and for which I can only profusely apologise for.

In drawing from the last two decades of my research, much of the research that informs this book was first published in my PhD and a range of other chapters and articles – although all of it has been reframed and updated for this new context. Nonethless, I want to acknowledge and thank my PhD supervisors, Andrea Durbach and Rosemary Rayfuse, my masters supervisor, Eileen Baldry, and all the editors and peer reviewers of those past publications, particularly including Alex Loftus and Farhana Sultana, for contributing to my thinking on these issues.

Relatedly, I have been absolutely blessed to work with many inspiring, kind, thoughtful, and incredibly talented collaborators, who have taught me so much. I am so grateful to each and every one of them for inspiring me. Thank you to Afshin Akhtar-Khavari, Jane Alver, Natalie Baird, Sam Bookman, Edward Challies, Julia Dehm, Nia Emmanouil, Karen Fisher, Beth Goldblatt, Elizabeth Hicks, Sarah Keenan, Rachel Killean, Sarah Laborde, Ron Levy, Elizabeth Macpherson, Rahkel Mercy, Paul Mitchell, Katie O'Bryan, Erin O'Donnell, John Page, Kavindra Paranage, Alessandro Pelizzon, Anne Poelina Martuwarra RiverofLife, Marc Tadaki, Hayden Turoa, and Julian Yates. I am particularly grateful to John for introducing me to legal geography and for being such a generous and inspiring co-author on our last book project (and many other publications), although this has been a double-edged sword because it made this solo project feel so much harder by comparison!

I also owe my particular interest in rivers to Alex, John, and Nia, and will never forget the joy of our collaborative project in the Byron Hinterlands. Relatedly, I learned so much from a long research collaboration with the Martuwarra, and am grateful to everyone in that project, but particularly to Anne and the Martuwarra for opening my world to the pluriverse. To Beth and Erin, thank you for being such great co-authors and friends. It never feels like work to write with you. Finally, I must single out Liz for being such an amazing collaborator, sounding board, and source of friendship and support. You are incredible.

Further thanks and acknowledgement go to the many people who supported my fieldwork through participating in an interview, connecting me to others, hosting me, and/or providing me with invaluable advice. For this support in South Africa (way back in 2006), I want to thank Patrick Bond, Jackie Dugard, Sandra Liebenberg, Tshepo Madlingozi, Jennifer Makoatsane, Dale McKinley, Paul Mitchell, Richard (Bricks) Mokolo, Gladys Mokolo, Sarrafina Morsopa, Mike Muller, Palesa, Silumko Radebe, and Jabulani Vincent. Thank you particularly to Jackie for all of your assistance, to Paul for accompanying me, to Bricks for taking us out to Orange Farm, and to Jennifer for hosting us in your home. For assistance in the Phillippines, my thanks go to Macra Cruz, Jude Esguerra, Mai Flor, Olim Gusi, Mary Ann Manahan, Bubut Palattao, a range of residents of informal settlements, and several senior officers at Manila Water and Maynilad. Enormous thanks to my lovely hosts at Miriam College. For support in the USA, I thank Nancy Burgher, Teresa Farley, Noah Hall, Peter Hammer, Rebecca Hardin, Leana Hosea, Alice Jennings, Darcey O'Callaghan, Makita Taylor, Mariah Urueta, and Meeko Williams. Thank you particularly to Rebecca for connecting me to such incredible people. For assistance in Ireland, I thank Kieran Allen, Lynn Boylan, Richard Boyd Barrett, Patrick Bresnihan, David Gibney, Oisin Kelly, Ruth Kelly, Mary Murphy, Paul Murphy, and Brid Smith. For your hospitality and sharing of expertise in Aotearoa New Zealand, my sincere thanks go to Gerard Albert, Liz Brown, Miriama Cribb, Elizabeth Macpherson, Hayden Potaka, John Reid, Ngā Tangata Tiaki, Te Pou Tupua (Turama Hawira, and Keria Ponga), Hayden Turoa, Te Atawhai o Te Ao (Rāwiri Tinirau and Graham Smith), and Raukura Naani Waitai. Thank you especially to Miriama and Liz for hosting me so generously. For your collegiality along the way, I'd also like to thank the whole Riverine Rights team, and particularly Rahul Ranjan, Rachel Sieder, and Gro Ween for your ongoing intellectual support. For support in Chile, I thank Camilla Boettiger, Natalia Dasenshich, Jorge Gonzalez, Michael Hantke Domas, Guillermo Donoso Harris, Dominique Hervé Espejo, José Hipolito, Zañartu Rosselot, Nicole Mansuy, Pilar Morgada, Manuel Núñez Poblete, Katie Panek, Denielle Perry, Tomas Soza, Francisca Vergara Diaz, and Pía Weber Salazar. Thank you especially to Pia and Francisca for being such kind hosts. For support in the UK, I'd like to thank the Oxford Centre for Socio-Legal Studies (and especially then-Director Linda Mulcahy and Academic Visitors coordinator Bettina Lange) for hosting me as an Academic Visitor in 2024 to work on this book. I also thank Pam Bell, Imogen Radford, Kate Rew, George Townsend, and Nathan Willmott. Finally, I could really write another entire book of thanks for all the support I have received in Australia, but I must at least acknowledge Kirsten Bauer, Nichola Lefroy, Erin O'Donnell, Anne Poelina, and Charlotte Sterrett. Thank you particularly to Erin for guiding me on such a beautiful day along the lovely Birrarung.

Finally, and most importantly, I must acknowledge and thank my family for their love and support – particularly my parents, David, Meg, Annemarie, and Sarah; my brother, Jonathan; and my children, Alexi and Charlie. My deepest gratitude of all goes to my partner, Paul. Thank you, darling, for everything.

1

MAPPING THE LEGAL GEOGRAPHIES OF WATER

Introduction

The global water crisis represents one of humanity's most pressing challenges. It is playing out through multiple, interconnected dimensions: inequitable access, growing scarcity, contaminated supplies, and intensifying conflicts over control. While communities have long faced localised water challenges, today's crisis exists on an unprecedented scale, fuelled by climate change, rising inequality, geopolitical instability, and the ongoing impacts of extractive development. Despite nearly five decades of international action aimed at expanding water access and addressing governance failure – from the 1977 Mar del Plata Conference to the 2010 recognition of the human right to water[1] – the situation has only deteriorated.[2]

This book argues that addressing the water crisis requires a fundamental reconceptualisation of human–water relationships through legal frameworks that recognise water's material agency and relational nature. Drawing on legal geography, it examines how law shapes human relationships with water while simultaneously being shaped by social relations and water's own materiality. This theoretical lens reveals the co-constitutive nature of legal frameworks, social arrangements, and water itself – challenging simplistic notions of water as merely an economic resource or abstract right.

Legal geography offers particularly valuable insights for analysing water governance because it focuses on how legal norms and institutions both reflect and shape the social, cultural, and material realities of specific places. This approach helps us to critically examine and understand several fundamental aspects of the water crisis.

DOI: 10.4324/9781003273219-1

In focusing on *space*, legal geography reveals how law shapes space in ways that mirror its underlying power dynamics and ideological biases. For water, this analysis reveals the way seemingly neutral legal mechanisms produce and legitimise spatial inequalities in water access and control. From Chile's water markets to Detroit's service shutoffs (discussed in the chapters that follow), legal frameworks often reinforce existing patterns of disadvantage along lines of race and class.

Legal geography's emphasis on *place* draws attention to how water's material properties and social values resist attempts to reduce it to an abstract commodity. Place has both physical and relational aspects, and its attention to context also highlights the ongoing reality and significance of pluralism. In addition to acknowledging legal pluralism, legal geography reveals a 'pluriverse' of water realities,[3] rather than assuming a universal 'one-world'[4] ontology where water is only a resource to be managed (or extracted).

Finally, this theoretical framework emphasises the role of *narrative* in constituting legal relations. While hegemonic narratives can operate to legitimise the spatial inequalities discussed above, counter-hegemonic narratives work to both open the conceptual space for radical alternatives and, through performance and prefigurative actions, to enact these into being.

Through case studies spanning four decades of water governance reforms, this book examines how different legal frameworks – from neoliberal water governance reforms to human rights to the emerging recognition of living water – reshape human-water relations while encountering both material and social resistance. The analysis reveals both the limitations of conventional regulatory approaches and the potential for more relational legal frameworks that recognise water's agency and plurality of values.

The chapters trace several key developments across time, space, and place: the emergence of neoliberal water governance in Chile and the UK in the 1980s (Chapter 2); its global proliferation and specific implementation in Manila in the 1990s (Chapter 3); the concurrent rise of water justice movements and human rights frameworks both globally and in South Africa (Chapters 4 and 5); the subsequent intensification of commodification through financialisation and its specific material and social effects in Detroit and Flint, Michigan (Chapter 6); and recent innovations in recognising living water and Indigenous water ontologies and legal orders, and how these have been developed in Aotearoa New Zealand for the Whanganui River (Chapter 7). Finally, in addition to synthesising the lessons from earlier chapters, Chapter 8 introduces a range of brief examples of new legal developments in Chile, Australia, and the UK to highlight the diverse range of potential pathways that exist for us to explore in adopting a more relational approach to water governance.

This introductory chapter develops the theoretical framework that guides the book's analysis. It begins by situating contemporary water governance challenges within their historical context, revealing the limitations of conventional regulatory approaches. Next, it establishes legal geography as an analytical lens that theorises how law shapes human relationships with water while being shaped by both social relations and water's material agency. Finally, it outlines the book's methodology and structure, explaining how this theoretical framework will be applied through detailed case studies.

Historical context and contemporary challenges

The contemporary global water crisis emerged against a backdrop of shifting governance paradigms that reveal a complex interplay between legal frameworks, social relations, and water's material agency. While communities have long faced localised water challenges, the 1970s marked a turning point in how these issues were conceptualised and addressed at the international level. The 1977 United Nations Water Conference in Mar del Plata represented the first coordinated global response to the (then) looming water crisis, establishing ambitious goals including universal access to clean drinking water by 1990.[5] However, the Mar del Plata framework was soon superseded by more fundamental transformations in water governance – transformations that continue to shape spatial patterns of access and control today.

The emergence of neoliberal water governance in the 1980s triggered a profound reconfiguration of human-water relations. This shift involved abstracting water from its social and material context, transforming it from a public good (or commons, kin, or ancestor) into an economic resource through new legal (and financial) frameworks. The theoretical foundations for this transformation were promulgated through influential policy documents like the 1992 Dublin Statement, which emphasised water's economic value,[6] and the World Bank's 1993 *Water Resources Management* report, which promoted privatisation and cost recovery.[7]

Paradoxically, given neoliberalism's anti-statist ideology, this legal-institutional restructuring required what has been called 'reregulation' rather than deregulation to actively create and maintain water markets through state intervention.[8] It also involved what David Harvey characterises as 'accumulation by dispossession' – in this case via the legal transformation of collective water resources into private assets.[9] In so doing, it entrenched and legitimised spatial inequalities in water services. Finally, the filtering of neoliberal logic down from international institutions to the national and local levels resulted in a complex scalar politics for water governance, meaning that local relationships with water are confronted with increasingly globalised legal and financial policy imperatives and pressures.

The human right to water emerged in part as a response to these market-based reforms, though its relationship with neoliberal governance frameworks proved complex and sometimes contradictory. While early water justice movements deployed rights discourse to contest commodification, institutional interpretations often proved compatible with market mechanisms.[10] This tension reflects broader theoretical debates about whether rights frameworks can effectively challenge the status quo or whether they actually operate to neutralise calls for radical change.

Finally, recent developments suggest growing recognition of water's relational values and living agency. The emergence of legal frameworks recognising rivers as living entities, particularly through Indigenous-led initiatives, also demonstrates the potential for pluralism – the coexistence of multiple, overlapping legal orders and water ontologies – to shape new, more sustainable water governance approaches.

This historical trajectory reflects several theoretical themes that inform the analysis that follows. First, that legal frameworks play an active role in producing spatial arrangements of water access and control rather than simply reflecting pre-existing conditions. Second, there is a persistent contest between attempts to abstract (and extract) water through legal mechanisms and material and social resistance to such abstraction. Finally, as a living, agentic entity, water plays its own role in this co-constitutive process. The following section sets out the theoretical framework that guides this book's exploration of these key theoretical themes.

Legal geography

Legal geography provides this book's overarching analytical framework for understanding how law shapes human relationships with water while simultaneously being shaped by both social relations and water's material agency. This theoretical framework emphasises the co-constitutive nature of legal mechanisms, spatial arrangements, and material realities – challenging notions of water governance as merely technical regulation or neutral administration.

At its core, legal geography examines how law and space 'co-inform and co-constitute' each other,[11] or the 'co-constitutive relationship of people, place and law.'[12] Luke Bennett and Antonia Layard argue that this interdisciplinary approach emerged from 'mutual curiosity' between legal scholars and geographers, addressing a 'deep-seated division of intellectual labour.'[13] As Nicholas Blomley's early work demonstrates, this approach disputes the 'aspatial language' of conventional legal frameworks that treat space as 'an objective and pregiven surface [...] something to be measured, contained, divided, manipulated, and crucially alienated.'[14] Instead, legal geography reveals how legal mechanisms actively produce spatial arrangements while being shaped by existing social and material relations.

In the context of water governance, this theoretical lens highlights how different legal frameworks generate distinct spatial configurations of access and control. Neoliberal reforms like Chile's water markets or England's privatised utilities do not simply regulate existing arrangements but fundamentally restructure human-water relationships through new legal geographies. In emphasising that law and place or space are co-constitutive, legal geography emphasises that 'place and law do not live in separate boxes,' and that law and space are instead 'conjoined and co-constitutive.'[15] As David Delaney explains,

> to legally constitute some entity X (space, the home, the corporation, appropriate sex, persons, events) means much more than to shape or influence it. In the strongest sense it is to call it into being or modify its social significance through the distinctive practices of naming, classifying, ruling, governing, or ordering associated with law most broadly conceived.[16]

This conceptualisation thus examines how law fundamentally shapes social reality. Here Delaney emphasises the mutual constitution of law and space, highlighting how 'law carves life-worlds into innumerable boxes and assembles and reassembles them in ways that structure experiences from the most mundane to the most extra-ordinary.'[17] Of course, the emphasis on co-constitution means that legal geography also observes the role of specific social and material realities in shaping law, in turn. Legal geography, thus, reveals how legal frameworks both shape and *are* shaped by specific geographical contexts and material realities. By emphasising the production of legal geographies through material and social processes, this analysis rejects law's claims to abstract universality. Within this co-constitutive process, three concepts are particularly significant – space, place, and narrative. Each of these concepts will be explored in turn.

Space and spatial justice

Within legal geography, space, including watery space, is not an abstract concept but a relational entity that is co-constituted and dynamic. Delaney's work, for example, emphasises the constitutive power of law in producing not just regulatory frameworks but spatial realities themselves.[18] This analysis seeks to counter the law's 'spatial blindness' and highlight the ongoing relevance of space to the law.[19] Here, legal geography is particularly concerned with issues of spatial justice and with revealing power dynamics in spatial arrangements. The field helps 'make plain the legal, spatial and power imbalances that pervade our lived environments, that both figuratively (and sometimes) literally concretise its injustices, and the resistances to this oppression.'[20]

This focus on spatial justice proves especially relevant for water governance given water's simultaneous necessity and finitude. In the story of the last four decades of water governance, we see a contest between highly unequal spatial entitlements – both historically grounded and newly (re)produced by market forces – and the prefigurative politics of the water justice movement with its reclaiming of the water commons and a more spatially just future. In critically reviewing the global influence of neoliberal theories of water governance, this book seeks to reveal its role in creating spatial injustice.

Legal geography not only reveals the processes through which this spatial injustice is created but also highlights the law's role in the legal legitimation, or naturalisation, of spatial inequality. As Delaney notes, '[c]ritical geography is indispensable for revealing the workings of power that conventional spatial imaginaries obscure and for identifying the whys, hows and wheres of injustice that are otherwise invisibilized and legitimized.'[21] Legal geography thus draws our attention to the way seemingly neutral legal mechanisms can reproduce and entrench unjust geographies of water distribution. Blomley's concept of 'legal violence,' for example, argues that technical regulations and administrative procedures often legitimise spatial inequalities along lines of race, class, and colonial relations.[22] This helps explain why market-based water reforms, despite claims of efficiency and universality, frequently reinforce existing patterns of advantage and exclusion.

The internal logic behind this process of enclosure (including the enclosure achieved through neoliberal water governance) is a 'winner takes all' logic that works to deliberately channel wealth and privilege to the few and away from the many, reflecting Harvey's notion of 'accumulation by dispossession.'[23] This process of extraction – the funnelling of wealth and power to an elite few – is both material and conceptual. In a material sense, it operates to ensure that water literally flows to power, away from the control and taps of communities. In a conceptual sense, it seeks to erase or render illegitimate alternative frameworks for governing water – frameworks that reflect and protect its relational values.

Place, materiality, and pluralism

While space provides a broad analytical frame for examining how legal mechanisms produce and legitimate inequality, place draws our attention to the specific material and social contexts where these processes unfold. This shift from abstract space to concrete place reveals how water governance encounters both physical resistance and social adaptation in specific settings. This concept of place is particularly important to legal geography, which notes that 'nearly every aspect of law is located, takes place, is in motion, or has some spatial frame of reference.'[24] As Irus Braverman and others observe, 'law is always "worlded" in some way,' and place brings a focus to the importance of context (social, cultural, environmental), highlighting that places 'are not simply the inert sites of the law but are inextricably implicated in how law happens.'[25]

Legal geography's emphasis on place provides a crucial analytical lens for understanding water governance. Place encompasses several key dimensions that shape legal frameworks: materiality, relationality, and plurality. These elements are deeply interconnected, with materiality being a key feature of place that grounds more abstract legal concepts in physical reality, relationality emphasising people's sense of belonging and their relationships to place in shaping law, and plurality drawing attention to the legal and ontological diversity of each place-based context.

The materiality of place, whether manifested through landscapes, waterscapes, or infrastructure networks, forms the physical foundation that both enables and constrains legal frameworks. As Tayanah O'Donnell and others note, the physical features of both land and waterscapes influence the development of law, while law, simultaneously, 'has an enormous power to transform the material (including landscapes) through fixing, labelling, restricting and ordering.'[26] This co-constitutive relationship is particularly evident in water governance, where physical infrastructure networks materially embed legal arrangements while also being shaped by them.

By focusing on materiality as a feature of place, legal geography examines how physicality intersects with social and legal arrangements in specific contexts. For example, water's material properties – its tendency to flow, its heaviness, its essential role in sustaining life – make it what Karen Bakker calls an 'uncooperative commodity' that resists legal attempts at abstraction and commodification.[27] As we will see in the case studies that follow, these material qualities perform differently across places, interacting with local social arrangements and legal frameworks to produce distinct water governance outcomes.

Beyond materiality, legal geography is also concerned with the social dimensions of place – or with relationality. Within this frame, a 'place is not just a thing or an entity. Place is a relational concept.'[28] Penny English, for example, notes that people are 'knitted into a network of locales [...] a series of places through which people's life histories are threaded.'[29] Similarly, Margaret Davies argues that property should be understood not through autonomous individual ownership but through networks of relations.[30]

The role of relationality is becoming an increasingly important focus in the analysis of water governance frameworks. Elizabeth Macpherson explains that relationality plays a role in both the substantive dimensions of water law (in recognising reciprocal relationships between water peoples and places) and in the law's procedural aspects (in enabling co-constitutive processes between multiple legal systems and knowledge frameworks).[31] Here Macpherson argues that the concept of '[r]elationality also helps us to understand how people (including, but not limited to, Indigenous peoples) relate to water places, to form a basis for water authority, use, rights and governance.'[32]

The interconnections between these material and social dimensions of place can be seen in the way private property and neoliberal water governance use two particular processes (one material, one conceptual) to transform the land and waterscape: exclusion and alienation.[33] In relation to land, private property excludes through the physical markers of 'fences, hedges, high walls and CCTV cameras.'[34] Similarly, it is the physical infrastructure of dams, reservoirs, treatment plants, and networks of pipes that serve this role in relation to water, operating to (re)direct water in a controlled manner that creates spatially unequal geographies. Alienation, on the other hand, relies on a conceptual process of dephysicalisation, where land or water is detached from place and transfigured into a commodity for the market. To describe the dephysicalising effects of the private property paradigm, Nicole Graham coins the term 'lawscape'[35] and notes that it inevitably encounters resistance because landscapes (as opposed to lawscapes) are 'complex networks of relationships . . . sites of spatial, temporal and legal connectivities . . . rather than ... two separate spheres: human and non-human, culture and nature.'[36] Similar dynamics play out in response to neoliberal water governance, both due to the materiality of water and its relational values – the deep sense of attachment that communities share with place and water that cannot be reduced to financial value.

Beyond materiality, water also resists commodification due to its own agency. As Davies argues, physical entities achieve 'a kind of subjectivity' that resists conventional legal frameworks based on subject-object distinctions.[37] Attachment to this dualism, particularly within Western legal frameworks, has played a significant role in creating the ecological crises we are now experiencing – crises that, significantly for this book, include the global water crisis. Davies observes that rejecting this dualism and '[u]nderstanding that human beings are enmeshed in the physical world and that any dominance we feel we have over it is both fragile and misguided may assist us in dealing with the imperatives of sustainable life and ecological resilience.'[38]

Legal geography's focus on place and context inherently challenges universalist frameworks, opening analytical space for examining multiple ways of knowing and relating to water. Rather than assuming a single modernist framework that knows water only as a resource to be managed and exploited, this approach reveals the existence of a 'pluriverse' of water realities.[39] This pluralism operates at both legal and ontological levels, though these dimensions are deeply intertwined.

Legal pluralism helps us to 'recognise multiple types of law, emphasise the heterogeneity of narratives constituting the law and identify several origins of law.'[40] In this sense, it can be contrasted with legal monism – a positivist understanding of law, which views it as a singular system of rules and principles imbued with legitimacy by a central state authority.[41] As Kirsten Anker argues, pluralism 'contests the idea that law is the normative product of the state alone, and that law can be comprehended solely according to statist precepts.'[42] The role of the state is thus an important site of analysis for legal pluralism, and, in the 1980s, John Griffiths distinguished between so-called 'weak legal pluralism' (an approach that does not fundamentally challenge the central legal authority of the state) and 'strong legal pluralism.'[43] Davies explains that strong legal pluralism refers to the situation 'where two or more "laws" exist in the one place and there is no dominant or overarching system which orders the relations between the different laws.'[44] Strong legal pluralism is thus particularly pertinent to the colonial context, where recognition by the colonial state is not centrally relevant to the question of the legitimacy or authority of Indigenous (or First) law (and, indeed, may be utterly irrelevant).

Whether in relation to its 'weak' or 'strong' forms, one of the central observations of legal pluralism is that law is constructed by a multiplicity of actors – a recognition that has led Sally Engle Merry to argue that legal pluralism is not a theory, as it is merely 'a description of what law is like.'[45] We can also observe the central importance of the legal subject in this analysis, and critical legal pluralism is particularly concerned with analysing the process by which the subject of law, in producing legal knowledge, engages in the transformative production of 'the very structures of law that contribute to their legal subjectivity.'[46]

Ontological pluralism is a broader concept than legal pluralism because ontology as a concept is the lens through which we understand what is real or, more simply, what is. Rather than emphasising multiple worldviews (or multiple perspectives on the one world), the concept of ontology acknowledges the existence of multiple worlds – or a 'pluriverse' (a concept to which we will return in Chapter 7).[47] This emphasis on ontological pluralism in both legal theory and other disciplines has been described as an 'ontological turn.'[48] Within legal theory, this has particularly involved an acknowledgement and critical analysis of the legal subjectivity of non-human entities (like rivers) alongside the fundamental reconsideration of the nature of human legal subjectivity, particularly through the theoretical disposition of 'posthuman legal theory,'[49] also known as 'new materialism,'[50] 'eco-legality,'[51] 'critical ecological jurisprudence,'[52] and decolonial theory.[53] Angela Harris describes this as 'legal-ontological work' and notes that it involves both the construction of new legal subjects and the deconstruction of old ones.[54]

The recognition of both legal and ontological pluralism proves critical for water governance because it reveals how different ways of knowing and relating to water generate distinct regulatory approaches. When water is understood solely as an economic resource, governance frameworks inevitably privilege market mechanisms and individual property rights. In contrast, ontologies that recognise water as a living entity with its own agency demand radically different legal arrangements – as evidenced by Aotearoa New Zealand's Te Awa Tupua legislation (considered in Chapter 7). Rather than being different perspectives on water, these competing ontologies represent fundamentally different water realities that shape governance outcomes. Understanding this plurality is essential for developing more equitable and sustainable approaches that can accommodate multiple ways of knowing and relating to water.

While this pluralism is relevant to the alter-narratives and legal orders that are maintained and enacted by communities globally, attention to pluralism demands a particular focus on Indigenous ontologies and legal orders. Of relevance to this book (and Chapter 7, in particular) is Nicole Latulipe's observation that many Indigenous worldviews understand that '[t]he not-only-human beings of Creation are agentic, willful, and intelligent [...] [and that t]he agency of land is rooted constitutionalism, the basis of Indigenous law.'[55] She goes on to argue that, when grounded in Indigenous worldviews, legal geography can help to reveal otherwise hidden 'pathways of resistance and worldbuilding, thus helping to disrupt settler-colonial power.'[56] In relation to water, this can help us to better understand Indigenous water ontologies and legal orders that know water as a living entity with its own agency and authority.[57]

While legal geography's focus on the specificities of place and context takes pluralism seriously, both private property paradigms and neoliberal water governance frameworks actively resist this plurality through what Blomley describes as a 'very conscious project' of asserting universal validity while simultaneously seeking to erase or discredit alternative approaches.[58] Hendrik Hartog describes this as the deliberate repression of 'the existence and relative autonomy of competing and conflicting socially constituted visions of legal order,'[59] while Blomley notes its erasure of 'the plurality and radical decentralization of [other] legal voices.'[60]

This universalist assertion operates to privilege state-based legal systems while delegitimising other normative orders, reduce place to an abstract economic resource stripped of social and cultural meaning, and present market mechanisms as natural and inevitable rather than historically contingent arrangements. This tension between pluralistic realities and universalist assertions is particularly evident in conflicts over water governance. Indigenous ontologies that recognise water as a living entity with its own agency fundamentally challenge both the conceptual foundations and material arrangements of market-based governance frameworks. The persistence of these alternative ways of knowing and relating to water, despite sustained attempts at erasure, demonstrates both the limitations of universalist approaches and the potential for continuing to develop and expand more pluralistic governance arrangements.

Narrative and performance

In the third and final theme of legal geography, we note that the material and social dimensions of space and place find expression and meaning through narrative. Legal geography observes the central role of narrative in both establishing and contesting legal frameworks – a dynamic particularly evident in water governance, where competing stories about water's nature and value shape regulatory approaches. This book examines the interaction between several of these narratives, including the hegemonic narrative of neoliberal water governance theory and the counter-hegemonic narratives extolled and enacted by communities on the ground. These community narratives emphasise justice, equality, and relationality and promote entirely different conceptions of water. Traversing this complex terrain is the narrative of the human right to water, which has often had a foot in each camp – depending on who is telling its story. This attention to narrative also reveals how communities strategically engage with different legal frameworks while maintaining more transformative political visions. From South African townships to Michigan cities, water justice movements have deployed rights discourse while simultaneously prefiguring alternative water relationships through direct action and mutual aid.

In critically analysing the historical foundations of our current (hegemonic) lawscape, legal geographers like Blomley highlight the role of the enclosure movement and its project of introducing and normalising the concept of private property – while simultaneously erasing or obscuring alternative understandings of property.[61] Here the link to the colonial project is visible, as the Western legal project is underwritten first by an organised forgetting of its own plurality (as discussed above), followed by a conscious process of erasing and rendering illegitimate the legal and ontological plurality it encountered in its colonial frontiers.[62] Like land, water was also subject to early processes of enclosure, but it was in the second wave that it became a key focus of updated modes of enclosure through privatisation and financialisation.[63] Similarly, we can observe the way that neoliberalism operates to contain and neutralise radical demands, sometimes through a process of 'reregulation.'[64]

Legal geography also helps us to understand how alternative property relations persist despite, and in resistance to, these dominant private property (and neoliberal) paradigms. Here we turn to a particular subspecies of narrative to examine the role of performance and similar acts of prefiguration.[65] This concept of 'acts of prefiguration' draws on prefigurative theory, which focuses particularly on the strategies and dynamics of counter-hegemonic movements, with scholars seeking to explain the power of prefigurative actions by social movements to enact long-lasting change through the temporary or small-scale enactment of alternative social orders such as occupations, camps, and 'everyday utopias.'[66] Davina Cooper, for example, argues that concrete sites of utopian dreaming can 'support new conceptual lines that lead to different forms of imagining.'[67] A common theme here is the role of performance in enacting a particular future into being.[68] However, Davies also reminds us of the prefigurative power of theory itself, noting that enacting a new world into being involves a fruitful 'oscillation between practice and concept-formation.'[69]

Legal geography thus draws on prefigurative theory to highlight the ways that performing and reimagining the world can work to bring it into being.[70] Returning briefly to space, legal geography scholars have repeatedly emphasised the role of performance in creating both spatial relations and property rights.[71] Blomley, for example, notes, '[t]hat which we designate as property… is "performed" into being through the arrangement of fences, the pronouncements of judges, the classifications of titling systems, the beliefs and practices of ordinary people, the growing of trees, and so on.'[72] This applies both to hegemonic and counter-hegemonic frameworks, and here he observes these frameworks (be they private property relations, neoliberal water governance reforms, or alternative approaches) have 'a relational effect, not a prior ground, brought into being by the very act of performance itself.'[73] In *The Lawful Forest*, John Page and I also note the role of performance in the counter-hegemonic enactment of communal property rights, which we describe as 'dynamic, performative, relational, co-constituted and inherently social.'[74] This reminds us of the dynamic nature of such legal relations and that, through this prefigurative process, alternative social relations can also shape power relations and, ultimately, law. As Sarah Keenan argues, critical property theory can help us to see how property's other 'can be productive of spaces … shaped differently from networks of hegemonic power relations.'[75]

This emphasis on narrative and performance provides insight into the relationship between legal mobilisation and social movements. Here both prefigurative and performance theory helps us to understand why winning or losing the case in court, for example, may not be the most significant outcome. Delaney, for example, notes that 'winning a case may not deliver substantive relief for plaintiffs and … losing a case might pay dividends in political organizing,' demonstrating the complex relationship between legal victories and social justice.[76] As we will see in Chapter 5, this complex relationship played out for the claimants in the Mazibuko water rights case, who lost in the Constitutional Court of South Africa but secured a wide range of 'wins' nonetheless.

Methodological approach

Having outlined the theoretical framework that guides this analysis, I now turn to the methodological approach that seeks to apply these concepts to detailed case studies. This mixed-methods approach combines critical doctrinal analysis with empirical investigation across multiple scales.

In 2010, Delaney introduced to legal geography the conceptual framework of 'nomosphere, nomic setting, and the nomoscape' as methodological tools for analysing legal-spatial relations.[77] If we consider these in increasing scale, nomic settings are individual case studies, nomoscapes are assemblages of case studies and the critical analysis of their processes, while the nomosphere describes an overarching theoretical framework. By starting with concrete or empirical case studies (nomic settings), this approach grounds a legal geographic study in the material – meaning that theory is extracted from place-based context rather than generated in the abstract.[78] The overarching theoretical framework described as the nomosphere also acknowledges 'the need to draw on other disciplines in order to generate a broader theoretical framework that deals with issues of race, gender, class, neoliberalism and so on (helping to construct a "fuller" nomosphere).'[79]

While not using these specific terms, this book draws from this methodological approach in presenting a series of empirical case studies, which are critically analysed in an attempt 'to "connect the dots," drawing lessons from these case studies to understand processes and systems of power.'[80] It then steps back once again, drawing on the theoretical insights of legal geography and other disciplines (including human rights, critical legal studies, posthumanism, and legal pluralism) to generate a broader theoretical analysis.

For the case studies themselves, this book employs a socio-legal approach, combining critical doctrinal analysis with the empirical investigation of their implementation and effects across multiple scales. The research draws on extensive fieldwork across multiple jurisdictions and includes semi-structured interviews with community members, activists, water managers, legal experts, and government officials. These empirical insights are complemented by the critical analysis of primary legal sources (including legislation, case law, treaties, tribunal judgments, and policy documents); archival research examining the historical development of different governance frameworks; government, United Nations, and civil society reports; and a wide range of secondary research (journal articles, books, and reports). This combination has enabled the investigation of both formal legal structures and their lived implications for communities (both human and more than human).

Importantly, this methodology acknowledges what Donna Haraway terms 'situated knowledge' – recognising that all analysis emerges from particular social and intellectual positions.[81] My own situated perspective has been shaped by 20 years of research into water governance issues, including fieldwork across multiple jurisdictions (for this book, this has included Chile, the UK, the Philippines, South Africa, the US, Ireland, Aotearoa New Zealand, and Australia). This research trajectory has been inevitably influenced by my position as a White, middle-class woman from Australia, educated in

Western legal traditions while simultaneously exposed to radical environmental movements and Indigenous water realities.

This positioning shapes both the strengths and limitations of the analysis in this book. My fieldwork and diverse theoretical engagement have (hopefully) supported a nuanced examination of how different legal frameworks reshape human-water relations. However, despite sustained engagement with communities across these jurisdictions, my understanding of their historical contexts, cultures, and legal systems remains necessarily partial. While I have restricted case studies to places where I have conducted fieldwork, I acknowledge the inherent limitations in analysing complex water governance issues from an external perspective.

These methodological constraints particularly impact the analysis of Indigenous water ontologies and legal orders. While working with Indigenous colleagues and communities has helped to inform my understanding, I cannot and do not claim to speak on their behalf. Instead, the analysis aims to foreground Indigenous scholarship while examining how state legal systems might better recognise and protect Indigenous relationships with water.

This methodology enables the critical examination of how legal frameworks shape human-water relations while remaining attentive to questions of positionality and the politics of knowledge production. Rather than attempting an impossible objective overview, this book offers a situated analysis of water governance transformations that aims to contribute to ongoing scholarly dialogues with colleagues and communities for whom I have the deepest of respect, while remaining mindful of its own limitations.

Chapter overview

The book examines the last four decades of water governance trends along largely chronical lines. Chapter 2 applies legal geography's focus on space to examine two pivotal early experiments in neoliberal water governance: Chile's water markets introduced by the Pinochet regime in 1981 and the full privatisation of water services in England and Wales under the Thatcher government in 1989. Through this analysis, the chapter reveals how legal mechanisms actively produce new spatial arrangements of water access and control rather than simply regulating existing conditions. The chapter also highlights several dynamics that came to characterise subsequent attempts at neoliberal water governance reform globally, including the persistent tension between abstract legal frameworks and water's material resistance and a paradox at the heart of neoliberal theory – rather than withdrawing, states must actively intervene to create and maintain water markets.

Chapter 3 deepens the examination of spatial justice by using Manila's experience with private sector participation to analyse how market-based reforms reshape urban space through infrastructure networks, producing differentiated service territories that reflect and reinforce existing socio-economic hierarchies. This case study particularly illustrates how apparently neutral legal mechanisms legitimise spatial inequalities while also encountering material and social resistance. The broader analysis in this chapter demonstrates how international financial institutions and corporate interests drove the global adoption of neoliberal water governance reforms through loan conditionalities and policy influence, even as growing evidence suggested that private sector participation exacerbated inequality while failing to reliably deliver promised efficiency gains.

Chapters 4 and 5 explore the messy interplay between competing legal frameworks through South Africa's attempt to implement both market mechanisms and rights-based approaches. Drawing on legal geography's attention to plurality and narrative, these chapters demonstrate how competing legal rationalities produce a hybrid governance system with inconsistent outcomes for water access. The chapters also track the way different actors strategically deploy competing narratives to both legitimise hegemonic politics and promote transformative political visions. The Mazibuko water rights case, considered in Chapter 5, alongside developments within the United Nations to recognise the human right to water, serves as a lens for analysing how rights frameworks can simultaneously legitimise market-based governance while providing tools for articulating alternative water relations and values.

Chapter 6 examines how financialisation represents both a continuation and evolution of neoliberal water reforms, transforming water from a public service into an abstract financial asset while reconfiguring institutional power structures and community relationships with water. Through detailed case studies of water crises in Detroit and Flint, Michigan, the chapter highlights how global and national financial imperatives interact with local materialities and social relations to produce new forms of spatial injustice. This analysis considers the scalar dimensions of contemporary water governance and explores the sophisticated forms of community resistance that operate across multiple scales to match financialisation's own scalar mobility.

Chapter 7 foregrounds legal geography's emphasis on place and pluralism to examine emerging frameworks that recognise rivers as living entities. The analysis of Aotearoa New Zealand's Te Awa Tupua legislation explores its sophisticated approach to embedding legal and ontological pluralism within water governance while protecting Indigenous relationships with water. This case study illustrates the significance of water's own agency within the co-constitution of legal frameworks and social relations of water governance while providing inspiration for pathways beyond both market mechanisms and individual rights frameworks.

Finally, Chapter 8 synthesises earlier theoretical insights to highlight multiple pathways towards more relational approaches to water governance. This chapter briefly examines several promising emerging initiatives towards more relational water governance from Chile, Australia, and the UK. Through examining these initiatives alongside persistent challenges around commodification and spatial justice, this concluding chapter considers how legal geography can inform the development of more equitable and sustainable approaches to water governance. Rather than prescribing universal solutions, it emphasises the importance of supporting place-based innovation while creating enabling conditions for transformation. The book concludes that water's essential qualities – its tendency to flow and connect, its resistance to abstraction, and its capacity to inspire alternative relationships – will continue shaping governance transformations, suggesting the need for more fluid and responsive legal frameworks that can recognise water's multiple values while protecting the plurality of human-water relations.

This book's contribution lies in demonstrating how legal geography can clarify both the limitations of conventional regulatory approaches and reveal the potential for more relational frameworks that recognise water's agency and plurality of values. This has practical implications for developing more equitable and sustainable approaches to water governance in an era of intensifying crises.

Notes

1 United Nations, *Report of the United Nations Water Conference, Mar Del Plata* (No U.N. Doc. E/CONF.70/29, United Nations, 1977); *Resolution 64/292 the Human Right to Water and Sanitation 2010* (UN GA Res 64/292, UN Doc A/RES/64/292, 28 July 2010).
2 UNESCO World Water Assessment Programme, *Water for Prosperity and Peace: UN World Water Development Report* (UN Water, 2024).
3 John Law, 'What's Wrong with a One-World World?' (2015) 12(1) *Distinktion: Journal of Social Theory* 126; Marisol de la Cadena and Mario Blaser (eds), *A World of Many Worlds* (Duke University Press, 2018).
4 Law, 'What's Wrong with a One-World World?' (n 3).
5 United Nations, *Report of the United Nations Water Conference, Mar Del Plata* (n 1).
6 United Nations, *The Dublin Statement on Water and Sustainable Development: Report of the International Conference on Water and the Environment* (U.N. Doc. A/CONF/151/PC/112, 1992).
7 World Bank, *Water Resources Management* (A World Bank policy paper, World Bank, 1993).
8 Karen Bakker, *An Uncooperative Commodity: Privatizing Water in England and Wales* (Oxford University Press, 2004).
9 David Harvey, *The New Imperialism: Accumulation by Dispossession* (Oxford University Press, 2003).
10 Cristy Clark, 'Of What Use Is a Deradicalized Human Right to Water?' (2017) 17(2) *Human Rights Law Review* 231.
11 Irus Braverman, Nicholas Blomley and David Delaney (eds), *The Expanding Spaces of Law: A Timely Legal Geography* (Stanford University Press, 2014) 11.
12 Luke Bennett and Antonia Layard, 'Legal Geography: Becoming Spatial Detectives' (2015) 9(7) *Geography Compass* 406.

13 Bennett and Layard, 'Legal Geography' (n 12) 407.
14 Nicholas Blomley, *Law, Space, and the Geographies of Power* (The Guildford Press, 1994) 91.
15 Jane Holder and Carolyn Harrison, 'Connecting Law and Geography' in Jane Holder and Carolyn Harrison (eds), *Law and Geography* (Oxford University Press, 2002) 1.
16 David Delaney, 'Legal Geography I: Constitutivities, Complexities, and Contingencies' (2015) 39(1) *Progress in Human Geography* 96, 98.
17 Delaney, 'Legal Geography I' (n 16) 99.
18 Delaney, 'Legal Geography I' (n 16) 100.
19 Bennett and Layard, 'Legal Geography' (n 12) 407.
20 Cristy Clark and John Page, 'Law and Geography' in Daniel Newman and Russell Sandberg (eds), *Law and Humanities* (Anthem Press, 2024) 69, 85.
21 David Delaney, 'Legal Geography II: Discerning Injustice" (2016) 40(2) *Progress in Human Geography* 267, 272.
22 Blomley, *Law, Space, and the Geographies of Power* (n 14).
23 David Harvey, *The New Imperialism: Accumulation by Dispossession* (Oxford University Press, 2003).
24 Braverman, Blomley and Delaney (eds), *The Expanding Spaces of Law* (n 11) 1.
25 Braverman, Blomley and Delaney (eds), *The Expanding Spaces of Law* (n 11) 1.
26 Tayanah O'Donnell, Daniel F. Robinson and Josephine Gillespie, 'An Australasian and Asia-Pacific Approach to Legal Geography' in Tayanah O'Donnell, Daniel F. Robinson and Josephine Gillespie (eds), *Legal Geography: Perspectives and Methods* (Routledge, 2020) 3, 9.
27 Bakker, *An Uncooperative Commodity* (n 8).
28 Penny English, 'Space and Time: The Genius Loci of Ancient Places' in Jane Holder and Carolyn Harrison (eds), *Law and Geography* (Oxford University Press, 2002) 465, 466.
29 English, 'Space and Time' (n 28).
30 Margaret Davies, 'Material Subjects and Vital Objects — Prefiguring Property and Rights for an Entangled World' (2016) 22(2) *Australian Journal of Human Rights* 37, 43.
31 Elizabeth Macpherson, 'Can Western Water Law Become More "Relational"? A Survey of Comparative Laws Affecting Water across Australasia and the Americas' (2022) *Journal of the Royal Society of New Zealand* 1, 4.
32 Macpherson, 'Can Western Water Law Become More "Relational"? A Survey of Comparative Laws Affecting Water across Australasia and the Americas' (n 31) 4.
33 Cristy Clark and John Page, *The Lawful Forest: A Critical History of Property, Protest, and Spatial Justice* (Edinburgh University Press, 2022) 50.
34 Clark and Page, *The Lawful Forest*' (n 33) 50; John Page, 'Property, Values, and the Empirics of Place' (2019) 28 *Griffith Law Review* 1.
35 Nicole Graham, *Lawscape: Property, Environment, Law* (Routledge, 2011).
36 Nicole Graham, 'Sydney's Drinking Water Catchment: A Legal Geographical Analysis of Coal Mining and Water Security' in Tayanah O'Donnell, Daniel F. Robinson and Josephine Gillespie (eds), *Legal Geography: Perspectives and Methods* (Routledge, 2020) 201, 201–202.
37 Davies, 'Material Subjects and Vital Objects — Prefiguring Property and Rights for an Entangled World' (n 30) 42.
38 Davies, 'Material Subjects and Vital Objects — Prefiguring Property and Rights for an Entangled World' (n 30) 38.
39 de la Cadena and Blaser (eds), *A World of Many Worlds* (n 3).
40 Margaret Davies, 'The Ethos of Pluralism' (2005) 27(1) *Sydney Law Review* 87, 88.

41 See, e.g., Davies, 'The Ethos of Pluralism' (n 40) 87; Martha-Marie Kleinhans and Roderick A. Macdonald, 'What Is a Critical Legal Pluralism' (1997) 12(1) *Canadian Journal of Law and Society* 25, 29.
42 Kirsten Anker, 'Plural Property' in Nicole Graham, Margaret Davies and Lee Godden (eds), *The Routledge Handbook of Property, Law and Society* (Routledge, 2022) 31, 131–132.
43 John Griffiths, 'What Is Legal Pluralism?' (1986) 18(24) *The Journal of Legal Pluralism and Unofficial Law* 1, 5.
44 Davies, 'The Ethos of Pluralism' (n 40) 95.
45 Sally Engle Merry, 'McGill Convocation Address: Legal Pluralism in Practice' 59 *McGill Law Journal* 1, 2; cited in Jeremy Webber et al, 'Sally Engle Merry, Legal Pluralism, and the Radicalization of Comparative Law' (2020) 54(4) *Law & Society Review* 846, 854.
46 Kleinhans and Macdonald, 'What Is a Critical Legal Pluralism' (n 41) 38.
47 See, e.g., Sarah Laborde and Sue Jackson, 'Living Waters or Resource? Ontological Differences and the Governance of Waters and Rivers' (2022) 27(3) *Local Environment* 357. For a debate on this issue, see Michael Carrithers et al, 'Ontology Is Just Another Word for Culture: Motion Tabled at the 2008 Meeting of the Group for Debates in Anthropological Theory, University of Manchester' (2010) 30(2) *Critique of Anthropology* 152.
48 See, e.g., Zoe Todd, 'An Indigenous Feminist's Take on the Ontological Turn: "Ontology" Is Just Another Word for Colonialism' (2016) 29(1) *Journal of Historical Sociology* 4; Emille Boulot and Joshua Sterlin, 'Steps Towards a Legal Ontological Turn: Proposals for Law's Place Beyond the Human' (2022) 11(1) *Transnational Environmental Law* 13; Rutgerd Boelens, Lena Hommes and Jaime Hoogesteger, 'Ontological Politics in River Defence Debates: Unpacking Fields of Contention in Eco-Centric and Non-Human Turns' (2024) 17(3) *Water Alternatives* 649.
49 See, e.g., Donna Haraway, *Staying with the Trouble* (Duke University Press, 2016); Anna Grear, 'Introduction: "Staying with the Trouble"*—Environmental Justice for the Anthropocene–Capitalocene' in *Environmental Justice* (Edward Elgar Publishing, 2020) <http://orca.cf.ac.uk/126039/>; Emily Jones, 'Posthuman International Law and the Rights of Nature' (2021) 12(Special Issue) *Journal of Human Rights and The Environment* 82; Jana Norman, *Posthuman Legal Subjectivity: Reimagining the Human in the Anthropocene* (Routledge, 2022).
50 See, e.g., Diana Coole and Samantha Frost, 'Introducing the New Materialisms' in Diana Coole and Samantha Frost (eds), *New Materialisms: Ontology, Agency, and Politics* (Duke University Press, 2010) 1; Anna Grear, 'Resisting Anthropocene Neoliberalism: Towards New Materialist Commoning?' in Anna Grear and David Bollier (eds), *The Great Awakening: New Modes of Life Amidst Capitalist Ruins* (Punctum Press, 2019) <http://orca.cf.ac.uk/122785/>; Grear 'Introduction' (n 49).
51 Margaret Davies, 'Re-Forming Property to Address Eco-Social Fragmentation and Rift' (2021) 12(Special Issue) *Journal of Human Rights and the Environment* 13, 14.
52 Boulot and Sterlin, 'Steps Towards a Legal Ontological Turn' (n 48) 31.
53 Boulot and Sterlin, 'Steps Towards a Legal Ontological Turn' (n 48) 32; Angela P. Harris, 'Decolonizing Legal Subjects in Climate Chaos' (2022) 121(2) *The South Atlantic Quarterly* 359.
54 Harris, 'Decolonizing Legal Subjects in Climate Chaos' (n 53) 371.
55 Nicole Latulippe, 'Indigenous Land Conflict and the Underlying Life of Laws: Lessons from the Ipperwash Crisis' in Robyn Bartel and Jennifer Carter (eds), *Research Handbook on Space, Place and Law* (Edward Elgar, 2021) 170, 174–175.

56 Latulippe, 'Indigenous Land Conflict and the Underlying Life of Laws' (n 55) 175.
57 See, e.g., Miriama Cribb, Elizabeth Macpherson and Axel Borchgrevink, 'Beyond Legal Personhood for the Whanganui River: Collaboration and Pluralism in Implementing the *Te Awa Tupua Act*' (2024) 0(0) *The International Journal of Human Rights* 1; Cristy Clark, Karen Fisher and Elizabeth Macpherson, 'Indigenous Rights and Ontological Plurality in the Institutional Arrangements for the Waikato and Waipā Rivers in Aotearoa' (2024) *The International Journal of Human Rights* 1; Karen Fisher et al, 'Broadening Environmental Governance Ontologies to Enhance Ecosystem-Based Management in Aotearoa New Zealand' (2022) 21(4) *Maritime Studies* 609; Samantha Muller, Steve Hemming and Daryle Rigney, 'Indigenous Sovereignties: Relational Ontologies and Environmental Management' (2019) 57(4) *Geographical Research* 399.
58 Blomley, *Law, Space, and the Geographies of Power* (n 14).
59 Hendrik Hartog, 'Pigs and Positivism' (1985) *Wisconsin Law Review* 899, 934.
60 Blomley, *Law, Space, and the Geographies of Power* (n 14).
61 Nicholas Blomley, 'Enclosure, Common Right and the Property of the Poor' (2008) 17 *Social & Legal Studies* 311, 322.
62 Clark and Page, *The Lawful Forest* (n 33).
63 Brett Christophers, *The New Enclosure: The Appropriation of Public Land in Neoliberal Britain* (Verso, 2018) (Brett Christophers argues that similar processes are operating to enact a new wave of enclosure over land).
64 Bakker, *An Uncooperative Commodity* (n 8).
65 Nicholas Blomley, 'Performing Property: Making the World' (2013) 26(1) *Canadian Journal of Law & Jurisprudence* 23.
66 Davina Cooper, *Everyday Utopias: The Conceptual Life of Promising Spaces* (Duke University Press, 2014); Clark and Page, *The Lawful Forest* (n 33); Amy J. Cohen and Bronwen Morgan, 'Prefigurative Legality' (2023) 48(3) *Law & Social Inquiry* 1053; Davina Cooper, Nikita Dhawan and Janet Newman (eds), *Reimagining the State: Theoretical Challenges and Transformative Possibilities* (Routledge, Taylor & Francis Group, a GlassHouse Book, 2020); Ruth Kinna, 'Utopianism and Prefiguration' in S.D. Chrostowska and James Ingram (eds), *Political Uses of Utopia: New Marxist, Anarchist and Radical Democratic Perspectives* (Columbia University Press, 2016) 198; Amelia Thorpe, *Owning the Street: The Everyday Life of Property* (MIT Press, 2020).
67 Cooper, *Everyday Utopias* (n 66) 14.
68 See, e.g., Clark and Page, *The Lawful Forest* (n 36); Davina Cooper, 'Towards an Adventurous Institutional Politics: The Prefigurative "as If" and the Reposing of What's Real' (2020) 68(5) *The Sociological Review* 893–916; Nicole Rogers, *Law, Fiction and Activism in a Time of Climate Change* (Routledge, 2020); Amelia Thorpe, 'Pop-Up Property: Enacting Ownership from San Francisco to Sydney: Pop-Up Property' (2018) 52(3) *Law & Society Review* 740; Tayanah O'Donnell, 'Legal Geography and Coastal Climate Change Adaptation: The Vaughan Litigation' (2016) 54(3) *Geographical Research* 301; Nicholas Blomley, 'The Boundaries of Property: Complexity, Relationality, and Spatiality' (2016) 50(1) *Law & Society Review* 224; Sarah Keenan, *Subversive Property: Law and the Production of Spaces of Belonging* (Routledge, 2014); Blomley, 'Performing Property' (n 65).
69 Davies, 'Material Subjects and Vital Objects — Prefiguring Property and Rights for an Entangled World' (n 30) 54.
70 Blomley, 'Performing Property' (n 65) 25.
71 Clark and Page, *The Lawful Forest* (n 34); Thorpe 'Owning the Street' (n 66); Thorpe 'Pop-Up Property' (n 68); Blomley, 'Boundaries of Property' (n 68); O'Donnell, 'Legal Geography and Coastal Climate Change Adaptation' (n 66); Keenan, *Subversive Property* (n 68); Blomley, 'Performing Property' (n 65).

72 Blomley, 'Boundaries of Property' (n 68) 250.
73 Blomley, 'Performing Property' (n 65) 32.
74 Clark and Page, 'Law and Geography' (n 20); Clark and Page, *The Lawful Forest* (n 33) 62.
75 Keenan, *Subversive Property* (n 68) 92.
76 Delaney, 'Legal Geography II' (n 21) 270.
77 David Delaney, *The Spatial, the Legal and the Pragmatics of World-Making: Nomospheric Investigations* (Routledge-Cavendish, 2010).
78 Clark and Page, 'Law and Geography' (n 20) 74.
79 Clark and Page, 'Law and Geography' (n 20) 74–75.
80 Clark and Page, 'Law and Geography' (n 20) 75.
81 Donna Haraway, 'Situated Knowledges: The Science Question in Feminism and the Privilege of Partial Perspective' (1988) 14(3) *Feminist Studies* 14, 3 575.

References

Anker, Kirsten, 'Plural Property' in Nicole Graham, Margaret Davies and Lee Godden (eds), *The Routledge Handbook of Property, Law and Society* (Routledge, 2022) 31

Bakker, Karen, *An Uncooperative Commodity: Privatizing Water in England and Wales* (Oxford University Press, 2004)

Bennett, Luke and Antonia Layard, 'Legal Geography: Becoming Spatial Detectives' (2015) 9(7) *Geography Compass* 406

Blomley, Nicholas, 'Enclosure, Common Right and the Property of the Poor' (2008) 17 *Social & Legal Studies* 311

Blomley, Nicholas, *Law, Space, and the Geographies of Power* (The Guildford Press, 1994)

Blomley, Nicholas, 'Performing Property: Making the World' (2013) 26(1) *Canadian Journal of Law & Jurisprudence* 23

Blomley, Nicholas, 'The Boundaries of Property: Complexity, Relationality, and Spatiality' (2016) 50(1) *Law & Society Review* 224

Boelens, Rutgerd, Lena Hommes and Jaime Hoogesteger, 'Ontological Politics in River Defence Debates: Unpacking Fields of Contention in Eco-Centric and Non-Human Turns' (2024) 17(3) *Water Alternatives* 649

Boulot, Emille and Joshua Sterlin, 'Steps Towards a Legal Ontological Turn: Proposals for Law's Place Beyond the Human' (2022) 11(1) *Transnational Environmental Law* 13

Braverman, Irus, Nicholas Blomley and David Delaney (eds), *The Expanding Spaces of Law: A Timely Legal Geography* (Stanford University Press, 2014)

de la Cadena, Marisol and Mario Blaser (eds), *A World of Many Worlds* (Duke University Press, 2018)

Carrithers, Michael et al, 'Ontology Is Just Another Word for Culture: Motion Tabled at the 2008 Meeting of the Group for Debates in Anthropological Theory, University of Manchester' (2010) 30(2) *Critique of Anthropology* 152

Christophers, Brett, *The New Enclosure: The Appropriation of Public Land in Neoliberal Britain* (Verso, 2018)

Clark, Cristy, 'Of What Use Is a Deradicalized Human Right to Water?' (2017) 17(2) *Human Rights Law Review* 231

Clark, Cristy, Karen Fisher and Elizabeth Macpherson, 'Indigenous Rights and Ontological Plurality in the Institutional Arrangements for the Waikato and Waipā Rivers in Aotearoa' (2024) *The International Journal of Human Rights* 1

Clark, Cristy and John Page, 'Law and Geography' in Daniel Newman and Russell Sandberg (eds), *Law and Humanities* (Anthem Press, 2024) 69

Clark, Cristy and John Page, *The Lawful Forest: A Critical History of Property, Protest, and Spatial Justice* (Edinburgh University Press, 2022)

Cohen, Amy J. and Bronwen Morgan, 'Prefigurative Legality' (2023) 48(3) *Law & Social Inquiry* 1053

Coole, Diana and Samantha Frost, 'Introducing the New Materialisms' in Diana Coole and Samantha Frost (eds), *New Materialisms: Ontology, Agency, and Politics* (Duke University Press, 2010) 1

Cooper, Davina, *Everyday Utopias: The Conceptual Life of Promising Spaces* (Duke University Press, 2014)

Cooper, Davina, 'Towards an Adventurous Institutional Politics: The Prefigurative "as If" and the Reposing of What's Real' (2020) 68(5) *The Sociological Review* 893–916

Cooper, Davina, Nikita Dhawan and Janet Newman (eds), *Reimagining the State: Theoretical Challenges and Transformative Possibilities* (Routledge, Taylor & Francis Group, a GlassHouse Book, 2020)

Cribb, Miriama, Elizabeth Macpherson and Axel Borchgrevink, 'Beyond Legal Personhood for the Whanganui River: Collaboration and Pluralism in Implementing the *Te Awa Tupua Act*' (2024) 0(0) *The International Journal of Human Rights* 1

Davies, Margaret, 'Material Subjects and Vital Objects — Prefiguring Property and Rights for an Entangled World' (2016) 22(2) *Australian Journal of Human Rights* 37

Davies, Margaret, 'Re-Forming Property to Address Eco-Social Fragmentation and Rift' (2021) 12(Special Issue) *Journal of Human Rights and the Environment* 13

Davies, Margaret, 'The Ethos of Pluralism' (2005) 27(1) *Sydney Law Review* 87

Delaney, David, 'Legal Geography I: Constitutivities, Complexities, and Contingencies' (2015) 39(1) *Progress in Human Geography* 96

Delaney, David, 'Legal Geography II: Discerning Injustice" (2016) 40(2) *Progress in Human Geography* 267

Delaney, David, *The Spatial, the Legal and the Pragmatics of World-Making: Nomospheric Investigations* (Routledge-Cavendish, 2010)

Engle Merry, Sally, 'McGill Convocation Address: Legal Pluralism in Practice' (2013) 59 *McGill Law Journal* 1

English, Penny, 'Space and Time: The Genius Loci of Ancient Places' in Jane Holder and Carolyn Harrison (eds), *Law and Geography* (Oxford University Press, 2002) 465

Fisher, Karen et al, 'Broadening Environmental Governance Ontologies to Enhance Ecosystem-Based Management in Aotearoa New Zealand' (2022) 21(4) *Maritime Studies* 609

Graham, Nicole, *Lawscape: Property, Environment, Law* (Routledge, 2011)

Graham, Nicole, 'Sydney's Drinking Water Catchment: A Legal Geographical Analysis of Coal Mining and Water Security' in Tayanah O'Donnell, Daniel F. Robinson and Josephine Gillespie (eds), *Legal Geography: Perspectives and Methods* (Routledge, 2020) 201

Grear, Anna, 'Introduction: "Staying with the Trouble"*—Environmental Justice for the Anthropocene–Capitalocene' in *Environmental Justice* (Edward Elgar Publishing, 2020) <https://orca.cf.ac.uk/126039/>

Grear, Anna, 'Resisting Anthropocene Neoliberalism: Towards New Materialist Commoning?' in Anna Grear and David Bollier (eds), *The Great Awakening: New

Modes of Life Amidst Capitalist Ruins (Punctum Press, 2019) <https://orca.cf.ac.uk/122785/>

Griffiths, John, 'What Is Legal Pluralism?' (1986) 18(24) *The Journal of Legal Pluralism and Unofficial Law* 1

Haraway, Donna, 'Situated Knowledges: The Science Question in Feminism and the Privilege of Partial Perspective' (1988) 14(3) *Feminist Studies* 575

Haraway, Donna, *Staying with the Trouble* (Duke University Press, 2016)

Harris, Angela P., 'Decolonizing Legal Subjects in Climate Chaos' (2022) 121(2) *The South Atlantic Quarterly* 359

Hartog, Hendrik, 'Pigs and Positivism' (1985) *Wisconsin Law Review* 899

Harvey, David, *The New Imperialism: Accumulation by Dispossession* (Oxford University Press, 2003)

Holder, Jane and Carolyn Harrison, 'Connecting Law and Geography' in Jane Holder and Carolyn Harrison (eds), *Law and Geography* (Oxford University Press, 2002) 1

Jones, Emily, 'Posthuman International Law and the Rights of Nature' (2021) 12(Special Issue) *Journal of Human Rights and The Environment* 82

Keenan, Sarah, *Subversive Property: Law and the Production of Spaces of Belonging* (Routledge, 2014)

Kinna, Ruth, 'Utopianism and Prefiguration' in S.D. Chrostowska and James Ingram (eds), *Political Uses of Utopia: New Marxist, Anarchist and Radical Democratic Perspectives* (Columbia University Press, 2016) 198

Kleinhans, Martha-Marie and Roderick A. Macdonald, 'What Is a Critical Legal Pluralism' (1997) 12(1) *Canadian Journal of Law and Society* 25

Laborde, Sarah and Sue Jackson, 'Living Waters or Resource? Ontological Differences and the Governance of Waters and Rivers' (2022) 27(3) *Local Environment* 357

Latulippe, Nicole, 'Indigenous Land Conflict and the Underlying Life of Laws: Lessons from the Ipperwash Crisis' in Robyn Bartel and Jennifer Carter (eds), *Research Handbook on Space, Place and Law* (Edward Elgar, 2021) 170

Law, John, 'What's Wrong with a One-World World?' (2015) 12(1) *Distinktion: Journal of Social Theory* 126

Macpherson, Elizabeth, 'Can Western Water Law Become More "Relational"? A Survey of Comparative Laws Affecting Water across Australasia and the Americas' (2022) *Journal of the Royal Society of New Zealand* 1

Muller, Samantha, Steve Hemming and Daryle Rigney, 'Indigenous Sovereignties: Relational Ontologies and Environmental Management' (2019) 57(4) *Geographical Research* 399

Norman, Jana, *Posthuman Legal Subjectivity: Reimagining the Human in the Anthropocene* (Routledge, 2022)

O'Donnell, Tayanah, 'Legal Geography and Coastal Climate Change Adaptation: The Vaughan Litigation' (2016) 54(3) *Geographical Research* 301

O'Donnell, Tayanah, Daniel F. Robinson and Josephine Gillespie, 'An Australasian and Asia-Pacific Approach to Legal Geography' in Tayanah O'Donnell, Daniel F. Robinson and Josephine Gillespie (eds), *Legal Geography: Perspectives and Methods* (Routledge, 2020) 3

Page, John, 'Property, Values, and the Empirics of Place' (2019) 28 *Griffith Law Review* 1

Resolution 64/292 the Human Right to Water and Sanitation 2010 UN GA Res 64/292, UN Doc A/RES/64/292, 28 July 2010)

Rogers, Nicole, *Law, Fiction and Activism in a Time of Climate Change* (Routledge, 2020)
Thorpe, Amelia, *Owning the Street: The Everyday Life of Property* (MIT Press, 2020)
Thorpe, Amelia, 'Pop-Up Property: Enacting Ownership from San Francisco to Sydney: Pop-Up Property' (2018) 52(3) *Law & Society Review* 740
Todd, Zoe, 'An Indigenous Feminist's Take on the Ontological Turn: "Ontology" Is Just Another Word for Colonialism' (2016) 29(1) *Journal of Historical Sociology* 4
UNESCO World Water Assessment Programme, *Water for Prosperity and Peace: UN World Water Development Report* (UN Water, 2024)
United Nations, *Report of the United Nations Water Conference, Mar Del Plata* (No U.N. Doc. E/CONF.70/29, United Nations, 1977)
United Nations, *The Dublin Statement on Water and Sustainable Development: Report of the International Conference on Water and the Environment* (U.N. Doc. A/CONF/151/PC/112, 1992)
Webber, Jeremy et al, 'Sally Engle Merry, Legal Pluralism, and the Radicalization of Comparative Law' (2020) 54(4) *Law & Society Review* 846
World Bank, *Water Resources Management* (A World Bank policy paper, World Bank, 1993)

2

THE INTRODUCTION OF WATER MARKETS

Introduction

This chapter examines how early experiments with neoliberal water governance in Chile and England/Wales reveal fundamental tensions between market abstraction and water's material and social properties. In both case studies, new legal frameworks sought to transform water into an economic good subject to the discipline of the market. However, these reforms were repeatedly confronted with water's material properties – its physical embeddedness, tendency to flow, and essential role in sustaining life – which make it what Karen Bakker terms an 'uncooperative commodity,' resistant to market abstractions.[1] An additional complication was water's relational characteristics, as these reforms also conflicted with the community's understandings of water's place-based values. These inherent tensions forced both the Chilean and British states to actively intervene to create and maintain water markets, leading to what scholars describe as 'reregulation' rather than deregulation,[2] or 'roll-out neoliberalism.'[3]

By examining how these tensions played out in Chile and England/Wales, and the international policy context from which they emerged, we can better understand why subsequent attempts to replicate these models globally encountered similar patterns of resistance and required continuous state intervention to maintain. This chapter demonstrates how legal frameworks and spatial relations continuously shape and reshape each other through complex material and social processes. These early experiments thus provide crucial insights into the spatial-legal transformations required to impose market logic on water governance and the inevitable conflict this creates with both water's materiality and communities' place-based water relationships.

DOI: 10.4324/9781003273219-2

Let's start first with a brief examination of the broader context of these two case studies, including the international response to the (then) looming water crisis beginning in the late 1970s and the ideology that came to dominate global economic policy by the 1990s – neoliberalism. As we will see in the case studies below, the concept of a 'water crisis' provided a scarcity narrative that served to justify dramatic policy shifts in relation to water governance, while neoliberalism provided an apparently coherent framework to guide the contours of this radical shift.

The looming 'global water crisis'

The threat of water scarcity and concerns around a looming 'water crisis' became an international focus in the 1970s, resulting in the first United Nations Water Conference in Mar del Plata, Argentina, in 1977.[4] At Mar del Plata, the international community committed to ambitious goals, including the provision of universal access to clean drinking water by 1990, alongside increased public participation, integrated water management, low-cost technologies, and international cooperation.[5] These goals were then taken up by the United Nations General Assembly with the declaration of an International Drinking Water and Sanitation (IDWS) Decade for the 1980s.[6] However, by the end of the decade, a new approach to water governance was beginning to shape global water policy – with the introduction of neoliberal (free market) reforms.

Despite the global commitments and scaled-up development programs introduced as part of the IDWS Decade, implementation fell well short of the articulated goals. While a significant number of people gained access to clean drinking water over the course of the 1980s, population increases meant coverage only increased from 70 to 76 percent in areas where reliable data were available, and even less success was recorded for expanding sanitation services.[7] Beyond population growth, these disappointing results have been attributed to a range of complex factors, including inappropriate technology, inadequate finance and maintenance, and an overly technical approach at the expense of institutional reform and community participation.[8]

The Mar del Plata recommendations had focused on the need to improve integrated water management through the formulation of national water policy statements and plans, with defined goals and targets, and supporting legislation.[9] However, many countries were slow to adopt national water policy statements, and those plans that were adopted tended to be overly technical in focus, with the result that more complex policy issues such as natural resource management and sustainability, equity, capacity building, and underlying structural issues received limited attention.[10] Community participation did receive attention, in part due to the broader trend towards participatory development (or 'community-driven development') in the 1970s and 1980s,[11] but its early institutional application did not reflect its radical roots.[12] Instead, participation was primarily employed as an instrument tool to achieve and sustain predetermined outcomes (including through cost recovery), and it resulted in minimal shifts in power dynamics or structural change.[13]

A closely related issue was the approach taken to human rights. Although Mar del Plata had recognised a human right to water, the IDWS Decade lacked a human rights framework, limiting the ultimate emphasis given to redistribution and community participation and empowerment. The more technical, efficiency-focused approach that was adopted instead paved the way for the ideological approach taken in the following decade – which intensified this focus on financial efficiency and technocratic solutions to the water crisis, sidelining the more complex and challenging policy issues posed by water governance.

By the early 1990s, the poor quality and uneven delivery of many public water services led to debates around the merits of public ownership and control. The public sector was increasingly portrayed as inefficient and prone to political interference and rent-seeking – leading to negative outcomes for public access, economic development, and environmental sustainability. In response, a new water governance approach came to dominate the policy agenda, informed by the prevailing economic ideology of the time – neoliberalism.

Neoliberalism

Neoliberalism was initially known as the 'Washington Consensus'[14] – so named by John Williamson because it included a range of policy prescriptions for fiscal discipline (or austerity), liberalisation, privatisation, and deregulation that were imposed on Latin America by 'Washington' (by which he meant 'Congress and senior members of the administration and the technocratic Washington of the international financial institutions, the economic agencies of the US government, the Federal Reserve Board, and the think tanks').[15] The theory was that these prescriptions were key to economic growth, or (at least) to creating open markets for US interests.[16] As these same policies were applied more broadly to other so-called developing countries, so too was the term Washington Consensus,[17] with the term *neoliberalism* beginning to supersede it by the early 2000s.[18]

Neoliberalism is based on the core belief that the retreat (or dismantling) of the state and related increased exposure of countries to market forces will result in prosperity through a process of economic liberalisation.[19] David Harvey describes it as 'a theory of political economic practices that proposes that human well-being can best be advanced by liberating individual entrepreneurial freedoms and skills within an institutional framework characterized by strong private property rights, free markets, and free trade.'[20] While this requires a retreat on the part of the state, particularly in relation to the regulation of the market and the provision of social welfare, neoliberalism still envisions a strong role for the state in 'creat[ing] and preserv[ing] an institutional framework' that facilitates the operation of the market by, for example, guaranteeing the 'quality and integrity of money... [and establishing] those military, defence, police, and legal structures and functions required to secure private property rights and to guarantee, by force if need be, the proper functioning of markets.'[21]

As we will see in Chile's transition (discussed below), neoliberalism also expects the state to play a positive role in creating markets for such things as 'land, water, education, health care, social security, or environmental pollution,' where they do not exist already.[22] Beyond this, states are expected to retreat because neoliberalism is informed by a deep suspicion of both the capacity and neutrality of the state and a belief that 'the state cannot possibly possess enough information to second-guess market signals (prices) and because powerful interest groups will inevitably distort and bias state interventions (particularly in democracies) for their own benefit'[23] – a concept known as 'rent seeking.'

The growing influence of neoliberal ideology can be observed in two prominent water policy documents of the early 1990s – the 1992 Dublin Statement and the World Bank's 1993 *Water Resources Management* report.[24] The Dublin Statement was the outcome of the International Conference on Water and Sustainable Development, and it set out four guiding principles, agreed to by the expert participants, to guide the 'concerted action . . . needed to reverse the present trends of overconsumption, pollution, and rising threats from drought and floods.'[25] These principles were (1) environmental sustainability, (2) participatory governance, (3) gender awareness, and (4) water as an economic good. While a human right to water was recognised in the Dublin Principles, it was buried within the explanatory text of Principle Four and employed as a key reason (alongside sustainability) for recognising the economic value of water. Ultimately, the headline of Principle Four – 'water as an economic good' – came to be known as *the* Dublin Principle, with human rights, environmental sustainability, participatory governance, and gender awareness receding into the background.

The following year, the World Bank published its *Water Resources Management* report, which stresses the increasing scarcity of water and argues that this 'resource' requires 'careful economic and environmental management.'[26] In relation to the urban water sector, the Bank particularly emphasised privatisation and cost recovery as key strategies 'both to ensure the financial sustainability of water supply systems and to ration the withdrawal of scarce water.'[27] As with the Dublin Statement, a range of challenges and approaches are considered by the Bank in this and other prominent water reports, but it was the focus on managing scarcity through the market (in both the rural and urban water sectors) that came to dominate the 1990s, particularly when it came to donor funding and loan conditionality (as we will consider further in Chapter 3).[28] Here we saw the increasing promotion of free-market water policies, including the liberalisation of water services (the reduction of government controls), private-sector participation, and full cost recovery (an arrangement under which consumers pay for the full cost of water services rather than receiving subsidies).

This commitment to neoliberal water governance that began to dominate global policy and development conditionality by the late 1990s was grounded in ideology and informed by the superficial and peremptory assessments of the 'success' of early experiments with free-market water policies in Chile, England and Wales. In truth, the implementation of abstract economic theory to the complex social and material dynamics of water encountered almost immediate challenges – challenges that were often minimised at the time. Free market theory may choose to define water as an economic resource – a commodity – detached from land and freely tradeable on the market, but community conceptions of water and their relationship with it are more complex than this. The materiality and even agency of water are significant in this process. You cannot, for example, freely trade water that is absent due to drought, and it is rarely frictionless to transfer such a fluid, heavy entity uphill or across long distances. Essentially, law does not operate in a vacuum – it is co-constituted by (and co-constitutive of) space and place. These were the lessons that ought to have been learned through the early experiments in Chile, England, and Wales, but ideology blinded those in power long enough for these models to be exported far and wide. Indeed, as we will see in Chapter 6, it appears these lessons still need learning.

The emergence of neoliberal water governance in the early 1990s represented a profound spatial-legal transformation in how water was conceptualised and regulated. The shift from understanding water as a public good to an economic resource demonstrates the co-constitutive relationship between legal frameworks and social constructions of water. This transformation found its first comprehensive expression in Chile's radical market reforms. As an early laboratory for neoliberal water governance, Chile's experience reveals the complex spatial and political dynamics that emerge when abstract market principles confront place-based water relationships and material realities. The attempt to create an 'aspatial' water rights framework ultimately revealed both the paradox of state intervention in market creation and the persistent resistance of water's materiality to commodification.

Chile's water markets

Chile has long been considered the paradigm example of neoliberal water governance, after the military junta overhauled the existing system of rural water rights with the introduction of a new Water Code in 1981, alongside a range of other radical free market economic policies.[29] This dramatic economic restructuring commenced immediately after the armed forces overthrew the socialist Allende government in a violent military coup on 11 September 1973, led by General Augusto Pinochet (and backed by the Nixon Administration of the US).[30] Carl Bauer argues,

> Chile is a textbook case not merely of neoliberal economic reform, but also of the 'Chicago' approach to law and institutions ... The Chilean Constitution exemplifies a legal and institutional framework designed to encourage a free market economy. The Constitution expands private economic rights and liberties, tightly restricts state economic activity and regulatory authority, and strengthens the courts' powers to enforce these principles.[31]

'Chicago' here refers to the Chicago School of Economics, originating at the University of Chicago prior to the 1970s, with leading contributions from theorists such as Milton Friedman, George Stigler, and Ronald Coase. The sweeping changes of the 1981 Water Code were underpinned by Chile's new Constitution, which established 'a legal and institutional framework intended to foster a free market economy, combining broad private property rights and economic liberties with a "subsidiary" state, whose economic and regulatory powers are restricted.'[32]

While ideologically driven, this new emphasis on a 'subsidiary' state also reflected a reaction to the interventions of the Chilean state under both the Christian Democrat government of Eduardo Frei Montalva (1964–1970) and Salvador Allende's Popular Unity government (1970–1973). Central to these interventions was a considerable increase in public spending on housing, poverty reduction, education, and agricultural subsidies funded by a progressive taxation system, alongside land (and water) reform, commencing with the 1967 *Agrarian Reform Act* and the 1967 *Water Code*. Under both 1967 Acts (supported by changes to the 1925 Constitution), the government was empowered to expropriate property and water rights without compensation.[33]

These 'statist' interventions were not only viewed as damaging to the economic fortunes of Chile as a nation but also created feelings of insecurity among many property holders, including farmers, particularly as the expropriations escalated under the socialist Allende government. The 'anti-statist' 1980 Constitution was thus framed as a 'Constitution of Liberty' – (with a nod to Chicago economist Friedrich Hayek) 'freeing' the population from the economic interventions of the state. With the introduction of the 1981 Water Code, the military junta sought to reform the water sector by providing strong security of property in water rights and by encouraging the development of an efficient water market. Deregulation was promoted as a means of taking politics out of water and allowing the market to 'allocate water apolitically toward the highest economic value uses while maximizing social welfare.'[34]

To support this agenda, government economists proposed auctioning off all new and cancelled water rights and taxing water rights separately from land to encourage 'rights-holders to regard water as a commodity and an economic good, rather than a free attribute of land ownership.'[35] However, these more market-oriented reforms were not popular amongst many in the agricultural sector. They were keen to see their water rights given greater security through strong protection as private property rights (now secure under the 1980 Constitution), but they did not anticipate demand for a water market, and many were not keen (or in a financial position) to pay for water that had always been free.[36]

A compromise(d) outcome

Bauer describes the 1981 Water Code as 'a compromise between the neoliberal economists and their more conservative opponents.'[37] It secured strong private property rights protection for water rights, decoupled these rights from land to enable them to be freely traded as commodities, and strictly limited the scope of government intervention.[38] On the other hand, it did not include many financial signals to promote market trading or to encourage investment in efficiency gains.[39]

The 1981 Water Code attempted to create what legal geographers call an 'aspatial' framework – one that treats water as abstract and detached from place. However, as Nicholas Blomley notes, such attempts at legal abstraction inevitably confront the 'geographical nonsense' of ignoring water's embedded relationships with communities and landscapes.

In the decade that followed Chile's neoliberal water governance reforms, they were touted as a success and model for addressing the looming global water crisis. Writing for the World Bank in 1995, Robert Hearne and William Easter begin their report on Chile's water markets by asserting that it,

> demonstrates that water can no longer be treated as a free good and better ways must be found to improve its allocation and use. Efficient water markets are one means of improving water allocation, while at the same time providing a mechanism to directly compensate existing water users. In addition, as the market value of water becomes clear to water users, they will use it more efficiently.[40]

In concluding their review, Hearne and Easter note a range of positive benefits of Chile's water markets, including that it has 'provided an enabling environment for investment in permanent fruit crops and improved irrigation technology,' contributed to the growth in value of Chile's agricultural output, made Chilean irrigators 'content,' and produced substantial economic gains from trade in some areas.[41] While they acknowledge some issues, including that, contrary to their expectations, only one of the four valleys they studied had active water trading, these are not presented as challenging the model. Instead, they prescribe additional market-based solutions such as the imposition of water fees and taxes.[42]

Monica Rios and Jorge Quiroz, also writing for the World Bank in 1995, similarly conclude, '[t]he system in Chile has worked reasonably well, especially in zones where water scarcity problems are more acute.'[43] They note that, in line with economic expectations, 'the private market has helped to avoid expensive new water infrastructure by allowing frictionless transfers of water rights from agricultural to urban sectors.'[44] While they acknowledge the system 'is not free of problems' (including challenges with implementation of non-consumptive uses and concerns around speculation), they conclude that 'solving each of them seems more a matter of "fine tuning" of the current system rather than a drastic reform of it.'[45] Like Hearne and Easter, to address these minor issues, they suggest the imposition of user fees.[46]

In considering negative environmental externalities, such as overextraction or contamination, Hearne and Easter claim there is 'little indication – from these case studies – that the 1981 Water Code needs to be modified in order to preserve the environment.'[47] Nonetheless, they note the likelihood of increased pressures due to economic growth and support increased environmental regulation (either by the Dirección General de Aguas 'DGA' or 'the proposed river basin management corporations') as a solution.[48] Arguably this is an acknowledgement that free market water policies, particularly including deregulation, are not, in fact, an effective solution to water sustainability challenges, but this conclusion is sidestepped entirely.

Material and social resistance

Other scholars have reached quite different conclusions about the efficacy of Chile's water markets. Writing in the late 1990s, Bauer notes the low level of trading and highlights the role of cultural values around water as a key barrier. The 1981 Water Code may have defined water as a commodity, detached from land, but Bauer argues that this definition did not match the dominant community understanding of water nor their relationship with it. Here Bauer highlights the influence of water scarcity and Chile's history of irrigated agriculture in shaping these water values,

> It would be hard to exaggerate the real and symbolic importance of irrigation in this semi-arid country, where it has taken centuries of labor and

> willpower to bring water to dry lands and transform them into productive fields. Spanish irrigation traditions have predominated, due to the long period of colonial rule and to the fact that central Chile's mediterranean climate is so similar to Spain's. This history, combined with the constant threat of drought, reinforces Chilean farmers' ingrained determination to hold onto their water supplies at almost any cost. They strongly resist selling water rights and returning land to its original non-irrigated condition.[49]

These alternative water values (or relations) were further reflected in community arguments that 'market logic is inappropriate for water precisely because it is so vital and scarce ... [and that as] "water is life" [it is] too fundamental to human existence to be entrusted to commercial motives.'[50] Mixed market signals (due to the absence of water fees or taxes, availability of free water from groundwater extraction, and the high value of irrigated land) and a practice of water speculation (encouraged by free water with no beneficial use obligations) also reduced the incentives for trade.[51]

As Chile's water markets evolved from theoretical model to lived reality, the spatial inequalities and resistance that emerged revealed the tensions between market logic and water's material and social properties. Writing in 2022, Manuel Prieto and others have taken earlier critiques further by arguing that Chile does not, in fact, have a deregulated water market.[52] Drawing on examples from the Antofagasta Region, located in the Atacama Desert of Northern Chile, Prieto and others demonstrate that Chile's market has both operated to entrench historic state allocations of water that privileged extractivism and has been subject to ongoing state interventions to reallocate rights in a manner that reinforces historical hierarchies of privileged access and control and to promote capital accumulation and extractivism.[53]

Particular water uses and users were directly disadvantaged by these interventions, particularly including 'traditional water management practices (e.g., irrigation of wetland, vernacular units of measurement of water flows, ways of organizing land ownership concerning irrigation)' and Indigenous communities and their traditional and cultural uses of water.[54] Prieto and others further argue, 'it is political interests, private agreements, and arbitrary state-centric decisions that have historically shaped water ownership ... [creating] a waterscape in which water is accumulated by extractive industries and indigenous peoples are dispossessed of their waters.'[55] In this context, they conclude that the 1981 Water Code 'has fossilized, under private ownership, historical power asymmetries that are rooted in colonial and extractive dynamics.'[56]

These state interventions are not new, either, with Bauer noting similarly politicised dynamics in the 1980s, when the military government intervened 'directly to prevent [water rights] auctions in several cases with intersectoral implications, particularly involving hydroelectric projects.'[57] Here Bauer notes, '[t]he government was unwilling to leave such crucial allocative decisions to the free market, and either denied the applications or simply assigned the rights to the applicant preferred on the basis of "exceptional circumstances and general interest."'[58] Prieto and others emphasise that 'markets are not separate from statecraft' and the state plays an active and ongoing role in reinforcing the commodification of water under neoliberal governance models.[59] Bakker calls this process 'reregulation,' describing it as the 'reconfiguration of the role of the state to ensure the continued functioning of capitalism.'[60]

Early economic reviews claimed that Chile's water market was not only likely to increase efficiency and productivity and stimulate private irrigation investment and economic growth but also 'reduce water conflicts, ... benefit the poor and ... help conserve natural resources.'[61] Once again, these claims have not been supported by empirical research. Instead, Jessica Budds, for example, found that Chile's market-based water regulation 'diminishes, rather than fosters, social equity and ecological concerns.'[62] She also reports high levels of water conflict (and illegal abstraction), which she argues was created or exacerbated by the 1981 Water Code and its market-based approach. Like others, Budds notes that water remains a highly politicised issue in Chile, with deeply polarised positions making legislative reform nearly impossible – a situation that is exacerbated by the status of water rights as constitutionally protected property.[63] While Bauer acknowledges that 'the Chilean model' has its strengths, he notes similar weaknesses to those observed by Budds, including 'social equity, environmental protection, river basin management, coordination of multiple water users, and resolution of water conflicts.'[64] Importantly, he argues these strengths and weaknesses are structurally connected – making them impossible to separate.[65]

Growing recognition of these weaknesses, particularly including distributional inequities and environmental concerns, led to amendments to the Water Code in 2005. Though significant, these amendments still sought to operate within rather than to fundamentally challenge the existing property rights paradigm (despite emerging from a post-Pinochet, democratic government).[66] The most significant and contentious element of these reforms was the introduction of 'fees for non-use' aimed at addressing water rights speculation. However, this measure had 'the perverse consequence of dispossessing small-scale users, often Indigenous peoples, who were causing the least water impact by leaving water in-stream or because they could not point to constructed water infrastructure to prove their productive use.'[67] The amendments also introduced some environmental protections, including a piecemeal minimum ecological flow regime.[68]

However, these provisions proved inadequate to address mounting environmental concerns because, precisely as Bauer had warned, strong property rights protections meant that they could have little impact in over-allocated basins – the model is predicated on limiting government interference, thus fundamentally limiting the government's capacity to regulate in favour of environmental protection.[69] As Elizabeth Macpherson has documented, the reforms' impacts on Indigenous communities were particularly problematic.[70] While a 2014 Supreme Court decision eventually held that Indigenous communities could retain water rights without being subject to non-use fees in certain circumstances, this came well after many communities had already been impacted by the 2005 provisions.[71]

The ongoing relevance of place

Later analysis of Chile's water markets has further emphasised the highly complex interactions of factors that have led to distinctive outcomes in different areas of Chile – with each valley having its own mix of geographic, social, and technical idiosyncrasies. Chloé Nicolas Artero, for example, has carried out extensive fieldwork in Chile's Elqui River basin and uses it as a case study to examine how technical water infrastructure, legal frameworks, and social practices intersect to produce distinctive market arrangements.[72] Through this analysis, she demonstrates the way water markets emerge through the 'joint and strategic reappropriation, by users, of law and space,' challenging both purely economic and institutional approaches to understanding water markets.[73]

Like Bauer and Budds, Artero is critical of studies that 'presuppose the existence of a water market in Chile since the promulgation of the 1981 Code' – or, at least, that this is a direct result of the Code itself.[74] Although she identifies five distinct types of water markets operating within the Elqui basin,[75] Artero emphasises that these markets are 'socially constructed' through a complex legal-spatial relationships – including the interaction between technical infrastructure, legal frameworks, and social practices.[76] Here, she notes the way 'technical water objects installed since the second half of the 20th century attract new investors and transform the political economy of the valley.'[77]

Artero's fieldwork observations in Chile's Elqui basin contradict the simplistic argument that the legal recognition of water rights as private property led to the emergence of a water market or the economic development of related sectors in Chile.[78] By using legal geography as a theoretical lens, she highlights the significance of 'relationships between legality, spatiality and power.'[79] A key takeaway from these observations is the near impossibility of extracting universal policy prescriptions from Chile's experience to guide the reform of water governance in other places – but this is exactly what has happened.

The World Bank, for example, 'has actively publicized the Chilean case as a model of success and an inspiration for water policy reforms in countries,' including to push for the establishment of tradable water rights in the global south.[80] This pressure to follow the 'Chilean model' has been particularly strong in Latin America, but it has also been influential in places such as Australia, Indonesia, South Africa, Spain, Taiwan, and Vietnam.[81] Bauer is particularly critical of superficial analysis by the World Bank and 'prominent international water economist working at or closely associated with the World Bank' for failing to recognise the complexity of implementing the 'Chilean model of water resources management' in practice. He argues that they tend to present it by sole reference to abstract economic theory and rely on 'assumptions that are rarely met in practice.'[82]

Pluralism

The ongoing reality of pluralism is one such complexity, and this is reflected in the way that communities have responded to state attempts to commodify water. This has particularly included some Indigenous communities who have traditionally held communal rights to water. Through his research on the Atacama Desert region, Prieto demonstrates how the resurgence of Atacameño Indigenous identity in the early 1990s enabled resistance to water privatisation.[83] Building on work by scholars like Rutgerd Boelens and Tom Perreault on the co-constitution of water politics and identity in the Andes, Prieto shows how 'indigeneity is a relational phenomenon that emerged from an ongoing tension between neoliberal water reforms and acts of Indigenous resurgence.'[84] He argues, '[b]y articulating a concrete identity difference, the Atacameños performed an act of anticommodification of water and ensured a common hydraulic property.'[85]

Boelens' work on water justice and territorial pluralism provides a useful theoretical lens for understanding this resistance. He uses the concept of 'hydraulic identity' to theorise how Indigenous communities assert alternative water ontologies that challenge market-based frameworks.[86] As he argues, water rights struggles are fundamentally about competing systems of meaning and authority, where Indigenous communities defend not just water access but entire 'hydrosocial territories' – spaces where water, power relations, cultural practices, and identity are deeply intertwined.[87] This framework helps explain why the Atacameño's resistance to water privatisation was inextricably linked to their broader struggle for territorial and cultural recognition.

The strategic deployment of Indigenous identity described by Prieto illustrates the performative dimension of legal (and property) relations. Rather than simply resisting commodification, communities actively performed alternative water relationships (back) into being. The persistence of these counter-hegemonic narratives about water's nature and value demonstrates how legal frameworks are shaped through ongoing processes of performance and contestation.

Temporality was an important factor in this process, as changing political contexts over time enabled different forms of resistance. In the 1980s, during the first period of attempted water privatisation under authoritarian rule, communities 'did see indigeneity as pejorative, rather than as an identity that would empower them.'[88] By the 1990s, during the second period of attempted water privatisation, Indigenous identity became 'a source of strength and a driver for the rejection of the privatization of water rights.'[89] Prieto emphasises the co-constitutive nature of these hydropolitics with Indigenous identity for the Atacameño, arguing that here 'indigeneity is a relational phenomenon that emerged from an ongoing tension between neoliberal water reforms and acts of Indigenous resurgence.' He elaborates that, in this context, 'the commodification of water is ... a productive political force of new identities that question the colonial conception of the "hopeless Indigenous."'[90] Prieto notes the paradox of this situation – 'although the neoliberal water reforms served as historical sediment that allowed the resurgence of Indigenous identity, it was this very identity that in turn allowed for the opposition and reversal of these reforms.'[91]

Prieto's analysis of Atacameño resistance provides another insight into the way that legal frameworks and water ontologies co-constitute each other. The resurgence of Indigenous identity in the early 1990s enabled resistance to water privatisation precisely because it manifested an alternative conceptualisation of water – not as detached commodity but as relational. This ontological conflict illustrates how seemingly technical water reforms inevitably confront resistance. The Atacameño's assertion of communal water values demonstrates how different legal orders produce and reflect distinct water realities, while also revealing the inherent tensions between market abstraction and place-based water relations. As Prieto points out, '[t]his resurgence [of indigenous identity] shows how market performance is rooted in differentiated ways across diverse places, identities, and natures, rather than being an abstract and ahistorical economic phenomenon.'[92]

The limitations of the 2005 amendments to the Water Code – particularly due to the challenges of addressing the weaknesses of the model without fundamentally overhauling its core commitment to strong private property rights and (ostensibly) limited government regulation – led to mounting pressure for more fundamental reform. This pressure ultimately culminated in a new 2022 Water Code amendment and attempts at constitutional transformation, but the time it took to pass the new Water Code (including over a decade of parliamentary debate and social mobilisation) and the failure of the new constitutional proposal highlight how contentious water remains in Chile.[93]

2022 amendments

The 2022 Water Code amendments marked a decisive shift from pure market ideology toward recognition of water's multiple values and functions, including through the recognition of the human right to water, the introduction of new protections for the environment and for Indigenous water relationships, and even the reclassification of water rights.[94] Although Chile has historically been described as 'rights-resistant' due to its pro-market orientation,[95] the 2022 reforms declared water access 'an essential and irrevocable human right that must be guaranteed by the State.'[96] New environmental protections were also passed, including a prohibition on granting water rights in glaciers, enhanced minimum ecological flow requirements, new state powers to create 'water reserves' for human consumption and ecosystem preservation, and the recognition of ecosystem preservation as a legitimate water use. The amendments sought to address Indigenous water relationships through 'substantive provisions protecting Indigenous rights to water... which attempt to reverse the separation of land and water in the Water Code, considered inconsistent with Indigenous ways of understanding the place-based connectedness and holism of land and water.'[97] Finally, in perhaps the most dramatic departure from the 1981 Code, the amendments transformed water rights from perpetual private property to 'administrative concessions granted for 30 years, subject to renewal in certain circumstances,' aiming to rebalance private and public interests while maintaining some market functions.[98]

Although these changes are substantial and meaningful, they suffer from some of the same limitations as the 2005 amendments in that pre-existing water rights remain private property and are protected under Chile's Pinochet-era Constitution. As such, many of the changes can only apply in relation to newly issued water rights, which is a significant limitation when many basins are already over-allocated. For this and other reasons, water reform remained on the agenda and was a key point of debate in the Constitutional Convention of 2021–2022.

Constitutional reform

The Constitutional Convention emerged from widespread social protests in 2019–2020 that represented Chile's most significant period of contestation since the dictatorship.[99] Following the November 2019 Agreement for Social Peace and a New Constitution,[100] nearly 80 percent of voters supported drafting a new constitution – a clear mandate for transformation.[101] The underlying grievances centred on Chile's Pinochet-era political-economic model, which had proven remarkably resistant to reform due to sophisticated institutional mechanisms embedded in the 1980 Constitution.[102] These mechanisms, which Hugo Rojas characterises as 'straitjackets' and 'locks,' include supermajority requirements for economic reforms and strategic use of the Constitutional Court, enabling a minority to maintain the neoliberal framework despite lacking majority support.[103] This institutional architecture proved particularly significant for water governance, as the constitutional protection of private property rights repeatedly constrained attempts to address growing social and environmental concerns through legislative reform.

The Chilean Constitutional Convention, designed to be broadly representative, included provisions for gender parity and Indigenous representation – symbolically marked by the election of Mapuche scholar Dr Elisa Loncon as the Convention's initial President.[104] Environmental and water rights were central to the Convention's agenda, with over two-thirds of members campaigning for enhanced environmental protections, including the human right to water, biodiversity protection, and climate action.[105] The resulting 2022 draft constitution proposed a radical reconceptualisation of human-water relationships, recognising both the human right to water and rights of nature while emphasising the 'inseparable connection' between people, communities, and nature.[106] Rather than maintaining the existing property rights framework, water was reconceptualised as 'common natural property' that 'could not be appropriated.'[107]

The draft constitution's rejection by 62 percent of voters in September 2022 revealed the persistent challenges of achieving transformative change within Chile's inherited institutional architecture. While various factors contributed to this outcome, including the draft constitution's complexity and scope,[108] the result also highlighted the durability of market-based conceptualisations of water. A second constitutional draft in late 2023, produced by a committee dominated by the far-right Republican Party, was also rejected by voters, leaving the Pinochet-era Constitution – and its strong protection of private water rights – in place.[109]

This constitutional impasse demonstrates how early neoliberal water reforms created enduring spatial-legal path dependencies that continue to constrain governance options. The challenge of reforming Chile's water governance regime illustrates what Petri Juuti and others argue about infrastructure and built environments being 'the results of decisions and efforts made decades and even centuries ago.'[110] This institutional stickiness shows how neoliberal water governance, once established, becomes embedded in both legal frameworks and spatial relations in ways that prove difficult to fundamentally reform.

Chile's experiment with water markets illustrates how legal frameworks attempting to treat water as a detached commodity confront deeply embedded place-based relationships with water. The spatial inequalities and ongoing resistance that emerged reveal the tension between abstract market principles and water's material and social properties. This demonstrates legal geography's key insight that law does not simply act upon space but is actively shaped by existing spatial relations and the agency of water itself.

While Chile's water markets emerged through authoritarian decree, the privatisation of water services in England and Wales followed a different spatial-legal trajectory. Yet despite these contrasting contexts, both cases demonstrate how attempts to impose market logic on water governance inevitably confront the 'geographical nonsense'[111] of treating water as detached from place.

The privatisation of water in England and Wales

While private enterprises were largely responsible for establishing modern urban water systems globally, ultimately most were brought under public control due to private failures to adequately protect public health or provide universal access.[112] Juuti and others argue that 'the decisions, arguments and policies' made in the 1990s to promote privatisation of these largely public utilities broadly resemble those made in the mid-to-late 1800s, in Europe in particular, to privatise water supply and sanitation (WSS) services, but that little attention has been paid to the historic lessons that ought to have been learned from the experiences of that time.[113] So, before we explore the (re) privatisation of WSS services in England and Wales, let's first briefly explore the early period of urban water provision and some of the lessons that could have been heeded.

Historical context

England has been described as the 'forerunner' of modern WSS systems, with households in London beginning to receive piped water to the home in the early 1600s, courtesy of several private water companies.[114] The most notable of these was the New River Company, which commenced operations in 1613 and became a corporation by royal charter in 1619.[115] Although households were initially slow to seek a connection, with just 360 connecting in 1613 and the number plateauing at around 1,500 for over a decade, demand started to increase around 1660 as wealthier households moved to London.[116] The Great Fire of 1666 also prompted new connections due to reconstruction work and the destruction of competing water infrastructure,[117] and, by 1670, the New River Company had 10,000 'tenants' (as they called consumers). This number rose to 17,000 by 1683,[118] and it is estimated that around 30–40 percent of buildings had a water connection by the 1700s,[119] a number that is estimated to have risen to 90 percent by 1850.[120]

These connection rates stand in stark contrast to those in most other European cities which largely relied on public fountains and water carriers until direct private was increased in the mid-1800s.[121] An important contrast between these two approaches was that public fountains provided water for free, so the widespread access to these fountains across Europe improved access for low-income households until it was reduced to support an increase in private connections.[122]

From around the mid-1800s, community attitudes began to change, and there was a growing expectation that the state should play a stronger role in the provision of WSS services to improve quality and better promote public health and hygiene.[123] Juuti and others cite the example of Joseph Chamberlain, a member of the Liberal Party, who argued in 1884, 'It is difficult, if not impossible, to combine the citizens' rights and interests and the private enterprise's interests, because the private enterprise aims at its natural and justified objective, the biggest possible profit.'[124] By 1902 London's WSS services were in public hands – after 50 years of public complaints and campaigns.[125] Similar shifts could be observed across much of the global north. In the US, for example, public ownership of water utilities went from around 20 percent in 1830, to 'about 50 per cent in 1880 and 70 per cent in 1924.'[126]

Full divestment

Despite these public health lessons having been learned by the turn of the 20th century, privatisation returned in 1989 under the Thatcher administration, when the British government took the unusual step of fully privatising the sector by floating the ten existing Regional Water Authorities (RWAs) on the London stock exchange.[127] The newly created utilities were vertically integrated – 'providing the entire cycle of services to their customers, from extraction of raw water, delivery of processed water, and collection, treatment and discharge of wastewater' – and were given monopoly rights in their regions for 25 years.[128] The one exception was 28 statutory water companies that had been operating since the 19th century, who kept their licenses to supply water services to their existing customer bases.[129]

The extreme nature of this neoliberal water governance reform – involving as it did the full divestiture of water utility assets – put England and Wales in the same category as Chile in terms of being a global outlier at the time. As in Chile, arguments in favour of privatisation included increased competition, the assumed greater efficiency of the private sector, and access to private sector investment – in this instance to finance much-needed improvements to deteriorated infrastructure and to meet new European water quality standards.[130]

Legislative groundwork

The foundations of water privatisation in Britain can be traced back to the introduction of a new Water Act in 1973, which nationalised the sector by merging the existing (largely municipally operated) 157 water and 1,398 sewerage entities into 10 RWAs, based on the ten major river basins in England and Wales.[131] Although they were charged with a wide range of functions, including water conservation, water supply, sanitation services, pollution control and environmental improvement, provision of recreation, and land drainage and flood protection, in addition to inheriting billions in debt,[132] the finances of these new RWAs were ring-fenced, and they were required to operate on a cost-recovery basis with caps imposed on expenditure and borrowing.[133] These conditions led to a sharp rise in water pollution incidents over the 1970s and into the 1980s. As the Office of Water Services (OFWAT) puts it (rather delicately),

> [i]n retrospect, the tight fiscal controls applied by central government ... led to insufficient expenditure to meet the capital maintenance and investment requirements of the industry. The resulting problems ... became progressively more unacceptable to the public given their heightened environmental awareness and increasingly stringent European legislation.[134]

Bakker is more blunt, reporting that,

> Britain earned the media label the "dirty man of Europe", dumping more sewerage sludge in the sea than any other country in the world, and failing to improve the condition of over 3,000 kilometres of river too polluted – with industrial effluent as well as sewerage – for any fish to survive.[135]

In response to these ongoing issues, a new Water Act was introduced in 1983 by the Thatcher government. In line with the government's commitment to neoliberalism, the new Act avoided injecting more public funds into the sector and instead 'gave the authorities scope to access the private capital markets.'[136] Further changes commercialised the operations of the RWAs, paving the way for privatisation.[137]

Despite commercialisation and access to private loans, RWA borrowing was tightly controlled, and investment remained insufficient to address the infrastructure upgrades and other compliance issues that were required. This gap was exacerbated by the need to comply with the European Union water quality standards,[138] and '[t]he decision by the EC [European Council] to start prosecution proceedings against the government for non-compliance with two EC Directives.'[139]

Bakker describes the environmental and fiscal crisis of the 1970s and 1980s as 'a powerful vehicle for legitimating change in the water industry.'[140] Despite being the direct result of inadequate public funding, the neoliberal perspective cast this twin crisis as 'evidence of the inefficiency of public water companies, and a justification for privatization.'[141] This historical trajectory illustrates how material conditions (deteriorating infrastructure and the resulting pollution), regulatory environment (new EU compliance requirements), and ideological shifts (neoliberalism) supported by the strategic narrative of 'crisis' combined to create the conditions for privatisation.

A new regulatory framework

The first government proposal for water privatisation, published in 1986, was widely criticised, particularly for its failure to separate WSS provision from environmental regulation.[142] Nonetheless, the Thatcher government took water privatisation to the 1987 national election, with a number of modifications on the original proposal, including the establishment of three new independent regulatory authorities – OFWAT (responsible for economic regulation), the Drinking Water Inspectorate, and the National Rivers Authority.[143] This created what Bakker calls a 'mix of command-and-control regulations and market mechanisms,'[144] and she argues it demonstrates one of the paradoxes of water privatisation – the need for increased rather than decreased regulatory oversight, contrary to neoliberal theory.[145] It is also notable that the government cancelled all long-term debt owned by the RWAs (at a total cost of £7.6bn in 2003–2004 prices) and invested a further £2.3bn into the sector on the eve of privatisation (known as a 'green dowry'), in addition to providing 'capital tax allowances of £12.0bn,' to set the newly privatised utilities up for success.[146]

Nonetheless, the implementation of privatisation proved more complex than anticipated for a range of reasons, including the challenges of balancing commercial imperatives with public service obligations (such as affordable universal access), of promoting competition in a natural monopoly, and the materiality of water itself. As noted above, these tensions led to 'reregulation' rather than deregulation, and instead of withdrawing, the state simply changed the nature of its interventions, with free market logic added alongside existing priorities.[147] Here Jamie Peck and Adam Tickell observe that, in response to resistance, neoliberal governance often shifts to more interventionist regulation to both institutionalise market logic while managing its social consequences – a stage they describe as 'roll-out' neoliberalism.[148]

Social and material resistance

As in Chile, only some of the neoliberal reforms were successfully implemented in this first stage of privatisation. While the WSS utilities were sold off, the legitimacy of the process was undermined by tensions between public perceptions of water as a public good (and entitlement) and the full commodification of water envisioned by the reforms. These tensions were exacerbated in the immediate aftermath due to early tariff increases of 67 percent. A compounding factor was the simultaneous growth in water company profits, with profit margins rising from 28.7 to 35.6 percent between 1990 and 1993.[149] Adding to this controversy was the sharp increase in water poverty and debt and the significant number of households who were disconnected for nonpayment during this period.[150]

Spatial inequality

The spatial concentration of this water poverty following privatisation illustrates the way legal frameworks can reinforce and reproduce existing socio-spatial inequalities. The uneven distribution of water access and affordability demonstrates how neoliberal water reforms intersect with and often exacerbate historical patterns of spatial disadvantage – a theme that was to be repeated globally (as we will explore in subsequent chapters).

Materiality and the Yorkshire drought

Water's material properties, and inherent unreliability, also made it resistant to market logic, as illustrated by the Yorkshire drought of 1995–1996. During this crisis, Yorkshire Water, the private utility for the region, attempted to operate on market logic, but this was undermined by water's material properties and infrastructure constraints, in addition to community outrage. The company's failure to make sufficient investments in water supply reflected unjustifiable assumptions of 'overall system stability,' ignoring water's inherent unpredictability. This resistance to market rationalities demonstrates how water's material properties necessarily shape legal and institutional arrangements.

Bakker reports that the drought 'took regulators, consumers, and [Yorkshire Water] by surprise' as reservoirs began to reach dangerously low levels by mid-1995.[151] Yorkshire Water responded by setting restrictions on water consumption and raising the prospect of cutting off water supply, with household provision to be replaced with public standpipes.[152] The public reaction was one of sustained outcry.[153] While both the company and the government attempted to frame the drought as 'an act of God,' the public blamed shortages on private mismanagement.[154]

Graham Haughton argues that the Yorkshire drought crisis is emblematic of fundamental tensions in neoliberal attempts to commodify water resources. His analysis emphasises the same intersecting tensions that we have already noted, including materiality, legitimacy, and regulation. The physical properties of water and water infrastructure collided with Yorkshire Water's profit-seeking imperatives, including, in this instance, the company's failure to make sufficient investments in water supply.[155] The company's privatised operations also conflicted with deeply held community views of water as a public good. As Labour MP, Helen Jackson, pointedly observed at the time, 'That's what went wrong with privatisation, they tried to turn one of the most essential public services of all into a commodity… [people] still feel it's their water but not that Yorkshire Water is their company.'[156]

There were also competing conceptions of the role and purpose of regulation, with the existing regulatory framework proving inadequate for balancing public and private interests – particularly as Yorkshire Water applied for increased abstractions from already stressed local rivers, having failed to invest in addressing leaks and other infrastructure issues.[157] '[M]edia coverage of Yorkshire Water was damning,' with 'imagery of environmental damage due to low river flows and visible leakage and waste.'[158] The company's continued profitability during this period also created controversy, particularly as OFWAT appeared impotent to address it. In November 1995, the public learned that the company 'had achieved half-yearly profits of £99.5 million, an increase of 48 per cent, leading to headlines such as "Obscene profits fuel water anger."'[159] News that the company's share price and profits were unaffected by the drought and service failures sparked further controversy.[160] Bakker argues that this reveals fundamental flaws in the regulatory framework, noting that Yorkshire Water's dependably 'good financial health during and after the drought is entirely consistent with the post-privatization regulatory framework' that privileged financial returns over infrastructure investment, to the detriment of the public and the environment.[161]

These tensions had spatial and temporal dimensions, with regional identity and media (particularly the *Yorkshire Post*) playing a crucial role in amplifying public resistance, particularly as Yorkshire Water was perceived as representing external interests.[162] There were also scalar tensions between expectations of local accountability (well established under the historic system of municipally supplied water services) and national regulation. Here we can also observe the role of temporarily, with pre-existing legitimacy issues creating conditions for crisis. These included earlier actions of Yorkshire Water in blocking attempts by Diana Scott from the community-based Yorkshire Water Watch to get elected to the company board.[163]

Contemporary media coverage highlighted these tensions. The Yorkshire Evening Post editorial noted the paradox of public resistance to water conservation messaging actually worsening the crisis: 'It seems that some people, relishing the company's problems are actually adding to them, by prodigal use of this wasting asset.'[164] Here public understanding of water as a public good manifested in resistance to Yorkshire Water Service's attempts to encourage them to conserve water – believing as they did that water shortages were the fault of the company.[165]

Fundamental contradictions

These fundamental contradictions in neoliberal water governance can be examined through the lens of the 'hydrosocial cycle' – a concept employed by scholars such as Erik Swyngedouw,[166] Boelens,[167] Budds,[168] and Jamie Linton.[169] This concept emphasises the way water circulation is simultaneously physical and social, shaped by power relations and political-economic structures. This lens highlights Yorkshire Water's role in exacerbating water shortages through capital accumulation, contrary to their attempts to frame the drought as purely 'an act of God'. The public's resistance thus represented not just opposition to service failures but a deeper contestation of water's commodification.

In the early years of the privatisation of England and Wales' WSS services, attempts to impose market rationalities on water governance were fundamentally constrained by water's material properties and social meanings. The Yorkshire drought provides a vivid illustration of how these tensions played out in practice, leading to both operational failures and public resistance. As Haughton concludes, 'Quite simply, in terms of popular acceptability and environmental management, the balance between relying on market mechanisms and state regulation proved to be unworkable.'[170]

Ultimately, these issues led to increased state intervention and the imposition of a range of restrictions on the sector, including a ban on disconnections for nonpayment and on the use of limiting devices, and restrictions on the imposition of volumetric (metred) charging.[171] Despite these early issues, in the years that followed this period of reregulation, the WSS services of England and Wales entered a new period of neoliberal reform with the financialisation of the sector (a stage that might be described as a new roll-out). We will consider this phase further in Chapter 6.

Discussion

This chapter's examination of early experiments with neoliberal water governance in Chile and England/Wales reveals the profound spatial-legal transformations required to impose market logic on water relationships. The theoretical tensions identified at the outset – between water's material properties, communities' place-based relationships, and the paradox of state intervention – manifested in distinct yet parallel ways across these contexts. The dialectic between reform attempts and local resistance particularly illustrates the dynamic interplay between law, space, and social relations.

The implementation of neoliberal water governance reforms in both contexts highlighted tensions between different scales of governance. Chile's water markets emerged through authoritarian national decree, imposing an ideology that originated in the US, but were resisted at the local level due to place-based realities and conceptions of water. England's privatisation followed a different trajectory involving local utilities, national regulation, and European Union water quality standards. However, again, resistance was strongest at the local level – particularly in the context of Yorkshire's drought.

If we return to the key themes of space, place, and narrative, we can draw several lessons from these case studies. Turning first to space, attempts to create 'aspatial' water markets inevitably confront the geographical realities of water. Chile's uneven market development particularly demonstrates how water's materiality forces the recognition of spatial relationships that market logic attempts to erase. The flipside is the observation that neoliberal water governance reforms have their own spatial effects. The early years of privatisation in England and Wales, for example, produced and entrenched spatial inequalities of access to affordable water, due to the prioritisation of profits over public access.

When we consider place, a key lesson from these case studies is the way resistance to neoliberal water governance reforms often emerges through what Prieto terms 'relational phenomena' – the way communities mobilise place-based identities and relationships to contest commodification. The resurgence of Indigenous identity in Chile's Atacama region and community resistance during the Yorkshire drought, for example, demonstrate how water's social meanings can generate powerful counter-narratives to market logic.

Speaking of narrative, our third lesson is that despite neoliberalism's narrative of dismantling the state and reducing regulation, neoliberal water governance reforms involve a roll-out of new regulatory infrastructure. Both cases reveal how states must actively intervene to create and maintain market conditions, challenging the rhetorical claims of 'market-based' governance. This paradox helps explain the persistent tensions in subsequent attempts to replicate these models globally.

The experiences in Chile and England/Wales highlight how attempts to impose market logic on water governance inevitably confront both material resistance and social contestation. As discussed above, these early experiments would nonetheless come to be portrayed as success stories by influential international institutions, particularly the World Bank, despite mounting evidence of their structural limitations. As we turn to examine the export of these models across the global south in the 1990s, the lessons from this chapter – about water's material resistance to commodification, the persistence of place-based water relationships, and the paradox of state intervention – take on renewed significance. The following chapter explores how these dynamics played out in Manila, where attempts to impose similar neoliberal water governance reforms (this time through a long-term private concession) created similar patterns of spatial inequality while encountering material and social resistance, albeit in distinctly local forms. Together, these case studies demonstrate the multiple ways that place-based context shapes local outcomes, even as proponents of neoliberal reform sought to present market logic as a universal solution to growing water governance challenges.

Notes

1 Karen Bakker, *An Uncooperative Commodity: Privatizing Water in England and Wales* (Oxford University Press, 2004).
2 Karen Bakker, 'Neoliberalizing Nature? Market Environmentalism in Water Supply in England and Wales' (2005) 95(3) *Annals of the Association of American Geographers* 542.
3 Jamie Peck and Adam Tickell, 'Neoliberalizing Space' (2002) 34(3) *Antipode* 380.
4 United Nations, *Report of the United Nations Water Conference, Mar Del Plata* (No U.N. Doc. E/CONF.70/29, United Nations, 1977).
5 United Nations, *Report of the United Nations Water Conference, Mar Del Plata.*
6 United Nations General Assembly (UNGA), *Proclamation of the International Drinking Water Supply and Sanitation Decade, U.N. Doc. A/RES/32/18* (United Nations, 1980).
7 Peter H. Gleick (ed), *The World's Water* (Island Press/Center for Resource Economics, 2011) 233–240 <http://link.springer.com/10.1007/978-1-59726-228-6>.
8 Asit K. Biswas, 'United Nations Water Conference Action Plan' (1988) 4(3) *International Journal of Water Resources Development* 148, 151–153; Gleick (ed), *The World's Water* (n 7) 233–240; E. O'Rourke, 'The International Drinking Water Supply and Sanitation Decade: Dogmatic Means to a Debatable End' (1992) 26(7–8) *Water Science and Technology* 1929; United Nations Development Programme, *The New Delhi Statement: Global Consultation on Safe Water and Sanitation for the 1990s* (UNDP, 1990); World Health Organization, 'Safe Water Supply and Sanitation: Prerequisites for Health for All' (1986) 39(1) *World Health Statistics Quarterly* 2; World Health Organization, *Evaluation of the International Drinking Water Supply and Sanitation Decade, 1981–1990* (89th Sess., U.N. Doc. EB89/24, 21 November 1991).
9 United Nations, *Report of the United Nations Water Conference, Mar Del Plata* (n 4) 30–34.
10 Biswas, 'United Nations Water Conference Action Plan' (n 8) 151; World Health Organization, 'Evaluation of the International Drinking Water Supply and Sanitation Decade, 1981–1990' (n 8) 7.
11 Samuel Paul, *Community Participation in Development Projects: The World Bank Experience* (No World Bank Discussion Paper No. 6, World Bank, 1987); Rosemary McGee, 'Participating in Development' in U. Kothari and M. Minogue (eds), *Development Theory and Practice: Critical Perspectives* (Palgrave Macmillan, 2002) 92, 92–95; Ghazala Mansuri and Vijayendra Rao, 'Evaluating Community-Based and Community-Driven Development: A Critical Review of the Evidence' (2003) *Economics, Sociology* <https://www.semanticscholar.org/paper/Evaluating-Community-Based-and-Community-Driven-%3A-A-Mansuri-Rao/3a38eceb5a202cd75b3ad4639ab326aee391a88d>; Rajesh Tandon, 'Participation, Citizenship and Democracy: Reflections on 25 Years' of PRIA' (2008) 43(3) *Community Development Journal* 284, 287; Jona Razzaque, 'Public Participation in Water Governance' in Joseph Dellapenna and Joyeeta Gupta (eds), *The Evolution of the Law and Politics of Water* (Springer, 2009) 353, 355 <https://papers.ssrn.com/abstract=1421227>.
12 Robert Chambers, *Rural Development: Putting the Last First* (Routledge, 1983); Michael Cernea (ed), *Putting People First: Sociological Variables in Rural Development* (Oxford University Press for the World Bank, 2nd edition, 1991); McGee, 'Participating in Development' (n 11) 94.
13 Paul, *Community Participation in Development Projects* (n 11); O'Rourke, 'The International Drinking Water Supply and Sanitation Decade (n 8); Andrea Cornwall

and John Gaventa, *From Users and Choosers to Makers and Shapers: Repositioning Participation in Social Policy* (IDS working papers No. 127, Institute of Development Studies, 2001) 4 <https://www.ids.ac.uk/publications/from-users-and-choosers-to-makers-and-shapers-repositioning-participation-in-social-policy/>; Mansuri and Rao, 'Evaluating Community-Based and Community-Driven Development' (n 11); Tandon, 'Participation, Citizenship and Democracy' (n 11) 289.

14 John Williamson, 'What Washington Means by Policy Reform' in John Williamson (ed), *Latin American Adjustment: How Much Has Happened?* (1990).

15 Williamson, 'What Washington Means by Policy Reform' (n 14) 1.

16 Williamson, 'What Washington Means by Policy Reform' (n 14) 1.

17 John Williamson, 'A Short History of the Washington Consensus' (Paper presented at the *From the Washington Consensus Towards a New Global Governance*, Barcelona, 24–25 September 2004).

18 See, e.g., Williamson, 'A Short History of the Washington Consensus' (n 17); Alfredo Saad-Filho and Deborah Johnston (eds), *Neoliberalism: A Critical Reader* (Pluto Press, 2005); Joseph Stiglitz, *Globalization and Its Discontents* (Penguin, 2002); Patrick Bond, *Elite Transition: From Apartheid to Neoliberalism in South Africa* (Pluto Press, 2nd ed, 2000).

19 Jagdish Bhagwati, *In Defence of Globalization* (Oxford University Press 2004) 66–67; Thomas Friedman, *The Lexus and the Olive Tree* (Harper Collins, 2000) 210, 442–444; Kenichi Ohmae, *The Borderless World: Power and Strategy in the Interlinked Economy* (Harper Collins, 1999) 11.

20 David Harvey, *A Brief History of Neoliberalism* (Oxford University Press, 2007) 2.

21 Harvey, *A Brief History of Neoliberalism* (n 20).

22 Harvey, *A Brief History of Neoliberalism* (n 20).

23 Harvey, *A Brief History of Neoliberalism* (n 20).

24 *The Dublin Statement on Water and Sustainable Development* (UN Doc. A/CONF/.151/PC/112, 26–31 January 1992); World Bank, *Water Resources Management* (A World Bank policy paper, World Bank, 1993).

25 *The Dublin Statement on Water and Sustainable Development* (n 24).

26 World Bank, *Water Resources Management* (n 24) 9.

27 World Bank, *Water Resources Management* (n 24) 126.

28 See, e.g., Kate Bayliss, *Privatisation and Poverty: The Distributional Impact of Utility Privatisation* (No Working Paper No. 16, Centre on Regulation and Competition, Institute for Development Policy and Management, 2002) 3; Stiglitz, *Globalization and Its Discontents* 53–78; WaterAid, *International Financial Institutions (IFI), Conditionality and Privatisation of Water and Sanitation Systems* (WaterAid, 2003) 2–3; Jomo Kwame Sundaram, Oliver Schwank and Rudiger von Arnim, *Globalization and Development in Sub-Saharan Africa* (UNDESA Working Paper No. 102, UNDESA, 2011).

29 Carl J. Bauer, *Against the Current: Privatization, Water Markets, and the State in Chile* (Springer, 1998) 1. Chile's urban water sector was not privatised until the late 1990s. See Madeline Baer, *Stemming the Tide: Human Rights and Water Policy in a Neoliberal World* (Oxford University Press, 2017).

30 Bauer, *Against the Current* (n 29) 4; Lubna Z. Qureshi, *Nixon, Kissinger, and Allende: U.S. Involvement in the 1973 Coup in Chile* (Lexington Books, 1st edition, 2009).

31 Bauer, *Against the Current* (n 29) 12.

32 Bauer, *Against the Current* (n 29) 24.

33 Bauer, *Against the Current* (n 29) 39.

34 Manuel Prieto et al, 'The (Not-so-Free) Chilean Water Model: The Case of the Antofagasta Region, Atacama Desert, Chile' (2022) 11 *The Extractive Industries and Society* 101081, 1; citing John Briscoe, *Water as an Economic Good: The Idea and What It Means in Practice* (The World Bank, 1996) 25.

35 Bauer, *Against the Current* (n 29) 43.
36 Bauer, *Against the Current* (n 29) 43–44.
37 Bauer, *Against the Current (n 29)* 44.
38 Bauer, *Against the Current* (n 29) 44–45.
39 Bauer, *Against the Current (n 29)* 44–45.
40 Robert R. Hearne and K. William Easter, *Water Allocation and Water Markets: An Analysis of Gains-from-Trade in Chile* (Text/HTML No World Bank technical paper no. WTP 315, World Bank, 31 December 1995) 1 (forward) <https://documents.worldbank.org/en/publication/documents-reports/documentdetail/168401468743722296/Water-allocation-and-water-markets-an-analysis-of-gains-from-trade-in-Chile>.
41 Hearne and Easter, *Water Allocation and Water Markets* (n 40) 38.
42 Hearne and Easter, *Water Allocation and Water Markets* (n 40) 38–39.
43 Monica Rios and Jorge Quiroz, *The Market for Water Rights in Chile: Major Issues* (World Bank Technical Paper No 285, World Bank, September 1995) 28 <https://documents1.worldbank.org/curated/en/254241468769894995/pdf/multi-page.pdf>.
44 Rios and Quiroz, *The Market for Water Rights in Chile* (n 43) 28.
45 Rios and Quiroz, *The Market for Water Rights in Chile* (n 43) 28.
46 Rios and Quiroz, *The Market for Water Rights in Chile* (n 43) 29.
47 Hearne and Easter, *Water Allocation and Water Markets* (n 41) 40.
48 Hearne and Easter, *Water Allocation and Water Markets* (n 41) 40.
49 Bauer, *Against the Current* (n 29) 63.
50 Bauer, *Against the Current* (n 29) 64.
51 Bauer, *Against the Current* (n 29) 65.
52 Prieto et al, 'The (Not-so-Free) Chilean Water Model' (n 34).
53 Prieto et al, 'The (Not-so-Free) Chilean Water Model' (n 34).
54 Prieto et al, 'The (Not-so-Free) Chilean Water Model' (n 34) 5.
55 Prieto et al, 'The (Not-so-Free) Chilean Water Model' (n 34) 6.
56 Prieto et al, 'The (Not-so-Free) Chilean Water Model' (n 34) 11.
57 Bauer, *Against the Current* (n 29) 66–67.
58 Bauer, *Against the Current* (n 29) 66–67.
59 Prieto et al, 'The (Not-so-Free) Chilean Water Model' (n 34) 11.
60 Bakker, 'Neoliberalizing Nature?' (n 2) 544.
61 Mateen Thobani, *Tradable Property Rights to Water: How to Improve Water Use and Resolve Water Conflicts* (No FPD Note No. 34, World Bank, February 1995) 4.
62 Jessica Budds, 'Power, Nature and Neoliberalism: The Political Ecology of Water in Chile' (2004) 25(3) *Singapore Journal of Tropical Geography* 322, 337.
63 Budds, 'Power, Nature and Neoliberalism' (n 62) 327.
64 Carl J. Bauer, *Siren Song: Chilean Water Law as a Model for International Reform* (Routledge, 2004) 2.
65 Bauer, (n 64) *Siren Song*.
66 Elizabeth Macpherson et al, 'Evolving Rights to (and of) Water in Chile: A Case for Relationship-Based Water Law and Governance' 0(0) *The International Journal of Human Rights* 1, 15.
67 Macpherson et al, 'Evolving Rights to (and of) Water in Chile' (n 66).
68 Macpherson et al, 'Evolving Rights to (and of) Water in Chile' (n 66) 19.
69 Carl J. Bauer, 'Water Conflicts and Entrenched Governance Problems in Chile's Market Model' (2015) 8(2) *Water Alternatives* 147, 149; Macpherson et al, 'Evolving Rights to (and of) Water in Chile' (n 66) 13.
70 Elizabeth Macpherson, *Indigenous Water Rights in Law and Regulation: Lessons from Comparative Experience* (Cambridge University Press, 2019) 161–212; Macpherson et al, 'Evolving Rights to (and of) Water in Chile' (n 66) 15.

71 Macpherson, *Indigenous Water Rights in Law and Regulation* (n 70) 161–212; Macpherson et al, 'Evolving Rights to (and of) Water in Chile' (n 66) 15.
72 Chloé Nicolas Artero, 'The Social Construction of Water Markets in Chile: An Approach from the Legal Geography' (2021) (79) *Revista de geografía Norte Grande* 163.
73 Artero, 'The Social Construction of Water Markets in Chile' (n 72) 164.
74 Artero, 'The Social Construction of Water Markets in Chile' (n 72) 172.
75 Artero, 'The Social Construction of Water Markets in Chile' (n 72) 169.
76 Artero, 'The Social Construction of Water Markets in Chile' (n 72) 164.
77 Artero, 'The Social Construction of Water Markets in Chile' (n 72) 163.
78 Artero, 'The Social Construction of Water Markets in Chile' (n 72) 172.
79 Artero, 'The Social Construction of Water Markets in Chile' (n 72) 164.
80 Bauer, *Siren Song* (n 64) [ft41].
81 Bauer, *Siren Song* (n 64) [ft41].
82 Bauer, *Siren Song* (n 64) [ft41].
83 Manuel Prieto, 'Indigenous Resurgence, Identity Politics, and the Anticommodification of Nature: The Chilean Water Market and the Atacameño People' (2022) 112(2) *Annals of the American Association of Geographers* 487, 501.
84 Prieto, 'Indigenous Resurgence, Identity Politics, and the Anticommodification of Nature' (n 83) 501 citing Tom Perreault, 'Custom and Contradiction: Rural Water Governance and the Politics of Usos y Costumbres in Bolivia's Irrigators' Movement' (2008) 98(4) *Annals of the Association of American Geographers* 834; Rutgerd Boelens, *Water, Power and Identity: The Cultural Politics of Water in the Andes* (Routledge, 2015).
85 Prieto, 'Indigenous Resurgence, Identity Politics, and the Anticommodification of Nature' (n 83) 501.
86 Rutgerd Boelens, 'Cultural Politics and the Hydrosocial Cycle: Water, Power and Identity in the Andean Highlands' (2014) 57 *Geoforum* 234.
87 Boelens, 'Cultural Politics and the Hydrosocial Cycle' (n 86).
88 Prieto, 'Indigenous Resurgence, Identity Politics, and the Anticommodification of Nature' (n 83) 495.
89 Prieto, 'Indigenous Resurgence, Identity Politics, and the Anticommodification of Nature' (n 84) 497.
90 Prieto, 'Indigenous Resurgence, Identity Politics, and the Anticommodification of Nature' (n 84) 501.
91 Prieto, 'Indigenous Resurgence, Identity Politics, and the Anticommodification of Nature' (n 84) 500.
92 Prieto, 'Indigenous Resurgence, Identity Politics, and the Anticommodification of Nature' (n 84) 489.
93 Macpherson, *Indigenous Water Rights in Law and Regulation* (n 71).
94 *Law No. 21.435 (Water Code Amendments) 2022*; Macpherson et al, 'Evolving Rights to (and of) Water in Chile' (n 67) 19.
95 Baer, *Stemming the Tide* (n 29) 15.
96 *Law No. 21.435 (Water Code Amendments)* (n 94) 5.
97 Macpherson et al, 'Evolving Rights to (and of) Water in Chile' (n 66) 19.
98 Macpherson et al, 'Evolving Rights to (and of) Water in Chile' (n 66) 19.
99 Hugo Rojas, 'Chile at the Crossroads: From the 2019 Social Explosion to a New Constitution' (2022) 20(4) *Seattle Journal for Social Justice* 981–1018.
100 Macpherson et al, 'Evolving Rights to (and of) Water in Chile' (n 66) 19–20.
101 Carlos García Soto, Miguel Ángel Martínez Meucci and Raúl Sánchez Urribarrí, 'Winds of Change: Comparing the Early Phases of Constitutional Redrafting in Chile and Venezuela' (2021) 13(2) *Hague Journal on the Rule of Law* 315.
102 Rojas, 'Chile at the Crossroads' (n 100) 986.

103 Rojas, 'Chile at the Crossroads' (n 99) 986.
104 Macpherson et al, 'Evolving Rights to (and of) Water in Chile' (n 66) 20.
105 Macpherson et al, 'Evolving Rights to (and of) Water in Chile' (n 66) 21.
106 Constitutional Convention of Chile, 'Consolidated Approved Norms: Constitutional Proposal by the Full Convention' 204.
107 Constitutional Convention of Chile, 'Consolidated Approved Norms: Constitutional Proposal by the Full Convention' 205–206.
108 Noam Titelman, 'Why Did Chileans Reject the Draft Constitution?', *NACLA* (8 September 2022) <https://nacla.org/why-did-chileans-reject-draft-constitution>; Camila Vergara, 'Chile's Rejection', *NLR Sidecar* (9 September 2022) <https://newleftreview.org/sidecar/posts/chiles-rejection>.
109 El Mercurio S.A.P., 'Boric cierra el proceso constitucional "en su Gobierno" y ante resultado afirma: "Ni celebración ni arrogancia"', *Emol* (17 December 2023) <https://www.emol.com/noticias/Nacional/2023/12/17/1116049/boric-proceso-constituyente.html>.
110 Petri S. Juuti, Tapio Katko and Heikki S. Vuorinen, *Environmental History of Water – Global Views on Community Water Supply and Sanitation* (IWA Publishing, 2007) 237.
111 Blomley, *Law, Space, and the Geographies of Power* (n 40) 53.
112 Juuti et al, *Environmental History of Water – Global Views on Community Water Supply and Sanitation* (n 110) 236.
113 Juuti et al, *Environmental History of Water – Global Views on Community Water Supply and Sanitation* (n 110) 237.
114 Juuti et al, *Environmental History of Water – Global Views on Community Water Supply and Sanitation* (n 110) 236.
115 Leslie Tomory, 'London's Water Supply before 1800 and the Roots of the Networked City' (2015) 56(3) *Technology and Culture* 704, 709.
116 Tomory, 'London's Water Supply before 1800 and the Roots of the Networked City' (n 115) 710–711.
117 Tomory, 'London's Water Supply before 1800 and the Roots of the Networked City' (n 115) 712.
118 Tomory, 'London's Water Supply before 1800 and the Roots of the Networked City' (n 115) 713.
119 Tomory, 'London's Water Supply before 1800 and the Roots of the Networked City' (n 115) 714.
120 Danis Bocquet, Konstantinos Chatzis and Agnes Sander, 'From Free Good to Commodity: Universalizing the Provision of Water in Paris (1830-1940)' (2008) 39(6) *Geoforum* 1821, 7.
121 Tomory, 'London's Water Supply before 1800 and the Roots of the Networked City' (n 115) 716.
122 Bocquet et al, 'From Free Good to Commodity (n 121) 3.
123 Juuti et al, *Environmental History of Water – Global Views on Community Water Supply and Sanitation* (n 110) 240.
124 Juuti et al, *Environmental History of Water – Global Views on Community Water Supply and Sanitation* (n 110) 240.
125 Juuti et al, *Environmental History of Water – Global Views on Community Water Supply and Sanitation* (n 110) 240.
126 Juuti et al, *Environmental History of Water – Global Views on Community Water Supply and Sanitation* (n 110) 243.
127 Karen J. Bakker, 'From Public to Private to … Mutual? Restructuring Water Supply Governance in England and Wales' (2003) 34(3) *Geoforum* 359, 361.
128 Bakker, 'From Public to Private to … Mutual?' (n 127).
129 Bakker, *An Uncooperative Commodity* (n 1) 60.

130 Bakker, 'Neoliberalizing Nature?' (n 2) 549.
131 *Water Act (UK) 1973* 2 (As Enacted); OFWAT, *The Development of the Water Industry in England and Wales* (Commissioned Report, OFWAT, 27 January 2006) 2, 13 <https://www.ofwat.gov.uk/publication/the-development-of-the-water-industry-in-england-and-wales/>.
132 OFWAT, *The Development of the Water Industry in England and Wales* (n 131) 22.
133 OFWAT, *The Development of the Water Industry in England and Wales* (n 131) 15–16; *Water Act (UK)* (n 132) 29.
134 OFWAT, *The Development of the Water Industry in England and Wales* (n 131) 2.
135 Bakker, *An Uncooperative Commodity* (n 1) 64.
136 OFWAT, *The Development of the Water Industry in England and Wales* (n 131) 27.
137 OFWAT, *The Development of the Water Industry in England and Wales* (n 131) 27–28.
138 Council of the European Union, 'Council Directive 76/160/EEC Concerning the Quality of Bathing Water, OJ L 31 of 5.2.1976'.
139 OFWAT, *The Development of the Water Industry in England and Wales* (n 131) 29.
140 Bakker, *An Uncooperative Commodity* (n 1) 64.
141 Bakker, *An Uncooperative Commodity* (n 1) 64.
142 OFWAT, *The Development of the Water Industry in England and Wales* (n 131) 30–32.
143 OFWAT, *The Development of the Water Industry in England and Wales* (n 131) 47; G. Walker, 'An Uncooperative Community: Revisiting Water Privatisation and Commoditisation in England and Wales' (http://purl.org/dc/dcmitype/Text, University of Oxford, 2014) 23 <https://ora.ox.ac.uk/objects/uuid:97e3c382-5475-4926-903f-0df327ebf720>.
144 Bakker, 'Neoliberalizing Nature?' (n 2) 559.
145 Bakker, *An Uncooperative Commodity* (n 1) 36–37.
146 OFWAT, *The Development of the Water Industry in England and Wales* (n 131) 38.
147 Graham Haughton, 'Private Profits – Public Drought: The Creation of a Crisis in Water Management for West Yorkshire' (1998) 23(4) *Transactions of the Institute of British Geographers* 419, 424; Bakker, *An Uncooperative Commodity* (n 1) 36–37.
148 Peck and Tickell, 'Neoliberalizing Space' (n 3).
149 John Middleton and Pat Saunders, 'Paying for Water' (1997) 19(1) *Journal of Public Health* 106, 108.
150 Middleton and Saunders, 'Paying for Water' (n 149).
151 Bakker, *An Uncooperative Commodity* (n 1) 105.
152 Haughton, 'Private Profits – Public Drought' (n 147) 419.
153 Haughton, 'Private Profits – Public Drought' (n 147) 419.
154 Haughton, 'Private Profits – Public Drought' (n 147) 420.
155 Haughton, 'Private Profits – Public Drought' (n 147) 431.
156 Haughton, 'Private Profits – Public Drought' (n 147) 430.
157 Haughton, 'Private Profits – Public Drought' (n 147) 433.
158 Walker, 'An Uncooperative Community' (n 143) 15.
159 Haughton, 'Private Profits – Public Drought' (n 147) 425 citing *The Guardian* (30 November 1995) 2.
160 Walker, 'An Uncooperative Community' (n 143) 15.
161 Bakker, *An Uncooperative Commodity* (n 1) 107.
162 Haughton, 'Private Profits – Public Drought' (n 147) 430.
163 Haughton, 'Private Profits – Public Drought' (n 147) 424, 429.
164 Haughton, 'Private Profits – Public Drought' (n 147) 426 citing *Yorkshire Evening Post* (1 September 1995).
165 Bakker, *An Uncooperative Commodity* (n 1) 111.

166 Erik Swyngedouw, 'The Political Economy and Political Ecology of the Hydro-Social Cycle' (2009) 142(1) *Journal of Contemporary Water Research & Education* 56.
167 Boelens, 'Cultural Politics and the Hydrosocial Cycle' (n 87).
168 Jessica Budds, 'Whose Scarcity? The Hydrosocial Cycle and the Changing Waterscape of La Ligua River Basin, Chile' in Michael Goodman, Maxwell Boykoff and Kyle Evered (eds), *Contentious Geographies: Environment, Meaning, Scale* (Ashgate Publishing, 2008) 59.
169 Jamie Linton, *What Is Water?* (UBC Press, 2010) <https://www.ubcpress.ca/what-is-water>.
170 Haughton, 'Private Profits – Public Drought' (n 147) 432.
171 *Water Industry Act (UK) 1999* 1, 2, 7.

References

Artero, Chloé Nicolas, 'The Social Construction of Water Markets in Chile: An Approach from the Legal Geography' (2021) 79 *Revista de geografía Norte Grande* 163

Baer, Madeline, *Stemming the Tide: Human Rights and Water Policy in a Neoliberal World* (Oxford University Press, 2017)

Bakker, Karen, *An Uncooperative Commodity: Privatizing Water in England and Wales* (Oxford University Press, 2004)

Bakker, Karen J., 'From Public to Private to … Mutual? Restructuring Water Supply Governance in England and Wales' (2003) 34(3) *Geoforum* 359

Bakker, Karen, 'Neoliberalizing Nature? Market Environmentalism in Water Supply in England and Wales' (2005) 95(3) *Annals of the Association of American Geographers* 542

Bauer, Carl J., *Against the Current: Privatization, Water Markets, and the State in Chile* (Springer, 1998)

Bauer, Carl J., *Siren Song: Chilean Water Law as a Model for International Reform* (Routledge, 2004)

Bauer, Carl J., 'Water Conflicts and Entrenched Governance Problems in Chile's Market Model' (2015) 8(2) *Water Alternatives* 147

Bayliss, Kate, *Privatisation and Poverty: The Distributional Impact of Utility Privatisation* (No Working Paper No. 16, Centre on Regulation and Competition, Institute for Development Policy and Management, 2002)

Biswas, Asit K., 'United Nations Water Conference Action Plan' (1988) 4(3) *International Journal of Water Resources Development* 148

Blomley, Nicholas, *Law, Space, and the Geographies of Power* (The Guildford Press, 1994)

Bocquet, Danis, Konstantinos Chatzis and Agnes Sander, 'From Free Good to Commodity: Universalizing the Provision of Water in Paris (1830-1940)' (2008) 39(6) *Geoforum* 1821

Boelens, Rutgerd, 'Cultural Politics and the Hydrosocial Cycle: Water, Power and Identity in the Andean Highlands' (2014) 57 *Geoforum* 234

Boelens, Rutgerd, *Water, Power and Identity: The Cultural Politics of Water in the Andes* (Routledge, 2015)

Briscoe, John, *Water as an Economic Good: The Idea and What It Means in Practice* (The World Bank, 1996) 25

Budds, Jessica, 'Power, Nature and Neoliberalism: The Political Ecology of Water in Chile' (2004) 25(3) *Singapore Journal of Tropical Geography* 322
Budds, Jessica, 'Whose Scarcity? The Hydrosocial Cycle and the Changing Waterscape of La Ligua River Basin, Chile' in Michael Goodman, Maxwell Boykoff and Kyle Evered (eds), *Contentious Geographies: Environment, Meaning, Scale* (Ashgate Publishing, 2008) 59
Cernea, Michael (ed), *Putting People First: Sociological Variables in Rural Development* (Oxford University Press for the World Bank, 2nd edition, 1991)
Chambers, Robert, *Rural Development: Putting the Last First* (Routledge, 1983)
Constitutional Convention of Chile, 'Consolidated Approved Norms: Constitutional Proposal by the Full Convention' (2021)
Cornwall, Andrea and John Gaventa, *From Users and Choosers to Makers and Shapers: Repositioning Participation in Social Policy* (IDS working papers No. 127, Institute of Development Studies, 2001) <https://www.ids.ac.uk/publications/from-users-and-choosers-to-makers-and-shapers-repositioning-participation-in-social-policy/>
Council of the European Union, 'Council Directive 76/160/EEC Concerning the Quality of Bathing Water, OJ L 31 of 5.2.1976' (1976)
El Mercurio S.A.P., 'Boric cierra el proceso constitucional "en su Gobierno" y ante resultado afirma: "Ni celebración ni arrogancia"', *Emol* (17 December 2023) <https://www.emol.com/noticias/Nacional/2023/12/17/1116049/boric-proceso-constituyente.html>
Gleick, Peter H. (ed), *The World's Water* (Island Press/Center for Resource Economics, 2011) <https://link.springer.com/10.1007/978-1-59726-228-6>
Harvey, David, *A Brief History of Neoliberalism* (Oxford University Press, 2007)
Haughton, Graham, 'Private Profits – Public Drought: The Creation of a Crisis in Water Management for West Yorkshire' (1998) 23(4) *Transactions of the Institute of British Geographers* 419
Hearne, Robert R. and K. William Easter, *Water Allocation and Water Markets: An Analysis of Gains-from-Trade in Chile* (Text/HTML No World Bank technical paper no. WTP 315, World Bank, 31 December 1995) <https://documents.worldbank.org/en/publication/documents-reports/documentdetail/168401468743722296/Water-allocation-and-water-markets-an-analysis-of-gains-from-trade-in-Chile>
Juuti, Petri S., Tapio Katko and Heikki S. Vuorinen, *Environmental History of Water – Global Views on Community Water Supply and Sanitation* (IWA Publishing, 2007)
Kwame Sundaram, Jomo, Oliver Schwank and Rudiger von Arnim, *Globalization and Development in Sub-Saharan Africa* (UNDESA Working Paper No 102, UNDESA, 2011)
Law No. 21.435 (Water Code Amendments) 2022
Linton, Jamie, *What Is Water?* (UBC Press, 2010) <https://www.ubcpress.ca/what-is-water>
Macpherson, Elizabeth et al, 'Evolving Rights to (and of) Water in Chile: A Case for Relationship-Based Water Law and Governance' (2023) *The International Journal of Human Rights* 1
Macpherson, Elizabeth, *Indigenous Water Rights in Law and Regulation: Lessons from Comparative Experience* (Cambridge University Press, 2019)
Mansuri, Ghazala and Vijayendra Rao, 'Evaluating Community-Based and Community-Driven Development: A Critical Review of the Evidence' (2003) *Economics, Sociology* <https://www.semanticscholar.org/paper/Evaluating-Community-Based-and-Community-Driven-%3A-A-Mansuri-Rao/3a38eceb5a202cd75b3ad4639ab326aee391a88d>

McGee, Rosemary, 'Participating in Development' in Uma Kothari and Martin Minogue (eds), *Development Theory and Practice: Critical Perspectives* (Palgrave Macmillan, 2002) 92
Middleton, John and Pat Saunders, 'Paying for Water' (1997) 19(1) *Journal of Public Health* 106
OFWAT, *The Development of the Water Industry in England and Wales* (Commissioned Report, OFWAT, 27 January 2006) <https://www.ofwat.gov.uk/publication/the-development-of-the-water-industry-in-england-and-wales/>
O'Rourke, Emily, 'The International Drinking Water Supply and Sanitation Decade: Dogmatic Means to a Debatable End' (1992) 26(7–8) *Water Science and Technology* 1929
Paul, Samuel, *Community Participation in Development Projects: The World Bank Experience* (No World Bank Discussion Paper No. 6, World Bank, 1987)
Peck, Jamie and Adam Tickell, 'Neoliberalizing Space' (2002) 34(3) *Antipode* 380
Perreault, Tom, 'Custom and Contradiction: Rural Water Governance and the Politics of Usos y Costumbres in Bolivia's Irrigators' Movement' (2008) 98(4) *Annals of the Association of American Geographers* 834
Prieto, Manuel, 'Indigenous Resurgence, Identity Politics, and the Anticommodification of Nature: The Chilean Water Market and the Atacameño People' (2022) 112(2) *Annals of the American Association of Geographers* 487
Prieto, Manuel et al, 'The (Not-so-Free) Chilean Water Model: The Case of the Antofagasta Region, Atacama Desert, Chile' (2022) 11 *The Extractive Industries and Society* 101081
Qureshi, Lubna Z., *Nixon, Kissinger, and Allende: U.S. Involvement in the 1973 Coup in Chile* (Lexington Books, 1st edition, 2009)
Razzaque, Jona, 'Public Participation in Water Governance' in Joseph Dellapenna and Joyeeta Gupta (eds), *The Evolution of the Law and Politics of Water* (Springer, 2009) 353 <https://papers.ssrn.com/abstract=1421227>
Rios, Monica and Jorge Quiroz, *The Market for Water Rights in Chile: Major Issues* (No World Bank Technical Paper No 285, World Bank, September 1995) <https://documents1.worldbank.org/curated/en/254241468769894995/pdf/multi-page.pdf>
Rojas, Hugo, 'Chile at the Crossroads: From the 2019 Social Explosion to a New Constitution' (2022) 20(4) *Seattle Journal for Social Justice* 981–1018
Soto, Carlos García, Miguel Ángel Martínez Meucci and Raúl Sánchez Urribarrí, 'Winds of Change: Comparing the Early Phases of Constitutional Redrafting in Chile and Venezuela' (2021) 13(2) *Hague Journal on the Rule of Law* 315
Stiglitz, Joseph, *Globalization and Its Discontents* (Penguin, 2002)
Swyngedouw, Erik, 'The Political Economy and Political Ecology of the Hydro-Social Cycle' (2009) 142(1) *Journal of Contemporary Water Research & Education* 56
Tandon, Rajesh, 'Participation, Citizenship and Democracy: Reflections on 25 Years' of PRIA' (2008) 43(3) *Community Development Journal* 284
The Dublin Statement on Water and Sustainable Development (UN Doc. A/CONF/. 151/PC/112, United Nations, 26–31 January 1992)
Thobani, Mateen, *Tradable Property Rights to Water: How to Improve Water Use and Resolve Water Conflicts* (No FPD Note No. 34, World Bank, February 1995)
Titelman, Noam, 'Why Did Chileans Reject the Draft Constitution?' *NACLA* (8 September 2022) <https://nacla.org/why-did-chileans-reject-draft-constitution>
Tomory, Leslie, 'London's Water Supply before 1800 and the Roots of the Networked City' (2015) 56(3) *Technology and Culture* 704

United Nations, *Report of the United Nations Water Conference, Mar Del Plata* (No U.N. Doc. E/CONF.70/29, United Nations, 1977)

United Nations Development Programme, *The New Delhi Statement: Global Consultation on Safe Water and Sanitation for the 1990s* (UNDP, 1990)

United Nations General Assembly (UNGA), *Proclamation of the International Drinking Water Supply and Sanitation Decade, U.N. Doc. A/RES/32/18* (United Nations, 1980)

Vergara, Camila, 'Chile's Rejection', *NLR Sidecar* (9 September 2022) <https://newleftreview.org/sidecar/posts/chiles-rejection>

Walker, G., 'An Uncooperative Community: Revisiting Water Privatisation and Commoditisation in England and Wales' (https://purl.org/dc/dcmitype/Text, University of Oxford, 2014) <https://ora.ox.ac.uk/objects/uuid:97e3c382-5475-4926-903f-0df327ebf720>

Water Act 1973 (UK) (As Enacted)

Water Industry Act 1999 (UK)

WaterAid, *International Financial Institutions (IFI), Conditionality and Privatisation of Water and Sanitation Systems* (WaterAid, 2003)

Williamson, John, 'What Washington Means by Policy Reform' in John Williamson (ed), *Latin American Adjustment: How Much Has Happened?* (Peterson Institute for International Economics, 1990)

World Bank, *Water Resources Management* (A World Bank policy paper, World Bank, 1993)

World Health Organization, *Evaluation of the International Drinking Water Supply and Sanitation Decade, 1981–1990* (89th Sess. U.N. Doc. EB89/24, 21 November 1991)

World Health Organization, 'Safe Water Supply and Sanitation: Prerequisites for Health for All' (1986) 39(1) *World Health Statistics Quarterly* 2

3

GLOBAL WATER GOVERNANCE REFORMS

Introduction

While Chile, England, and Wales were outliers in their early implementation of neoliberal water governance reforms, by the late 1990s market-based approaches had become increasingly influential in shaping global water governance. Through examining Manila's experiment with private sector participation (PSP) in urban water provision, introduced in 1997, this chapter explores how market mechanisms generate differentiated service territories that reflect and reinforce existing socio-spatial inequalities.

The privatisation of Manila's Metropolitan Waterworks and Sewerage System (MWSS) emerged at the intersection of colonial legacies, domestic political imperatives, and international policy pressures. As a former Spanish and American colony, Manila's water infrastructure reflected deeply embedded spatial inequalities with services historically concentrated in elite enclaves. These historical patterns were reinforced rather than transformed by neoliberal reforms promoted by international financial institutions (IFIs) as part of a broader development agenda. Manila's experience reveals how the commercial logic of PSP creates what Steve Graham and Simon Marvin term 'splintered urbanism' – where infrastructure networks fragment along socio-economic lines, producing distinct service levels calibrated to anticipated returns rather than social need.[1]

Here we can observe that infrastructure networks (whether for water or other urban services) not only reflect power relations but also entrench and create them through the physical arrangement of pipes, meters, and treatment facilities. In Manila, the material properties of water infrastructure, from bulk supply points to household connections, shaped patterns of access and control.

DOI: 10.4324/9781003273219-3

As we saw in Chapter 2, the temporal implications of this are also important, with the physicality of infrastructure networks creating enduring spatial-legal arrangements that constrain future governance possibilities. The emergence of so-called 'micro-networks' in informal settlements (discussed below) demonstrates how material configurations of infrastructure both enable and limit service provision while institutionalising spatial hierarchies through differentiated service territories.

As discussed in Chapter 2, the rising dominance of neoliberal approaches to water governance by the 1990s can be explained by several factors, including domestic politics in the UK and US and related waves of neoliberal reform across Latin America. Perhaps even more significant was the enthusiastic uptake of neoliberal theory by IFIs and the influence this had on loan conditionality. The poor state of urban water supply and sanitation (WSS) systems, particularly in the global south, provided fertile ground for market-based solutions. By 1992, 1.3 billion people were unable to access sufficient quantities of safe water to meet their basic needs.[2] This crisis created political momentum for dramatic reform, with neoliberal theory providing an apparently clear pathway forward for governments and donors looking to deliver change.

Drawing on Manila's experience with PSP in urban water provision, this chapter examines how neoliberal governance reforms reshape urban space through water infrastructure. It reveals the complex ways market mechanisms interact with existing social and spatial inequalities to produce differentiated forms of service delivery that reflect underlying power relations. The analysis further demonstrates how regulatory frameworks, while theoretically designed to ensure public benefit, often operate to legitimise these spatial disparities of water access. Through a close examination of Manila's experience, the chapter develops broader theoretical insights about the spatial politics of water governance and the limitations of market-based reforms in ensuring equitable service provision.

The political economy of water reform

By the 1990s, many urban water systems had suffered from decades of poor governance. It was widely acknowledged that WSS services were managed inefficiently, poorly regulated, unresponsive to community needs, and plagued by financial deficits and corruption.[3] Most had initially been constructed only to service elite enclaves of the population, and this legacy was carried forward into the modern era.[4] Pipes were old, with leaks causing systems to lose over 50 percent of water – resulting in high levels of non-revenue water (essentially the difference between water supplied to the system and water billed to consumers, representing both physical losses through leaks and commercial losses through theft or unbilled consumption).[5] Constrained finances also meant that many systems lacked the means to conduct necessary maintenance or to extend services to low-income communities. This lack of maintenance and failure to expand meant that many water systems provided either unreliable service or none at all to large sections of the community,[6] while also failing to meet health and safety standards.[7]

While high levels of non-revenue water contributed to the financial issues of many public water systems, these issues were also the result of inadequate public investment exacerbated by political pressure to keep tariffs low. This status quo benefitted those wealthy households already receiving good services at low prices but left many households to the mercy of the informal sector with its significantly higher prices and lower standards of service. Public water systems were in crisis.

These financial and governance failures help to explain the attractiveness of neoliberal water governance reforms in the 1990s. When a system is plagued by inefficiency and inadequate finance, reforms that both prioritise and promise to deliver both efficiency and financial sustainability make a lot of sense. Neoliberal liberal theory dictates that treating water as an economic good will encourage people to manage it in a more sustainable manner – both economically and for the environment. While England and Wales had achieved this in the 1980s through full divestment, under which the entire system and its assets were sold off to the private sector, a more common approach is a so-called 'public-private partnership' involving a long-term concession or a management contract – often called 'private sector participation.'

In the second half of the 1990s, long-term concessions were created in Buenos Aires (Argentina),[8] Manila (the Philippines),[9] Jakarta (Indonesia),[10] and Cochabamba (Bolivia)[11] – all influenced by policy advice from, and loan conditionalities imposed by, the IFIs. As we saw in Chile, many assumptions are built into this neoliberal approach, particularly that the private sector will necessarily manage water more efficiently and effectively than the public sector (or the community). However, as will become clear below, these assumptions are not always borne out in practice.

Role of International Financial Institutions

A key reason for the adoption of neoliberal water reforms by governments across the global south has been pressure from the IFIs to open their WSS markets to private water corporations – pressure that was particularly potent in the 1990s and early 2000s.[12] The most significant mechanism used by the IFIs to impose PSP on governments of the global south is loan conditionalities. These conditionalities are mostly administered through the International Bank for Reconstruction and Development (IBRD), a division of the World Bank that provides low-interest loans to governments for developmental purposes. For example, in 1999 the IBRD provided a US$117 million loan to Mozambique to finance infrastructure development.[13] The condition attached to this loan and to the extension of the country's debt relief package was that Mozambique open up its WSS system to PSP.[14] The same kinds of conditions were also imposed on Burkina Faso, Ghana, and Nigeria.[15] During this same period, the International Monetary Fund (IMF) also imposed similar loan conditions on countries in the global south. For example, 'a random review of IMF loan documents involving 40 countries revealed that the IMF imposed conditions requiring water privatisation or cost recovery on 12 countries in the year 2000.'[16]

This trend continued across public service provision more broadly (including health, education, water, and sanitation).[17] For example, in 2006, a 'study of 20 countries receiving World Bank and IMF loans found that privatisation was a condition in 18 of them,'[18] and a 'study of debt cancellation found that reforms requiring some form of privatisation were a pre-condition for debt relief in over half the [qualifying] countries.'[19] This issue is not limited to the global south. In the wake of the EU financial crisis, the European Commission and the IMF also imposed PSP as a condition of the bailouts provided to countries such as Greece and Portugal.[20] These conditions were imposed despite strong public opposition.[21]

Donors also wield considerable influence over the policies of governments in the global south even when conditionalities are not imposed. As Oxfam points out, '[f]or some of the poorest countries, donor aid is equivalent to half the national budget. Advice from outside experts, funded by aid, is highly influential in determining the kinds of reforms a government adopts.'[22] While sometimes this advice involves explicit directions to privatise water systems, it can also influence policy in more subtle ways by prescribing reforms to the public sector that are more geared towards creating future potential for private sector investment than they are with ensuring the ongoing viability of the public operator.[23]

As we will explore further below, Manila's experience with water privatisation in 1997 provides an illustrative case study of how these global policy prescriptions materialise in specific urban contexts, highlighting both the institutional mechanisms through which neoliberal reforms are implemented and the spatial inequalities they produce and legitimise. The privatisation of MWSS emerged at the intersection of domestic political imperatives and international policy diffusion, making it a fitting case study for examining how global pressures for market-based reform interact with local governance arrangements.

Corporate interests and policy influence

It is worth noting that these neoliberal water reforms created new commercial opportunities for large water corporations and have been shaped by their lobbying and influence.[24] By the early 2000s, the private sector was describing water as the oil of the 21st century and as an 'exciting investment opportunity.'[25] For example, ABN AMRO Private Banking Asia released an investment brochure in July 2006 that starts by noting, '[n]o other commodity is experiencing such a rise in demand juxtaposed with declining supply.'[26] In the brochure, they reassure investors that the private water market is opening up: 'We see governments across the world increasingly privatising their water infrastructures, which has been a boon to industrial companies the like of Suez and Veolia Environment.'[27] Finally, and relevantly to this case study, ABN AMRON describes Asia as a 'sweet spot' for investors because companies will be subject to less pricing regulation and able to make substantial profits.[28]

To increase and exploit this investment opportunity, large water corporations, such as Veolia, Suez, RWE-Thames Water, Bechtel-United Utilities, and Enron-Azurix, actively lobbied national governments and the IFIs to ensure favourable policy decisions were adopted.[29] At times these private firms were able to take an active role in determining the content of water policy, both at a domestic and global level, through their participation in organisations such as the World Water Council (which 'aims to reach a common strategic vision on water resources and water services management amongst all stakeholders in the water community' and organises the triennial World Water Forum),[30] and through a variety of lobby groups such as the International Private Water Association, the National Association of Water Companies, and the International Federation of Private Water Operators (AquaFed).[31]

Tension between financial sustainability and social equity

As we saw in Chapter 2, neoliberal theory was already informing the practice of the World Bank and IMF by the 1980s and into the 1990s and shaping the structural adjustment programs prescribed for developing countries.[32] However, many recipient countries (particularly those in sub-Saharan Africa) experienced a period of decelerated economic growth during this period,[33] instead of the prosperity that had been predicted.[34] In response, the World Bank began to look for reasons to explain why their predictions for growth had been incorrect and why some countries, in particular, had experienced such negative results from the prescribed structural adjustment programs.[35] This review led the Bank to the conclusion that the quality of the domestic governance environment is an essential precondition for effective economic development and aid effectiveness.[36] In response, it began promoting 'good governance' as a central part of its mandate, particularly in the areas of 'public sector management, accountability, the legal framework for development, and information and transparency.'[37]

The World Bank's new focus on improving the quality of governance in recipient countries spread quickly, with many development organisations adopting their own approaches to 'good governance.' These approaches had their roots in each organisation's historical (and ideological) approach to development, which perhaps explains the lack of a single agreed-upon definition of the term itself.[38] Nonetheless, the underlying motivation from the perspective of the World Bank and many other major donors remained grounded in ensuring the success of neoliberal economic reforms. Therefore, while non-economic issues were included in the theory of good governance, the emphasis and key criteria for success focused on financial sustainability and efficiency, while other considerations were primarily valued for their contribution towards these fundamental goals.[39] As a result, while the theory of good governance encompasses considerations of equity, transparency, accountability, and participation, the practical application by the IFIs and other major donors reflected neoliberal ideology and primarily focused on increasing the financial sustainability and efficiency of water governance.[40] An awareness of this gap between the rhetoric (or narrative) of good governance and its practical application is useful for understanding the realities and impacts of neoliberal water governance reforms at the turn of the century. It also helps to explain the phenomenon of reregulation or roll-out neoliberalism observed earlier.

One benefit of this era was that investment increased, and this did have the benefit of reducing non-revenue water and enabling the extension of services. It also focused attention on the importance of effective regulation. Nonetheless, comprehensive research conducted in the early 2000s demonstrated that the private sector was no more efficient than the public sector in water management.[41] More concerningly, accessibility for low-income communities decreased under PSP, and community participation was also compromised, as privity of contract (a legal doctrine limiting enforcement rights to direct parties to a contract) left the public with no standing to challenge decisions or seek accountability from private providers.[42] As discussed below, the increase in inequality under a system that rhetorically claims to be focused on universal provision can be explained by returning to this gap between the rhetoric and practice of neoliberal governance. The foundational principles of neoliberalism operate to produce and entrench inequality, often along spatial lines, and to create regulatory biases towards the private sector, which then serve to legitimise these unequal outcomes.

While these regulatory challenges highlight the institutional tensions inherent in market-based water governance, they also point towards deeper patterns of spatial differentiation that emerged through Manila's experiment with PSP. As we will consider below, the concessionaires' approach to service provision, particularly in informal settlements, reveals how regulatory frameworks can legitimise and institutionalise spatial inequalities through seemingly technical decisions about infrastructure investment and service delivery models.

Theorising neoliberal water governance

Neoliberal water reforms can be examined across multiple theoretical dimensions, including their spatial implications, reconfiguration of regulatory frameworks, and intersection with community relationships. While often presented as technical solutions to inefficient public provision, closer analysis reveals how these reforms fundamentally reshape human-water relations along ideological lines.

Production and legitimation of spatial inequality

A key feature of neoliberal governance is its creation of differentiated service territories that reflect and reinforce existing socio-spatial hierarchies. The mechanisms through which this socio-spatial inequality is both produced and entrenched have been extensively examined in the urban context. In their wide-ranging analysis of the political and economic significance of urban infrastructure landscapes, for example, Graham and Marvin argue that infrastructure networks fragment along socio-economic lines as a direct result of service levels being driven by private profit rather than social needs.[43] They describe this as 'splintered urbanism.'[44]

Writing specifically about urban water governance, Karen Bakker describes this process as 'market environmentalism', where the commodification of water services creates distinct spatial territories of value and investment.[45] This marketisation process produces differentiated service levels as providers segment urban space according to commercial logic. The resulting spatial arrangements both reflect pre-existing inequalities and actively reshape urban territories through infrastructure investment decisions and service delivery models.

This process has been legitimatised, in part, through the strategic deployment of 'informality,' with providers deliberately maintaining certain spaces as 'informal' to justify differentiated service provision. In Manila's case, Deborah Cheng has argued that informality in certain areas has become 'a mode of urban governance' driven by the logic of liberalisation.[46] As we will discuss below, in Manila, this resulted in the emergence of what Cheng terms 'micro-networks' – locations where private providers outsourced service provision to informal settlements to small-scale providers in order to maximise profits and reduce risk, while simultaneously entrenching existing spatial inequalities in access to safe and affordable water services.[47] This strategic deployment of informality resulted in more than service differentiation; it also produced hybrid governance frameworks that combined market logic with community management.

David Harvey describes this process as 'uneven geographical development,' arguing that market mechanisms necessarily produce and reproduce spatial disparities through the concentrated accumulation of capital investment in particular territories.[48] Rather than viewing differentiated service provision as an unintended consequence, he argues it is a structural feature of neoliberal governance. Harvey also highlights the flipside of this uneven investment – noting that it is facilitated by the privatisation of public assets and services through a process of 'accumulation by dispossession,' which further concentrates (formerly public) benefits in private hands while dispersing costs and risks across marginalised communities.[49] This is often described as the privatisation of profits coupled with the socialisation of risk. These insights are useful frameworks for examining how market-based reforms reshape urban space through water infrastructure while also helping to explain the limitations of conventional regulatory solutions in ensuring equitable service provision.

Regulatory legitimation

In addition to entrenching and producing spatial inequality, neoliberal governance operates to legitimise these outcomes through appeals to market efficiency and shallow forms of community participation. This process of legitimation often relies on regulatory frameworks that, while theoretically designed to ensure public benefit, operate to naturalise service differentiation and protect corporate interests. As Erik Swyngedouw demonstrates, the technical language of efficiency and financial sustainability can obscure how regulatory mechanisms validate and entrench spatial inequalities through differentiated service standards and pricing models.[50] This regulatory legitimation helps explain the persistence of spatial disparities even in contexts of substantial private sector investment and formal commitments to universal service provision. As we will see below, this is particularly evident in Manila's experience with risk allocation during financial crises, where the spatial distribution of service improvements closely tracked patterns of existing socio-economic advantage, and these adjustments to earlier commitments to universal provision were frequently legitimated by the regulator.

Regulatory legitimation also operates through the strategic deployment of 'participation' by using community engagement rhetoric to mask fundamentally unequal power relations. Participatory mechanisms can serve to support rather than challenge market logic, transforming citizens into consumers (or even sub-contractors) while limiting their capacity for meaningful engagement or control. The 'water for poor' projects in Manila particularly illustrate this approach, as the participation of residents was largely confined to accepting responsibility for bill collection and the construction and cost of water pipes to connect individual households to the water main.[51]

The transformation of Manila's water governance through PSP followed a classic pattern, starting with so-called 'roll-back' neoliberalism (focused on dismantling existing institutions) and moving on to 'roll-out' neoliberalism (characterised by the introduction of new institutions and regulatory responses, including legitimating responses).[52] This analysis helps to explain how spatial inequalities are both produced and legitimated through seemingly technical regulatory decisions about infrastructure investment and service provision.

Multi-scalar governance challenges

Finally, the implementation of neoliberal water reforms also highlights the complex dynamics between governance mechanisms across multiple spatial scales. As Swyngedouw has emphasised through his concept of 'glocalisation,' water governance simultaneously operates through highly localised infrastructure networks while being shaped by global flows of capital, policy models, and institutional power.[53] This rescaling of governance produces new tensions between local service provision, national regulatory frameworks, and transnational policy (and financial) regimes, resulting in 'new geometries of social power' where different scales of authority compete and collaborate in ways that often reinforce existing inequalities.[54] Swyngedouw's theoretical framework (including the emphasis on complexity) is particularly relevant to Manila's experience, where global policy prescriptions from IFIs intersected with national regulatory structures and local infrastructure legacies to entrench spatial inequalities – albeit while simultaneously expanding water access.

Neoliberal water reforms in the global south – Manila's experience

The reform of Manila's public WSS system took place in 1997 during the peak of the policy trend for the adoption of PSP across the global south. It was a significant project and initially held up as the model for all future projects of a similar nature. Since then, it has been variously described as either a notable success[55] or a notorious failure,[56] and there is truth in both descriptions. While the specific historical context, local conditions, and place-based dynamics of Manila make its experience with PSP unique, the first decade of this experiment still provides an illustrative case study of many of the larger themes discussed above – particularly including spatial politics, regulatory legitimation, and multi-scalar governance challenges. Before we further examine these themes, allow me to set the scene.

Water governance in the Philippines

The MWSS of the greater city of Manila was established in 1878, making it the oldest WSS system in Asia.[57] By the mid-1990s, its coverage area included 14 adjoining cities and municipalities and a population of about 11 million people.[58] By this time, MWSS was largely failing in its duty to provide WSS services to the people of Metro Manila. [59] Only two-thirds of its coverage population were receiving water services, and then only for an average of 16 hours per day, while just eight percent of its coverage population were receiving sanitation services.[60]

MWSS was a government corporation, operating independently of the national legislature (Congress), but often turning to Congress for subsidies to assist it in its operations.[61] Despite these subsidies, MWSS was unable to afford to expand its operations to cover the growing population of Metro Manila or to pay for repairs and maintenance for its ageing infrastructure.[62] These financial problems were primarily the result of inefficiency.[63] Non-revenue water was somewhere between 56 and 63 percent.[64] The staff-per-1,000-connections ratio[65] was the highest in Asia.[66] Additionally, and perhaps most crucially, MWSS had reached the point where it was struggling to service its debts of USD800 million.[67]

Due to the political pressure not to raise tariffs, service quality was deliberately reduced whenever MWSS was placed under financial pressure.[68] This default solution meant that new revenue was never available to increase efficiency or to expand services to the 33 percent of the population relying on alternative sources of water. While wealthier residents could afford to dig private wells and purchase bottled water, it was the urban poor who suffered the most under the status quo. Unserved poor households were forced to pay small-scale water providers up to 13 times as much as those households with piped water.[69]

Policy identification – private sector participation

In January 1997, the Government of the Philippines privatised the MWSS through a competitive bidding process.[70] Several years earlier, investors from Malaysia (in partnership with British water firm Biwater) had presented privatisation to the Philippine government as the solution to all of the problems of MWSS.[71] The claim was that through private investment and the injection of private sector efficiency, it would be possible to expand distribution services, provide new water supply sources, and reduce non-revenue water all at a lower tariff than was currently being charged to consumers.[72] In 1993, the government had solved a power supply crisis in Manila through PSP, and its experience in this industry made it predisposed to adopting a similar approach to reforming the WSS sector.[73] In 1995, Congress passed the *National Water Crisis Act*,[74] which reorganised MWSS, authorised the retrenchment of personnel, criminalised water theft, and gave the President the authority to privatise the company.[75]

Mark Dumol reports that after learning about the early success of the privatisation of the Buenos Aires' WSS system,[76] the administration was encouraged to pursue a similar model of privatisation (a long-term concession agreement (CA)) and a similar bidding process.[77] Unlike the model adopted in Buenos Aires, the national government also decided to divide MWSS into two concessions, as had been done in Paris when it privatised its WSS system in 1861.[78] The decision to create two concessions was designed to enable regulators to make comparisons between the two zones, thus overcoming some of the information asymmetry inherent in a privatised arrangement.[79] It was also expected to provide the government with more leverage in negotiations with concessionaires.[80]

Another difference between the Buenos Aires concession and the privatisation of MWSS was the requirement under the Philippine Constitution that all public utilities be owned and controlled by Filipinos.[81] This meant that 60 percent of each of the concessionaires had to be owned by a local corporation and that its officers were required to be Filipinos.[82] Since no local firm had any previous experience in running a water utility, joint venture arrangements between domestic companies and multinational water corporations were the only realistic option.[83] The size of the undertaking and the pre-qualification restrictions imposed by the government[84] also meant that only a small number of domestic companies were big enough to bid for the concession.[85]

Every effort was made to ensure that the privatisation process was a success. The MWSS Board hired the International Finance Corporation (IFC) in November 1995 as lead advisors for the design and implementation of the privatisation project.[86] In drafting the concession contract, the IFC and the government sought to balance the need to attract private investors by minimising the risks involved to the concessionaires and the need to guarantee improvements in efficiency, financial sustainability, and access.[87] To this end, the CA included ambitious service expansion targets, the establishment of a Regulatory Office (Regulator), clear dispute resolution mechanisms, and specific procedures for contract amendment and termination (including a requirement for the concessionaires to deposit a substantial performance bond – a financial guarantee deposited by concessionaires that the regulator could claim if they failed to meet contractual obligations).[88] After the bidding process, the deal was viewed as a genuine success and a model to be emulated internationally.[89]

Although neoliberal theory promotes PSP as a means of increasing cost recovery and, thus, financial sustainability, Manila's privatisation process was designed to ensure that tariffs would go down – at least in the initial five-year period. This was done to avoid any public backlash against the process.[90] A range of tariff adjustment mechanisms were then incorporated into the CA to protect concessionaires against the risk of failure while ensuring that the public would continue to enjoy lower prices.[91] These mechanisms recognised three grounds for adjusting rates: inflation,[92] extraordinary price adjustment (a mechanism allowing tariff increases outside regular adjustments to account for unexpected events like currency fluctuations)[93] and rate rebasing (a periodic review process where tariffs are recalculated based on past investments and future projections to ensure both cost recovery and reasonable returns).[94] While rate-rebasing was scheduled to take place once every five years, the first was made optional at the discretion of the Regulator.[95] This was to discourage the prospective concessionaires from deliberately bidding at a level that would require them to operate at a loss under the assumption that a better rate could be negotiated further down the track – a practice known as 'dive bidding.'[96]

Crucially, for the financial sustainability of the system, the CA also committed the winning bidders to pay concession fees amounting to around USD1.2 billion over the life of the concession period, which would be used to service the existing debts of MWSS and to finance the operations of the new Regulator.[97] The CA imposed obligations to maintain existing assets and to significantly expand the service coverage in each zone from 67 percent in 1997 to 96 percent by 2006 and universal coverage thereafter.[98] The concessionaires also committed themselves to maintaining and upgrading existing infrastructure, with the expectation that they would then recoup this investment by expanding their customer base and by increasing the efficiency of the system through the reduction of non-revenue water.[99]

Regulatory design and implementation challenges

Good governance theory recognises the need for regulatory independence to ensure both transparency and accountability.[100] Under a privatised system, independent regulation can also help to ensure the public interest is not compromised in the pursuit of profit.[101] As government officials involved in the privatisation process considered it essential to complete the process well before the next congressional elections,[102] the constrained timetable meant that there was insufficient time to pass legislation necessary to create an independent Regulator.[103] Instead the Regulator was set up within MWSS, under the Board, meaning that it was forced not only to rely on the government for cooperation but also on the fees of the concessionaires to pay its costs, including salaries.[104] As will be discussed below, this lack of independence had implications for the transparency of negotiations that subsequently took place, the role the public interest was able to play in the outcomes of these negotiations, and the influence of short-term political interests on both tariffs and service commitments.[105]

The institutional design of Manila's regulatory framework reflects the fundamental tensions within neoliberal theory that result in its need for strong state institutions to create and maintain markets (as discussed above). This contradiction creates challenges for regulatory design, where agencies must balance market facilitation with public interest protection. By default, this tension tends to be resolved by neoliberal theory's privileging of market efficiency over social equity, creating an inherent regulatory bias toward private sector interests. This bias operates not just through obvious mechanisms like regulatory capture but also through the metrics and frameworks used to evaluate regulatory decisions. When regulators adopt market-based criteria for assessing outcomes, they implicitly prioritise commercial viability over public values, even as they seek to balance multiple objectives. Manila's experience reveals how this theoretical contradiction shapes regulatory practice, as the Regulator repeatedly legitimated decisions that prioritised concessionaire interests over public accountability.

One of the key roles of the Regulator was to regulate the tariffs charged by the Concessionaires. To assist this process, the CA carefully defined the tariff adjustment mechanisms for the regulator to follow when reviewing the tariffs set by the concessionaires and sought to stabilise tariffs in the initial decade of the concession period. The government expected this would provide a commercial incentive for the concessionaires to increase the efficiency of the water service,[106] because (in theory) this would be the only viable method of increasing profits.[107]

Several incentives were built into the bidding process and the design of the CA to encourage potential concessionaries to commit to lowering tariffs (at least for the initial period of the concession),[108] including a six-year income tax holiday,[109] and a significant delay in heavy investment commitments.[110] MWSS also increased water tariffs by 38 percent just months before the bid submission date.[111] Nonetheless, when the envelopes were opened, everyone was surprised at just how low the bids were.[112] In the end, the Manila Water Company, Inc. (Manila Water – owned by investors that include transnational United Utilities and local firm Ayala Corporation) won the east zone concession with a bid to cut tariffs by 72 percent, while Maynilad Water Services, Inc. (Maynilad – a partnership between Lyonnaise des Eaux[113] and local company Benpres Holdings[114]) won the west zone concession with a bid to cut tariffs by 43 percent.[115]

Jude Esguerra argues that the reason that the initial tariffs were so low is that they were deliberate dive bids.[116] He points out,

> Aggressive dive bidding, or bidding at such a low level that will require the company to operate at a loss, is not irrational behaviour, at least when the bidder expects to be able to renegotiate once the contract is signed. [...] The gamble will have a greater propensity of paying off if regulatory structures are weak, or if there is a greater role for non-formal political interference to play a role in future decisions.[117]

A similar argument has been made by Raul Fabella, who points out that the local partners of both winning consortiums were such large companies as to enjoy the status of being 'too big to fail,' the 'type of enterprise [which], when distressed, implicitly become wards of the state for systemic stability reasons,'[118] increasing the likelihood of an early and favourable rate rebasing exercise (to raise tariffs before the first five-year period was complete). An inevitable outcome of this situation was regulatory capture, a process where regulatory agencies come to serve the interests of the companies they are meant to regulate rather than the public interest.[119]

Contract renegotiation and regulatory capture

Manila's PSP process was a classic example of neoliberal water governance reform, in that PSP was selected for its assumed capacity to deliver increased investments, efficiency gains, and service expansions. Despite the attempts made to draft a CA that guaranteed these targets while protecting the concessionaires from risk, two unexpected events in late 1997 placed considerable financial strain on the newly privatised utilities. The first related to water's materiality, when an unprecedented drought reduced available water by 30 percent, meaning the concessionaires had less revenue than they had originally anticipated.[120] Then the Asian Financial Crisis, in late 1997, caused a dramatic devaluation of the peso, essentially doubling the financial obligations under the debt service agreement and making it far more expensive and difficult to obtain finance to pay for the promised improvements.[121] These events placed significant pressure on tariffs and threw Maynilad, which controlled the west zone and had accepted 90 percent of the former MWSS' debt burden, into a financial crisis from which it never recovered.[122] This financial crisis also triggered a series of contractual amendments that significantly undermined the balance created under the original CA and exposed some of the limitations and risks of privatisation.

The first amendment (Amendment No.1) was implemented in October 2001, after a series of controversial renegotiations between Maynilad and the Regulator in the first half of 2001, during which Chief Regulator Tantiongco advocated strongly for Maynilad's proposal to amend the contract to allow for an automatic currency exchange rate adjustment to tariffs and for the postponement of some service obligations.[123] This advocacy led to serious conflict within the Regulatory Office, with two other regulators, Alojipan, the deputy for financial regulation, and Ocaya, the deputy for administration and legal affairs, expressing concern that the Chief Regulator was making decisions without consulting the rest of the team in contravention of the terms of the CA,[124] and 'undermining the independence and the integrity of the regulatory office' by adopting such a partisan position.[125] More controversially, Ocaya accused the Chief Regulator and Maynilad of outright corruption, stating, '[a] few millions in grease money for a corrupt director could be considered a justified expense by a Concessionaire and its stakeholders.'[126]

The controversy ultimately led the President to intervene,[127] and the Chief Regulator to resign,[128] but Maynilad responded to calls to uphold the contract by announcing it would be forced to impose water blackouts within the west zone.[129] It also stopped paying its concession fees, claiming that its financial troubles gave it no option.[130] By October, the government had bowed to the pressure to preserve the viability of Maynilad and agreed to amend the contract.[131] Alojipan and Ocaya (the two regulators who had opposed the amendments) were served with termination letters stating that they had lost the 'trust and confidence' of the MWSS Board of Trustees,[132] and by early 2002 rates had risen by 211 percent,[133] despite the government's promise that there would be no significant rate increase in the first ten years.[134] Perhaps most importantly, MWSS made these amendments without conducting the requisite public hearings required under section 9 of the 1987 *Administrative Code*.[135] MWSS also failed to follow a transparent process of amendment, meaning there was inadequate public scrutiny and accountability. For these reasons, Amendment No. 1 elicited public protest and scrutiny.[136]

Public bailouts, private profit

Despite the increase in tariffs that it enabled, Amendment No. 1 was insufficient to guarantee Maynilad's financial stability. When the Regulator was not willing to approve its proposed 75 percent tariff increase in the 2002 rate rebasing exercise, Maynilad wrote to the government, claiming that due to the government's breach of contract, they no longer had the necessary funds to carry out the project.[137]

In December, when talks had failed to resolve the situation, Maynilad filed for arbitration, seeking an early contract termination and USD300 million in compensation for MWSS' failure to assist the company in resolving its financial problems.[138] Article 12 of the CA provided for arbitration under UNCITRAL Arbitration Rules 1976,[139] introducing the jurisdiction of the Permanent Court of Arbitration into the multi-scalar governance arrangements of Manila's WSS system. In this instance, Maynilad's claims were unsuccessful, and the arbitrator authorised MWSS to draw on the USD120 million performance bond if Maynilad failed to pay its unpaid concession fees of USD127 million within 15 days.[140] Nonetheless, Maynilad responded by filing for corporate rehabilitation (a legal process allowing financially distressed companies to restructure debts and operations under court supervision) in a local trial court, seeking a temporary restraining order on its creditors.[141] This new phase of litigation pushed the government into negotiations with Maynilad, and together they agreed on a corporate rehabilitation plan designed to save Maynilad from insolvency.[142] The rehabilitation plan, announced to the public in March 2004 as Amendment No. 2, converted 71 percent of Maynilad's unpaid concession fees into a 63 percent equity for MWSS and enabled MWSS to draw on USD50 million of Maynilad's performance bond.[143] Additionally, Maynilad's local partner, Benpres Holdings, was to be relieved of all its guarantees.[144]

Media and civil society were critical of the proposed Amendment No. 2, which they perceived to be a corporate 'bailout' of a politically well-connected family company.[145] Civil society contended that the proposed plan would result in MWSS purchasing Maynilad's shares for well over double their real value[146] and would involve the government exposing taxpayers to Maynilad's outstanding debts of almost PhP11 billion (or around USD195 million).[147] As a result, the amendment was renegotiated, resulting in the Debt Capital and Restructuring Agreement (DCRA), which included a full draw on the USD120 million performance bond[148] and, significantly for poor communities, allowed Maynilad to prioritise 'opportunity areas' rather than focusing on supplying water to poor areas.[149]

On 24 November 2004, the Regulatory Office issued Resolution No. 04-014 increasing tariff rates from PhP19.92 to PhP30.19 (or by 52 percent), effective 1 January 2005. This tariff hike was again approved without any public consultation, despite legislative requirements to the contrary.[150] In response, a group of petitioners consisting of several public interest groups and consumers lodged a complaint with the National Water Resources Board (NWRB) requesting that they stop the implementation of the tariff increase.[151] In response, Maynilad and MWSS moved to have the complaint dismissed on the ground that NWRB had no jurisdiction over the concessionaires.[152] They argued that the 'water tariffs are governed by the concession agreement and it would be an impairment of contract if its implementation would be stayed.'[153] However, the NWRB dismissed their arguments and ruled in favour of the complainants.[154] Maynilad then appealed to the Supreme Court. However, by this time the Deputy Administrator for Administration and Legal Affairs (DA) had already provided advice to MWSS reaffirming the jurisdiction of the NWRB, and so MWSS did not join Maynilad in its suit.[155]

The DA's advice was substantiated when the Supreme Court dismissed Maynilad's petition for lack of merit after finding that the NWRB's jurisdiction over public utilities clearly covered the two concessionaires, who were agents of MWSS.[156] Gonzales-Sison J also found that Maynilad's 'business operations is imbued with public interest [and, therefore] the regulatory and adjudicatory power of the NWRB over water rates on all public utilities established by existing laws is deemed read into the CA.'[157] Nonetheless, the case remained pending as of February 2010,[158] by which point a new ownership structure was in place. This outcome highlights Maynilad's capacity to engage in regulatory shopping to obtain the most favourable result – or to delay unfavourable outcomes (sometimes permanently). The multi-scalar governance tensions of private sector provision provide fertile ground for this kind of behaviour, as jurisdictional boundaries are blurred by the selective roll-back of existing regulatory mechanisms coupled with the roll-out of new institutional mechanisms to support neoliberal agendas.

These developments demonstrate that commercial incentives, harnessed by market-based solutions like PSP, cannot by themselves guarantee improvements in efficiency, investment, or service. The market is unpredictable and influenced by both external events, such as drought and currency fluctuations, and internal issues, such as corruption, regulatory capture, and poor management. It also illustrates a common pattern with privatisation, where only the profits are privatised, while the public is still left carrying the financial risk. This is a weakness in the neoliberal approach to water reform and highlights the ongoing need for transparency and accountability through both public participation and state intervention (via a strong, *independent* regulator – or an alternative governance approach).

Spatial politics of service provision

Despite these problematic developments in the early years of Manila's experience with PSP, both concessionaires had positive achievements in relation to investment and efficiency (although this came later in Maynilad's case), and it is necessary to take these into account to make a balanced assessment of the full impact of PSP in Manila. It is notable, for example, that both concessions did ultimately achieve universal service provision. Manila has also been reported as a particular 'success story' for its innovative approaches to delivering water services to informal settlements, which are occupied by around a third of Metro Manila's population.[159] However, the detail of these innovative programs raises questions about the spatial politics of PSP and the ways that informality has been deployed to justify highly unequal tariffs and service levels.

In contrast to Maynilad, Manila Water fared well even in the early years of the concession, both financially and in terms of improving efficiency. By 2007, the east concessionaire had reduced non-revenue water to 22 percent.[160] The company's profits also grew steadily (even at the conclusion of their income tax holiday), and its stock price increased by 100 percent between 2006 and 2007.[161] By 2010, Manila Water claimed to have expanded 24-hour water services to 99 percent of its coverage area and reduced non-revenue water to just 11 percent.[162] Developments since 2007 also paint a more positive picture of Maynilad's performance. In January 2007, a new private consortium purchased 84 percent of Maynilad shares in a public bidding.[163] Within a year, the new firm had paid off Maynilad's outstanding debts of USD240 million and begun to invest in infrastructure maintenance and improvements.[164] By 2012, Maynilad claimed to have expanded 24-hour water services to 83 percent of its coverage area (from a low of 32 percent in 2006),[165] and reduced non-revenue water to 51 percent (from a high of 67 percent).[166]

As mentioned above, the provision of water to informal settlements has also been touted as a key success of Manila's experience with PSP. Many public water systems, including MWSS, had long refused to provide water connections to households living in informal settlements.[167] In contrast, the private concessionaires in Manila initiated a range of programs to expand connections in partnership with development agencies.[168] For example, between 1997 and 2000, an additional 35,000 poor urban households were provided with connections under Manila Water's *Water for the Poor* program (*Tubig para se Baraguay*).[169] According to Manila Water's website, this figure rose to a total of 1.6 million people by 2012.[170] This expansion of WSS services into informal settlements offered significant benefits. The water is safer and more reliable than the water residents were previously forced to purchase from small-scale water providers.[171] Many residents also saved a lot of time by having water connections in their homes rather than having to travel and queue for water.[172] The program was also sold as enabling many of these communities to directly manage their own water services, thus empowering them to 'participate' in water governance at the highly local level – although these claims will be further interrogated below.[173]

While these benefits of cleaner, safer household water are undeniable, the way that water services were delivered to informal settlements also served to entrench existing spatial inequalities in a range of ways. Under Manila Water's *Water for the Poor* project, water pipes were built up to the edge of informal settlements and community water organisations were required to arrange and pay to have the water connected from this bulk water outlet to individual households.[174] They also had to organise to collect the money from households to pay Manila Water.[175]

Like Manila Water, Maynilad also developed a program for providing water to poor communities, including informal settlements, known as *Bayan Tubig* (which translates as something akin to 'Water for the Nation').[176] In the early period of the concession, Maynilad mostly provided individual connections under this program, but from 2009, 'after new investors had taken over, Maynilad shifted its approach in low-income areas towards one that resembled Manila Water's bulk supply scheme.'[177] Named *Samahang Tubig Maynilad* (Water Association of Maynilad), this new program used the same techniques as Manila Water to provide bulk water connections to community-based associations, who are then responsible for providing individual connections.[178]

While this approach did mean that the residents of the poorest areas of Manila did not have to raise the large amount of cash required to pay for an individual household connection (which, at over USD100, was unaffordable for many households),[179] it also provided significant financial benefits to the private providers. Participant communities in both bulk water projects were required to take complete financial responsibility for all non-revenue water.[180] In the first decade of the concession, Manila Water also billed these customers at the highest bulk water rate, meaning they paid as much as four times per cubic meter than they would if they were being provided with an individual connection.[181] Under the terms of the CA, Manila Water could have exercised its discretion and applied the lowest bulk rate in recognition of low household usage, but it chose not to and received financial benefits from this decision.[182] Many communities were also required to pay additional levies (increasing the cost by up to seven times the original price) to cover extra expenses and to generate a profit for the community water organisation.[183] Sometimes this profit was reinvested in the community in the form of paving or childcare facilities (outcomes that Manila Water then claimed credit for),[184] while sometimes a private entity acted as the on-seller and the increased charges left the community as profit.[185]

These 'pro-poor' programs became key features of the public relations messaging of both concessionaires.[186] During my fieldwork in 2006, a Manila Water project officer took me on a tour of several *Water for the Poor* project locations where I could witness the new connections in person and speak to (pre-selected) grateful community members about their improved situations.[187] The project was also featured in World Bank and IFC reports about how privatised WSS systems can benefit the poor and finance universal access to safe and affordable water.[188] However, beyond the public relations messaging, the details of these projects reveal a different story about the role of PSP in delivering universal and equal water access.

Production of differential service territories

Many commentators have been critical of the fact that the level of service being offered to poor communities with new connections was inferior to that offered to those already connected.[189] Arthur McIntosh points out that by permitting the concessionaires to outsource the work of providing individual connections (and allowing them to count these connections as part of their service targets), the CA provides incentives for the concessionaires to only sell bulk water to poor urban households.[190] He is also critical of the design of the rising block tariff, which subsidises wealthy households with individual connections while penalising poor households with shared connections or those without connections who are forced to purchase their water from SSWPs.[191] Another problematic element of these bulk water connections is that while the tariffs charged to individual consumers by the concessionaires are regulated, on-sellers are not properly monitored.[192] Instead, the Regulator relies on self-reporting and does not have the capacity to verify the information provided.[193]

The unequal results of the 'Water for the Poor' project (particularly the decision to charge the highest bulk tariff rates) were the subject of congressional hearings in 2002, leading to a request for the Regulator to draft proposals for a more equitable method of calculating tariff rates.[194] From 2005, Manila Water gradually began providing individual household connections to low-income communities, and by 2010 it had replaced 62 percent of community connections with individual ones (although communities living in areas of uncertain land tenure continued to be offered only bulk connections).[195] A 'social rate' was also introduced for the community connections that better reflected the low household usage.[196] However, according to Petr Matous, these changes were driven in good part by the IFC's decision in 2007 to provide significant subsidies to support the provision of individual connections to low-income households – an approach then followed by the Philippines government and the Asian Development Bank.[197] Of course, these subsidies could just as easily been afforded to a publicly (or community) owned and operated provider.

Matous notes that instead of providing the necessary investments (a key justification for PSP), Manila Water 'was successful in mobilising large funds from the public sector and international donors' while reducing its own expenses.[198] He goes on to conclude,

> The company increased the reported efficiency of its operations by shifting problematic tasks and accountability for water losses onto groups of low-income residents in the unmonitored and unregulated sphere of informal settlements. The perceived intrinsic value of participation helped to brand this profitable approach as the building of active civil society and helped to mask the actual situation within the communities. In particular, the poor had to carry out the water service tasks by themselves and still pay higher tariffs than ordinary consumers because of the actual low efficiency of their operations and elite capture.[199]

Micro-networks and spatial inequality

In an in-depth 2010–2011 study, Cheng documented the way the concessionaires used small-scale water providers to outsource the costs and risks involved in expanding access to informal settlements, highlighting the ways this process enabled the entrenchment of existing spatial inequalities in access to affordable water. She observes here that, despite the rhetoric of the public relations messaging, '[a]ccess, then, is not flat and uniform, as the utilities would have us believe, but selective and contingent, based largely on a calculus of anticipated cost recovery.'[200] Cheng describes the resultant community bulk water schemes as 'micro-networks' and argues they are 'one manifestation of lingering informality [that] can be used to interpret the ways in which space is treated differentially.'[201] Here she notes, '[b]y examining the historical production of micro-networks in Manila's post-privatisation era, we begin to understand the ways in which the expansion of formal infrastructure replaces some forms of informality, while producing others.'[202] A further issue revealed through this analysis is the production of various forms of informality, classified by class and the deliberate 'unmapping' of urban space.[203] Here informality is 'a mode of urban governance' driven by the logic of liberalisation.[204]

The emergence of these 'micro-networks' in informal settlements represents more than just service differentiation. It demonstrates how neoliberal reforms produced hybrid governance forms that combined market logic with community management. These arrangements simultaneously enabled service expansion while institutionalising spatial inequality through differentiated service standards. Cheng is also critical of the way these schemes have exploited the concept of 'community participation' to romanticise the provision of second-class service to poor communities.[205] While water tariffs are lower under these community-based connections than they were when communities were only served by tankers operated by SSWPs, they still receive a markedly lower level of service (often at a higher price) than wealthier households, and the private providers are able to count these connections as part of their contractual achievements in addition to promoting their 'pro-poor' achievements.

Participation and power in water governance

This gap between the rhetoric of participation and the reality on the ground is a wider problem under private sector provision. The transformation of citizens into consumers under neoliberal governance represents more than a semantic shift by fundamentally restructuring the relationship between communities and infrastructure provision. This reconstitution of political subjectivity operates through both legal mechanisms and institutional practices that privilege market relations over democratic participation. Although community participation (including in tariff adjustment decisions) was formally required in Manila, regulatory capture and private sector bias enabled these to be bypassed. Perhaps most significantly, privity of contract then operated to prevent the public from enforcing the CA – leaving the community with few options to hold private providers to account. These issues played out in Manila when the community responded to contract renegotiations triggered by the Asian Financial Crisis and Maynilad's subsequent bankruptcy.

Legal frameworks and public exclusion

In 2005, a coalition of public interest groups and affected individuals filed a Petition for Certiorari filed with the Supreme Court to stop the new rehabilitation plan (the DCRA) from being approved.[206] The petition contained three main arguments. First, the petitioners argued that the 2005 Rehabilitation

Plan and the DCRA were not in the public interest because they allowed Maynilad to substantially modify its contractual obligations.[207] As a result, the delays permitted by the DCRA would substantially improve Maynilad's position vis-à-vis its original bidding commitments and negatively affect the quality of water services received in the west zone.[208] For many residents (and particularly those living in poor communities), the terms of the DCRA further delayed their access to any formal water services at all.

Second, the petitioners argued that the rehabilitation plan was contrary to public policy as it involved 'a scheme to bail out Benpres Holdings Corporation (Benpres) using USD60 million in public funds derived from the draw on the USD120 million performance bond.'[209] Under the deal, Benpres would lose its entire stockholdings in, and receivables from, Maynilad worth around USD44.2 million, but it was to be absolved from its guarantees of more than USD130 million.[210] The petitioners also argued that this deal placed MWSS in an unsound financial position by being forced to loan additional money to, and forego receivables from, Maynilad instead of paying off its own maturing loan obligations.[211] According to a manager from the MWSS Financial Department, this was likely to cause MWSS to post negative cash balances from 2006 to 2008 and again in 2011.[212] MWSS would also have to secure a new World Bank loan, which would further add to its debt.[213]

Finally, the petitioners challenged the 52 percent tariff that had taken place in 2005 without the period of public consultation required under section 9 of the *Administrative Code of 1987*.[214] The petitioners argued that compliance with these public consultation requirements 'is a condition precedent for the validity of rate increases granted by government agencies.'[215] To support their arguments, they cited *Manila International Airport Authority v. Airspan Corporation*,[216] which had found that a similar rate increase was invalid for lack of the required prior notice and public hearing.[217]

Initially, the court allowed the petitioners to participate in the rehabilitation case by allowing their arguments to be heard and giving them the opportunity to submit their evidence (including a valuation of Maynilad's shares that they had obtained from expert witnesses).[218] However, in response to all of their claims, both MWSS and Maynilad argued that the petitioners should be denied standing since they were not parties to the CA. This argument was successful, and the judge declared that the petitioners were 'barred from further participating in the proceedings since they [were] not interested parties-of-record, citing section 6, rule 4 of the Interim Rules.'[219] Nonetheless, the government did respond to the petition by requiring Maynilad to file yet another revised rehabilitation plan on 29 April 2005.[220] This new plan substantially adopted the petitioners' valuation of Maynilad's shares, and MWSS' 84.4 percent interest was now to be purchased for USD22.67 million (or just over one-third of the previous valuation).[221]

This ultimately positive outcome demonstrates the importance of public participation in bringing otherwise hidden issues into the public domain, forcing the government to justify its actions to the public and, ultimately, to amend them. However, the issues raised by the litigation and the responses of the government and the concessionaries to the claims raised also highlight a concerning feature of Manila's approach to PSP, namely a tendency to exclude the public from the water governance process by decreasing transparency, accountability, and reducing the available avenues for community participation. While the public have a direct stake in the water governance process and should, therefore, have the capacity to challenge bad policy decisions, privity of contract arguments were successfully used to shut down community engagement.

The contractual amendments contained in the rehabilitation agreement (and challenged in this case) had direct impacts on the right to water for many in the community, particularly for poorer households. Delaying the service expansion targets directly affected the rights of unserviced communities to physically (and affordably) access the water system, particularly as Maynilad was permitted to prioritise 'opportunity areas.' While the private providers were keen on 'community participation' in the context of the water for the poor program – where participatory mechanisms operated to outsource financial risk to, and extract free labour from, poor communities – they simultaneously benefitted from bypassing legally required public consultation requirements for tariff increases and actively excluded the community from the process of balancing financial sustainability with affordability.

Regulatory legitimation

Another issue that tested MWSS' commitment to transparency and public participation came out of the Regulator's resolution (of 30 July 2004) not to treat the concessionaires as public utilities.[222] This was relevant because under section 12 of the MWSS Charter, a public utility is not permitted to exceed a return on rate base (RORB – a measure of profit margin calculated as the percentage return on a utility's capital investments) of more than 12 percent.[223] It was also relevant due to a 2003 finding within the energy sector that private entities acting as public utilities were not allowed to pass on their corporate income tax to consumers.[224]

In 2002, the Commission on Audit had investigated the financial operations of the two concessionaires at the request of the Regulator.[225] The Commission found that in 1999 Manila Water had incurred a RORB of 41 percent, exceeding its allowable RORB by 29 percent.[226] Initially, the Regulator attempted to sanction Manila Water for exceeding their allowable RORB. However, after a period of negotiations with Manila Water and a review of the CA by a newly created Technical Working Group, the Regulator declared that the concessionaires were actually agents of MWSS and, as such, not to be considered public utilities for the purposes of the RORB cap.[227] This declaration was made despite the fact that Article 9 of the CA itself provides that water tariff adjustments were to be made subject to the limitation that the concessionaires' rate of net return shall not exceed 12 percent per annum (as required by section 12 of the MWSS Charter).[228]

In June 2006, this regulatory declaration was challenged in the Supreme Court by a group of non-government organisations, led by the Freedom from Debt Coalition.[229] In this case, the applicants argued that the *Public Service Act* explicitly states that WSS services are included in the list of public services.[230] They also pointed out that the Regulator's Technical Regulation Administrator had refused to endorse the declaration because he believed it to be in conflict with existing legal opinions.[231] The public interest in this case was fairly evident since allowing the concessionaires to increase their profit levels affected both the price of water for all users and the amount of money the concessionaires would be required to reinvest in the water system to both maintain and expand services (affecting the rights of unserved and underserved sections of the community).[232] However, the Regulator argued that the Supreme Court should dismiss the petition for want of merit.[233]

Ultimately, the Supreme Court dismissed the petition on three grounds.[234] First, that the petition should have been lodged with the NWRB, which had exclusive original jurisdiction over all cases contesting the rates or fees of water and sanitation services.[235] Second, that the concessionaires were indispensable parties to the proceedings and that their non-inclusion rendered the petition defective.[236] Finally, that the petition was barred under the doctrine of hierarchy of courts.[237] Despite the Supreme Court's concurrent original jurisdiction with the Regional Trial Court and the Court of Appeals, it cannot address issues of fact, and this petition raised several that needed to be determined.[238] On 28 January 2008, the Freedom from Debt Coalition and the other parties to the case asked the Supreme Court to reconsider its ruling, but this appeal was denied.[239]

The facts set out in these cases reveal that the technical language of regulatory oversight in Manila served to obscure fundamentally political decisions about resource allocation and service provision. This technocratic legitimation represents a key feature of the roll-out of neoliberalism, where market ideology and its highly political biases are institutionalised through seemingly neutral administrative mechanisms.

Discussion

Within Manila's experience, we can observe legal geography's central argument about the co-constitutive relationship between law and space. The legal frameworks that established, enabled, and regulated PSP in the WSS sector actively produced new spatial arrangements through seemingly technical decisions about infrastructure investment and service delivery while encountering resistance from water's material and social properties. The resulting governance arrangements emerged through the dynamic interaction between formal regulations, corporate power, physical infrastructure networks, and social practices – demonstrating how law and space continuously shape and reshape each other through dynamic material and social processes.

When MWSS was privatised in 1997, it was facing a serious financial crisis. As a result, the millions of households who were unserved and underserved by the public system were relying on expensive (and poorly regulated) SSWPs, and there was no reason to believe the situation would improve. Within a decade of privatisation, the Concessionaires had increased efficiency and made significant new investments in the Metro Manila WSS system. As a result, the overall financial position of MWSS and the levels of service being delivered to the people of Manila improved – particularly in the east concession area. Nonetheless, Maynilad's financial crisis also demonstrated that market-based reforms do not guarantee financial success, in part because they are vulnerable to external events like currency fluctuations.

Manila's experience with privatised water provision also reflects the spatial politics of neoliberal governance reform. As we have seen above, water infrastructure networks materialise power relations in urban space, with decisions about investment and service provision actively producing distinct 'spatial power geometries.'[240] This helps to explain why Manila's concessionaires developed differentiated service territories that reflected and reinforced existing socio-spatial hierarchies. Rather than viewing the emergence of micro-networks and bulk water schemes as pragmatic responses to service delivery challenges, we can understand them as manifestations of power relations that produce new forms of spatial inequality through infrastructure provision. The commercial logic of PSP, legitimated through regulatory frameworks and participatory rhetoric, created distinct service levels attuned to anticipated returns rather than social need. As Cheng's analysis highlights, the deliberate 'unmapping' of certain urban spaces represents not a failure of neoliberal governance but rather its spatial rationality at work. This calculated informality enables providers to maintain differentiated service levels while shifting risks and costs onto marginalised communities. This spatial differentiation is thus a structural feature of neoliberal governance and reflects the way market mechanisms necessarily result in 'uneven geographical development.'[241]

While Manila's experience reflects specific spatial politics, it also reveals features inherent to market-based water provision with implications that extend well beyond this particular case. This conclusion points toward the limits of conventional regulatory solutions in ensuring equitable service provision. Manila's experience reveals that regulation alone cannot resolve the fundamental tensions between profit-seeking behaviour and universal service provision. Rather, regulatory frameworks themselves can become sites where spatial inequalities are institutionalised and legitimated through technical language and market rationalisation.

The uneven outcomes of neoliberal water reforms have also triggered new forms of resistance and contributed to the demand for alternative governance frameworks. As we will see in Chapter 4, the emergence of a global water justice movement, particularly visible in Cochabamba's 'water war,' represents a direct challenge to the commodification of water and its spatial inequalities. Meanwhile, experiments with corporatised utilities in Johannesburg demonstrate ongoing state attempts to reconcile social imperatives with market rationalities, even as financialisation introduces new forms of abstraction and value capture into urban water systems. These evolving governance arrangements take place against the backdrop of an emerging human right to water – a framework that simultaneously challenges and risks being co-opted by neoliberal ideology. The tensions revealed in Manila's case are thus a preview of broader contestations over water's status as an economic good and a human right (and as a living, relational entity).

Notes

1 Steve Graham and Simon Marvin, *Splintering Urbanism: Networked Infrastructures, Technological Mobilities and the Urban Condition* (Routledge, 2001). See also Stephen Graham and Simon Marvin, 'Splintering Urbanism at 20 and the "Infrastructural Turn"' (2022) 29(1) *Journal of Urban Technology* 169; Timothy Moss, 'Refracting Urbanism: The Multiple Histories (as Well as Geographies) of the Networked City' (2022) 29(1) *Journal of Urban Technology* 127; Kristian Karlo Saguin and Maria Khristine Alvarez, '"Danger Zones," "Death Zones," and Paradoxes of Infrastructural Space-Making in Manila' (2022) 29(1) *Journal of Urban Technology* 145; Omar Jabary Salamanca and Jonathan Silver, 'In the Excess of Splintering Urbanism: The Racialized Political Economy of Infrastructure' (2022) 29(1) *Journal of Urban Technology* 117; Alan Wiig et al, 'From the Guest EditorsSplintering Urbanism at 20: Mapping Trajectories of Research on Urban Infrastructures' (2022) 29(1) *Journal of Urban Technology* 1.

2 United Nations Development Programme (UNDP), *Human Development Report* (Oxford University Press, 1992) 14.

3 See United Nations Development Programme (UNDP), *Human Development Report: Beyond Scarcity – Power, Poverty and the Global Water Crisis* (UNDP, 2006) 2 <http://hdr.undp.org/en/content/human-development-report-2006>.

4 United Nations Development Programme (UNDP), *Human Development Report* (n 3) 86, 89.

5 These problems exist in both the global south and the global north. For example, in United Nations Development Programme (UNDP), *Human Development Report* (n 3) 89 noted that water utilities in the UK are frequently being fined for failing to reduce water leakage. On the broader issue, see also Bill Kingdom, Roland Liemberger and Philippe Marin, *The Challenge of Reducing Non-Revenue Water (NRW) in Developing Countries: How the Private Sector Can Help: A Look at Performance-Based Service Contracting* (Water Suppy

and Sanitation Board Discussion Paper Series No Volume 8, World Bank, 2006) <http://siteresources.worldbank.org/INTWSS/Resources/WSS8fin4.pdf>.

6 World Bank, *The World Bank Group's Program for Water Supply and Sanitation* (World Bank, 2004) 13; James Winpenny, *Financing Water for All: Report of the World Panel on Financing Water Infrastructure* (World Water Council, 2003) 21.

7 World Bank, 'Program for WSS' (n 6) 13; Winpenny, *Financing Water for All* (n 6) 21.

8 Alexander Loftus and David A. McDonald, 'Of Liquid Dreams: A Political Ecology of Water Privatization in Buenos Aires' (2001) 13(2) *Environment & Urbanization* 179.

9 Mark Dumol, *The Manila Water Concession: A Key Government Official's Diary of the World's Largest Water Privatization* (World Bank Publications, 2000).

10 Karen Bakker, 'Trickle Down? Private Sector Participation and the pro-Poor Water Supply Debate in Jakarta, Indonesia' (2007) 38(5) *Geoforum* 855.

11 Oscar Olivera and Tom Lewis, *Cochabamba!: Water War in Bolivia* (South End Press, 2004).

12 Maude Barlow and Tony Clarke, *Blue Gold: The Battle against Corporate Theft of the World's Water* (Stoddart, 2002) 156–161; Kate Bayliss, *Privatisation and Poverty: The Distributional Impact of Utility Privatisation* (No Working Paper No. 16, Centre on Regulation and Competition, Institute for Development Policy and Management, 2002) 3; Bethan Emmett, *In the Public Interest: Health, Education, and Water and Sanitation for All* (Oxfam and WaterAid, 2006) 9.

13 Barlow and Clarke, *Blue Gold* (n 12) 161.

14 Barlow and Clarke, *Blue Gold* (n 12) 161.

15 WaterAid, *International Financial Institutions (IFI), Conditionality and Privatisation of Water and Sanitation Systems* (WaterAid, 2003) 6.

16 Barlow and Clarke, *Blue Gold* (n 12) 163.

17 Emmett, *In the Public Interest: Health, Education, and Water and Sanitation for All* (n 12).

18 Emmett, *In the Public Interest: Health, Education, and Water and Sanitation for All* (n 12) 9.

19 Angela Wood, *Tightening the Chains or Cutting the Strings: The Status of HIPC Conditionality in 2006* (Jubilee Debt Campaign, 2006) 17.

20 Corporate Europe Observatory, 'EU Commission Forces Crisis-Hit Countries to Privatise Water' (2012) <http://corporateeurope.org/pressreleases/2012/eu-commission-forces-crisis-hit-countries-privatise-water>.

21 Wood, *Tightening the Chains or Cutting the Strings* (n 19) 5.

22 Emmett, *In the Public Interest: Health, Education, and Water and Sanitation for All* (n 12) 9.

23 WaterAid, *International Financial Institutions (IFI), Conditionality and Privatisation of Water and Sanitation Systems* (n 15) 4, 9–10; Deborah Moore and Penny Urquhart, *Global Water Scoping Project* (WaterAid, 2004) 19.

24 See, e.g., Anna F.S. Russell, 'Incorporating Social Rights in Development: Transnational Corporations and the Right to Water' (2011) 7(1) *International Journal of the Law in Context* 1, 9.

25 See, e.g., Fred Pearce, *When the Rivers Run Dry: Water-the Defining Crisis of the Twenty-First Century* (Beacon Pr, 2006).

26 Alex Kwan and Roger Groebil, 'Water as an Investment Theme: It's Scarce and ABN AMRO Private Banking Asia Thinks Water Is a Great Investment' (5 July 2006) *Finance Asia* 1 <https://www.financeasia.com/article/water-as-an-investment-theme/39520>.

27 Kwan and Groebil, 'Water as an Investment Theme' (n 26) 2.

28 Kwan and Groebil, 'Water as an Investment Theme' (n 26) 3.

29 Russell, 'Incorporating Social Rights in Development' (n 24) 10–13; Barlow and Clarke, *Blue Gold* (n 12) 156–157.
30 World Water Council, *Giving an Audible Voice to Water* (World Water Council) <www.worldwatercouncil.org/about-us/vision-mission-strategy/>.
31 Russell, 'Incorporating Social Rights in Development' (n 24) 10–13; Barlow and Clarke, *Blue Gold* (n 12) 157–158.
32 World Bank, *Assessing Aid: What Works, What Doesn't and Why* (World Bank, 1998). Neoliberal theory also informed many of the conditions that these institutions continued to attach to their loans and development assistance programs well into the 2000s: see, e.g., Hetty Kovach and Yasmina Lansman, *World Bank and IMF Conditionality: A Development Injustice* (European Network on Debt and Development (Eurodad), 2006); Jomo Kwame Sundaram, Oliver Schwank and Rudiger von Arnim, *Globalization and Development in Sub-Saharan Africa* (UNDESA Working Paper No 102, UNDESA, 2011).
33 For a detailed analysis of how and why this occurred see Kwame Sundaram, Schwank and von Arnim, *Globalization and Development in Sub-Saharan Africa* (n 32). See also Joseph Stiglitz, *Globalization and Its Discontents* (2002); Patrick Bond, 'Neoliberalism in Sub-Saharan Africa: From Structural Adjustment to NEPAD' in Alfredo Saad-Filho and Deborah Johnston (eds), *Neoliberalism: A Critical Reader* (2005) 232; Alfredo Saad-Filho, 'The Political Economy of Neoliberalism in Latin America' in Alfredo Saad-Filho and Deborah Johnston (eds), *Neoliberalism: A Critical Reader* (2005) 227.
34 See, e.g., Kwame Sundaram, Schwank and von Arnim, *Globalization and Development in Sub-Saharan Africa* (n 32).
35 World Bank, 'Assessing Aid' (n 32).
36 World Bank, *Governance and Development* (World Bank, 1992) 3. For a critical analysis of the World Bank's adoption of the good governance agenda, see also Bidyut Chakrabarty and Mohit Bhattacharya, 'Introduction' in Bidyut Chakrabarty and Mohit Bhattacharya (eds), *Governance Discourse: A Reader* (2008) 1.
37 World Bank, 'Governance and Development' (n 36) 2.
38 Julie Aubut, *The Good Governance Agenda: Who Wins and Who Loses. Some Empirical Evidence for 2001* (Working Paper Series, Development Studies Institute, London School of Economics and Political Science, 2004).
39 Chakrabarty and Bhattacharya, 'Introduction' (n 36) 2.
40 Chakrabarty and Bhattacharya, 'Introduction' (n 36) 2.
41 Emanuele Lobina and David Hall, *Problems with Private Water Concessions: A Review of Experience* (Public Services International Research Unit, University of Greenwich, 2003); David Hall and Emanuele Lobina, *Water Privatisation* (Public Services International Research Unit (PSIRU), 2008).
42 Lobina and Hall, *Problems with Private Water Concessions* (n 41); Hall and Lobina, *Water Privatisation* (n 41).
43 Graham and Marvin, 'Splintering Urbanism at 20 and the "Infrastructural Turn"' (n 1).
44 Graham and Marvin, 'Splintering Urbanism at 20 and the "Infrastructural Turn"' (n 1).
45 Karen J. Bakker, *Privatizing Water: Governance Failure and the World's Urban Water Crisis* (Cornell University Press, 2010).
46 Deborah Cheng, 'The Persistence of Informality: Small-Scale Water Providers in Manila's Post-Privatisation Era' (2014) 7(1) *Water Alternatives* 54.
47 Cheng, 'The Persistence of Informality' (n 46).
48 David Harvey, *Spaces of Global Capitalism* (Verso, 2006).
49 David Harvey, *The New Imperialism: Accumulation by Dispossession* (Oxford University Press, 2003).

50 Erik Swyngedouw, *Social Power and the Urbanization of Water*, ed. Gordon Clark, Andrew Goudie and Ceri Peach (Oxford University Press, 2004).
51 Jocelyn C. Cuaresma, *Pro-Poor Water Services in Metro Manila: In Search for Greater Equity* (Working Paper Series No 81, Centre on Regulation and Competition, June 2004).
52 Jamie Peck and Adam Tickell, 'Neoliberalizing Space' (2002) 34(3) *Antipode* 380.
53 Erik Swyngedouw, 'Globalisation or "Glocalisation"? Networks, Territories and Rescaling' (2004) 17(1) *Cambridge Review of International Affairs* 25.
54 Swyngedouw, 'Globalisation or "Glocalisation"?'.
55 See, e.g., Dumol, *The Manila Water Concession* (n 9); Raul Fabella, 'The Privatization of the Metropolitan Waterworks and Sewerage System: How and Why It Was Won' in The Asia Foundation (ed), *Built on Dreams, Grounded in Reality: Economic Policy Reform in the Philippines* (2011) 65; Mai Flor, *MWSS Privatization: Lessons on Good Governance* (Asian Development Bank (ADB), 2009).
56 See, e.g., Jude Esguerra, 'The Corporate Muddle of Manila's Water Concessions' in Eric Gutierrez et al (eds), *New Rules, New Roles: Does PSP Benefit the Poor?* (WaterAid and Tearfund, 2003); Mae Buenaventura and Bubut Palattao, 'Taking Stock of Water Privatization in the Philippines – The Case of the Metropolitan Waterworks and Sewerage System (MWSS)' (2004) 14 *PAID!* 12; Freedom from Debt Coalition, *Recalibrating the Meter: A Ten Year Overview of the MWSS Privatization Deal* (FDC, 2008).
57 Dumol, *The Manila Water Concession* (n 9) 5.
58 Dumol, *The Manila Water Concession* (n 9) 5.
59 Dumol, *The Manila Water Concession* (n 9) 5.
60 Dumol, *The Manila Water Concession* (n 9) 5.
61 Dumol, *The Manila Water Concession* (n 9) 5.
62 Dumol, *The Manila Water Concession* (n 9) 5.
63 Dumol, *The Manila Water Concession* (n 9) 5.
64 See Dumol, *The Manila Water Concession* (n 9) 5; Arthur McIntosh, *Asian Water Supplies – Reaching the Urban Poor* (Asian Development Bank (ADB), 2003) 175 (who gives a figure of 63 percent).
65 Staff-to-connections ratios are considered to be a strong measurement of 'efficiency', as employing a larger number of staff per 1,000 connections is more expensive. Obviously, lower ratios also result in a reduction of employment and available staff for service, which has separate implication.
66 Dumol, *The Manila Water Concession* (n 9) 40.
67 Dumol, *The Manila Water Concession* (n 9) 19.
68 Raul Fabella, *Shifting the Boundary of the State: The Privatization and Regulation of Water Service in Metropolitan Manila* (No Paper No 123, Centre on Regulation and Competition, Institute for Development Policy, University of Manchester, 2006) 18.
69 Xun Wu and Nepomuceno A. Malaluan, 'A Tale of Two Concessionaires: A Natural Experiment of Water Privatisation in Metro Manila' (2008) 45(1) *Urban Studies* 207, 213.
70 Dumol, *The Manila Water Concession* (n 9).
71 Dumol, *The Manila Water Concession* (n 9) 9–11.
72 Dumol, *The Manila Water Concession* (n 9) 9.
73 Dumol, *The Manila Water Concession* (n 9) 9–10; Interview with Bubut Palattao, 'Advocacy Coordinator at Freedom from Debt Coalition' (Cristy Clark, Manila, 1 November 2006).
74 *Constitution of the Republic of the Philippines 1987*; *An Act to Address the National Water Crisis and for Other Purposes (The Republic of the Philippines) 1995* (*National Water Crisis Act*).

75 Dumol, *The Manila Water Concession* (n 9).
76 Water privatisation in Buenos Aires started out as a success until the Argentinean currency crisis in 2000 when the water utility began to experience serious liquidity problems. See, e.g., Loftus and McDonald (n 8); Florencia Almansi et al, 'Everyday Water Struggles in Buenos Aires: The Problem of Land Tenure in the Expansion of Potable Water and Sanitation Service to Informal Settlements' in Eric Gutierrez et al (eds), *New Rules, New Roles: Does PSP Benefit the Poor?* (WaterAid and Tearfund, 2003) 24; Ariel A. Casarin, Jose A. Delfino and Maria Eugenia Delfino, 'Failures in Water Reform: Lessons from the Buenos Aires's Concession' (2007) 15 *Utilities Policy* 234; Wu and Malaluan, 'A Tale of Two Concessionaires' (n 69) 211.
77 Dumol, *The Manila Water Concession* (n 9) 12.
78 Dumol, *The Manila Water Concession* (n 9) 12.
79 Dumol, *The Manila Water Concession* (n 9) 12.
80 Dumol, *The Manila Water Concession* 45–49; Wu and Malaluan, 'A Tale of Two Concessionaires' (n 69) 213.
81 *Constitution of the Republic of the Philippines* (n 74) 11.
82 Dumol, *The Manila Water Concession* (n 9) 38.
83 Dumol, *The Manila Water Concession* (n 9) 38–39.
84 Dumol, *The Manila Water Concession* (n 9) 29.
85 Dumol, *The Manila Water Concession* (n 9) 38–39; McIntosh, *Asian Water Supplies – Reaching the Urban Poor* (n 64) 175. The IFC is the member of the World Bank Group that finances private sector investments and advisory services to business and government in order build the private sector in developing countries.
86 Dumol, *The Manila Water Concession* (n 9) 29.
87 Esguerra, 'The Corporate Muddle of Manila's Water Concessions' (n 56) 13; Dumol, *The Manila Water Concession* (n 9) 13.
88 Metropolitan Waterworks and Sewerage System (MWSS), 'Concession Agreement' arts 5 (service obligations), 6.4 (concession fees), 6.9 (performance bond), 7 (obligations of MWSS), 10 (events of early termination, penalties), 11 (regulatory office), 12 (dispute resolution), 16.10 (force majeure), schs 2 (water service expansion targets), 3 (sewerage service expansion targets).
89 Dumol, *The Manila Water Concession* (n 9) 29; Fabella, *Shifting the Boundary of the State* (n 68) 15.
90 Dumol, *The Manila Water Concession* (n 9) 42.
91 Dumol, *The Manila Water Concession* (n 9) 55; Metropolitan Waterworks and Sewerage System (MWSS) (n 88) arts 2.4 (CPI adjustments), 9.3 (extraordinary price adjustments), 9.4 (rate rebasing).
92 Metropolitan Waterworks and Sewerage System (MWSS) (n 88) art 2.4 (inflation was to be calculated using the consumer price index).
93 Ibid 9.3.
94 Ibid 9.2–9.4; Dumol, *The Manila Water Concession* (n 9) 51; Esguerra, 'The Corporate Muddle of Manila's Water Concessions' (n 56) 14–15; Wu and Malaluan, 'A Tale of Two Concessionaires' (n 69) 215.
95 *Metropolitan Waterworks and Sewerage System (MWSS)* (n 88) 9.3.4.
96 Esguerra, 'The Corporate Muddle of Manila's Water Concessions' (n 56) 16.
97 Wu and Malaluan, 'A Tale of Two Concessionaires' (n 69) 215.
98 *Metropolitan Waterworks and Sewerage System (MWSS)* (n 88) art 6.5 (asset management obligations), schs 2 (water service expansion targets), 3 (sewerage service expansion targets), sch 2. See, also, Esguerra, 'The Corporate Muddle of Manila's Water Concessions' (n 56) 5–6; Wu and Malaluan, 'A Tale of Two Concessionaires' (n 69) 215.
99 Dumol, *The Manila Water Concession* (n 9) 29, 53, 63–64, 82, 107.

100 See, e.g., Sophie Trémolet and Catherine Hunt, *Taking Account of the Poor in Water Sector Regulation* (Water Supply and Sanitation Working Notes No Note No 11, World Bank, 2006).
101 See, e.g., Dumol, *The Manila Water Concession* (n 9) 56; Winpenny, *Financing Water for All* (n 6) 10; Selim Jahan and Robert McCleery, *Making Infrastructure Work for the Poor – Synthesis Report of Four Country Studies (Bangladesh, Senegal, Thailand and Zambia)* (United Nations Development Programme (UNDP), 2005) 19–20; Wu and Malaluan, 'A Tale of Two Concessionaires' (n 69) 207.
102 Dumol, *The Manila Water Concession* (n 9) 56.
103 Dumol, *The Manila Water Concession* (n 9) 56; Interview with Mai Flor, 'Lawyer for Ondeo (Maynilad)' (Cristy Clark, Manila, 24 October 2006).
104 Interview with Mary Ann Manahan, 'Advocacy Coordinator at Focus on the Global South' (Cristy Clark, Manila, 31 October 2006); Interview with Bubut Palattao, 'Advocacy Coordinator at Freedom from Debt Coalition' (n 73).
105 Esguerra, 'The Corporate Muddle of Manila's Water Concessions' (n 56) 25–26.
106 Dumol, *The Manila Water Concession* (n 9) 107.
107 Dumol, *The Manila Water Concession* (n 9) 52; Esguerra, 'The Corporate Muddle of Manila's Water Concessions' (n 56) 14.
108 Dumol, *The Manila Water Concession* (n 9) 44.
109 Dumol, *The Manila Water Concession* (n 9) 44.
110 Dumol, *The Manila Water Concession* (n 9) 44.
111 Dumol, *The Manila Water Concession* (n 9) 44.
112 Dumol, *The Manila Water Concession* (n 9) 97.
113 Lyonnaise des Eau is a French company that is now called Suez, and their water division was renamed Ondeo in 2001. 'Suez Creates ONDEO', *WaterWorld* (23 March 2001) <https://www.waterworld.com/home/article/16208281/suez-creates-ondeo>.
114 Benpres Holdings is part of the Lopez Group of Companies.
115 Dumol, *The Manila Water Concession* (n 9) 84, 97.
116 Esguerra, 'The Corporate Muddle of Manila's Water Concessions' (n 56) 16. See *contra* 'Ondeo's response to this case study' on page 12 (In which Ondeo argues that Maynilad's bid was based on highly inaccurate 'technical and operational data provided' by the government and that the financial situation was exacerbated by the currency devaluation and the government's unwillingness to renegotiate to appropriately accommodate these changed circumstances.).
117 Esguerra, 'The Corporate Muddle of Manila's Water Concessions' (n 56) 16.
118 Fabella, *Shifting the Boundary of the State* (n 55) 48.
119 Ernesto Dal Bó, 'Regulatory Capture: A Review' (2006) 22(2) *Oxford Review of Economic Policy* 203, 203.
120 Wu and Malaluan, 'A Tale of Two Concessionaires' (n 69) 215. *Metropolitan Waterwords and Sewerage Systems (MWSS) v Maynilad Water Services Inc (Maynilad) in the matter of an ad hoc arbritration under the UNCITRAL Rules* (2003) UNC47/KGA (Unreported) 20; *Metropolitan Waterworks And Sewerage System (MWSS) v Hon Judge Daway* (Unreported Regional trial court of Quezon City, Branch 90 G.R. No 160732, 20, 2004) (*Rehab Case*).
121 Wu and Malaluan, 'A Tale of Two Concessionaires' (n 69) 215; *Metropolitan Waterwords and Sewerage Systems (MWSS) v Maynilad Water Services Inc (Maynilad) in the Matter of an Ad Hoc Arbritration under the UNCITRAL Rules* (n 120) 19.
122 Wu and Malaluan, 'A Tale of Two Concessionaires' (n 69) 215; *Metropolitan Waterwords and Sewerage Systems (MWSS) v Maynilad Water Services Inc (Maynilad) in the Matter of an Ad Hoc Arbritration under the UNCITRAL Rules* (n 120) 19.
123 Esguerra, 'The Corporate Muddle of Manila's Water Concessions' (n 56) 18. The proposed tariff adjustment would allow Maynilad to recover foreign exchange

losses from consumers by adjusting rates monthly without the need for evaluation and approval by the regulatory office – rather than having to wait until the end of each calendar year as provided for in the contract. The postponed service obligations were those that Maynilad's creditors were concerned that it would not meet – thus running the risk of forfeiting its performance bond.

124 Esguerra, 'The Corporate Muddle of Manila's Water Concessions' (n 56) 18.

125 Esguerra, 'The Corporate Muddle of Manila's Water Concessions' (n 56) 25–26.

126 Personal communication cited in Buenaventura and Palattao, 'Taking Stock of Water Privatization in the Philippines – The Case of the Metropolitan Waterworks and Sewerage System (MWSS)' (n 56) 47.

127 Romel Bagares, 'MSWW Disallows Maynilad Rate Hike', *Philippine Star* (Manila, 25 August 2001); Esguerra, 'The Corporate Muddle of Manila's Water Concessions' (n 56).

128 Bagares, 'MSWW Disallows Maynilad Rate Hike' (n 127); Interview with Macra Cruz, 'Senior Administrator of MWSS' (Cristy Clark, Manila, 30 October 2006).

129 Interview with Macra Cruz, 'Senior Administrator of MWSS' (n 128); Interview with Bubut Palattao, 'Advocacy Coordinator at Freedom from Debt Coalition' (n 73).

130 Interview with Macra Cruz, 'Senior Administrator of MWSS' (n 128); Interview with Bubut Palattao, 'Advocacy Coordinator at Freedom from Debt Coalition' (n 73).

131 Bagares, 'MSWW Disallows Maynilad Rate Hike' (n 127); Interview with Macra Cruz, 'Senior Administrator of MWSS' (n 128).

132 Ledivia V Carino, *Regulatory Governance in the Philippines: A Profile* (Working Paper Series No Paper No.44, Institute for Development, Policy & Managment, University of Manchester, 2002) 68; Romel Bagares, 'QC Court to Rule Today on 2 MWSS Executives', *Philippine Star* (Manila, 6 November 2001).

133 Philippine Star, 'No Improvement after 5 Years of MWSS Privatization – Solon', *Philippine Star* (Manila, 11 April 2002).

134 Buenaventura and Palattao, 'Taking Stock of Water Privatization in the Philippines – The Case of the Metropolitan Waterworks and Sewerage System (MWSS)' (n 56) 26–28.

135 *Administrative Code (The Republic of the Philippines) 1987* 9.

136 Buenaventura and Palattao, 'Taking Stock of Water Privatization in the Philippines – The Case of the Metropolitan Waterworks and Sewerage System (MWSS)' (n 56) 28; Mayen Jaymalin et al, 'Water Rate Hike Opposed', *The Philippine Star* (Manila, 5 October 2001).

137 Interview with Bubut Palattao, 'Advocacy Coordinator at Freedom from Debt Coalition' (n 73). Maynilad's rate at the time of bidding was just over 19 pesos per cubic litres and it wanted to increase this rate to 34 pesos. After reviewing Maynilad's investments and financial management to date the Regulatory Office was only willing to approve a new rate of 26.75 pesos to be implemented in stages over a two-year period.

138 *Metropolitan Waterwords and Sewerage Systems (MWSS) v Maynilad Water Services Inc (Maynilad) in the Matter of an Ad Hoc Arbritration under the UNCITRAL Rules* (n 120) 30.

139 *Metropolitan Waterworks and Sewerage System (MWSS)* (n 88) 12.2.

140 *Metropolitan Waterwords and Sewerage Systems (MWSS) v Maynilad Water Services Inc (Maynilad) in the Matter of an Ad Hoc Arbritration under the UNCITRAL Rules* (n 120) 35.

141 *Rehab Case* (n 120); Interview with Macra Cruz, 'Senior Administrator of MWSS' (n 128).

142 *Petition for Certiorari (with Application for Preliminary Injuction and Motion for Consolidation), Action for Economic Reforms v Hon Judge Daway (G.R. No. 167418)* (2005) 17–19; Nepomuceno Malaluan, *Maynilad Rehab Plan: Timbang Ka Ngunit Kulang* (Action for Economic Reforms, 2005).

143 Buenaventura and Palattao, 'Taking Stock of Water Privatization in the Philippines – The Case of the Metropolitan Waterworks and Sewerage System (MWSS)' (n 56) 51; Oscar M. Lopez, 'Remarks of Oscar M. Lopez, Chairman, Benpres Holdings Corporation at the Annual Stockholders Meeting' (2004).

144 Lopez, 'Remarks of Oscar M. Lopez, Chairman, Benpres Holdings Corporation at the Annual Stockholders Meeting' (n 143); Alexander Martin Remollino, 'GMA Faces New Suit Over Maynilad Bailout', *Bulatlat* (2004).

145 Buenaventura and Palattao, 'Taking Stock of Water Privatization in the Philippines – The Case of the Metropolitan Waterworks and Sewerage System (MWSS)' (n 56) 51.

146 Buenaventura and Palattao, 'Taking Stock of Water Privatization in the Philippines – The Case of the Metropolitan Waterworks and Sewerage System (MWSS)' (n 56) 51.

147 Lopez, 'Remarks of Oscar M. Lopez, Chairman, Benpres Holdings Corporation at the Annual Stockholders Meeting' (n 143); Remollino, 'GMA Faces New Suit Over Maynilad Bailout' (n 144).

148 Buenaventura and Palattao, 'Taking Stock of Water Privatization in the Philippines – The Case of the Metropolitan Waterworks and Sewerage System (MWSS)' (n 56) 52; *Rehab Case* (n 120); William Kingdom, *Project Information Document – PH-PSD for MWSS Financial Rehab* (World Bank, 2006) 2.

149 Benpress Holdings Corporation, *Quarterly Report Pursuant to Section 17 of the Securities Regulation Code and SRC Rule 17(2)(b) Thereunder* (The Securities and Exchange Commission, 2006); Kingdom, *Project Information Document – PH-PSD for MWSS Financial Rehab* (n 148) 2; Buenaventura and Palattao, 'Taking Stock of Water Privatization in the Philippines – The Case of the Metropolitan Waterworks and Sewerage System (MWSS)' (n 56) 52–53.

150 *Petition for Certiorari (with Application for Preliminary Injuction and Motion for Consolidation), Action for Economic Reforms v Hon Judge Daway (G.R. No. 167418)* (n 142) 5; *Administrative Code (The Republic of the Philippines)* (n 135) 9 ('Public Participation. – [1] If not otherwise required by law, an agency shall, as far as practicable, publish or circulate notices of proposed rules and afford interested parties the opportunity to submit their views prior to the adoption of any rule. [2] In the fixing of rates, no rule or final order shall be valid unless the proposed rates shall have been published in a newspaper of general circulation at least two [2] weeks before the first hearing thereon.').

151 The tariff increase was authorised by MWSS-RO Resolution No. 04-014. For further information about the petitioners' arguments, see *Center for Popular Empowerment v Maynilad Water Services Inc WRC/WUC* (Unreported NWRB Case No.05-062c, 2005); *Maynilad Water Services Inc v National Water Resources Board* (Unreported Court of Appeals Manila 15th Division CA-G.R. SP No 92743, 2007).

152 *Maynilad Water Services Inc v National Water Resources Board* (n 151).

153 *Maynilad Water Services Inc v National Water Resources Board* (n 151) 2.

154 *Maynilad Water Services Inc v National Water Resources Board* (n 151).

155 Atty Estrella T. Decena-Zalidivar, *Legal Opinion on the Concession Agreement Ruling on the NWRB Jurisdiction* (No Legal Opinion No. 07-001, 2007).

156 *Maynilad Water Services Inc v National Water Resources Board* (n 151) 9.

157 *Maynilad Water Services Inc v National Water Resources Board* (n 151) 9.

158 Maynilad, *Annual Report, 2009* (Maynilad, 2010) 64.
159 NEDA (National Economic and Development Institute), *Philippine Development Plan 2011–2016* (NEDA, 2011).
160 Rhys Owen, 'Manila Water Goes from Strength to Strength' (2008) 9(3) *Global Water Intelligence*.
161 Owen, 'Manila Water Goes from Strength to Strength' (n 160).
162 Marianne Go, 'Metro Water Firms Reduce System Losses', *The Philippine Star* (Manila, 14 January 2011).
163 Maynilad, 'History', *Maynilad Water* (Company, 2009) <http://www.mayniladwater.com.ph/about01.php>.
164 Maynilad, 'History' (n 163).
165 Maynilad, 'Maynilad Marks Fifth Year of Reprivatization; Significantly Improves Services', *Maynilad Water* (2012) <https://www.mayniladwater.com.ph/maynilad-marks-fifth-year-of-reprivatization-significantly-improves-services/>
166 Go Metro Water Firms Reduce System Losses (n 162).
167 Catarina de Albuquerque, *Stigma and the Realization of the Human Rights to Water and Sanitation* (HRC, 21st Sess., U.N. Doc. A/HRC/21/42, Human Rights Council, 2012) 30, 35, 53, 56.
168 See, e.g., PPIAF and Asian Development Bank, 'The Design of the Manila Concessions and Implications for the Poor' (The Asian Perspective, 2002); V.C. Rivera, Group Director, Regulatory and Planning, Manila Water Company cited in McIntosh, *Asian Water Supplies – Reaching the Urban Poor* (n 64) 169–172; Carlo Berina-Kim (NGO liaison, Manila Water), 'Personal Communication'; Interview with Perry Riveria, 'Director of Regulation and Corporate Development, Manila Water' (Cristy Clark, Manila, 3 November 2006).
169 See, e.g., PPIAF and Asian Development Bank, 'The Design of the Manila Concessions and Implications for the Poor' (n 168); V.C. Rivera, Group Director, Regulatory and Planning, Manila Water Company cited in McIntosh, *Asian Water Supplies – Reaching the Urban Poor* (n 64) 169–172; Carlo Berina-Kim (NGO liaison, Manila Water) (n 168); Interview with Perry Riveria, 'Director of Regulation and Corporate Development, Manila Water' (n 168).
170 Manila Water Company Inc, 'Corporate Social Responsibility', *Manila Water* (23 May 2012) <http://www.manilawater.com/section.php?section_id=4&category_id=23>.
171 Maria Lourdes Baclagon, *Water for the Poor Communities (TPSB)* (United Nations Economic and Social Commission for Asia and the Pacific, 2004) 22.
172 Baclagon, *Water for the Poor Communities (TPSB)* (n 171).
173 Jude Esguerra, *Universal Service Coverage after the Crisis?* (United Nations Research Institute for Social Development, 2005).
174 Interview with Mary Ann Manahan, 'Advocacy Coordinator at Focus on the Global South' (n 104); Interview with Bubut Palattao, 'Advocacy Coordinator at Freedom from Debt Coalition' (n 73); Interview with Jude Esguerra, 'Economist at the Institute for Popular Democracy' (Cristy Clark, Manila, 25 October 2006); Esguerra, *Universal Service Coverage after the Crisis?* (n 173) 31; Wu and Malaluan, 'A Tale of Two Concessionaires' (n 69) 222–223.
175 Interview with Mary Ann Manahan, 'Advocacy Coordinator at Focus on the Global South' (n 104); Interview with Bubut Palattao, 'Advocacy Coordinator at Freedom from Debt Coalition' (n 73); Interview with Jude Esguerra, 'Economist at the Institute for Popular Democracy' (n 174); Esguerra, *Universal Service Coverage after the Crisis?* (n 173) 31; Wu and Malaluan, 'A Tale of Two Concessionaires' (n 69) 222–223.
176 Cheng, 'The Persistence of Informality' (n 46) 60.
177 Cheng, 'The Persistence of Informality' (n 46) 60.
178 Cheng, 'The Persistence of Informality' (n 46) 60.
179 Metropolitan Waterworks and Sewerage System (MWSS), 'Concession Agreement' 9.5. See also Shane Rosenthal, 'The Manila Water Concessions and Their

Impact on the Urban Poor' (The average monthly income in Manila was USD260, and so this figure represents several times the monthly income of poor households in Manila); Wu and Malaluan, 'A Tale of Two Concessionaires' (n 69) 222–223.

180 McIntosh, *Asian Water Supplies – Reaching the Urban Poor* (n 54) 2, 175.

181 Freedom from Debt Coalition, 'Recalibrating the Meter: A Ten Year Overview of the MWSS Privatization Deal' (n 56) 5; Interview with Jude Esguerra, 'Economist at the Institute for Popular Democracy' (n 174); Interview with Bubut Palattao, 'Advocacy Coordinator at Freedom from Debt Coalition' (n 73); Interview with Mary Ann Manahan, 'Advocacy Coordinator at Focus on the Global South' (n 104); Esguerra, *Universal Service Coverage after the Crisis?* (n 173) 16, 31; Wu and Malaluan, 'A Tale of Two Concessionaires' (n 69) 222–223.

182 Esguerra, *Universal Service Coverage after the Crisis?* (n 173) 16, 31.

183 Esguerra, *The Corporate Muddle of Manila's Water Concessions* (n 56) 31; Interview with Jude Esguerra, 'Economist at the Institute for Popular Democracy' (n 174); Interview with Bubut Palattao, 'Advocacy Coordinator at Freedom from Debt Coalition' (n 73); Interview with Mary Ann Manahan, 'Advocacy Coordinator at Focus on the Global South' (n 104); Wu and Malaluan, 'A Tale of Two Concessionaires' (n 69) 222–223.

184 Interview with Mary Ann Manahan, 'Advocacy Coordinator at Focus on the Global South' (n 104).

185 Interview with Mary Ann Manahan, 'Advocacy Coordinator at Focus on the Global South' (n 104).

186 See, e.g., Manila Water Company Inc, 'Manila Water's TPSB Program Brings 24/7 Water Supply to Marginalized Communities', *Manila Water Company, Inc.* <https://www.manilawater.com/customer/agos/2022-10-27/manila-water-s-tpsb-program-brings-24-7-water-supply-to-marginalized-communities>; Independent Expert on the issue of human rights obligations related to access to safe drinking water and sanitation, *'Good Practices' Related to Access to Safe Drinking Water and Sanitation Questionnaire: Philippines Manila Water – Water Provision for the Poor Program* (OHCHR, February 2010) <https://www.ohchr.org/sites/default/files/english/issues/water/iexpert/docs/questionnaires2010/Philippines_Manila_Water_Water_Provision_for_the_Poor_Program.pdf>; Business Fights Poverty, 'Water for the Poor Prorgamme', *Business Fights Poverty* (29 June 2016) <https://businessfightspoverty.org/water-for-the-poor/>; Perfecto Raymundo, '2M Marginalized Customers given Clean Water: Manila Water' <https://www.pna.gov.ph/articles/1187205>; Maynilad News, 'Indigent Community Benefits from Maynilad Project – Maynilad Water Services, Inc.', *Maynilad News* (7 July 2010) <https://www.mayniladwater.com.ph/indigent-community-benefits-from-maynilad-project/>; Maynilad, 'Maynilad Doubles Coverage of Poor Communities – Maynilad Water Services, Inc.', *Maynilad News* (9 September 2009) <https://www.maynilad-water.com.ph/maynilad-doubles-coverage-of-poor-communities/>.

187 Interview with Informal settlement residents, 'Water for the Poor Program' (Cristy Clark, Manila, 27 October 2006); Interview with Informal settlement residents, 'Water for the Poor Program' (Cristy Clark, Manila, 3 November 2006).

188 IFC (International Finance Corporation), *Public-Private Partnership Stories – Philippines: Manila Water* (IFC, 2010) <https://documents1.worldbank.org/curated/en/788771542141840115/pdf/96924-BRI-PUBLIC-PPPStories-Philippines-ManilaWater.pdf>; Iain Menzies and Mario Suardi, *Output-Based Aid in the Philippines: Improved Access to Water Services for Poor Households in Metro Manila | The Global Partnership for Results-Based Approaches (GPRBA)* (No Note Number 28, The Global Partnership on Output-Based Aid, July 2009) <https://www.gprba.org/knowledge/resources/output-based-aid-philippines-improved-access-water-services-poor-households>.

189 McIntosh, *Asian Water Supplies – Reaching the Urban Poor* (n 64) 2, 175; Esguerra, *Universal Service Coverage after the Crisis?* (n 173) 25.

190 McIntosh, *Asian Water Supplies – Reaching the Urban Poor* (n 64) 2, 175.
191 McIntosh, *Asian Water Supplies – Reaching the Urban Poor* (n 64) 2, 175.
192 Interview with Jude Esguerra, 'Economist at the Institute for Popular Democracy' (n 174); Interview with Mary Ann Manahan, 'Advocacy Coordinator at Focus on the Global South' (n 104).
193 Interview with Jude Esguerra, 'Economist at the Institute for Popular Democracy' (n 174); Interview with Mary Ann Manahan, 'Advocacy Coordinator at Focus on the Global South' (n 104).
194 Esguerra, *Universal Service Coverage after the Crisis?* (n 173) 25.
195 Petr Matous, 'The Making and Unmaking of Community-Based Water Supplies in Manila' (2013) 23(2) *Development in Practice* 217, 225; Cheng, 'The Persistence of Informality' (n 46) 60.
196 Matous, 'The Making and Unmaking of Community-Based Water Supplies in Manila' (n 195) 224.
197 Matous, 'The Making and Unmaking of Community-Based Water Supplies in Manila' 227; Asian Development Bank, *In the Pipeline: Water for the Poor: Investing in Small Piped Water Networks* (Asian Development Bank, 2009) <https://www.adb.org/publications/pipeline-water-poor-investing-small-piped-water-networks>; Menzies and Suardi, *Output-Based Aid in the Philippines* (n 188).
198 Matous, 'The Making and Unmaking of Community-Based Water Supplies in Manila' (n 195) 229.
199 Matous, 'The Making and Unmaking of Community-Based Water Supplies in Manila' (n 195) 229.
200 Cheng, 'The Persistence of Informality' (n 46) 56.
201 Cheng, 'The Persistence of Informality' (n 46) 56.
202 Cheng, 'The Persistence of Informality' (n 46) 56.
203 Ananya Roy, 'Urban Informality: Toward an Epistemology of Planning' (2005) 71(2) *Journal of the American Planning Association* 147, 149.
204 Cheng, 'The Persistence of Informality' (n 46) 57 citing; Ananya Roy and Nezar AlSayyad (eds), *Urban Informality: Transnational Perspectives from the Middle East, Latin America, and South Asia* (Rowman & Littlefield, 2003).
205 Cheng, 'The Persistence of Informality' (n 46) 61.
206 *Action for Economic Reforms v Hon Judge Daway (2005) GR No 167418 (Unreported)* (Republic of the Philippines Supreme Court); Interview with Bubut Palattao, 'Advocacy Coordinator at Freedom from Debt Coalition' (n 73).
207 *Action for Economic Reforms v Hon Judge Daway (2005) G.R. No. 167418 (Unreported)* (n 206) 5, 21b.
208 *Action for Economic Reforms v Hon Judge Daway (2005) G.R. No. 167418 (Unreported)* (n 206) 5, 21b.
209 *Action for Economic Reforms v Hon Judge Daway (2005) G.R. No. 167418 (Unreported)* (n 206) 5, 21a.
210 Benpress Holdings Corporation, *Quarterly Report Pursuant to Section 17 of the Securities Regulation Code and SRC Rule 17(2)(b) Thereunder* (n 149) 4–5.
211 *Action for Economic Reforms v Hon Judge Daway (2005) G.R. No. 167418 (Unreported)* (n 206) 34.
212 *Action for Economic Reforms v Hon Judge Daway (2005) G.R. No. 167418 (Unreported)* (n 206) 34.
213 *Action for Economic Reforms v Hon Judge Daway (2005) G.R. No. 167418 (Unreported)* (n 206) 34; Kingdom, *Project Information Document – PH-PSD for MWSS Financial Rehab* (n 148).
214 *Petition for Certiorari (with Application for Preliminary Injuction and Motion for Consolidation), Action for Economic Reforms v Hon Judge Daway (G.R. No. 167418)* (n 142) 5; *Administrative Code (The Republic of the Philippines)* (n 135) 9 ('Public Participation. – [1] If not otherwise required by law, an agency

shall, as far as practicable, publish or circulate notices of proposed rules and afford interested parties the opportunity to submit their views prior to the adoption of any rule. [2] In the fixing of rates, no rule or final order shall be valid unless the proposed rates shall have been published in a newspaper of general circulation at least two [2] weeks before the first hearing thereon.').

215 *Petition for Certiorari (with Application for Preliminary Injuction and Motion for Consolidation), Action for Economic Reforms v Hon Judge Daway (G.R. No. 167418)* (n 142) 38–39.

216 *Manila International Airport Authority v Airspan Corporation* (2004) (G.R. No 157581, 2004).

217 *Petition for Certiorari (with Application for Preliminary Injuction and Motion for Consolidation), Action for Economic Reforms v Hon Judge Daway (G.R. No. 167418)* (n 142) 38–39.

218 Interview with Bubut Palattao, 'Advocacy Coordinator at Freedom from Debt Coalition' (n 73).

219 *Action for Economic Reforms v Hon Judge Daway (2005) G.R. No. 167418 (Unreported)* (n 206) 22; Interview with Bubut Palattao, 'Advocacy Coordinator at Freedom from Debt Coalition' (n 73).

220 Action for Economic Reforms, *Maynilad Rehab Plan Is Anti-Consumer* (2005).

221 *Petition for Certiorari (with Application for Preliminary Injuction and Motion for Consolidation), Action for Economic Reforms v Hon Judge Daway (G.R. No. 167418)* (n 142) 24.

222 Interview with Bubut Palattao, 'Advocacy Coordinator at Freedom from Debt Coalition' (n 73); *Freedom from Debt Coalition v Metropolitan Waterworks and Sewerage System (MWSS)* (2007) Unreported Supreme Court G.R. No 173044, 38–42.

223 *An Act Creating The Metropolitan Waterworks and Sewerage System and Dissolving The National Waterworks and Sewerage Authority; and for Other Purposes (The Republic of the Philippines) 1971*; Freedom from Debt Coalition, 'Water Advocates Picket MWSS over Public Utility Issue', *Freedom from Debt Coalition* (2006) <http://www.fdc.ph/index.php?view=article&catid=36%3Aadvocacy-on-water&id=159%3Awater-advocates-picket-mwss-over-public-utility-issue&option=com_content&Itemid=87>; Interview with Bubut Palattao, 'Advocacy Coordinator at Freedom from Debt Coalition' (n 73).

224 *Republic v Manila Electric Company (MERALCO)* (2003) 410 SCRA Supreme Court G.R. Nos. 141314 & 141369, 130.

225 Interview with Bubut Palattao, 'Advocacy Coordinator at Freedom from Debt Coalition' (n 73).

226 Interview with Bubut Palattao, 'Advocacy Coordinator at Freedom from Debt Coalition' (n 73).

227 Interview with Bubut Palattao, 'Advocacy Coordinator at Freedom from Debt Coalition' (n 73).

228 Metropolitan Waterworks and Sewerage System (MWSS) (n 179) 9.

229 *Freedom from Debt Coalition v Metropolitan Waterworks and Sewerage System (MWSS)* (n 222); Interview with Bubut Palattao, 'Advocacy Coordinator at Freedom from Debt Coalition' (n 73).

230 Freedom from Debt Coalition, 'FDC to Ask SC Invalidate MWSS Board Resolution', *Freedom from Debt Coalition* (2006) <http://www.fdc.ph/index.php?view=article&catid=36%3Aadvocacy-on-water&id=152%3Afdc-to-ask-sc-invalidate-mwss-board-resolution&option=com_content&Itemid=87>.

231 Freedom from Debt Coalition, 'FDC to Ask SC Invalidate MWSS Board Resolution'; *Freedom from Debt Coalition v Metropolitan Waterworks and Sewerage System (MWSS)* (n 222).

232 Esguerra, *Universal Service Coverage after the Crisis?* (n 173) 20–23.

233 *Freedom from Debt Coalition v Metropolitan Waterworks and Sewerage System (MWSS)* (n 222) 11.
234 *Freedom from Debt Coalition v Metropolitan Waterworks and Sewerage System (MWSS)* (n 222) 11–16.
235 *Freedom from Debt Coalition v Metropolitan Waterworks and Sewerage System (MWSS)* (n 222) 11–12 Despite this advice, the petitioners did not lodge a case with the NWRB.
236 *Freedom from Debt Coalition v Metropolitan Waterworks and Sewerage System (MWSS)* (n 222) 13–14.
237 *Freedom from Debt Coalition v Metropolitan Waterworks and Sewerage System (MWSS)* (n 222) 15–16.
238 *Freedom from Debt Coalition v Metropolitan Waterworks and Sewerage System (MWSS)* (n 222) 16.
239 Tetch Torres, 'SC Asked to Reconsider Ruling on MWSS Row', *Inquirer.net* (Manila, online, 28 January 2008) <http://newsinfo.inquirer.net/breakingnews/metro/view/20080128-115321/SC-asked-to-reconsider-ruling-on-MWSS-row>; Freedom from Debt Coalition, 'National Advocacy against the Privatization of Essential Services and Commons (Water)', *Freedom from Debt Coalition* (2008) <http://www.fdc.ph/index.php?option=com_content&view=article&id=50:advocacy-on-water&catid=77:our-advocacies&Itemid=91>.
240 Swyngedouw, 'Globalisation or "Glocalisation"?' (n 50).
241 Harvey, *The New Imperialism* (n 48).

References

Action for Economic Reforms, *Maynilad Rehab Plan Is Anti-Consumer* (2005)

Action for Economic Reforms v Hon Judge Daway (2005) GR No 167418 (Unreported) (Republic of the Philippines Supreme Court, 2005)

Administrative Code 1987 (The Republic of the Philippines)

de Albuquerque, Catarina, *Stigma and the Realization of the Human Rights to Water and Sanitation* (HRC, 21st Sess., U.N. Doc. A/HRC/21/42, Human Rights Council, 2012)

Almansi, Florencia et al, 'Everyday Water Struggles in Buenos Aires: The Problem of Land Tenure in the Expansion of Potable Water and Sanitation Service to Informal Settlements' in Eric Gutierrez et al (eds), *New Rules, New Roles: Does PSP Benefit the Poor?* (WaterAid and Tearfund, 2003) 24

An Act Creating the Metropolitan Waterworks and Sewerage System and Dissolving the National Waterworks and Sewerage Authority; and for Other Purposes 1971 (The Republic of the Philippines)

An Act to Address the National Water Crisis and for Other Purposes 1995 (The Republic of the Philippines)

Asian Development Bank, *In the Pipeline: Water for the Poor: Investing in Small Piped Water Networks* (Asian Development Bank, 2009) <https://www.adb.org/publications/pipeline-water-poor-investing-small-piped-water-networks>

Aubut, Julie, *The Good Governance Agenda: Who Wins and Who Loses. Some Empirical Evidence for 2001* (Working Paper Series, Development Studies Institute, London School of Economics and Political Science, 2004)

Bagares, Romel, 'QC Court to Rule Today on 2 MWSS Executives', *Philippine Star* (Manila, 6 November 2001)

Bagares, Romel, 'MSWW Disallows Maynilad Rate Hike', *Philippine Star* (Manila, 25 August 2001)

Bakker, Karen J., *Privatizing Water: Governance Failure and the World's Urban Water Crisis* (Cornell University Press, 2010)

Bakker, Karen, 'Trickle Down? Private Sector Participation and the pro-Poor Water Supply Debate in Jakarta, Indonesia' (2007) 38(5) *Geoforum* 855

Barlow, Maude and Tony Clarke, *Blue Gold: The Battle against Corporate Theft of the World's Water* (Stoddart, 2002)

Bayliss, Kate, *Privatisation and Poverty: The Distributional Impact of Utility Privatisation* (No Working Paper No. 16, Centre on Regulation and Competition, Institute for Development Policy and Management, 2002)

Benpress Holdings Corporation, *Quarterly Report Pursuant to Section 17 of the Securities Regulation Code and SRC Rule 17(2)(b) Thereunder* (The Securities and Exchange Commission, 2006)

Bond, Patrick, 'Neoliberalism in Sub-Saharan Africa: From Structural Adjustment to NEPAD' in Alfredo Saad-Filho and Deborah Johnston (eds), *Neoliberalism: A Critical Reader* (Pluto Press, 2005) 232

Buenaventura, Mae and Bubut Palattao, 'Taking Stock of Water Privatization in the Philippines – The Case of the Metropolitan Waterworks and Sewerage System (MWSS)' (2004) 14 *PAID!* 12

Business Fights Poverty, 'Water for the Poor Prorgamme', *Business Fights Poverty* (29 June 2016) <https://businessfightspoverty.org/water-for-the-poor/>

Carino, Ledivia V., *Regulatory Governance in the Philippines: A Profile* (Working Paper Series No Paper No. 44, Institute for Development, Policy & Managment, University of Manchester, 2002)

Carlo Berina-Kim (NGO liaison, Manila Water), 'Personal Communication'

Casarin, Ariel A., Jose A. Delfino and Maria Eugenia Delfino, 'Failures in Water Reform: Lessons from the Buenos Aires's Concession' (2007) 15 *Utilities Policy* 234

Center for Popular Empowerment v Maynilad Water Services Inc WRC/WUC (Unreported NWRB Case No.05-062c, 2005)

Chakrabarty, Bidyut and Mohit Bhattacharya, 'Introduction' in Bidyut Chakrabarty and Mohit Bhattacharya (eds), *Governance Discourse: A Reader* (Oxford University Press, 2008)

Cheng, Deborah, 'The Persistence of Informality: Small-Scale Water Providers in Manila's Post-Privatisation Era' (2014) 7(1) *Water Alternatives* 54

Constitution of the Republic of the Philippines 1987 (The Republic of the Philippines)

Corporate Europe Observatory, 'EU Commission Forces Crisis-Hit Countries to Privatise Water' (2012) <https://corporateeurope.org/pressreleases/2012/eu-commission-forces-crisis-hit-countries-privatise-water>

Cuaresma, Jocelyn C., *Pro-Poor Water Services in Metro Manila: In Search for Greater Equity* (Working Paper Series No. 81, Centre on Regulation and Competition, June 2004)

Dal Bó, Ernesto, 'Regulatory Capture: A Review' (2006) 22(2) *Oxford Review of Economic Policy* 203

Decena-Zalidivar, Atty Estrella T., *Legal Opinion on the Concession Agreement Ruling on the NWRB Jurisdiction* (No Legal Opinion No. 07-001, 2007)

Dumol, Mark, *The Manila Water Concession: A Key Government Official's Diary of the World's Largest Water Privatization* (World Bank Publications, 2000)

Emmett, Bethan, *In the Public Interest: Health, Education, and Water and Sanitation for All* (Oxfam and WaterAid, 2006)
Esguerra, Jude, 'The Corporate Muddle of Manila's Water Concessions' in Eric Gutierrez et al (eds), *New Rules, New Roles: Does PSP Benefit the Poor?* (WaterAid and Tearfund, 2003)
Esguerra, Jude, *Universal Service Coverage after the Crisis?* (United Nations Research Institute for Social Development, 2005)
Fabella, Raul, *Shifting the Boundary of the State: The Privatization and Regulation of Water Service in Metropolitan Manila* (No Paper No. 123, Centre on Regulation and Competition, Institute for Development Policy, University of Manchester, 2006)
Fabella, Raul, 'The Privatization of the Metropolitan Waterworks and Sewerage System: How and Why It Was Won' in Raul Fabella et al (eds), *Built on Dreams, Grounded in Reality: Economic Policy Reform in the Philippines* (The Asia Foundation, 2011) 65
Flor, Mai, *MWSS Privatization: Lessons on Good Governance* (Asian Development Bank (ADB), 2009)
Freedom from Debt Coalition, 'FDC to Ask SC Invalidate MWSS Board Resolution', *Freedom from Debt Coalition* (2006) <https://www.fdc.ph/index.php?view=article&catid=36%3Aadvocacy-on-water&id=152%3Afdc-to-ask-sc-invalidate-mwss-board-resolution&option=com_content&Itemid=87>
Freedom from Debt Coalition, 'National Advocacy against the Privatization of Essential Services and Commons (Water)', *Freedom from Debt Coalition* (2008)
Freedom from Debt Coalition, *Recalibrating the Meter: A Ten Year Overview of the MWSS Privatization Deal* (FDC, 2008)
Freedom from Debt Coalition, 'Water Advocates Picket MWSS over Public Utility Issue', *Freedom from Debt Coalition* (2006)
Freedom from Debt Coalition v Metropolitan Waterworks and Sewerage System (MWSS) (Unreported Supreme Court G.R. No 173044, 2007)
Go, Marianne, 'Metro Water Firms Reduce System Losses', *The Philippine Star* (Manila, 14 January 2011)
Graham, Steve and Simon Marvin, *Splintering Urbanism: Networked Infrastructures, Technological Mobilities and the Urban Condition* (Routledge, 2001)
Hall, David and Emanuele Lobina, *Water Privatisation* (Public Services International Research Unit (PSIRU), 2008)
Harvey, David, *Spaces of Global Capitalism* (Verso, 2006)
Harvey, David, *The New Imperialism: Accumulation by Dispossession* (Oxford University Press, 2003)
IFC (International Finance Corporation), *Public-Private Partnership Stories – Philippines: Manila Water* (IFC, 2010) <https://documents1.worldbank.org/curated/en/788771542141840115/pdf/96924-BRI-PUBLIC-PPPStories-Philippines-ManilaWater.pdf>
Independent Expert on the issue of human rights obligations related to access to safe drinking water and sanitation, *'Good Practices' Related to Access to Safe Drinking Water and Sanitation Questionnaire: Philippines Manila Water – Water Provision for the Poor Program* (OHCHR, February 2010) <https://www.ohchr.org/sites/default/files/english/issues/water/iexpert/docs/questionnaires2010/Philippines_Manila_Water_Water_Provision_for_the_Poor_Program.pdf>

Interview with Macra Cruz, 'Senior Administrator of MWSS' (Cristy Clark, Manila, 30 October 2006)

Interview with Jude Esguerra, 'Economist at the Institute for Popular Democracy' (Cristy Clark, Manila, 25 October 2006)

Interview with Mai Flor, 'Lawyer for Ondeo (Maynilad)' (Cristy Clark, Manila, 24 October 2006)

Interview with Informal settlement residents, 'Water for the Poor Program' (Cristy Clark, Manila, 27 October 2006)

Interview with Informal settlement residents, 'Water for the Poor Program' (Cristy Clark, Manila, 3 November 2006)

Interview with Mary Ann Manahan, 'Advocacy Coordinator at Focus on the Global South' (Cristy Clark, Manila, 31 October 2006)

Interview with Bubut Palattao, 'Advocacy Coordinator at Freedom from Debt Coalition' (Cristy Clark, Manila, 1 November 2006)

Interview with Perry Riveria, 'Director of Regulation and Corporate Development, Manila Water' (Cristy Clark, Manila, 3 November 2006)

Jahan, Selim and Robert McCleery, *Making Infrastructure Work for the Poor – Synthesis Report of Four Country Studies (Bangladesh, Senegal, Thailand and Zambia)* (United Nations Development Programme (UNDP), 2005)

Jaymalin, Mayen et al, 'Water Rate Hike Opposed', *The Philippine Star* (Manila, 5 October 2001)

Kingdom, William, *Project Information Document – PH-PSD for MWSS Financial Rehab* (World Bank, 2006)

Kingdom, Bill, Roland Liemberger and Philippe Marin, *The Challenge of Reducing Non-Revenue Water (NRW) in Developing Countries: How the Private Sector Can Help: A Look at Performance-Based Service Contracting* (Water Suppy and Sanitation Board Discussion Paper Series No Volume 8, World Bank, 2006) <https://siteresources.worldbank.org/INTWSS/Resources/WSS8fin4.pdf>

Kovach, Hetty and Yasmina Lansman, *World Bank and IMF Conditionality: A Development Injustice* (European Network on Debt and Development (Eurodad), 2006)

Kwame Sundaram, Jomo, Oliver Schwank and Rudiger von Arnim, *Globalization and Development in Sub-Saharan Africa* (UNDESA Working Paper No. 102, UNDESA, 2011)

Kwan, Alex and Roger Groebil, 'Water as an Investment Theme: It's Scarce and ABN AMRO Private Banking Asia Thinks Water Is a Great Investment', *Finance Asia* (5 July 2006) <https://www.financeasia.com/article/water-as-an-investment-theme/39520>

Lobina, Emanuele and David Hall, *Problems with Private Water Concessions: A Review of Experience* (Public Services International Research Unit, University of Greenwich, 2003)

Loftus, Alexander and David A. McDonald, 'Of Liquid Dreams: A Political Ecology of Water Privatization in Buenos Aires' (2001) 13(2) *Environment & Urbanization* 179

Lopez, Oscar M., 'Remarks of Oscar M. Lopez, Chairman, Benpres Holdings Corporation at the Annual Stockholders Meeting' (Benpress Holdings Corporation, 2004)

Lourdes Baclagon, Maria, *Water for the Poor Communities (TPSB)* (United Nations Economic and Social Commission for Asia and the Pacific, 2004)

Malaluan, Nepomuceno, *Maynilad Rehab Plan: Tinimbang Ka Ngunit Kulang* (Action for Economic Reforms, 2005)

Manila International Airport Authority v Airspan Corporation (G.R. No 157581, 2004)
Manila Water Company Inc, 'Corporate Social Responsibility', *Manila Water* (23 May 2012)
Manila Water Company Inc, 'Manila Water's TPSB Program Brings 24/7 Water Supply to Marginalized Communities', *Manila Water Company, Inc.* <https://newsinfo.inquirer.net/1685641/manila-waters-tpsb-program-brings-24-7-water-supply-to-marginalized-communities>
Matous, Petr, 'The Making and Unmaking of Community-Based Water Supplies in Manila' (2013) 23(2) *Development in Practice* 217
Maynilad, *Annual Report, 2009* (Maynilad, 2010)
Maynilad, 'History', *Maynilad Water Company* (2009)
Maynilad, 'Maynilad Doubles Coverage of Poor Communities – Maynilad Water Services, Inc.', *Maynilad News* (9 September 2009) <https://www.mayniladwater.com.ph/maynilad-doubles-coverage-of-poor-communities/>
Maynilad, 'Maynilad Marks Fifth Year of Reprivatization; Significantly Improves Services', *Maynilad Water* (2012)
Maynilad News, 'Indigent Community Benefits from Maynilad Project – Maynilad Water Services, Inc.', *Maynilad News* (7 July 2010) <https://www.mayniladwater.com.ph/indigent-community-benefits-from-maynilad-project/>
Maynilad Water Services Inc v National Water Resources Board (Unreported Court of Appeals Manila 15th Division CA-G.R. SP No 92743, 2007)
McIntosh, Arthur, *Asian Water Supplies – Reaching the Urban Poor* (Asian Development Bank (ADB), 2003)
Menzies, Iain and Mario Suardi, *Output-Based Aid in the Philippines: Improved Access to Water Services for Poor Households in Metro Manila | The Global Partnership for Results-Based Approaches (GPRBA)* (No Note Number 28, The Global Partnership on Output-Based Aid, July 2009) <https://www.gprba.org/knowledge/resources/output-based-aid-philippines-improved-access-water-services-poor-households>
Metropolitan Waterworks and Sewerage System (MWSS), 'Concession Agreement'
Metropolitan Waterworks and Sewerage System (MWSS) v Hon Judge Daway (Unreported Regional trial court of Quezon City, Branch 90 G.R. No. 160732, 2004)
Metropolitan Waterwords and Sewerage Systems (MWSS) v Maynilad Water Services Inc (Maynilad) in the Matter of an Ad Hoc Arbitration under the UNCITRAL Rules (Unreported UNC47/KGA, 2003)
Moore, Deborah and Penny Urquhart, *Global Water Scoping Project* (WaterAid, 2004)
NEDA (National Economic and Development Institute), *Philippine Development Plan 2011–2016* (NEDA, 2011)
Olivera, Oscar and Tom Lewis, *Cochabamba!: Water War in Bolivia* (South End Press, 2004)
Owen, Rhys, 'Manila Water Goes from Strength to Strength' *Global Water Intelligence* (20 March 2008) <https://www.globalwaterintel.com/articles/manila-water-goes-from-strength-to-strength>
Pearce, Fred, *When the Rivers Run Dry: Water-the Defining Crisis of the Twenty-First Century* (Beacon Pr, 2006)
Peck, Jamie and Adam Tickell, 'Neoliberalizing Space' (2002) 34(3) *Antipode* 380

Petition for Certiorari (with Application for Preliminary Injuction and Motion for Consolidation), Action for Economic Reforms v Hon Judge Daway (GR No. 167418) (2005)

Philippine Star, 'No Improvement after 5 Years of MWSS Privatization–Solon', *Philippine Star* (Manila, 11 April 2002)

PPIAF and Asian Development Bank, *The Design of the Manila Concessions and Implications for the Poor* (The Asian Perspective, 2002)

Raymundo, Perfecto, '2M Marginalized Customers given Clean Water: Manila Water' <https://www.pna.gov.ph/articles/1187205>

Remollino, Alexander Martin, 'GMA Faces New Suit over Maynilad Bailout', *Bulatlat* (2004)

Republic v Manila Electric Company (MERALCO) (410 SCRA Supreme Court G.R. Nos. 141314 & 141369, 2003) 130

Rosenthal, Shane, 'The Manila Water Concessions and Their Impact on the Urban Poor' Yale School of Forestry and Environmental Studies (2001) < https://hixon.yale.edu/sites/default/files/files/fellows/paper/rosenthal_shane_2001_report.pdf >

Roy, Ananya, 'Urban Informality: Toward an Epistemology of Planning' (2005) 71(2) *Journal of the American Planning Association* 147

Roy, Ananya and Nezar AlSayyad (eds), *Urban Informality: Transnational Perspectives from the Middle East, Latin America, and South Asia* (Rowman & Littlefield, 2003)

Russell, Anna F.S., 'Incorporating Social Rights in Development: Transnational Corporations and the Right to Water' (2011) 7(1) *International Journal of the Law in Context* 1

Saad-Filho, Alfredo, 'The Political Economy of Neoliberalism in Latin America' in Alfredo Saad-Filho and Deborah Johnston (eds), *Neoliberalism: A Critical Reader* (Pluto Press, 2005) 227

Stiglitz, Joseph, *Globalization and Its Discontents* (Penguin, 2002)

'Suez Creates ONDEO', *WaterWorld* (23 March 2001) <https://www.waterworld.com/home/article/16208281/suez-creates-ondeo>

Swyngedouw, Erik, 'Globalisation or "Glocalisation"? Networks, Territories and Rescaling' (2004) 17(1) *Cambridge Review of International Affairs* 25

Swyngedouw, Erik, *Social Power and the Urbanization of Water*, ed Gordon Clark, Andrew Goudie and Ceri Peach (Oxford University Press, 2004)

Torres, Tetch, 'SC Asked to Reconsider Ruling on MWSS Row', *Inquirer.net* (Manila, online, 28 January 2008) <https://newsinfo.inquirer.net/breakingnews/metro/view/20080128-115321/SC-asked-to-reconsider-ruling-on-MWSS-row>

Trémolet, Sophie and Catherine Hunt, *Taking Account of the Poor in Water Sector Regulation* (Water Supply and Sanitation Working Notes No Note No 11, World Bank, 2006)

United Nations Development Programme (UNDP), *Human Development Report* (Oxford University Press, 1992)

United Nations Development Programme (UNDP), *Human Development Report: Beyond Scarcity – Power, Poverty and the Global Water Crisis* (UNDP, 2006) <https://hdr.undp.org/en/content/human-development-report-2006>

WaterAid, *International Financial Institutions (IFI), Conditionality and Privatisation of Water and Sanitation Systems* (WaterAid, 2003)

Winpenny, James, *Financing Water for All: Report of the World Panel on Financing Water Infrastructure* (World Water Council, 2003)
Wood, Angela, *Tightening the Chains or Cutting the Strings: The Status of HIPC Conditionality in 2006* (Jubilee Debt Campaign, 2006)
World Bank, *Assessing Aid: What Works, What Doesn't and Why* (World Bank, 1998)
World Bank, *Governance and Development* (World Bank, 1992)
World Bank, *The World Bank Group's Program for Water Supply and Sanitation* (World Bank, 2004)
World Water Council, *Giving an Audible Voice to Water* (World Water Council, 2021) < https://www.worldwatercouncil.org/en/vision-mission>
Wu, Xun and Nepomuceno A. Malaluan, 'A Tale of Two Concessionaires: A Natural Experiment of Water Privatisation in Metro Manila' (2008) 45(1) *Urban Studies* 207

4

THE HUMAN RIGHT TO WATER

Introduction

While the neoliberal water governance reforms carried out in Chile, England, Wales, and the Philippines emphasised the economic value of water and sought to mediate distribution via the market, concerns around affordability of access and equitable distribution increased during the 1990s, ultimately leading to the recognition of an international human right to water. This recognition represented an important turning point in the production of new legal geographies of water access, but the effects of the right to water were often contradictory.

This chapter begins with an introduction to the legal basis for the eventual international recognition of the human right to water, before exploring the emergence of a global water justice movement. We will then explore some of the debates that took place both within civil society (and ultimately the United Nations) around the compatibility of both water justice and the human right to water with neoliberal water governance (particularly private sector participation or 'PSP'), before examining how the issues highlighted by these debates played out in the domestic context of post-apartheid South Africa from 1996 to around 2008. South Africa provides a paradigmatic case study of the compatibility of neoliberal water governance with the human right to water because the government attempted to implement both simultaneously, with mixed results.

The legal implications of this apparent clash of values ultimately came to a head in 2009 in the Constitutional Court of South Africa when five applicants from the suburb of Phiri in Soweto challenged the City of Johannesburg's forced installation of prepaid water meters into their community.[1] This case, along with the United Nations debates and resolutions around the human to water, will be examined in Chapter 5.

DOI: 10.4324/9781003273219-4

This chapter examines how the emergence of the human right to water produced new spatial-legal relations around water governance. By analysing the interplay between rights-based approaches and market mechanisms through the lens of legal geography, we can better understand how these distinct legal frameworks shape both material access to water and the social relations that mediate this access. The South African case study provides a vivid illustration of how competing legal frameworks – human rights and market efficiency – produced distinct legal geographies of water access, while also highlighting the complex scalar dynamics between international, national, and local governance frameworks. Through this analysis, the chapter demonstrates how legal mechanisms can simultaneously challenge and reinforce existing spatial inequalities while also showing how different actors strategically deploy competing legal frameworks (and narratives) to advance particular visions of water justice. This analysis highlights both the practical challenges of implementing the human right to water and the deeper structural tensions between rights-based and market-based approaches to water governance.

The human right to water

The evolution of the human right to water in international law reveals how legal frameworks produce (and are produced by) distinct ways of knowing and governing water resources. While early recognition emerged through specialised treaties protecting particular groups, there was a gradual expansion toward the universal application of this right.[2] A key moment in this evolution was the 2002 adoption of General Comment No. 15 by the Committee on Economic, Social, and Cultural Rights (CESCR), which declared that a universal human right to water could be implied under articles 11 and 12 of the International Covenant on Economic, Social and Cultural Rights (ICESCR), guaranteeing access for everyone to 'sufficient, safe, acceptable, physically accessible and affordable water for personal and domestic uses.'[3]

CESCR noted that while ICESCR did not specifically list access to water as a protected right, article 11(1) guarantees the right to an adequate standard of living and those rights that are indispensable to the realisation of this right, 'including' food and housing. The word 'including' indicates this is intended to be a non-exhaustive list, and it is undeniable that access to water and sanitation is equally indispensable to the realisation of the right to an adequate standard of living. Similarly, the right to the highest attainable standard of health, guaranteed in article 12(1) of ICESCR, was also found to impliedly guarantee access to an adequate amount of safe water necessary to provide for the highest attainable standard of health. Thus, the right to water can be understood as a prerequisite for the realisation of other human rights.

While the status of the right to water remained unsettled in the aftermath of General Comment No. 15, the focus began to shift towards questions around its scope and normative content. There was also widespread debate over the implications of the right for neoliberal water governance reforms, particularly PSP, and whether framing water as a human right adequately protects its environmental and social values.[4]

The recognition of the human right to water has fundamentally reshaped legal geographies of access and control, but not always in the ways that we might expect. For example, the spatial dimension of rights implementation operates in surprisingly similar ways to neoliberal governance, including through the legitimation of spatial inequality through the application of seemingly neutral technical criteria, such as 'progressive realisation' and 'reasonableness,' and through the simultaneous creation of new spaces of contestation generated by rights mobilisation.

The global water justice movement

Civil society played a central role in the debate around the interpretation and implications of, and the need for, a human right to water. To understand the early focus of these civil society organisations and individuals, who came to form a global water justice movement, it is necessary to go back to the roots of this movement, which arguably lie in Cochabamba, Bolivia.

In 1990, the city of Cochabamba's water supply system was in critical need of repair and expansion.[5] When the Bolivian government approached the World Bank for a loan to upgrade the city's water system, the Bank made privatisation a condition.[6] The resulting tender received just one bid, from Aguas del Tunari (a subsidiary of Bechtel), and it was so bad the Bank itself recommended against it.[7] Nonetheless, the government decided to go ahead and, in 1999, it granted Aguas del Tunari a 40-year concession to provide the city with water and passed legislation to facilitate the legality and profitability of the concession.[8]

To ensure the company would collect the 16 percent annual return on investment guaranteed by the contract, water rates were tripled,[9] and bills rose to around USD20 per month – one fifth of the minimum wage.[10] Before long, many people were unable to afford sufficient water to meet their basic needs, and this was compounded by new laws that imposed charges for collecting rainwater and accessing water from community wells.[11] A community organisation, the *Coordinadora de Defensa del Agua y de la Vida* (Coalition for the Defence of Water and Life), was formed to bring together a range of social movements to challenge the privatisation project and to organise public protests and blockades.[12] As protests escalated, the government imposed martial law and authorised police to fire at protesters.[13] The death of an unarmed teenager brought an end to the conflict,[14] and Aguas del Tunari was forced to withdraw from Cochabamba (although it then sued Bolivia for compensation through international arbitration relying on the terms of a Bolivia-Netherlands bilateral investment treaty).[15]

The dramatic events in Cochabamba became known as the 'Bolivian Water Wars' and catalysed the emergence of a global water justice movement.[16] A central focus of the movement was to challenge the dominant legal framework that positioned water primarily as an economic good subject to market logic. By advocating for water as a *commons* and human right,[17] these activists produced alternative legal rationalities that emphasised water's social and ecological dimensions. This conceptual shift had material consequences by creating new shared narratives (alongside new legal rights) through which communities could contest market-based water governance reforms and assert collective rights to water management.

While the struggle began at the local level in Cochabamba, activists deliberately scaled up their resistance to engage with international legal frameworks. These scalar politics were evident in how the movement simultaneously pursued local direct action, national legal reforms, and international advocacy for the human right to water. This multi-scalar approach connected local water struggles to global rights frameworks. By promoting community control over water resources, activists advanced a legal geography of water that emphasised democratic decision-making at the local scale, contesting the consolidation of control over water resources by both state and private institutions.

The birth of this water justice movement coincided with renewed energy at the international level to formally recognise a human right to water, including the publication of General Comment 15. In this early period, many water justice activists joined with other campaigners to push for this international recognition.[18] A key motivation was the belief that a human right to water would be a potential defence against commodification, including the imposition of PSP and other neoliberal reforms.[19] However, this understanding of the right was not shared by everyone. There were some in the campaign who embraced neoliberal water governance reforms as being necessary to successfully address the crisis of water access,[20] as well as organisations like WaterAID and the Centre on Housing Rights and Evictions (COHRE), who framed the human right to water as a mechanism for promoting access and affordability while remaining circumscribed about the legal compatibility of the right with PSP and similar reforms.[21]

This debate, and underlying legal ambiguity,[22] led to a further proposed approach to pursuing water justice that eschewed rights discourse altogether. Karen Bakker, for example, argued that human rights were inherently compatible with neoliberal water governance reforms while also being anthropocentric and thus unhelpful in promoting the broader ecological values of water.[23] In lieu of a rights-based approach, Bakker promoted a *commons*-based approach to water governance,[24] grounded in Nobel laureate Ostrom's work on the commons.[25] Ostrom's research demonstrated that, contrary to the 'tragedy of the commons' narrative,[26] cooperative institutions to manage local common property resources were widespread and often highly successful.[27] In championing this approach, Bakker shared similar anti-commodification goals to many promoting the human right to water but questioned whether framing water as a human right was the best way of protecting all of its eco-social values.[28]

In many respects, these early debates around water justice divided along two fault lines: one focused on the characterisation of water, the other on human rights. The central fault line was whether to characterise water as an economic good or a commons. As we have seen, a water-as-economic-good approach prioritises water's productive value and emphasises the importance of financial sustainability and economic efficiency in water governance. In contrast, a commons view of water recognises its social values as 'a flow resource essential for life and ecosystem health: non-substitutable and tightly bound to communities and ecosystems through the hydrological cycle.'[29] This distinction leads to particular political decisions around the kind of water governance that will be adopted, including the appropriate level of community control, the role of the private sector, and the degree of cost recovery imposed on the poor.

While this debate focused on the specific context of urban water supply and sanitation (WSS) services, the core distinction reflects a broader ideological contest over the political and economic system – with the water-as-economic-good approach aligning with a broader hegemonic neoliberal worldview and the commons approach aligning with a more counter-hegemonic, utopian worldview concerned with the progressive transformation of society.[30] Here, water is just one component of a larger struggle over the imposition of a top-down, market-dominated development agenda (and wider political economic system) and the alter-globalisation movement's demands for a more democratic, inclusive system.

Within the second fault line, relating to the characterisation of human rights, we can observe that human rights have been used to justify a hegemonic neoliberal approach to water governance, while many civil society groups have also used human rights to support a more counter-hegemonic, commons approach. Sitting somewhere in the middle, the pragmatic rights approach adopted by WaterAid and COHRE views human rights as being more neutral in relation to economic and political systems. Finally, a more critical counter-hegemonic approach rejects human rights as an appropriate tool for social transformation precisely because they understand rights as inherently hegemonic. The sceptical view of rights, illustrated by the arguments of Bakker and a range of other activists and scholars,[31] echoes critical legal theory in arguing that 'rights talk' is in fact grounded in (neo)liberalism, as well as being irredeemably anthropocentric.[32] It is because of this critical understanding of rights that these rights-sceptics argued that water justice activists should focus instead on grassroots community campaigning for the (re)establishment of the commons.[33]

The right to water in South Africa

While much of this debate took place at the international level, especially as the United Nations moved towards formally adopting a human right to water (discussed further in Chapter 5), it also played out at the domestic level in South Africa, which was the first country in the world to explicitly recognise a human right to water in its Constitution.[34] The 1996 Constitution also recognises a right of participation in governance,[35] and the African National Congress (ANC), South Africa's governing party, has recognised the interdependence of participatory rights to both the realisation of socioeconomic rights and the process of social and economic transformation envisioned for post-apartheid South Africa.[36]

These constitutionally recognised rights to water and participation have been given legislative force,[37] and have been implemented through a series of water governance reforms, including decentralisation and the provision of free basic water (FBW).[38] However, the realisation of these rights has also been compromised by the cost recovery imperatives embraced by the government and the challenges of overcoming entrenched class and racial divisions in South African society.

South Africa's attempt to implement both human rights and market-based approaches to water governance provides a valuable case study in the production of hybrid legal spaces. The country's constitutional recognition of the right to water, coupled with its embrace of neoliberal reforms, created complex and contradictory outcomes. While the implementation of the human right to water, including through a program of FBW, was designed to transform the historically unequal patterns of water access, the simultaneous implementation of neoliberalism had countervailing effects. This hybridity helps to explain why rights-based approaches in South Africa both transformed and reinforced existing patterns of inequality.

Historical background

Two centuries of colonial rule followed by 50 years of formal apartheid left South Africa with a legacy of extreme polarisation.[39] In 1993, shortly before the adoption of the new Constitution, the Gini coefficient – a World Bank measure of (in)equality[40] – was estimated to be 0.61, placing South Africa in a tie with Brazil as the most unequal country in the world.[41] The 1998 Human Development Report ranked South Africa's Black population 100 places lower than its White population on the human development index.[42] The ongoing legacy of apartheid policies meant that although Black South Africans were given formal equality in 1994, by the end of the 20th century, they remained significantly disadvantaged in comparison to White South Africans in terms of income, employment, and access to resources and essential services.[43]

Apartheid housing policies also meant that these racial inequalities had a distinctly spatial quality and could be mapped along geographic lines, with rural inequalities in access adding a further layer of distinction.[44] These racial and spatial inequalities were starkly reflected in municipal water services. In 1993, only 43 percent of Black South Africans had on-site access to running water as compared to 99 percent of White South Africans.[45] For women in households without running water, this meant travelling an average of 500 meters to access potable water from communal taps or natural sources.[46]

South Africa's historic constitutional recognition of the right to water was largely the result of two features of the context in which the Constitution was drafted. At the international level, socioeconomic rights had just started to receive a wider level of recognition and acceptance. The creation of CESCR in 1987,[47] and the publication of *General Comment No 3* in 1990,[48] had begun to shift the perception of socioeconomic rights from intangible and aspirational to concrete and justiciable.[49] At the domestic level, the end of apartheid and the ascendance of the ANC to government were the culmination of a long struggle on behalf of South Africa's majority population for equality and full citizenship. Apartheid laws had denied the Black population access not only to civil and political rights but also to socioeconomic rights in a manner that had underscored the interdependent nature of these rights.[50] A lack of democratic rights had disempowered the population from demanding access to socioeconomic rights, while their everyday struggle for survival in the face of systematic deprivation had limited their capacity to demand political freedom.[51]

Sandra Liebenberg believes this history indicates that the Constitution was designed to play a transformative role, both in terms of promoting the realisation of socioeconomic rights and in terms of empowering South Africans to play an active role in the transformation of South African society.[52] She argues that,

> [t]he ability of ordinary people to invoke civil and political rights such as the right of freedom of association and speech as well as socio-economic rights was seen as integral to their active participation in the process of reconstruction and development.[53]

This was also reflected in the drafting process for the new Constitution, which was highly participatory.[54] Nonetheless, there was significant debate in South Africa over the inclusion of socioeconomic rights in the Constitution.

Concerns were raised about the state's financial capacity to meet the cost burden of realising these rights and the judiciary's institutional capacity to consider the budgetary and polycentric[55] issues raised by their adjudication.[56]

Codifying the right to water

The right to water is recognised in section 27 of the South African Constitution, which states that '[e]veryone has the right to have access to ... sufficient food and water.'[57] Section 27 also lays out the state's responsibilities, stating that it 'must take reasonable legislative and other measures, within its available resources, to achieve the progressive realisation of each of these rights.'[58] As the Constitution allocates responsibility for the provision of water services to local government,[59] it binds all levels of government to take 'reasonable legislative and other measures' to progressively realise the right to water.

The policy background to the ANC's promotion of socioeconomic rights was the Reconstruction and Development Plan (RDP), which the ANC adopted in the lead up to the April 1994 elections.[60] The RDP declared that the state was going to provide equal access to essential services that had long been denied to Black South Africans under apartheid.[61] Amongst many other promises, the RDP committed the government to providing 20–30 litres per capita per day (Lpcpd) as a matter of priority, with a medium-term goal of 50–60 Lpcpd, and installing waterborne sanitation in every house.[62]

The government codified the constitutional right to water through the *Water Services Act* 1997,[63] which regulates water services, including the provision of domestic WSS services.[64] Section 3 of the Act provides:

1 Everyone has the right of access to basic water supply and basic sanitation.
2 Every water services institution must take reasonable measures to realise these rights.
3 Every water services authority must, in its water services development plan, provide for measures to realise these rights.

'Basic water supply' is defined as 'the prescribed minimum standard of water supply services necessary for the reliable supply of a sufficient quantity and quality of water to households, including informal households, to support life and personal hygiene.'[65]

The Department of Water Affairs and Forestry (DWAF)[66] published a number of regulations to the *Water Services Act*, including the *Compulsory National Standards*,[67] section 3(b) of which sets out the minimum standard for basic water supply services as:

b) A minimum quantity of potable water of 25 litres per person per day or six kilolitres per household per month:

i at a minimum flow rate of not less than ten litres per minute;

ii within 200 meters of a household; and
iii with an effectiveness such that no consumer is without a supply for more than seven full days in any year.

Participatory rights in both the implementation and the monitoring and evaluation stages of policy are also enshrined in the Constitution. Section 33(1) entitles everyone to administrative action that is lawful, reasonable, and procedurally fair.[68] This right is given legislative effect through the *Promotion of Administrative Justice Act 2000* (PAJA),[69] which states that administrative action that materially and adversely affects the rights or legitimate expectations of any person must be procedurally fair.[70] Section 3(2) elaborates that a person affected by a decision must be given,

> adequate notice of the nature and purpose of the proposed administrative action; a reasonable opportunity to make representations; a clear statement of the administrative action; adequate notice of any right of review or internal appeal, where applicable; and adequate notice of the right to request reasons...[71]

The Constitution further protects public participation in the legislative process by creating a duty on legislative bodies to facilitate public involvement.[72] In *Doctors for Life International v The Speaker of the National Assembly*,[73] the Constitutional Court set out a test for determining whether a legislative body had acted reasonably in the fulfilment of this duty and stated that this would be assessed against the specific context of the case, but that issues such as the nature and importance of the legislation concerned and the intensity of its impact on the public were particularly relevant.[74] The Court also emphasised that this obligation required that legislative bodies provide opportunities for *meaningful* participation and that they ensure that people have the capacity to take advantage of these opportunities.[75]

However, in her 2008 analysis of the Constitutional Court's judgment in the case of *Merafong Demarcation Forum v President of Republic of South Africa*,[76] Nyati argues that 'the test for reasonableness in the duty to facilitate public involvement has no procedural safeguards' and has set such a low standard that the legislature is able to pass after practicing only a 'minimalist approach to public participation' rather than engaging meaningfully with the community.[77] She argues further that '[s]etting such low standards means that judicial review of the other branches of government is ineffective.'[78] As we will consider below, Nyati's critique proved apt in relation to the Constitutional Court's judgment in the Mazibuko water rights case[79] – although whether the outcome was ultimately 'ineffective' remains the subject of debate.

The legal mechanisms established to realise the right to water in post-apartheid South Africa exposed complex dynamics between spatial inequality, scalar politics, and competing legal frameworks. While these mechanisms were ostensibly designed to transform apartheid's geographies of exclusion, their implementation often reproduced existing spatial inequalities. Examples of this include the grandfathering of existing water rights, which effectively preserved apartheid's hydro-geographic inequalities by protecting historical patterns of unequal water access; the devolution of service provision responsibilities to resource-poor municipalities; and the imposition of cost recovery requirements, with disproportionate effects on poor communities.

The scalar dynamics of implementation proved particularly significant. While the right to water was constitutionally enshrined at the national level, its realisation was fundamentally shaped by interactions between different scales of governance. National (and, indeed, international) policy frameworks emphasised cost recovery and efficiency while simultaneously devolving implementation responsibilities to local governments. However, this rescaling of responsibility was not matched by corresponding financial or technical capacity, meaning that local governments bore increasing responsibility without commensurate resources or authority. This reflects what J. Christopher Brown and Mark Purcell call the 'local trap' – the tendency to assume that local-scale arrangements are inherently more democratic, sustainable, and socially just, without considering that scale is socially produced – 'constructed through contingent political struggle'.[80]

These contradictions were carefully negotiated by different actors deploying competing legal frameworks and narratives to advance their interests. The national government strategically invoked both rights-based and market-based legal frameworks, using rights discourse to legitimate its authority while employing market mechanisms to manage implementation (and international pressures). Local governments, constrained by limited resources, often privileged financial sustainability over social equity and the realisation of human rights. Civil society organisations, meanwhile, strategically deployed rights-based frameworks to contest market-based governance approaches, particularly around issues of affordability and disconnection. This complex interplay produced a landscape of water access that reflected neither pure market logic nor a full commitment to human rights, but rather the spatial manifestation of these competing legal rationalities and their associated power relations.

The political economic context of South Africa's water governance reforms

Despite the ambitious goals set out in the RDP and enshrined in the new Bill of Rights, the new South African government (generally referred to as the ANC due to its dominant role in the Tripartite Alliance with the South African Communist Party (SACP) and the Congress of South African Trade Unions (COSATU)) came to power facing constrained economic conditions and during the global ascendancy of neoliberalism.[81] As a result, water governance reform in South Africa was ultimately informed just as much (if not more) by the broader macroeconomic policies adopted after 1993 than by the transformative vision set out in the Constitution and the RDP.

The ANC was limited in its capacity to redistribute resources by the concessions made as part of the transition to democracy,[82] meaning it had to shift its attention to rapidly expanding the economy. Adopting neoliberal policies in this context came with a range of incentives, including World Bank and IMF approval, increased access to finance, and the promise of increased foreign investment.[83] The ANC has been criticised for these compromises,[84] particularly given its ongoing alliance with the SACP, but others argue this approach was critical to the success of the relatively peaceful transition.[85]

By 1996, the ANC had made a policy shift from the equity orientation of the RDP to the Growth, Employment and Redistribution strategy (GEAR),[86] which has been described as 'South Africa's own, "home-grown" structural adjustment programme.'[87] GEAR covered a range of policy areas, including trade liberalisation, tax breaks for big business, labour market adjustments, and cuts in social spending – all designed to expand the South African economy and make it competitive in the international market.[88] In relation to the provision of essential services, GEAR adopted policies of 'fiscal responsibility,' including cost recovery, PSP,[89] and corporatisation.[90] As discussed in Chapter 3, these are the kind of policies that are encouraged by the World Bank, which has stated that only a 'fee reflecting the costs will encourage users to correctly value the service they receive, [... and] help reverse the "entitlement mentality" that has been the historical result of subsidising public services.'[91]

A key result of these economic policies was that despite a transition to democracy, the dramatic economic and spatial polarisation of South African society remained entrenched, and gaining the vote did not significantly improve the real political power or the standard of living of poor communities.[92] An illustration of this effect is that between 1995 and 2005, South Africa went down by almost three-quarters of a point on UNDP's Human Development Index (HDI) from 0.745 to 0.674.[93]

This process of entrenching inequality was compounded by the challenges posed by the water scarcity that prevails in South Africa.[94] The decision to grandfather the water rights of large commercial farms by exempting them from the new water licence rules exacerbated existing levels of inequality.[95] There was simply not enough water left for the majority of South Africa's population to experience the same levels of water use that were the norm in White households.[96] Despite accounting for only 10 percent of the population, White urban households accounted for more than 50 percent of residential water use in 2000.[97] In Johannesburg, for example, these households used an average of 3,000 litres per household per day, while 27 percent of Black households did not have access to piped water within the guaranteed radius of 200 meters of their homes.[98]

These spatial manifestations of water inequalities in South Africa can be described as forms of 'legal violence' – seemingly neutral legal mechanisms that operate to entrench and legitimise spatial inequality and deprivation.[99] The grandfathering of White farmers' water rights is a classic example of how the law can naturalise historical patterns of dispossession while appearing procedurally neutral.

The government acknowledged the imperative of addressing historic inequality in the 1997 *White Paper on National Water Policy*,[100]

> It is important that the introduction of realistic pricing for water does not further penalise disadvantaged communities who were already penalised during the apartheid era. White communities were given a strong economic advantage under apartheid through access to cheap water, while economic development in black communities was restricted by a variety of factors, one of which was lack of access to affordable water. In the interests of equity and social justice, this aspect will have to be considered in the question of water pricing. The price to be levied for water reserved to meet basic needs must merit particular attention.

Despite this acknowledgement, the government instituted a policy of marginal cost recovery for basic water (high enough to cover operation and maintenance).[101] It did so without first investigating whether the resulting price would be affordable for poor households.[102]

This efficiency-focused approach to water governance was also reflected in the ANC's focus on ensuring that new water-use allocations prioritised 'highly valued economic uses.'[103] The 1997 Water Policy document also states that 'water is valued as an economic resource, ... it is widely agreed that the setting of the appropriate price for a natural resource such as water can be an effective mechanism to achieve its efficient and productive use.'[104] In line with this approach, bulk water charges were steadily increased to raise money for infrastructure investment and to ensure the market reflected the scarcity of the resource.[105]

The provision of WSS services is the constitutional responsibility of local government in South Africa.[106] In theory, decentralised delivery should encourage a responsive and participatory style of water management. However, its application in South Africa was compromised by the national government's decision to simultaneously withdraw financial and technical support from the water sector.[107]

Local governments in South Africa receive funding from the national government through several mechanisms outlined in the Constitution.[108] From 1991 to 1998, funding to local governments was reduced by 85 percent, while an additional 55 percent was withheld from 1997 to 2000.[109] After 2000, some efforts were made to increase the level of funding provided to local governments for water management.[110] However, even by 2008, national government funds remained insufficient to ensure universal access to adequate and affordable WSS services, particularly in uniformly poor municipalities (which cannot cross-subsidise from wealthy consumers).[111]

When responsibility for WSS services was devolved to municipalities, staff had little relevant technical experience. Since insufficient funds were made available for capacity building or wage increases necessary to attract skilled staff,[112] by 2008 many municipalities still lacked the technical capacity to adequately carry out the responsibilities of water sector management.[113] The former Director-General of DWAF recognised this problem,[114] and argued that 'many municipalities are in a state of crisis because they do not have enough [appropriately qualified] people on their staff.'[115]

Prior to 2001, the policy response to the need to facilitate the realisation of South Africa's constitutional right to water focused on increasing efficiency and financial sustainability in order to increase physical access,[116] while less attention was paid to affordability, equity, or participation.[117] In response to the pressure of trying to meet an increasing demand with severely limited funds and capacity, local governments began to commercialise their WSS services.[118] The imperative to raise funds brought an increased focus on cost recovery, and tariffs were increased in order to ensure the financial sustainability of WSS systems and to enable them to expand services.[119]

For households that could not afford these rising costs, this approach had a devastating effect on their ability to maintain access to water.[120] Significant water tariff increases between 1996 and 2000 led to unprecedented levels of household debt and to millions of people having their water cut off for non-payment.[121] Women were forced to bear a disproportionate burden of increased cost recovery measures.[122] As the traditional caregivers for the elderly and the sick (a significant issue with the high prevalence of HIV and AIDS at the time), it fell to women to source enough water to meet these responsibilities and to meet the needs of the household.[123]

Some government officials argued that the policies of the apartheid government, along with the payment boycotts used against them (in the mid-1980s, the ANC called for South African townships to become 'ungovernable' in part by refusing to pay rent or service fees),[124] had created a 'culture of non-payment' in South Africa.[125] A related argument was that Black South Africans refuse to pay for services due to a so-called 'culture of entitlement.'[126] However, these criticisms fail to account for the issue of affordability. In a 2003 study, the number one reason given for non-payment of bills was an 'incapacity to pay due to insufficient income.'[127] Even by 2012, somewhere between 25 and 40 percent of South Africans were unemployed (with the 40 percent figure including those who were no longer actively looking for work).[128] The rate of unemployment was also considerably higher amongst Black South Africans,[129] with some townships, like Soweto, having rates of 53 percent and higher.[130]

In a 2000 study of household affordability,[131] 90 percent of low-income households gave unemployment, no income, or too low an income as the main reason for the non-payment of water tariffs. Although providers were required to make arrangements with households to manage their repayments, many of these arrangements left households permanently in debt, while others imposed unrealistic payment schedules and then imposed disconnections or more serious action, such as eviction proceedings, when they were unmet.[132]

Water disconnections are permissible under the 2003 Strategic Framework for Water Services, but only intended as a last resort.[133] Additionally, section 4(3) of the *Water Services Act* states that procedures for the limitation or discontinuation of water services must not result in a person who is unable to pay being denied access to basic water services.[134] In practice, however, researchers in 2005 and 2008 found that water service disconnections were the most common response to a poor household's failure to pay their water bills, even when this failure was clearly the result of an inability to pay.[135] This uncompromising approach to disconnections was a direct result of the preoccupation with cost recovery that was imposed on municipalities by national government policies.[136]

In 1994, when the ANC first came to power, 12 million South Africans did not have access to clean drinking water.[137] While the ANC was able to provide an additional seven million people with access to water by 2002, the imposition of disconnection as a means of credit control also meant that at least that same number (if not many more) had their water cut off for non-payment.[138] Additionally, over two million people had been evicted from their homes for failing to pay their accumulated debts on either their water or electricity bills.[139]

The effects of these early policies eventually forced authorities to reconsider their approach. Households who could not afford to purchase sufficient water, or whose water services were cut off for non-payment, were forced to use water from untreated natural sources like streams, ponds, or muddy puddles.[140] Often these natural sources were polluted and unsafe, and households experienced negative health consequences as a result of consuming contaminated water.[141] One consequence was cholera, which saw an upsurge in cases after the introduction of cost recovery and credit control policies.[142] In one area of KwaZulu-Natal, one such cholera outbreak became one of the worst in Africa.[143]

Poor communities in areas like Nqutshini, Matshana, Shakashead, and Nkobongo in KwaZulu-Natal had been receiving free water since the 1980s until the local government and a private water provider increased cost recovery efforts in mid-2000.[144] In Nqutshini and Matshana, a flat rate of R20 per month [USD3.2] was imposed on households seeking to access the communal standpipes.[145] This new charge presented a barrier for many households due to high rates of unemployment,[146] forcing some to turn to untreated water sources and others to default on their bills.[147] In order to enforce payment, authorities cut the supply of water to all the standpipes in early August.[148]

During the same period, the WSS systems of Shakashead and Nkobongo were contracted out to a private concessionaire, and prepaid meters were installed for the purposes of tariff collection.[149] Instead of continuing to receive free water, residents had to purchase tokens to activate their water supply.[150] Many households could not afford to purchase the necessary tokens and began using untreated natural sources of water.[151]

On 22 August 2000, the first reported case of cholera in the area was diagnosed.[152] By the end of the month, there were a total of 62 cases.[153] Cholera spread to other parts of the country, infecting a total of 117,147 and killing 265 people.[154] These tragic results of imposing inflexible cost recovery policies led to a re-examination of the issue of affordability and a new approach of delivering on the constitutional promise of basic water for all.[155] As the then-Director-General of DWAF put it, '[p]erhaps we were being a little too market-oriented.'[156]

Cost recovery and the right to water

The introduction of FBW in South Africa emerged at the intersection of competing legal rationalities – human rights and market efficiency – creating what could be called a hybrid legal space where different conceptual frameworks for understanding and governing water coexist in dynamic tension. The cholera outbreak that precipitated this policy shift vividly illustrated the material consequences of these competing frameworks while also highlighting the spatial politics of rights implementation.

The cholera outbreak was a dramatic turning point in South Africa's experience with attempting to implement the human right to water by rapidly expanding access to poor communities while simultaneously complying with neoliberal cost recovery principles. Despite its early adoption of a marginal cost recovery approach to all water services, by 2001 the South African government realised that, in the context of the apartheid legacies of widespread unemployment, geographic clusters of poverty, and low levels of education, affordability for the poor meant that a lifeline amount needed to be free.[157] The Minister for Water, Ronnie Kasrils, tells a story of the moment when he realised this fact,

> Last year, I visited a newly installed water supply scheme in a typical South African rural village called Lutsheko. The project was well run by a village water committee and had improved the lives of 3,000 people. But when I went down to see the borehole, on the banks of a dried out riverbed, I found a young woman, with a three-week old baby on her back, scooping water out of a hole she had dug in the riverbed. She told me she could not afford to use the taps.[158]

Free basic water

The 1997 White Paper on National Water Policy had envisioned a *lifeline tariff* to provide a reserve of free water for basic human need.[159] This vision was realised in February 2001 when President Mbeki announced a new national policy of Free Basic Services (FBS), which included water.[160] The 'FBW' allocation was set at six kilolitres per household per month, which was designed to provide a household of eight people with 25 Lpcpd.[161]

While the need for water affordability has widespread international support,[162] providing water for free is a more controversial approach.[163] Mike Muller argues that the FBW policy was controversial for going against the conventional wisdom that water, as an economic good, should be paid for.[164] Critics saw it as a populist political ploy, particularly because it was introduced on the eve of local government elections.[165] The introduction of a free lifeline amount was a progressive policy in this context. The FBW policy thus represents an approach to water services in which affordability is acknowledged as a central element in South Africa's constitutionally enshrined right to water.[166]

However, while the FBW policy emerged from rights-based imperatives – particularly following the cholera outbreak – its implementation was fundamentally shaped by market logic, creating contradictory approaches to water delivery with highly uneven socio-spatial consequences. One such contradiction was the policy's household-based allocation system, which failed to account for variations in household size and composition. As these variations largely reflect apartheid-era economic inequalities, the outcome of this policy mapped neatly onto existing patterns of spatial disadvantage.

Scalar politics also affected the implementation of FBW. While the policy was nationally mandated, its realisation was fundamentally shaped by local government capacity and resource constraints, including inadequate national funding.[167] This led to a slow rollout in many areas.[168] Inadequate funding also entrenched existing spatial inequalities, as municipalities with limited revenue bases struggled to finance the policy's implementation and were forced to cross-subsidise from poor communities themselves, meaning they imposed significant tariff increases in the second block of consumption (immediately above the FBW amount) in order to recover the cost of providing the first six kilolitres free.[169] In some areas, such as Durban, this resulted in water tariffs actually doubling for poor consumers after the introduction of FBW.[170]

A further response to local resource constraints was the increased reliance on punitive cost recovery and demand management measures,[171] such as water restriction devices (metal discs with a small hole in the centre, which reduces the diameter of the pipe and restricts the flow of water),[172] prepaid meters (devices that are programmed to dispense the monthly FBW amount and then to cut off the water supply unless additional water credit tokens are purchased),[173] and lower levels of water service, such as a yardpipe or standpipe rather than a household water connection.[174]

Most municipalities also restricted access to FBW to those who are registered as indigent.[175] This is problematic because the various indigent registers (which vary from municipality to municipality) are highly under-representative of the true numbers of poor households in South Africa.[176] There are no national criteria for indigent status,[177] but the criteria set by each municipality are typically onerous and exclusionary.[178] Requirements of proof of income and account-holder status exclude many poor tenants, all informal occupiers, and many undocumented poor people.[179] People are also required to re-register every six months or two years, with the result that many find their registration lapses before they are able to arrange to resubmit all required documentation.[180]

Civil society contested these mechanisms through both legal channels and direct action, producing new spaces of resistance (at the local, national, and international levels). Meanwhile, the national government maintained an ambiguous position, promoting both rights realisation and cost recovery without resolving their fundamental tensions.

Discussion

These fundamental tensions in South Africa's attempts to implement the human right to water alongside neoliberal water governance reforms illustrate many of the compatibility issues that were debated within the campaign for a right to water and within the water justice movement. While the government's emphasis on expanding access and its adoption of the FBW program were tangible positive outcomes of the right to water, they were undermined by the punitive approach adopted to cost recovery.

Beyond this question of compatibility, the dual implementation of these approaches also provides an illustration of how they operate to shape people's relationship with water. We have seen that commodification – including cost recovery – alienates people from water, casting them into the role of water consumers whose relationship is mediated entirely through the market. The ANC attempts to realise the human right to water alongside commodification meant that it framed it largely as a consumer right, but the community did not share this interpretation. Instead, many community members understood that the human right to water guaranteed a more communitarian relationship with water by ensuring both affordability and protecting the community's right to participate in the management of water resources in order to make decisions focused on the public good.

This chapter highlights how the emergence of the human right to water produced complex new legal geographies, and we can consider these outcomes in relation to space, place, and narrative. Attention to space highlights the way competing legal rationalities – rights-based and market-based approaches – produced 'hybrid legal spaces' where rights discourse and market logic coexist in dynamic tension. While these hybrid spaces were given concrete form through technologies like prepaid meters, which simultaneously enable rights realisation (through FBW) and market discipline (through automated disconnection), their contradictory rationalities also challenge and reinforce existing spatial patterns of water inequality.

If we turn our attention to place, we can reflect on the complex scalar politics of rights implementation in South Africa. The rescaling of service delivery responsibilities to local governments, without corresponding fiscal and technical capacity, created a misalignment between rights obligations and implementation capabilities. Once again, this misalignment produced distinctly uneven geographies of water access, often reinforcing historical patterns of spatial inequality despite the transformative aspirations of the Constitution and the RDP.

Finally, attention to narrative draws our attention to the strategic deployment of competing legal discourses by different actors and the inherently political nature of the realisation of the human right to water. Various stakeholders, from municipal authorities to civil society, actively engaged in producing new legal relations around water through the rationalising language of both neoliberalism and rights.

Together, these observations help explain why rights-based approaches can simultaneously transform and reinforce existing patterns of water inequality. As we will see in Chapter 5, these tensions would ultimately be tested in the Constitutional Court of South Africa through the Mazibuko case,[181] raising fundamental questions about the capacity of rights-based approaches to challenge the spatial-legal relations produced by neoliberal water governance.

Notes

1 *Mazibuko v City of Johannesburg* [2009] ZACC 28; 2010 4 SA 1, Constitutional Court of South Africa (8 October 2009).

2 For specific groups, see, e.g., the *Geneva Convention relative to the Treatment of Prisoners of War (Third Geneva Convention)*, opened for signature 12 August 1949, 75 UNTS 135 (entered into force 21 October 1950) art 26 (which requires that prisoners of war be supplied with '[s]ufficient drinking water', and art 29 requires that prisoners of water be supplied with 'sufficient water and soap for their personal toilet and for washing their personal laundry'); the *Convention on the Elimination of All Forms of Discrimination Against Women*, opened for signature 18 December 1979, 1249 UNTS 13 (entered into force 3 September 1981) art 14(2) (which requires that state parties ensure women in rural areas have the right to 'enjoy adequate living conditions, particularly in relation to . . . water supply'); the *Convention on the Rights of the Child*, opened for signature 20 November 1989, 1577 UNTS 3 (entered into force 2 September 1990)

art 24(2) (which requires states parties to combat disease and malnutrition in children 'through the provision of adequate nutritious foods and clean drinking-water'); the *Convention on the Rights of Persons with Disabilities*, opened for signature 13 December 2006, 2515 UNTS 3 (entered into force 3 May 2008) art 28(2)(a) (which recognises a right of 'equal access by persons with disabilities to clean water services.'). For broader protections, see, e.g., the *Arab Charter on Human Rights*, signed 22 May 2004, official translated version reprinted in [ST/HR/]CHR/NONE/2004/40/Rev.1 (entered into force 15 March 2008) art 39 (which recognises the right to 'highest attainable standard of physical and mental health' and, subsection 2(e), makes specific mention of including the 'provision of the basic nutrition and safe drinking water for all.'); United Nations, *Report of the United Nations Water Conference, Mar Del Plata, 14–25 March 1977* (E/CONF.70/29, 1977), 11(a) (which recognized the principle that 'all people . . . have the right to have access to drinking water in quantities and of a quality equal to their basic needs').

3 United Nations Committee on Economic, Social and Cultural Rights (CESCR), *General Comment No. 15: The Right to Water (Arts. 11 and 12 of the International Covenant on Economic, Social and Cultural Rights)*, 29th sess, UN Doc E/C.12/2002/11 (20 January 2003).

4 Karen Bakker, 'Commons versus Commodities: Debating the Human Right to Water' in Farhana Sultana and Alex Loftus (eds), *The Right to Water* (Routledge, 1st edition, 2011); Cristy Clark, 'Of What Use Is a Deradicalized Human Right to Water?' (2017) 17(2) *Human Rights Law Review* 231.

5 World Bank, *Bolivia: Major Cities Water and Sewerage Rehabilitation Project* (Report No. 18009, Implementation Completion Report, 12 June 1998).

6 World Bank, *Bolivia – Major Cities Water Supply and Sewerage Rehabilitation Project: Credit 2187 – Credit Agreement – Conformed* (Legal ISC Files, 1990) as amended by Legal Department of World Bank, *Conformed Copy – C2187 – Major Cities Water Supply and Sewerage Rehabilitation Project – Amendment 3* (24 May 1996).

7 See, for example, Christopher Neal, 'Letter to the Democracy Centre' (2000) reprinted in Jim Shultz and Tom Kruse, *Water Revolt: The World Bank Letters* (The Democracy Centre, 2000) <https://www.democracyctr.org/the-world-bank-letters> (last accessed 26 March 2025).

8 *Aguas del Tunari, SA v Republic of Bolivia* (ICSID Case No. ARB/02/3, 2005) 52. See also *Law No. 2029: Potable Water and Sanitary Law* (Ley de Servicios de Agua Potable y Alcantarillado Sanitario, 29 October 1999) (Bolivia) art 19.

9 *Aguas del Tunari, SA v Republic of Bolivia* (n 8) 57 and 66.

10 Vandana Shiva, *Water Wars: Privatization, Pollution, and Profit* (Pluto Press, 2002) 102.

11 Shiva, *Water Wars* (n 10).

12 Olivera Terhorst and Alexander Dwinell, 'Social Movements, Left Governments, and the Limits of Water Sector Reform in Latin America's Left Turn' (2013) 40(4) *Latin American Perspectives* 55, 64.

13 *Aguas Del Tunari, SA v Republic of Bolivia* (n 8) 73.

14 Oscar Olivera and Tom Lewis, *Cochabamba!: Water Rebellion in Bolivia* (South End Press, 2004) 43.

15 *Aguas Del Tunari, SA v Republic of Bolivia* (n 8) 73. (The Bolivia-Netherlands bilateral investment treaty applied because 55% of Aguas de Tunari was owned by Dutch company International Water. Bechtel, a US company, owned a 50% share of International Water.)

16 Luis Sánchez Gómez and Philipp Terhorst, 'Cochabamba, Bolivia: Public-Collective Partnership after the Water War' in Belén Balanyá et al (eds), *Reclaiming Public Water: Achievements, Struggles and Visions from Around the World* (Transnational

Institute and Corporate Europe Observatory, 2007). See, for example, Philippe Marin, *Public-Private Partnerships for Urban Water Utilities: A Review of Experiences in Developing Countries* (World Bank, 2009) 17–37.

17 Cristy Clark, 'Water Justice Struggles as a Process of Commoning' (2019) 54(1) *Community Development Journal* 80.

18 Friends of the Right to Water, *Key Principles for an International Treaty on the Right to Water: Draft Work in Progress for Consultation* (Friends of the Right to Water, 2005); Maude Barlow, *The Right to Water: The Campaign for a United Nations Treaty* (Council of Canadians, 2006).

19 For a discussion of this approach, see, for example, Karen Bakker, 'The "Commons" Versus the "Commodity": Alter-Globalization, Anti-Privatization and the Human Right to Water in the Global South' (2007) 39(3) *Antipode* 430; Adam Davidson-Harden, Anil Naidoo and Andi Harden, 'The Geopolitics of the Water Justice Movement' (2007) 11 *Peace Conflict & Development* 1; Oriol Mirosa and Leila M Harris, 'Human Right to Water: Contemporary Challenges and Contours of a Global Debate' (2012) 44(3) *Antipode* 932.

20 Green Cross International et al, *Fundamental Principles for a Global Framework Convention on the Right to Water* (Green Cross International, 2004) <www.cawater-info.net/library/eng/right_to_water.pdf> (last accessed 2 March 2017) art 10.

21 WaterAid, *International Financial Institutions (IFI), Conditionality and Privatisation of Water and Sanitation Systems* (Water Aid, 2003); Langford et al, *Legal Resources for the Right to Water: International and National Standards* (Centre on Housing Rights and Evictions, 2004).

22 See, e.g., Steven Shrybman, *Critical Review of the 'Green Cross' Proposal for a Global Framework Convention on the Right to Water* (2005) <goldblattpartners.com/wp-content/uploads/00128085.pdf> (last accessed 2 March 2017).

23 Bakker, 'The "Commons" Versus the "Commodity"' (n 19).

24 See, for example, Bakker, 'The "Commons" Versus the "Commodity"' (n 19).

25 Elinor Ostrom, *Governing the Commons: The Evolution of Institutions for Collective Action* (Cambridge University Press, 1990); Elinor Ostrom and Roy Gardner, 'Coping with Asymmetries in the Commons: Self-Governing Irrigation Systems Can Work' (1993) 7(4) *Journal of Economic Perspectives* 93.

26 Garrett Hardin, 'The Tragedy of the Commons' (1968) 162(3859) *Science* 1243.

27 Hardin, 'The Tragedy of the Commons' (n 26).

28 Bakker, 'The "Commons" Versus the "Commodity"' (n 19).

29 Bakker, 'The "Commons" Versus the "Commodity"' (n 19) 441.

30 Madeline Baer and Andrea Gerlak, 'Implementing the Human Right to Water and Sanitation: A Study of Global and Local Discourses' (2015) 36(8) *Third World Quarterly* 1527.

31 See, for example, Daria Roithmayr, 'Lessons from Mazibuko: Persistent Inequality and the Commons' (2010) 3 *Constitutional Court Review* 317; Patrick Bond, 'The Right to the City and the Eco-Social Commoning of Water: Discursive and Political Lessons from South Africa' in Farhana Sultana and Alex Loftus (eds), *The Right to Water: Politics, Governance and Social Struggles* (Routledge, 1st edition, 2011) 190.

32 Bakker, 'The "Commons" Versus the "Commodity"' (n 19) 441.

33 Bakker, 'The "Commons" Versus the "Commodity"' (n 19); Cf. Bakker, 'The "Commons" Versus the "Commodity"' (n 4) 19 where she modifies her view and argues that a human right to water has some value as a campaigning tool.

34 *Constitution of the Republic of South Africa 1996*, s 27.

35 *Constitution of the Republic of South Africa 1996*, s 33(1).

36 See, e.g., Sandra Liebenberg, *Socio-Economic Rights: Adjudication under a Transformative Constitution* (Juta, 2010) 9.

37 *Water Services Act 1997* (South Africa); *Promotion of Administrative Justice Act (PAJA) 2000* (South Africa).
38 See below. See also Department of Water Affairs and Forestry (DWAF), *Free Basic Water* (2012) <http://www.dwaf.gov.za/dir_ws/fbw/#> (last accessed April 2012); *Constitution of the Republic of South Africa 1996*, Schedule 4, Part B – 'The following local government matters to the extent set out in section 155 (6) (a), (7): [...] Water and sanitation services limited to potable water supply systems and domestic waste-water and sewage disposal systems.'
39 Rose Francis, 'Water Justice in South Africa: Natural Resources Policy at the Intersection of Human Rights, Economics, and Political Power' (2005) 18(1) *Georgetown International Environmental Law Review* 149, 149–150.
40 World Bank, *GINI index* (2012) <http://data.worldbank.org/indicator/SI.POV.GINI/> (last accessed 10 December 2012). ('Gini index measures the extent to which the distribution of income (or, in some cases, consumption expenditure) among individuals or households within an economy deviates from a perfectly equal distribution. A Lorenz curve plots the cumulative percentages of total income received against the cumulative number of recipients, starting with the poorest individual or household. The Gini index measures the area between the Lorenz curve and a hypothetical line of absolute equality, expressed as a percentage of the maximum area under the line. Thus a Gini index of 0 represents perfect equality, while an index of 100 implies perfect inequality.').
41 Stephan Klasen, 'Social, Economic, and Environmental Limits for the Newly Enfranchised in South Africa?' (2002) 50(3) *Economic Development and Cultural Change* 607, 608–609.
42 Klasen, 'Social, Economic, and Environmental Limits for the Newly Enfranchised in South Africa?' (n 41) 609, citing UNDP, *Human Development Report – Consumption for Human Development* (1998).
43 Klasen, 'Social, Economic, and Environmental Limits for the Newly Enfranchised in South Africa?' (n 41) 608–609, 615.
44 Klasen, 'Social, Economic, and Environmental Limits for the Newly Enfranchised in South Africa?' (n 41) 608–609, 615.
45 Klasen, 'Social, Economic, and Environmental Limits for the Newly Enfranchised in South Africa?' (n 41) 609.
46 Francis, 'Water Justice in South Africa' (n 39) 150 (citations omitted); David A. McDonald, 'The Bell Tolls for Thee: Cost Recovery, Cutoffs, and the Affordability of Municipal Services in South Africa' in David A. McDonald and John Pape (eds), *Cost Recovery and the Crisis of Service Delivery in South Africa* (Zed Books, 2002) 161, 163.
47 Philip Alston, 'Out of the Abyss? The Challenges Confronting the New U.N. Committee on Economic, Social and Cultural Rights' (1987) 9 *Human Rights Quarterly* 332; Philip Alston, 'The Committee on Economic, Social and Cultural Rights' in Philip Alston (ed), *The United Nations and Human Rights* (Oxford University Press, 1992) 473; UN Committee on Economic, Social and Cultural Rights (CESCR), *The Limburg Principles on the Implementation of the International Covenant of Economic Social and Cultural Rights,* 43rd sess, UN Doc E/CN.4/1987/17 (8 January 1987).
48 United Nations Committee on Economic, Social and Cultural Rights (CESCR), *General Comment No. 3: The Nature of Sates Parties Obligations (Art 2, Para 1, of the Covenant)*, 5th sess, UN Doc E/1991/23 (14 December 1990); International Commission of Jurists (ICJ), *Maastricht Guidelines on Violations of Economic, Social and Cultural Rights* (United Nations, 1997); Scott Leckie, 'Another Step Towards Indivisibility: Identifying the Key Features of Violations of Economic, Social and Cultural Rights' (1998) 20 *Human Rights Quarterly* 81.

49 Malcolm Langford, 'The Justiciability of Social Rights: From Practice to Theory' in Malcolm Langford (ed), *Social Rights Jurisprudence – Emerging Trends in International and Comparative Law* (Cambridge University Press, 2008) 3.
50 See, e.g., Liebenberg, *Socio-Economic Rights* (n 36) xxi.
51 Nelson Mandela, 'Address: On the Occassion of the ANC's Bill of Rights Conference' in *A Bill of Rights for a Democratic South Africa: Papers and Report of a Conference Convened by the ANC Constitutional Committee* (1991) 9, 12, cited in Liebenberg, *Socio-Economic Rights* (n 36) 9.
52 Liebenberg, *Socio-Economic Rights* (n 36) 9.
53 Liebenberg, *Socio-Economic Rights* (n 36) 9.
54 Jeremy Sarkin, 'The Drafting of South Africa's Final Constitution from a Human-Rights Perspective' (1999) 47(1) *The American Journal of Comparative Law* 67, 70–72.
55 'Polycentric' refers to issues that involve a complex range of interlocking and interacting interests and potential repercussions. See Lon L. Fuller, 'The Forms and Limits of Adjudication' (1978) 92 *Harvard Law Review* 353, 394–398.
56 Liebenberg, *Socio-Economic Rights* (n 36) 11–12, citing SALC, *Interim Report: Project 58 Group and Human Rights* (1991) 533–537; Hugh Corder et al, *A Charter for Social Justice: A Contribution to the South African Bill of Rights Debate* (Department of Public Law, University of Cape Town and Department of Public Law, University of the Western Cape ; Cape Town Legal Resources Centre, 1992).
57 *Constitution of the Republic of South Africa 1996*, s 27.
58 *Constitution of the Republic of South Africa 1996*, s 27.
59 *Constitution of the Republic of South Africa 1996*, s 27, Schedule 4, Part B – 'The following local government matters to the extent set out in section 155 (6)(a), (7): [...] Water and sanitation services limited to potable water supply systems anddomestic waste-water and sewage disposal systems.'
60 African National Congress (ANC), *Reconstruction and Development Programme* (1994) South Africa.
61 African National Congress (ANC), *Reconstruction and Development Programme* (1994) South Africa.
62 African National Congress (ANC), *Reconstruction and Development Programme* (1994) South Africa 2.6.6–2.6.7.
63 *Water Services Act 1997* (South Africa) s 3.
64 *Water Services Act 1997* (South Africa) s 3.
65 *National Water Act 1998* (South Africa) s 1(iii).
66 DWAF is now known as the Department of Water Affairs (DWA) but will be referred to as DWAF throughout this chapter for the purposes of consistency.
67 Department of Water Affairs and Forestry (DWAF), *Guidelines for Compulsory national standards (Regulations under Section 9 of the Water Services Act (Act 108 of 1997)) and Norms and standards for water services tariffs (Regulations under Section 10 of the Water Services Act (Act 108 of 1997)) and Water Services Provider Contract Regulations (in terms of s19(5) of the Water Services Act, 1997)* (South Africa, 2002).
68 *Constitution of the Republic of South Africa 1996*, s 33(1).
69 *Promotion of Administrative Justice Act (PAJA) 2000* (South Africa).
70 *Promotion of Administrative Justice Act (PAJA) 2000* (South Africa) s 3(1).
71 *Promotion of Administrative Justice Act (PAJA) 2000* (South Africa) s 3(2).
72 *Constitution of the Republic of South Africa 1996*, ss 59(1)(a), 72(1)(a), 118(1)(a).
73 [2006] ZACC 11; 2006 6 SA 416, Constitutional Court of South Africa (South Africa, 17 August 2006).

74 *Doctors for Life International v The Speaker of the National Assembly* [2006] ZACC 11; 2006 6 SA 416, Constitutional Court of South Africa (South Africa, 17 August 2006) [128].
75 *Doctors for Life International v The Speaker of the National Assembly* (n 74) [129].
76 [2008] ZACC 10, Constitutional Court of South Africa (South Africa, 13 June 2008).
77 Linda Nyati, 'Public Participation: What Has the Constitutional Court Given the Public?' (2008) 12(2) *Law, Democracy & Development* 102, 109.
78 Nyati, 'Public Participation' (n 77) 109.
79 It is worth noting that the Constitutional Court's judgment in *Occupiers of 51 Olivia Road Berea Township and 197 Main Street Johannesburg v City of Johannesburg and Others* CCT24/07 [2008] ZACC 1, 2008 (3) SA 208 (CC) established a more robust approach to requiring 'meaningful engagement' in response to a forced eviction case.
80 J. Christopher Brown and Mark Purcell, 'There's Nothing Inherent about Scale: Political Ecology, the Local Trap, and the Politics of Development in the Brazilian Amazon' (2005) 36(5) *Geoforum* 607, 609.
81 For a thorough (and insider) description of the hegemonic power of the neoliberal approach to development in the 1990s, see Joseph Stiglitz, *Globalization and Its Discontents* (Penguin, 2002). For a defence of this approach to economic governance, see Jagdish Bhagwati, *In Defence of Globalization* (Oxford University Press, 2004); Thomas Friedman, *The Lexus and the Olive Tree* (HarperCollins, 2000); Nancy Birdsall, 'Life Is Unfair: Inequality in the World' in Karen Mingst and Jack Snyder (eds), *Essential Readings in World Politics* (W.W. Norton & Company, 2001). For a strong critique of this approach, see Walden Bello, *Deglobalization: Ideas for a New World Economy* (Zed Books, 2002); John Cavanagh and Jerry Mander (eds), *Alternatives to Economic Globalization: A Better World Is Possible* (Berrett-Koehler Publishers, 2004). For critiques of this approach in specific relation to South Africa, see Patrick Bond, *Elite Transition: From Apartheid to Neoliberalism in South Africa* (2nd edition, Pluto Press, 2000); Richard Peet, 'Ideology, Discourse and the Geography of Hegemony: From Socialist to Neoliberal Development in Post Apartheid South Africa' (2002) 34(1) *Antipode* 54.
82 See Bond, *Elite Transition* (n 81). See also Francis, 'Water Justice in South Africa' (n 39) 159.
83 See, e.g., Bond, *Elite Transition* (n 81) 58–62; Klasen, 'Social, Economic, and Environmental Limits for the Newly Enfranchised in South Africa?' (n 41) 621; Francis, 'Water Justice in South Africa' (n 39) 155–159.
84 See, e.g., Bond, *Elite Transition* (n 81) 63; John Pilger, 'Freedom Next Time', *Guardian* (11 April 1998).
85 See, e.g., Francis, 'Water Justice in South Africa' (n 39) 159.
86 Department of Finance, *Growth, Employment and Redistribution: A Macroeconomic Strategy (GEAR)* (1996) South Africa. For a critical discussion of the impact of GEAR on South Africa's poor, see Bond, *Elite Transition* (n 81), (especially 58–62); David A. McDonald, 'No Money, No Service: South Africa's Attempts to Recover Costs for Water and Power are Harming its Poorest Citizens' (2002) (Spring) *Alternatives Journal* 16; Peet, *Ideology, Discourse and the Geography of Hegemony* (n 81).
87 Coalition Against Water Privatisation (CAWP), Anti-Privatisation Forum (APF) and Public Citizen, *Nothing for Mahala: The Forced Installation of Prepaid Water Meters in Stretford, Extension 4, Orange Farm, Johannesburg, South Africa* (Research Report No. 16, Centre for Civil Society, 2004) 5.

88 Department of Finance, *Growth, Employment and Redistribution* (n 86).
89 The adoption of PSP in the water sector in South Africa was fairly short-lived. When new pro-poor policies were introduced in 2000/2001, including the policy of Free Basic Water (discussed below), it became unprofitable for the private sector to invest in South Africa's water sector and it mostly pulled out. See Mike Muller, 'Public-Private Partnerships in Water: A South African Perspective on the Global Debate' (2003) 15(8) *Journal of International Development* 1115.
90 Department of Finance, *Growth, Employment and Redistribution* (n 86) 2.3, 3.2, 3.4, 7.1, 9, 10. For critical discussions of the impact of GEAR on access to basic services for the poor in South Africa, see McDonald, 'No Money, No Service' (n 86); Michael Kidd, 'Not a Drop to Drink: Disconnection of Water Services for Nonpayment and the Right of Access to Water' (2004) 20(1) *South African Journal on Human Rights* 119.
91 World Bank, *World Development Report: Infrastructure for Development* (World Bank, 1994) 44.
92 See, e.g., Bond, *Elite Transition* (n 81); Klasen, 'Social, Economic, and Environmental Limits for the Newly Enfranchised in South Africa?' (n 41) 607, 618. See also World Bank, *World Development Report: Equity and Development* (World Bank, 2006) 201 (although the Bank only mentions the impact in relation to policy responses to 'crises'). But see *contra* Brian Crisp and Michael Kelly, 'The Socioeconomic Impacts of Structural Adjustment' (1999) 43 *International Studies Quarterly* 533, 544.
93 United Nations Development Programme (UNDP), *National Human Development Reports for South Africa* (International Human Development Indicators) <http://hdrstats.undp.org/en/countries/profiles/ZAF.html> (last accessed 10 December 2012). In January 2012, the IMF itself came out against austerity, indicating a shift in accepted economic theory: Larry Elliott, 'IMF Warns of Threat to Global Economies Posed by Austerity Drives', *The Guardian* (20 January 2012). See also Olivier Blanchard and Daniel Leigh, *Growth Forecast Errors and Fiscal Multipliers* (IMF Working Paper 13/1, 2013).
94 Department of Water Affairs and Forestry (DWAF), *Overview of Water Resource Availability and Utilisation in South Africa* (1997) South Africa; Department of Water Affairs and Forestry (DWAF), *White Paper on National Water Policy for South Africa* (1997) South Africa.
95 See, e.g., Klasen, 'Social, Economic, and Environmental Limits for the Newly Enfranchised in South Africa?' (n 41) 618; Francis, 'Water Justice in South Africa' (n 39) 155.
96 See Department of Environmental Affairs and Tourism, *White Paper on Environmental Management Policies for South Africa* (1997) South Africa 79; Department of Water Affairs and Forestry (DWAF), *A Pricing Strategy for Raw Water Use Charges* (1999) South Africa. See also Klasen, 'Social, Economic, and Environmental Limits for the Newly Enfranchised in South Africa?' (n 41) 618–619; Francis, 'Water Justice in South Africa' (n 39) 155; Mike Muller, 'Free Basic Water – A Sustainable Instrument for a Sustainable Future in South Africa' (2008) 20 *Environment and Urbanization* 67, 69.
97 Francis, 'Water Justice in South Africa' (n 39) 150 (citations omitted).
98 Klasen, 'Social, Economic, and Environmental Limits for the Newly Enfranchised in South Africa?' (n 41) 609.
99 Nicholas Blomley, 'Law, Property, and the Geography of Violence: The Frontier, the Survey, and the Grid' (2003) 93(1) *Annals of the Association of American Geographers* 121.
100 DWAF, *A Pricing Strategy for Raw Water Use Charges* (n 96) [6.5.2].

101 Patrick Bond, *Johannesburg's Water Wars: Soweto verus Suez* (2006) <http://www.passant-ordinaire.com/revue/48-611-en.asp> (last accessed 26 March 2025) 6; Muller, 'Free Basic Water' (n 96) 72.
102 Bond, *Johannesburg's Water Wars* (n 101) 6; Muller, 'Free Basic Water' (n 96) 72.
103 DWAF, *A Pricing Strategy for Raw Water Use Charges* (n 96).
104 DWAF, *White Paper on National Water Policy for South Africa* (n 94) [6.5].
105 DWAF, *White Paper on National Water Policy for South Africa* (n 94).
106 *Constitution of the Republic of South Africa 1996*, Schedule 4, Part B – 'The following local government matters to the extent set out in section 155 (6) (a), (7): [...] Water and sanitation services limited to potable water supply systems and domestic waste-water and sewage disposal systems.'
107 See, e.g., Kate Tissington et al, *Water Service Fault Lines: An Assessment of South Africa's Water and Sanitation Provision across 15 Municipalities* (Centre for Applied Legal Studies (CALS), Centre on House Rights and Evictions (COHRE), and Norwegian Centre for Human Rights (NCHR), 2008) 57–59; Laila Smith, *Neither Public nor Private: Unpacking the Johannesburg Water Corporatisation Model* (Programme Paper Number 27, United Nations Research Institute for Social Development Social Policy and Development, 2006) 5; Francis, 'Water Justice in South Africa' (n 39) 165–166; Alix Gowlland-Gualtieri, *South Africa's Water Law and Policy Framework – Implications for the Right to Water* (IELRC Working Paper, International Environmental Law Research Centre, 2007) 6.
108 These include the Municipal Infrastructure Grant and the Local Government Equitable Share: *Constitution of the Republic of South Africa 1996*, s 214(I).
109 McDonald, 'No Money, No Service' (n 86); Laila Smith and Susan Hanson, 'Access to Water for the Urban Poor in Cape Town: Where Equity Meets Cost Recovery' (2003) 40(8) *Urban Studies* 1517, 1522.
110 Francis, 'Water Justice in South Africa' (n 39) 168–169.
111 See, Francis, 'Water Justice in South Africa' (n 39) 168–169; Tissington et al, *Water Service Fault Lines* (n 107) 57–61; Gowlland-Gualtieri, *South Africa's Water Law and Policy Framework* (n 108) 6.
112 Tissington et al, *Water Service Fault Lines* (n 107) 60. Muller argues that the initial skills shortage in South African municipalities was the result of 'many, mainly white, technically qualified officials [being] encouraged to take 'voluntary severance packages' and leave municipal service – often signing agreements which excluded them from future employment by the state – and since there were no black skills to replace them, allowing less qualified or often completely unqualified candidates to take up positions.' Muller, 'Free Basic Water' (n 96) 37. As a (White) outsider to South Africa, I do not intend to engage any further with this argument.
113 Tissington et al, *Water Service Fault Lines* (n 107) 57; Muller, 'Free Basic Water' (n 96) 37–38.
114 *Interview with Mike Muller, former Director-General of the Department of Water Affairs and Forestry* (Cristy Clark, Johannesburg, 4 October 2006).
115 Mike Muller, quoted in 'Developing Crisis Number Two' *The Weekender* (17–18 May 2008) note 7, cited in Tissington et al, *Water Service Fault Lines* (n 107) 59.
116 See Patrick Bond and Jackie Dugard, 'Water, Human Rights and Social Conflict: South African Experiences' (2008) 1 *Law, Social Justice and Global Development* 2.
117 See Bond and Dugard, 'Water, Human Rights and Social Conflict' (n 116) 2.
118 See, e.g., Laila Smith and Ahmedi Vawda, 'Citizen vs. customer—Different Approaches to Public Participation in Service Delivery in Cape Town' (2003) 14(1) *Urban Forum* 26.

119 See, e.g., David A. McDonald and John Pape (eds), *Cost Recovery and the Crisis of Service Delivery in South Africa* (Zed Books, 2002).
120 See, e.g., Smith and Hanson, 'Access to Water for the Urban Poor in Cape Town' (n 110) 1528.
121 See, e.g., Patrick Bond and Jackie Dugard, 'The Case of Johannesburg Water: What Really Happened at the Pre-paid Parish Pump' (2008) 12(1) *Law, Democracy and Development* 1, 17; Smith and Hanson, 'Access to Water for the Urban Poor in Cape Town' (n 110) 1533; McDonald, 'No Money, No Service' (n 86) 168; Hameda Deedat, 'Viva Prepaids, Viva! Assessing New Technology for Cost Recovery in the Rural Northern Cape' in David A. McDonald and John Pape (eds), *Cost Recovery and the Crisis of Service Delivery in South Africa* (2002)143, 154.
122 See Jackie Dugard and Nthabiseng Mohlakoana, 'More Work for Women: A Rights-based Analysis of Women's Access to Basic Services in South Africa' (2009) 28(3) *South African Journal on Human Rights (SAJHR)* 546.
123 See, e.g., Dugard and Mohlakoana, 'More Work for Women'; CAWP, APF and Public Citizen, *Nothing for Mahala* (n 87) 10.
124 Richard Tomlinson et al, 'The Postapartheid Struggle for an Integrated Johannesburg' in Richard Tomlinson (ed), *Emerging Johannesburg: Perspectives on the Postapartheid City* (Routledge, 2003) 3, 9.
125 This is reported (in a critical manner) by McDonald, 'No Money, No Service' (n 86) 16.
126 This is reported (in a critical manner) by Patrick Bond, *South Africa's 'rights culture' of Water Consumption: Breaking Out of the Liberal Box and into the Commons?* (UNESCO, 2010) 1, 14. It is also discussed in relation to the depoliticisation of poverty and the creation of the concept of the 'undeserving poor' in Danie Brand, 'The "Politics of Need Interpretation" and the Adjudication of Socio-economic Rights Claims in South Africa' in A.J. van deer Wait (ed), *Theories of Social and Economic Justice* (Sun Press, 2005) 17, where he refers to the government's 'fear that a basic income grant would breed in poor people a "culture of entitlement" or dependency'.
127 Smith and Hanson, 'Access to Water for the Urban Poor in Cape Town' (n 110) 1540–1541.
128 *Quarterly Labour Force Survey: Quarter 4 (October to December), 2012* (Statistics South Africa, 2013); Ethel Hazelhurst, *SA Unemployment Gets Worse* (Business Report, 31 October 2012).
129 Hazelhurst, *SA Unemployment Gets Worse.*
130 *The Five Year Soweto Economic Development Plan 2008 – 2013* (City of Johannesburg, 2008) 85; *Strategic Analysis Paper – Food and Water Security in South Africa: Present and Future* (Future Directions International, 2012) 3.
131 Embrahim Harvey, *Researching the Public's Perceptions, Views and Concerns about the Planned Installation of Pre-Paid Water Meters in Soweto, South Africa* (African Studies Association Conference, Boston, 30 October–2 November 2003) 7.
132 Mthetho Xali, '"They are Killing us Alive" A Case Study of the Impact of Cost Recovery on Service Provision in Makhaza Section, Khayelitsha' in David A. McDonald and John Pape (eds), *Cost Recovery and the Crisis of Service Delivery in South Africa* (2002) 101, 113. See also Smith and Hanson, 'Access to Water for the Urban Poor in Cape Town' (n 110) 1533.
133 Department of Water Affairs and Forestry (DWAF), *Strategic Framework for Water Services* (September 2003) 4.5.8.
134 *Water Services Act 1997* (South Africa) s 4(3).
135 Tissington et al, *Water Service Fault Lines* (n 107) 50–53; Francis, 'Water Justice in South Africa' (n 39) 170–173.

136 See, eg, Tissington et al, *Water Service Fault Lines* (n 107) 52; Bond and Dugard, 'The Case of Johannesburg Water' (n 121) 16–21.

137 ANC, *Reconstruction and Development Programme* (n 60). See also McDonald, 'No Money, No Service' (n 86).

138 Precise data on water disconnections in South Africa are not possible to obtain. This is because local governments rarely collect data on disconnections, nor are they willing to share this information - see Tissington et al, *Water Service Fault Lines* (n 107); Jackie Dugard, 'Can Human Rights Transcend the Commercialization of Water in South Africa? Soweto's Legal Fight for an Equitable Water Policy' (2010) 42(2) *Review of Radical Political Economics* 175. Furthermore, with the introduction of prepaid water meters (discussed below), households 'self-disconnect,' and there is no notification to any authority on these occurrences. Nevertheless, a figure of ten million disconnections between 1994 and 2004 is cited by CAWP, APF and Public Citizen, *Nothing for Mahala* (n 87) 5, citing Statistics SA, *Census* (2001) <http://www.stassa.gov.za/defaul3.asp>. See also Bond and Dugard, 'The Case of Johannesburg Water' (n 121) 17, who argue for a figure of 1.5 million people a year, based on the fact that former director-general of DWAF Mike Muller has 'conceded that in 2003 alone, 275,000 households were disconnected from water services at least once due to inability to pay, which amounts to 1.5 million or more people, and these do not include people whose pre-paid meters ran out at a time of insufficient funds to replenish water supplies (i.e., self-disconnection)' – citing Mike Muller, 'Turning on the Taps', *Mail and Guardian* (South Africa, 25 June 2004). Muller has subsequently disputed these figures, claiming that he was misinterpreted. Instead he argues that out of the seven million people who experienced water interruptions in 2003, only 7 percent (490,000 people) of these were for non-payment, while 38.9 percent (2.723 million people) were for repairs and 39.7 percent (2.779 million people) responded that their supply 'just stopped': Mike Muller, 'Parish Pump Politics: The Politics of Water Supply in South Africa' (2007) 7(1) *Progress in Development Studies* 41. However, Bond and Dugard, 'The Case of Johannesburg Water' (n 121) 17 challenge this reinterpretation, arguing that it is not unreasonable to believe that some of the 2.779 million people whose water 'just stopped' did have their supply disconnected for nonpayment, 'Given the chaotic status of municipal billing…'
Other research also supports a figure of between 1 and 1.5 million disconnections per year. See, e.g., Smith and Hanson, 'Access to Water for the Urban Poor in Cape Town' (n 110) 1533; McDonald, 'No Money, No Service' (n 86) 168; Deedat, 'Viva Prepaids, Viva!' (n 121) 154.

139 See, e.g., McDonald, 'No Money, No Service' (n 86) ft 12.

140 See, e.g., David Hemson et al, *Still Paying the Price: Revisiting the Cholera Epidemic of 2000 – 2001 in South Africa* (Municipal Services Project, 2006); Hameda Deedat and Eddie Cottle, 'Cost Recovery and Prepaid Water Meters and the Cholera Outbreak in KwaZulu-Natal: A Case Study in Madlebe' in David A. McDonald and John Pape (eds), *Cost Recovery and the Crisis of Service Delivery in South Africa* (2002); Farah Khan, *Health – South Africa: High Water Fees Cited in Cholera Outbreak* (Inter Press Services, 17 October 2000); Francis, 'Water Justice in South Africa' (n 39) 175 (citations omitted).

141 See, e.g., Hemson et al, 'Still Paying the Price' (n 140); Deedat and Cottle, 'Cost Recovery and Prepaid Water Meters and the Cholera Outbreak in KwaZulu-Natal' (n 140); Khan, 'Health – South Africa (n 140); Francis, 'Water Justice in South Africa' (n 39) 175 (citations omitted).

142 See, e.g., Hemson et al, 'Still Paying the Price' (n 140); Deedat and Cottle, 'Cost Recovery and Prepaid Water Meters and the Cholera Outbreak in KwaZulu-Natal' (n 140); Khan, *Health – South Africa* (n 140); Francis, 'Water Justice in South

Africa' (n 39) 175 (citations omitted); Bond and Dugard, 'The Case of Johannesburg Water' (n 121) 8.

143 Hemson et al, 'Still Paying the Price' (n 140) 4 ('According to the World Health Organization this was the biggest outbreak of cholera in Africa for that reporting period, accounting for 80 percent of all cases worldwide.' [citing World Health Organization (WHO) 2001. Communicable Disease Surveillance and Response (CSR). Cholera outbreaks reporting.]).

144 Hemson et al, 'Still Paying the Price' (n 140) 12–15. See also Bond and Dugard, 'The Case of Johannesburg Water' (n 121) 8.

145 Hemson et al, 'Still Paying the Price' (n 140) 12–13. See also Bond and Dugard, 'The Case of Johannesburg Water' (n 121) 8.

146 Hemson et al, 'Still Paying the Price' (n 140) 12.

147 Hemson et al, 'Still Paying the Price' (n 140) 12.

148 Hemson et al, 'Still Paying the Price' (n 140) 12.

149 Hemson et al, 'Still Paying the Price' (n 140) 12–15. See also Bond and Dugard, 'The Case of Johannesburg Water' (n 121) 8.

150 Hemson et al, 'Still Paying the Price' (n 140) 12–15. See also Bond and Dugard, 'The Case of Johannesburg Water' (n 121) 8.

151 Hemson et al, 'Still Paying the Price' (n 140) 12–15. See also Bond and Dugard, 'The Case of Johannesburg Water' (n 120) 8; Heidi Vogt, 'Environmental Justice in South Africa: Water Sanitation, Privatization, and the Legacy of Apartheid' (2003) *Dollars & Sense* 8, 9.

152 Hemson et al, 'Still Paying the Price' (n 140) 16.

153 Hemson et al, 'Still Paying the Price' (n 140) 16.

154 Hemson et al, 'Still Paying the Price' (n 140) 3. See also Deedat and Cottle, 'Cost Recovery and Prepaid Water Meters and the Cholera Outbreak in KwaZulu-Natal (n 140) 96; Vogt, 'Environmental Justice in South Africa' (n 151) 9.

155 See, e.g., Hemson et al, 'Still Paying the Price' (n 140) 3; Paulina Calfucoy et al, *Improving Free Basic Water Provision in South Africa – Prepared for the Financial and Fiscal Commission* (La Follette School of Public Affairs University of Wisconsin-Madison, 2009) 7; Bond and Dugard, 'The Case of Johannesburg Water' (n 121) 8–9, Gowlland-Gualtieri, *South Africa's Water Law and Policy Framework* (n 107) 12.

156 Mike Muller, *Interview on 'News Maker'*, (2001) cited in Harvey, *Researching the Public's Perceptions, Views and Concerns about the Planned Installation of Pre-Paid Water Meters in Soweto, South Africa* (n 132) 4.

157 Muller, *Interview on 'News Maker'* (n 156) 72.

158 Ronnie Kasrils, 'The Value and Price of Water (The Women of Lutsheko)' (2001) 43(4) *Water Science and Technology* 51.

159 DWAF, *Strategic Framework for Water Services* (n 133) [6.5.3].

160 Department of Water Affairs and Forestry (DWAF), *Free Basic Water Implementation Strategy* (Version One, 2001) South Africa.

161 Department of Water Affairs and Forestry (DWAF), *Free Basic Water Implementation Strategy* (Version Two, 2002) South Africa [3.3]; (DWAF), *Strategic Framework for Water Services* (n 133) [4.4.1]; *Regulation Relating to Compulsory National Standards and Measures to Conserve Water 2001* (South Africa).

162 See, e.g., James Winpenny, *Financing Water for All: Report of the World Panel on Financing Water Infrastructure* (World Water Council, 2003) 18–19.

163 See, e.g., Vivien Foster, Andres Gomez-Lobo and Jonathan Halpern, *Designing Direct Subsidies for the Poor – A Water and Sanitation Case Study* (World Bank, 2000) 4, who argue that, 'a subsidy that covers the full cost of the service will eliminate incentives for the efficient use of water, and is likely to create

a non-payment habit that may be difficult to break at a later date. Therefore, full- scale subsidies should be avoided.' See also Rachel Cardone and Catarine Fonseca, *Financing and Cost Recovery* (International Water and Sanitation Centre, 2003) 31, 47, 88 (where free water is described as the result of unhelpful 'political interference.').

164 Muller, *Interview on 'News Maker'* (n 156) 67.

165 Muller, *Interview on 'News Maker'* (n 156) 67.

166 *Constitution of the Republic of South Africa 1996*, ch. 2, Section 27.

167 Gowlland-Gualtieri, *South Africa's Water Law and Policy Framework* (n 107) 6.

168 DWAF, *Free Basic Water* (n 109). See also Hemson et al, 'Still Paying the Price' (n 140) 7.

169 Bond and Dugard, 'The Case of Johannesburg Water' (n 121) 21.

170 Bond and Dugard, 'The Case of Johannesburg Water' 20–21.

171 DWAF, *Free Basic Water* (n 109) [4.5.8]. For a discussion of the impact of these measures, see, e.g., Xali, '"They are Killing us Alive"' (n 132) 106; CAWP, APF and Public Citizen, *Nothing for Mahala* (n 87) 20; Tissington et al, *Water Service Fault Lines* (n 107) 31.

172 Alex Loftus, '"Free Water" as Commodity: The Paradoxes of Durban's Water Service Transformations' in David A. McDonald and Greg Ruiters (ed), *The Age of Commodity: Water Privatization in Southern Africa* (2005) 194; Tissington et al, *Water Service Fault Lines* (n 107) 33.

173 *Mazibuko v City of Johannesburg* (2008) 4 All SA 471; Bond and Dugard, 'The Case of Johannesburg Water' (n 121); *Interview with Jennifer Makoatsane, Applicant in Mazibuko Water Rights case* (Phiri, South Africa, 5 October 2006).

174 See, e.g., *City of Johannesburg Metropolitan Municipality Water Services By-Laws* (Provincial Gazette Extraordinary No. 179, Notice No. 835, 2004) s 3; *City of Johannesburg Metropolitan Municipality Water Services By-Laws* (Gauteng Provincial Gazette extranordinary no. 162, 2008) s 3.

175 Tissington et al, *Water Service Fault Lines* (n 107) 34. Department of Provision and Local Government (DPLG), *Guidelines for the Implementation of the National Indigent Policy by Municipalities* (2005) 2.1 (According to these Guidelines the purpose of an indigent policy is to ensure that those households and citizens who are unable to access or pay for basic services can have access to the packages of services in the FBS programme.).

176 Tissington et al, *Water Service Fault Lines* (n 107) 34.

177 DPLG, *Guidelines for the Implementation of the National Indigent Policy by Municipalities* (n 175) 2.7.

178 See, e.g., Calfucoy et al, *Improving Free Basic Water Provision in South Africa – Prepared for the Financial and Fiscal Commission* (n 155) 9; DPLG, *Guidelines for the Implementation of the National Indigent Policy by Municipalities* 2.7; Francis, 'Water Justice in South Africa' (n 39); Tissington et al, *Water Service Fault Lines* (n 107) 4, 34, 37.

179 This problem was identified in the 2005 DPLG Guidelines, which noted, 'A further approach needs to be adopted by municipalities to ensure that these citizens are not excluded from access to FBS.' – DPLG, *Guidelines for the Implementation of the National Indigent Policy by Municipalities* (n 175) 2.2. See also DPLG, *Guidelines for the Implementation of the National Indigent Policy by Municipalities* (n 175) 2.7; Calfucoy et al, *Improving Free Basic Water Provision in South Africa* (n 155) 9; Bond and Dugard, 'The Case of Johannesburg Water' (n 121) ft 69; Tissington et al, *Water Service Fault Lines* (n 107) 37.

180 Tissington et al, *Water Service Fault Lines* (n 107) 38.

181 *Mazibuko v City of Johannesburg* (n 1).

References

African National Congress (ANC), *Reconstruction and Development Programme* (1994) South Africa

Aguas del Tunari, SA v Republic of Bolivia (ICSID Case No. ARB/02/3, 2005)

Alston, Philip, 'Out of the Abyss? The Challenges Confronting the New U.N. Committee on Economic, Social and Cultural Rights' (1987) 9 *Human Rights Quarterly* 332

Alston, Philip, 'The Committee on Economic, Social and Cultural Rights' in Philip Alston (ed), *The United Nations and Human Rights* (Oxford University Press, 1992) 473

Arab Charter on Human Rights, signed 22 May 2004, official translated version reprinted in [ST/HR/]CHR/NONE/2004/40/Rev.1 (entered into force 15 March 2008)

Baer, Madeline and Andrea Gerlak, 'Implementing the Human Right to Water and Sanitation: A Study of Global and Local Discourses' (2015) 36(8) *Third World Quarterly* 1527

Bakker, Karen, 'Commons versus Commodities: Debating the Human Right to Water' in Farhana Sultana and Alex Loftus (eds), *The Right to Water* (Routledge, 1st edition, 2011)

Bakker, Karen, 'The "Commons" Versus the "Commodity": Alter-Globalization, Anti-Privatization and the Human Right to Water in the Global South' (2007) 39(3) *Antipode* 430

Barlow, Maude, *The Right to Water: The Campaign for a United Nations Treaty* (Council of Canadians, 2006)

Bello, Walden, *Deglobalization: Ideas for a New World Economy* (Zed Books, 2002)

Birdsall, Nancy, 'Life Is Unfair: Inequality in the World' in Karen Mingst and Jack Snyder (eds), *Essential Readings in World Politics* (W.W. Norton & Company, 2001)

Bhagwati, Jagdish, *In Defence of Globalization* (Oxford University Press, 2004)

Blanchard, Olivier, and Daniel Leigh, Growth Forecast Errors and Fiscal Multipliers (IMF Working Paper 13/1, 2013)

Blomley, Nicholas, 'Law, Property, and the Geography of Violence: The Frontier, the Survey, and the Grid' (2003) 93(1) *Annals of the Association of American Geographers* 121

Bond, Patrick, and Jackie Dugard, 'The Case of Johannesburg Water: What Really Happened at the Pre-paid Parish Pump' (2008) 12(1) *Law, Democracy and Development* 1

Bond, Patrick, and Jackie Dugard, 'Water, Human Rights and Social Conflict: South African Experiences' (2008) 1 *Law, Social Justice and Global Development* 2

Bond, Patrick, *Elite Transition: From Apartheid to Neoliberalism in South Africa* (2nd edition, Pluto Press, 2000)

Bond, Patrick, *Johannesburg's Water Wars: Soweto verus Suez* (2006) <http://www.passant-ordinaire.com/revue/48-611-en.asp> (last accessed 26 March 2025)

Bond, Patrick, *South Africa's 'rights culture' of Water Consumption: Breaking Out of the Liberal Box and into the Commons?* (UNESCO, 2010)

Bond, Patrick, 'The Right to the City and the Eco-Social Commoning of Water: Discursive and Political Lessons from South Africa' in Farhana Sultana and Alex Loftus (eds), *The Right to Water: Politics, Governance and Social Struggles* (Routledge, 1st edition, 2011) 190

Brand, Danie, 'The "Politics of Need Interpretation" and the Adjudication of Socio-economic Rights Claims in South Africa' in A.J. van deer Wait (ed), *Theories of Social and Economic Justice* (Sun Press, 2005) 17

Brown, J. Christopher and Mark Purcell, 'There's Nothing Inherent about Scale: Political Ecology, the Local Trap, and the Politics of Development in the Brazilian Amazon' (2005) 36(5) *Geoforum* 607

Calfucoy, Paulina, et al, *Improving Free Basic Water Provision in South Africa – Prepared for the Financial and Fiscal Commission* (La Follette School of Public Affairs University of Wisconsin-Madison, 2009)

Cardone, Rachel, and Catarine Fonseca, *Financing and Cost Recovery* (International Water and Sanitation Centre, 2003)

Cavanagh, John, and Jerry Mander (eds), *Alternatives to Economic Globalization: A Better World Is Possible* (Berrett-Koehler Publishers, 2004)

City of Johannesburg Metropolitan Municipality Water Services By-Laws (Provincial Gazette Extraordinary No. 179, Notice No. 835, 2004)

City of Johannesburg Metropolitan Municipality Water Services By-Laws (Gauteng Provincial Gazette extranordinary no. 162, 2008)

Clark, Cristy, 'Of What Use Is a Deradicalized Human Right to Water?' (2017) 17(2) *Human Rights Law Review* 231

Clark, Cristy, 'Water Justice Struggles as a Process of Commoning' (2019) 54(1) *Community Development Journal* 80

Coalition Against Water Privatisation (CAWP), Anti-Privatisation Forum (APF) and Public Citizen, *Nothing for Mahala: The Forced Installation of Prepaid Water Meters in Stretford, Extension 4, Orange Farm, Johannesburg, South Africa* (Research Report No. 16, Centre for Civil Society, 2004)

Constitution of the Republic of South Africa 1996 (South Africa)

Convention on the Elimination of All Forms of Discrimination Against Women, opened for signature 18 December 1979, 1249 UNTS 13 (entered into force 3 September 1981)

Convention on the Rights of Persons with Disabilities, opened for signature 13 December 2006, 2515 UNTS 3 (entered into force 3 May 2008)

Convention on the Rights of the Child, opened for signature 20 November 1989, 1577 UNTS 3 (entered into force 2 September 1990)

Crisp, Brian, and Michael Kelly, 'The Socioeconomic Impacts of Structural Adjustment' (1999) 43 *International Studies Quarterly* 533

Davidson-Harden, Adam, Anil Naidoo and Andi Harden, 'The Geopolitics of the Water Justice Movement' (2007) 11 *Peace Conflict & Development* 1

Deedat, Hameda, and Eddie Cottle, 'Cost Recovery and Prepaid Water Meters and the Cholera Outbreak in KwaZulu-Natal: A Case Study in Madlebe' in David A. McDonald and John Pape (eds), *Cost Recovery and the Crisis of Service Delivery in South Africa* (2002)

Deedat, Hameda, 'Viva Prepaids, Viva! Assessing New Technology for Cost Recovery in the Rural Northern Cape' in David A. McDonald and John Pape (eds), *Cost Recovery and the Crisis of Service Delivery in South Africa* (2002)143

Department of Environmental Affairs and Tourism, *White Paper on Environmental Management Policies for South Africa* (1997) South Africa

Department of Finance, *Growth, Employment and Redistribution: A Macroeconomic Strategy (GEAR)* (1996) South Africa

Department of Provision and Local Government (DPLG), *Guidelines for the Implementation of the National Indigent Policy by Municipalities* (2005)

Department of Water Affairs and Forestry (DWAF), *A Pricing Strategy for Raw Water Use Charges* (1999) South Africa

Department of Water Affairs and Forestry (DWAF), *Free Basic Water* (2012) <http://www.dwaf.gov.za/dir_ws/fbw/#> (last accessed April 2012)

Department of Water Affairs and Forestry (DWAF), *Free Basic Water Implementation Strategy* (Version One, 2001) South Africa

Department of Water Affairs and Forestry (DWAF), *Free Basic Water Implementation Strategy* (Version Two, 2002) South Africa

Department of Water Affairs and Forestry (DWAF), *Guidelines for Compulsory national standards (Regulations under Section 9 of the Water Services Act (Act 108 of 1997)) and Norms and standards for water services tariffs (Regulations under Section 10 of the Water Services Act (Act 108 of 1997)) and Water Services Provider Contract Regulations (in terms of s19(5) of the Water Services Act, 1997)* (2002) South Africa

Department of Water Affairs and Forestry (DWAF), *Overview of Water Resource Availability and Utilisation in South Africa* (1997) South Africa

Department of Water Affairs and Forestry (DWAF), *Strategic Framework for Water Services* (September 2003)

Department of Water Affairs and Forestry (DWAF), *White Paper on National Water Policy for South Africa* (1997) South Africa

Doctors for Life International v The Speaker of the National Assembly [2006] ZACC 11; 2006 6 SA 416, Constitutional Court of South Africa (South Africa, 17 August 2006)

Dugard, Jackie, 'Can Human Rights Transcend the Commercialization of Water in South Africa? Soweto's Legal Fight for an Equitable Water Policy' (2010) 42(2) *Review of Radical Political Economics* 175

Dugard, Jackie, and Nthabiseng Mohlakoana, 'More Work for Women: A Rights-based Analysis of Women's Access to Basic Services in South Africa' (2009) 28(3) *South African Journal on Human Rights (SAJHR)* 546

Elliott, Larry, 'IMF Warns of Threat to Global Economies Posed by Austerity Drives', The Guardian (20 January 2012)

Foster, Vivien, Andres Gomez-Lobo and Jonathan Halpern, *Designing Direct Subsidies for the Poor – A Water and Sanitation Case Study* (World Bank, 2000)

Francis, Rose, 'Water Justice in South Africa: Natural Resources Policy at the Intersection of Human Rights, Economics, and Political Power' (2005) 18(1) *Georgetown International Environmental Law Review* 149

Friedman, Thomas, *The Lexus and the Olive Tree* (HarperCollins, 2000)

Friends of the Right to Water, *Key Principles for an International Treaty on the Right to Water: Draft Work in Progress for Consultation* (Friends of the Right to Water, 2005)

Fuller, Lon L., 'The Forms and Limits of Adjudication' (1978) 92 *Harvard Law Review* 353

Geneva Convention relative to the Treatment of Prisoners of War (Third Geneva Convention), opened for signature 12 August 1949, 75 UNTS 135 (entered into force 21 October 1950)

Gowlland-Gualtieri, Alix, *South Africa's Water Law and Policy Framework – Implications for the Right to Water* (IELRC Working Paper, International Environmental Law Research Centre, 2007)

Green Cross International et al, *Fundamental Principles for a Global Framework Convention on the Right to Water* (Green Cross International, 2004) <www.cawater-info.net/library/eng/right_to_water.pdf> (last accessed 26 March 2025)

Hardin, Garrett, 'The Tragedy of the Commons' (1968) 162(3859) *Science* 1243

Harvey, Embrahim, *Researching the Public's Perceptions, Views and Concerns about the Planned Installation of Pre-Paid Water Meters in Soweto, South Africa* (African Studies Association Conference, Boston, 30 October–2 November 2003)

Hazelhurst, Ethel, *SA Unemployment Gets Worse* (Business Report, 31 October 2012)

Hemson, David, et al, *Still Paying the Price: Revisiting the Cholera Epidemic of 2000 – 2001 in South Africa* (No Occasional Papers No. 10, Municipal Services Project, 2006)

International Commission of Jurists (ICJ), *Maastricht Guidelines on Violations of Economic, Social and Cultural Rights* (United Nations, 1997)

Interview with Jennifer Makoatsane, Applicant in Mazibuko Water Rights case (Phiri, South Africa, 5 October 2006)

Interview with Mike Muller, former Director-General of the Department of Water Affairs and Forestry (Johannesburg, 4 October 2006)

Kasrils, Ronnie, 'The Value and Price of Water (The Women of Lutsheko)' (2001) 43(4) *Water Science and Technology* 51

Khan, Farah, *Health – South Africa: High Water Fees Cited in Cholera Outbreak* (Inter Press Services, 17 October 2000)

Kidd, Michael, 'Not a Drop to Drink: Disconnection of Water Services for Nonpayment and the Right of Access to Water' (2004) 20(1) *South African Journal on Human Rights* 119

Klasen, Stephan, 'Social, Economic, and Environmental Limits for the Newly Enfranchised in South Africa?' (2002) 50(3) Economic Development and Cultural Change 607

Langford, Malcolm et al, *Legal Resources for the Right to Water: International and National Standards* (Centre on Housing Rights and Evictions, 2004)

Langford, Malcolm 'The Justiciability of Social Rights: From Practice to Theory' in Malcolm Langford (ed), *Social Rights Jurisprudence – Emerging Trends in International and Comparative Law* (Cambridge University Press, 2008) 3

Law No. 2029: Potable Water and Sanitary Law (Ley de Servicios de Agua Potable y Alcantarillado Sanitario, 29 October 1999) (Bolivia)

Leckie, Scott, 'Another Step Towards Indivisibility: Identifying the Key Features of Violations of Economic, Social and Cultural Rights' (1998) 20 *Human Rights Quarterly* 81

Liebenberg, Sandra, *Socio-Economic Rights: Adjudication under a Transformative Constitution* (Juta, 2010)

Loftus, Alex, '"Free Water" as Commodity: The Paradoxes of Durban's Water Service Transformations' in David A. McDonald and Greg Ruiters (ed), *The Age of Commodity: Water Privatization in Southern Africa* (2005) 194

Mandela, Nelson, 'Address: On the Occassion of the ANC's Bill of Rights Conference' in *A Bill of Rights for a Democratic South Africa: Papers and Report of a Conference Convened by the ANC Constitutional Committee* (1991) 9

Marin, Philippe, *Public-Private Partnerships for Urban Water Utilities: A Review of Experiences in Developing Countries* (World Bank, 2009)

Mazibuko v City of Johannesburg (2008) 4 All SA 471

Mazibuko v City of Johannesburg [2009] ZACC 28; 2010 4 SA 1, Constitutional Court of South Africa (8 October 2009)

McDonald, David A., and John Pape (eds), *Cost Recovery and the Crisis of Service Delivery in South Africa* (Zed Books, 2002)

McDonald, David A., 'No Money, No Service: South Africa's Attempts to Recover Costs for Water and Power are Harming its Poorest Citizens' (2002) (Spring) *Alternatives Journal* 16

McDonald, David A., 'The Bell Tolls for Thee: Cost Recovery, Cutoffs, and the Affordability of Municipal Services in South Africa' in David A. McDonald and John Pape (eds), *Cost Recovery and the Crisis of Service Delivery in South Africa* (Zed Books, 2002) 161

Merafong Demarcation Forum v President of Republic of South Africa [2008] ZACC 10, Constitutional Court of South Africa (South Africa, 13 June 2008)

Mirosa, Oriol and Leila M. Harris, 'Human Right to Water: Contemporary Challenges and Contours of a Global Debate' (2012) 44(3) *Antipode* 932

Muller, Mike, 'Free Basic Water – A Sustainable Instrument for a Sustainable Future in South Africa' (2008) 20 *Environment and Urbanization* 67

Muller, Mike, 'Parish Pump Politics: The Politics of Water Supply in South Africa' (2007) 7(1) *Progress in Development Studies* 41

Muller, Mike, 'Public-Private Partnerships in Water: A South African Perspective on the Global Debate' (2003) 15(8) *Journal of International Development* 1115

Muller, Mike, 'Turning on the Taps', *Mail and Guardian* (South Africa, 25 June 2004)

National Water Act 1998 (South Africa)

Neal, Christopher, 'Letter to the Democracy Centre' (2000) reprinted in Jim Shultz and Tom Kruse, *Water Revolt: The World Bank Letters* (The Democracy Centre, 2000) <https://www.democracyctr.org/the-world-bank-letters> (last accessed 26 March 2025)

Linda Nyati, 'Public Participation: What Has the Constitutional Court Given the Public?' (2008) 12(2) *Law, Democracy & Development* 102

Peet, Richard, 'Ideology, Discourse and the Geography of Hegemony: From Socialist to Neoliberal Development in Post Apartheid South Africa' (2002) 34(1) *Antipode* 54

Pilger, John, 'Freedom Next Time', *The Guardian* (11 April 1998).

Promotion of Administrative Justice Act (PAJA) 2000 (South Africa)

Occupiers of 51 Olivia Road Berea Township and 197 Main Street Johannesburg v City of Johannesburg and Others CCT24/07 [2008] ZACC 1, 2008 (3) SA 208 (CC)

Olivera, Oscar and Tom Lewis, *Cochabamba!: Water Rebellion in Bolivia* (South End Press, 2004)

Ostrom, Elinor, *Governing the Commons: The Evolution of Institutions for Collective Action* (Cambridge University Press, 1990)

Ostrom, Elinor and Roy Gardner, 'Coping with Asymmetries in the Commons: Self-Governing Irrigation Systems Can Work' (1993) 7(4) *Journal of Economic Perspectives* 93

Quarterly Labour Force Survey: Quarter 4 (October to December), 2012 (Statistics South Africa, 2013)

Regulation Relating to Compulsory National Standards and Measures to Conserve Water 2001 (South Africa)

Roithmayr, Daria, 'Lessons from Mazibuko: Persistent Inequality and the Commons' (2010) 3 *Constitutional Court Review* 317

Sánchez Gómez, Luis and Philipp Terhorst, 'Cochabamba, Bolivia: Public-Collective Partnership after the Water War' in Belén Balanyá et al (eds), *Reclaiming Public Water: Achievements, Struggles and Visions from Around the World* (Transnational Institute and Corporate Europe Observatory, 2007)

Sarkin, Jeremy, 'The Drafting of South Africa's Final Constitution from a Human-Rights Perspective' (1999) 47(1) *The American Journal of Comparative Law* 67

Shiva, Vandana, *Water Wars: Privatization, Pollution, and Profit* (Pluto Press, 2002)

Shrybman, Steven, *Critical Review of the 'Green Cross' Proposal for a Global Framework Convention on the Right to Water* (2005) <goldblattpartners.com/wp-content/uploads/00128085.pdf> (last accessed 2 March 2017)

Smith, Laila, *Neither Public nor Private: Unpacking the Johannesburg Water Corporatisation Model* (Programme Paper Number 27, United Nations Research Institute for Social Development Social Policy and Development, 2006)

Smith, Laila and Ahmedi Vawda, 'Citizen vs. customer—Different Approaches to Public Participation in Service Delivery in Cape Town' (2003) 14(1) *Urban Forum* 26

Smith, Laila, and Susan Hanson, 'Access to Water for the Urban Poor in Cape Town: Where Equity Meets Cost Recovery' (2003) 40(8) *Urban Studies* 1517

Strategic Analysis Paper – Food and Water Security in South Africa: Present and Future (Future Directions International, 2012)

Stiglitz, Joseph, *Globalization and Its Discontents* (Penguin, 2002)

Terhorst, Olivera and Alexander Dwinell, 'Social Movements, Left Governments, and the Limits of Water Sector Reform in Latin America's Left Turn' (2013) 40(4) *Latin American Perspectives* 55

The Five Year Soweto Economic Development Plan 2008 – 2013 (City of Johannesburg, 2008)

Tissington, Kate, et al, *Water Service Fault Lines: An Assessment of South Africa's Water and Sanitation Provision across 15 Municipalities* (Centre for Applied Legal Studies (CALS), Centre on House Rights and Evictions (COHRE), and Norwegian Centre for Human Rights (NCHR), 2008)

Tomlinson, Richard, et al, 'The Postapartheid Struggle for an Integrated Johannesburg' in Richard Tomlinson (ed), *Emerging Johannesburg: Perspectives on the Postapartheid City* (Routledge, 2003) 3

United Nations Committee on Economic, Social and Cultural Rights (CESCR), *General Comment No. 3: The Nature of Sates Parties Obligations (Art 2, Para 1, of the Covenant)*, 5th sess, UN Doc E/1991/23 (14 December 1990)

United Natioins Committee on Economic, Social and Cultural Rights (CESCR), *General Comment No. 15: The Right to Water (Arts. 11 and 12 of the International Covenant on Economic, Social and Cultural Rights)*, 29th sess, UN Doc E/C. 12/2002/11 (20 January 2003)

United Nations Committee on Economic, Social and Cultural Rights (CESCR), *The Limburg Principles on the Implementation of the International Covenant of Economic Social and Cultural Rights*, 43rd sess, UN Doc E/CN.4/1987/17 (8 January 1987)

United Nations, *Report of the United Nations Water Conference, Mar Del Plata, 14-25 March 1977* (E/CONF.70/29, 1977)

United Nations Development Programme (UNDP), *National Human Development Reports for South Africa* (International Human Development Indicators) <http://hdrstats.undp.org/en/countries/profiles/ZAF.html> (last accessed 10 December 2012)

Vogt, Heidi, 'Environmental Justice in South Africa: Water Sanitation, Privatization, and the Legacy of Apartheid' (2003) *Dollars & Sense* 8

WaterAid, *International Financial Institutions (IFI), Conditionality and Privatisation of Water and Sanitation Systems* (Water Aid, 2003)

Water Services Act 1997 (South Africa)

Winpenny, James, *Financing Water for All: Report of the World Panel on Financing Water Infrastructure* (World Water Council, 2003)

World Bank, Bolivia: Major Cities Water and Sewerage Rehabilitation Project (Report No. 18009, Implementation Completion Report, 12 June 1998)

World Bank, Bolivia – Major Cities Water Supply and Sewerage Rehabilitation Project: Credit 2187 – Credit Agreement – Conformed (Legal ISC Files, 1990) as amended by Legal Department of World Bank, Conformed Copy – C2187 – Major Cities Water Supply and Sewerage Rehabilitation Project – Amendment 3 (24 May 1996)

World Bank, *GINI index* (2012) <http://data.worldbank.org/indicator/SI.POV.GINI/> (last accessed 10 December 2012)

World Bank, *World Development Report: Infrastructure for Development* (World Bank, 1994)

World Bank, *World Development Report: Equity and Development* (World Bank, 2006)

Xali, Mthetho, "They are Killing us Alive" A Case Study of the Impact of Cost Recovery on Service Provision in Makhaza Section, Khayelitsha' in David A. McDonald and John Pape (eds), *Cost Recovery and the Crisis of Service Delivery in South Africa* (2002) 101

5

COMPETING CONCEPTIONS OF THE HUMAN RIGHT TO WATER

Introduction

The fundamental tensions in South Africa's attempts to implement the human right to water alongside neoliberal water governance reforms, considered in Chapter 4, also played out on the international stage in debates around the normative content of the emerging human right to water. In South Africa, these debates came to a head in the *Mazibuko* water rights case, in which five applicants from the suburb of Phiri, Soweto, challenged the City of Johannesburg's forced installation of prepaid water meters as being incompatible with their constitutionally protected human right to water. Through analysing South Africa's Mazibuko water rights case alongside parallel international developments around the recognition of the human right to water, this chapter considers how rights frameworks can simultaneously legitimise neoliberal water governance while providing strategic tools for articulating alternative water relations and ontologies. The analysis builds on the patterns of institutional adaptation and resistance observed in earlier chapters while exploring how these dynamics operate differently across scales of governance.

The tensions explored here are central themes in the ongoing debates about the emancipatory potential of human rights discourse, particularly for water. Critics argue that rights-based approaches risk depoliticising fundamental struggles over resources and entrenching individualistic, Eurocentric worldviews that conceptualise water primarily as an economic good. As we will consider, the *Mazibuko* case seemingly confirms these concerns, with South Africa's Constitutional Court adopting a deferential approach that effectively sanctioned the installation of prepaid water meters and insufficient free basic water allocations in Phiri's impoverished communities.

DOI: 10.4324/9781003273219-5

Yet, as this chapter demonstrates, rights-based resistance also created spaces for articulating more radical and relational understandings of water justice. Through strategic litigation combined with direct action, community movements challenged not only specific policies but also the underlying logic of water commodification. Their activism embodied alternative ontological frameworks that recognise water's deep connections to dignity, community solidarity, and cultural practice.

This analysis contributes to broader theoretical debates about legal mobilisation, neoliberal governance, and the decolonisation of rights discourse. By examining how communities tactically engaged with rights while maintaining more transformative political horizons, it suggests possibilities for reimagining rights-based approaches in ways that centre collective struggles and challenge market fundamentalism. The chapter thus offers insights into both the limitations and strategic potential of human rights frameworks in advancing water justice.

Operation Gcin'amanzi

In November 2000, Johannesburg's public water utility incorporated as Johannesburg Water, adopting a neoliberal water governance reform that echoed earlier experiments in Manila (discussed in Chapter 3). Corporatisation allowed the utility to remain publicly owned while reorienting operations along market principles. The spatial politics of this reform were particularly significant. Just as Chile's water markets and Manila's concessions produced distinct geographies of water access, the market-based reforms in Johannesburg targeted historically Black townships like Soweto, reinforcing apartheid's legacy of spatial inequality. The installation of prepaid meters in Phiri – one of Soweto's poorest suburbs – exemplifies another mechanism through which technical decisions about infrastructure can materialise power relations in urban space.

As part of the corporatisation process, Johannesburg Water's finances were ring-fenced, meaning that its budget was separated from the budgets of other government departments so it could not be subsidised or have its profits diverted for other purposes.[1] The general idea is that ring-fencing enables the collection of more accurate data regarding the performance of water utilities and the true costs of operations and maintenance to enable operators to increase efficiency and to set tariffs at 'financially sustainable' levels.[2] The downside is that this can serve to mask the inherently interconnected nature of public service provision and create the potential for negative externalities, particularly in relation to health care. For example, as we saw in Chapter 4, while increasing tariffs can reduce the amount of government subsidies that are needed to provide water supply and sanitation services, it can also force people to turn to untreated natural sources – leading to disease outbreaks (such as cholera) and creating significant public health expenses.[3]

To support this corporate transition, in April 2001, a five-year management contract was granted to the Johannesburg Water Management Company – a joint venture between Suez and its two subsidiaries, Northumbrian Water and Water and Sanitation Services South Africa. The following year, Johannesburg Water began experimenting with prepaid water meters and launched 'Operation Gcin'amanzi' (an isiZulu term for 'conserving water'),[4] starting with a pilot project in Stretford, Extension 4, Orange Farm – a township 45 kilometers from Johannesburg.[5] The following year, to tackle high levels of non-revenue water in Soweto (which were caused by a combination of physical losses from ageing infrastructure and low levels of bill payment), Johannesburg Water expanded Operation Gcin'amanzi to Soweto, starting with a pilot project in Phiri, one of Soweto's poorest suburbs.[6] Despite its claim that 'an exceptionally high premium has been placed on involving the affected communities at every step' of the 'so-called Phiri Prototype,'[7] the policy details of Operation Gcin'amanzi, including the decision to use prepaid meters as the preferred method of 'demand management,' were decided by Johannesburg Water without consultation.[8]

Material effects

Community members in both Orange Farm and Phiri reported a range of negative effects from the imposition of prepaid water meters on their communities. One women's empowerment leader, for example, noted that the meters had the biggest impact on women, as it is they who are responsible for the household tasks that require water and who have to walk for kilometers in search of it when their credit runs out.[9] Several civil society organisers also highlighted the impact that the manufactured water scarcity had had on community relations, with one noting, 'suspicion and individualism have replaced a sense of community now that people are concerned about running out of water to drink and are more reluctant to share with their neighbours.'[10] Another emphasised the barrier to hospitality and mutual aid created by the meters, commenting that people now hesitated to invite people over due to concern over the impact on their limited water credit.[11]

One of the reasons that the free basic water (FBW) allowance was so inadequate in Phiri was that it was provided at the household level and calculated to provide 25 litres of water per person per day (Lpppd) to a household of eight people. The City of Johannesburg was well aware that most households in Phiri had a large household living in the main house and one or more additional households living in a backyard shack, but the City decided against providing a larger household allowance to reflect these facts. Since the average household size in Phiri, including the backyard shacks, was 16, this meant that the FBW allowance worked out to just 12.5 Lpppd. To put this figure in perspective, it is less water than an average shower uses per minute.

Vusimuzi Paki was a resident of Phiri during this period, who lived with his brother in the main house on his block. His backyard had four shacks, with a total of ten residents. Around 2:00am, on 27 March 2005, Paki was woken by one of his tenants, Victoria Mavuso, to let him know that a fire had broken out in the shack belonging to Malefo Tamane. The residents of the other shacks were all attempting to fight the blaze with rainwater from a nearby ditch. Paki worked with the tenants to connect a hosepipe, but the water pressure was low (due to the prepaid meters) and the household ran out of water before the fire was extinguished. By the time the police arrived at 4:00am, the fire had been extinguished, but Ms Tamane's two children, aged two and nine, had tragically died in the fire.[12]

Another Phiri resident affected by the prepaid meters was Jennifer Makoatsone. It was her father who agreed to have a prepaid meters installed on their property. In true patriarchal style, he did not consult her or her mother, despite having very little to do with the house and care work that relies on a ready supply of tap water. Several months later, he died, and the household went into debt just to afford water for his funeral – a water-intensive cultural ritual that involves hosting guests for multiple days.[13] The meters had a dramatic effect on the behaviour of Makoatsone's neighbours, who ordinarily would have supported the family during such a time. Instead, Makoatsone reports,

> We went through hell ... we took out the fence next door so that we can use their yard, and some people would go to their loo and use their loo. They just locked their water so that we couldn't use it. You know. It becomes difficult.[14]

The material effects of prepaid meters in Phiri demonstrate how attempts to impose market logic on water can have devastating material consequences. Phiri residents experienced the stark reality that water's essential role in sustaining life, conducting cultural practices, and maintaining community relations cannot be reduced to mere commodity transactions. The tragic death of two children in a fire due to insufficient water pressure starkly illustrates this point. The prepaid meters also transformed neighbourly water sharing into a commodified transaction, or stifled it altogether. However, as in previous cases, water's social significance also shaped resistance on the streets and ultimately in court.

Community resistance

The adoption of punitive austerity policies by the ANC, including Operation Gcin'amanzi, initially caught the community off-guard.[15] Progressive activism in South Africa's Black community had historically been led by the ANC, and when it was unbanned towards the end of the apartheid era, community organisations were demobilised or co-opted, creating a civil society vacuum.[16] When the ANC became the party of government and took on the role of the establishment, people initially responded to unpopular policies by raising their concerns with local councillors, but they were dismissed and labelled 'ultra-leftists' or 'counter-revolutionaries.'[17] Eventually, local community movements started mobilising. In Orange Farm, this mobilisation took the form of the Orange Farm Water Crisis Committee (OFWCC), which began organising community resistance to the prepaid meters.[18] The OFWWC adopted a multifaceted approach to fighting the meters, employing women's empowerment projects (including free childcare), community education, and direct action (the destruction of water meters and 'toyi-toyi' – a South African dance used in political protests and blockades, often accompanied with chanting).[19] Their slogan – which could be seen painted on walls around the township – was, 'Destroy The Meter. Enjoy the water.'[20] The government responded to the community's protests by calling them 'radicals' and 'counter-revolutionaries.'[21] Local organisations in Phiri also adopted a similar approach, blockading the streets to stop the installation process and digging up the new pipes during the night. So-called 'struggle plumbers' also offered up their services to support households to bypass the meters and enjoy free water in their homes.[22]

Phiri resident Sarrafina Morsopa, for example, refused to have a prepaid meter installed, and so Johannesburg Water disconnected her water altogether.[23] In response, she called on Soweto's 'Struggle Plumbers,' who came and installed an illegal, unmetered yard tap.[24] In line with the heavy-handed response that was to play out across the community, the City responded to Morsopa's new connection by sending police to dig out her new pipes with a machine.[25] But, unlike the wider Phiri community, Morsopa, who was in her mid-70s, successfully resisted their efforts by sleeping over her pipes and refusing to be moved for days.[26]

Morsopa's resistance benefitted her whole community. When I visited in 2006, neighbours, including Jennifer Makoatsone, came to her yard tap for water when they ran out of credit or needed to get their laundry properly clean.[27] It became a community hub of sorts, where women gathered to rinse their washing and discuss the next steps in their anti-prepaid meter campaign. Water has always drawn people together. As Morsopa told me,

> That's why I say that I am going to fight 'till they cut the neck and the head is not there, like that [she flops her head side to side], but I'm going to fight. Because the water is life. If you haven't got water, you got nothing, nothing.[28]

The OFWWC was one of around 30 community affiliates of the Anti-Privati sation Forum (APF), an umbrella organisation formed in 2000 by activists who were struggling against the privatisation of basic services within the City of

Johannesburg.[29] While community-based organisations, such as the OFWCC, engaged in targeted action against prepaid meters (and similar policies), the APF sought to unite these struggles into a broader radical political project – one that would create 'working class alternatives to capitalism.'[30] The APF was one of the few social movements of its time that was openly critical of the ANC and overt in its political agenda to challenge the capitalist status quo.[31]

The community response in Orange Farm and Phiri echoed patterns of resistance seen in earlier chapters – from Chile's Atacameño communities to Manila's civil society campaigns. Like these earlier movements, Phiri residents articulated alternative water ontologies that emphasised relationality over market efficiency. Their combination of direct action and strategic litigation demonstrates how communities navigate multiple legal orders while maintaining more transformative political horizons. The OFWCC's multifaceted approach – combining women's empowerment projects, community education, and direct action – exemplifies what Lefebvre terms 'the right to the city' in action: a collective claim to reshape both the material infrastructure and social relations of urban space.[32] Their slogan, 'Destroy The Meter. Enjoy the water,' articulates a radical critique of water commodification that transcends traditional rights discourse to assert alternative modes of valuation and distribution.

The spatial dynamics of this resistance are particularly significant. The persistence of apartheid geography meant that prepaid meters were exclusively installed in historically Black townships, making water infrastructure a material manifestation of an ongoing landscape of structural inequality. Community resistance thus operated simultaneously at multiple scales – challenging both the immediate spatial control enacted through prepaid meters and the broader geographies of racial capitalism.

At first, these coordinated protest actions appeared to be successful. Construction work was disrupted, and Johannesburg Water was forced to bring in private security to protect their work from sabotage and from residents physically blocking their attempts to dig the trenches and lay new pipes.[33] However, these attempts did not deter Johannesburg Water or encourage dialogue. Instead, it applied to the court for an interdict to prevent residents from interfering with the construction work.[34] In the following months, 14 people were arrested on charges of public violence, incitement, and malicious damage to property, while many more were fined for bypassing their meters.[35]

Faced with the alternative of total disconnection (and the impossibility of further direct action), by the end of 2004 most households in Phiri had either accepted prepaid meters or standpipes.[36] Those with prepaid meters soon found that their FBW allocation lasted until around the 12–15th of the month.[37] Many were unable to afford more credit and had to go without water until the following month when their next allocation became available.[38] Another difficulty with the prepaid meters was that they provided no clear notice that the water was about to be disconnected and no opportunity for households to make representations to Johannesburg Water that they were unable to afford the additional water necessary to meet their basic needs.[39]

The APF's decision to pursue rights-based litigation, despite their radical political orientation, reflects complex tensions that Critical Legal Studies (CLS) scholars have long grappled with. The shift from direct resistance to constitutional litigation raises fundamental questions about the emancipatory potential and limitations of rights discourse. As David Kennedy argues, rights frameworks can simultaneously offer strategic tools for marginalised communities while risking the containment of more radical political demands.[40] This tension becomes particularly acute in the context of socioeconomic rights, where, as Marius Pieterse notes, the institutional enforcement of rights claims often produces an 'abstract and conceptually empty' jurisprudence that can serve to legitimise rather than challenge existing power relations.[41] The Mazibuko case would prove to be a powerful illustration of these concerns.

The APF's combination of direct action and rights-based strategies parallels earlier patterns of resistance seen in Chile and Manila. However, South Africa's unique constitutional framework and historical context shaped how these strategies evolved. In response to the transformative promise of South Africa's Constitution and its inclusion of socioeconomic rights, like the human right to water, South African activists strategically engaged with rights discourse while maintaining more radical political horizons focused on systemic transformation.

The Mazibuko water rights case

It was against the backdrop of a community that had run out of options for direct resistance that the APF decided to pursue rights-based litigation on behalf of the Phiri community, leading to South Africa's first Constitutional Court judgment on the human right to water.[42] In July 2006, five residents of Phiri,[43] including Jennifer Makoatsone and Vusimuzi Paki, launched a legal challenge in the Witwatersrand High Court against the City of Johannesburg, Johannesburg Water, and the Department of Water Affairs and Forestry (DWAF), seeking a declaration that the government's policies of capping the FBW allowance and installing prepaid meters were unlawful and unconstitutional.[44] The applicants sought to 'review and set aside the City and Johannesburg Water's decisions, to set the amount of free water at 6 kilolitres per stand; and to introduce pre-paid water meters in Phiri.'[45] If either of those challenges were successful, the applicants asked,

> the Court to order the City and Johannesburg Water to provide [them], and others who are in the same position ..., with 50 litres free water per person per day and the option of water on credit afforded to the wealthier and largely white residents of Johannesburg.[46]

The applicants based their case on sections 27(1)(b), 33(1), 9, and 10 of the Constitution, as well as *The Promotion of Administrative Justice Act 3 of 2000* (PAJA), *The Water Services Act 108 of 1997* (WSA), and *The Johannesburg Water Services By-Laws*. Several of their claims related to the content of the right to water, including the definition of sufficiency,[47] and its relationship with the rights to equality[48] and participation.[49] They argued that the definition of 'sufficient water' under section 27(1)(b) of the Constitution should be at least 50 Lpcpd – the amount of water necessary for dignified human existence for those households with waterborne sanitation.[50] They also challenged the City's decision not to factor in the comparatively larger size of poor households (particularly those with backyard shacks) in the formulation of the FBW policy.[51]

The applicants made several arguments based on procedural justice, including the fact that the prepaid meters discontinued water services without the procedural protection afforded by s 4(3) of the WSA,[52] meaning the disconnection was unfair and inequitable and executed without notice or any opportunity to make representations regarding capacity to buy more credit.[53] They argued further that the decision to impose prepaid meters on the Phiri community and the manner of their introduction was a breach of the right to procedural justice contained in section 33(1) of the Constitution[54] and outlined in section 3 of the PAJA.[55]

The answering affidavit of the City of Johannesburg

In answer to the applicant's claims, the City of Johannesburg argued that it was not obliged to provide any water for free and that 'free' water and 'access to' water should not be conflated.[56] Central to the City's response was the fact that it was faced with a significant challenge of managing its finances and that providing a more generous FBW allocation would place an excessive strain on its budget.[57] The City also argued that a significant amount of money had been spent on installing prepaid meters in Soweto (almost R336 million, or around USD58 million), and the cost of removing them and installing a new system in their place would have a negative effect on the financial sustainability of Johannesburg Water.[58]

The City argued that the prepaid meters do not disconnect households in a manner prohibited by section 4(3) of the WSA, because the prepaid meters were always credited with each month's FBW amount, and thus access to a 'basic service' was never denied.[59] The City also argued that the installation of the prepaid meters was a necessary response to the high level of non-revenue water in the deemed consumption areas, which it claimed was due 'to leaks, collapsing infrastructure, the culture of non-payment and water wastage.'[60]

Despite their arguments against the key points in the applicant's case, the City did change their FBW policy in response to the litigation by using the indigency register as the mechanism for increasing flexibility,[61] and increasing the per household allocation to ten kilolitres,[62] with the capacity for this to be increased further in special circumstances.[63] The applicants noted that these were significant improvements, but that two main problems remained. The first was that the FBW amount was still set at 25 Lpcpd, despite the fact that this amount is insufficient to cover the basic needs of poor urban households living with waterborne sanitation. The second problem was that this policy was only available to those households who registered as indigents. At the time of the application, 72 percent of households with prepaid meters were not registered as indigent (despite the majority qualifying).[64] The City acknowledged this fact and the under-representative nature of the indigency system.[65]

High Court judgment

The *Mazibuko* case was heard in December 2007 before Tsoka J in the High Court of South Africa (Witwatersrand Local Division). Justice Tsoka handed down his judgment on 30 April 2008, ordering the respondents to provide each applicant and other similarly placed residents of Phiri Township with FBW of 50 Lpcpd;[66] to permit the option of a metered supply installed at the costs of the City;[67] and to pay for the costs of the application.[68] Tsoka J found that the obligation under the Constitution to provide access to sufficient water must include economic access to such water.[69] He also found that 'it is obvious that the 25 Lpcpd is insufficient for the residents of Phiri,'[70] and accepted Peter Gleick's expert evidence that 50 Lpcpd was a more appropriate amount and was within the financial resources of the City to provide.[71]

Justice Tsoka agreed with the applicants that the limitation or discontinuation of water services by the prepaid meter was a breach of s 4(3) of the WSA.[72] Surveying international case law on the issue of disconnections and prepaid meters, he concluded that '[i]t is apparent that in the established democracies, prepayment meters are illegal as they violate the procedural requirements of fairness by cutting off or discontinuing the supply of water without notice and representation.'[73]

Justice Tsoka also accepted the applicants' claims that the manner in which the prepaid meters were introduced into Phiri was a violation of their right to participation (or procedural justice) under section 33, in that they were not consulted or advised of their rights to request reasons for the decision or to challenge the decision.[74] The judge dismissed the City's claims that such consultations did take place, finding the evidence that they submitted in this regard was unreliable.[75] In reviewing the notice provided to the applicants regarding the installation of the prepaid meters, Tsoka J found Johannesburg Water's manner to be 'both intimidatory and presumptive,'[76] concluding 'that the actions of the respondents, were not consultative but a publicity drive for the prepayment measuring systems.'[77]

Supreme Court judgment

The City (along with Johannesburg Water and the Minister for Water Affairs and Forestry) appealed the High Court's judgment in the Supreme Court of Appeal. The appeal was heard before five judges in February 2009, and the Court handed down a unanimous judgment by Streicher JA on 25 March 2009. The Court made similar findings to Tsoka J regarding the City's obligation to supply a sufficient amount of water free to the applicants and that the disconnection of water supply effected by the prepaid meters breached the procedural safeguards contained in section 4(3) of the WSA.[78] However, in relation to the quantification of what amounted to sufficient water for the applicants and people in similar situations, the Court accepted the evidence of the City's expert that 42 Lpcpd would be sufficient.[79] The Court was also more deferential regarding orders made against the City and chose to 'suspend the order of unlawfulness for a period of two years to enable the City to take such steps as it may be advised to take to legalise the use of prepayment water meters.'[80]

Constitutional Court judgment

Despite being successful on both of their main claims against the City, the Phiri residents appealed the Supreme Court of Appeal's judgment to the Constitutional Court of South Africa. They were concerned that the two-year suspension of the order of invalidity seemed to imply that the City could simply amend its bylaws in order to make the installation of the prepaid meters lawful.[81] They were also concerned by the Supreme Court's acceptance of the indigency register as the most appropriate means of delivering the FBW allocation of 42 Lpcpd.[82] The City and Johannesburg Water applied to cross-appeal, and the case was heard in September 2009.

The Constitutional Court handed down a unanimous judgment by O'Regan J on 8 October 2009, ruling against the applicants on all grounds.[83] In summary, the Court disagreed with both lower courts and found that the City's FBW policy fell 'within the bounds of reasonableness' and was therefore 'not in conflict with either section 27 of the Constitution or with the national legislation regulating water services.'[84] The Court also found that the installation of prepaid meters in Phiri was lawful,[85] and accordingly set aside all of the Supreme Court's orders.[86]

Unlike the lower courts, the Constitutional Court found that the City was not under a constitutional obligation to provide any particular amount of free water to citizens per month.[87] Instead, the Court rejected the applicants' argument that it should determine a quantified amount of water as 'sufficient' within the meaning of section 27 of the Constitution,[88] stating that the right to water,

> does not require the state upon demand to provide every person with sufficient water ...; rather it requires the state to take reasonable legislative

> and other measures progressively to realise the achievement of the right to access to sufficient water, within available resources.[89]

The Court expressed concern that any order that obliged the state to provide a specific amount of water would go beyond both the text of the Constitution and the appropriate role of the judiciary,[90] who are not best placed 'to determine what the achievement of any particular social and economic right entails and what steps government should take to ensure the progressive realisation of the right.'[91] The Court held that the obligation of progressive realisation could not impose an immediate obligation to provide a fixed quantified content.[92] The Court also rejected the applicants' arguments that the FBW policy was insufficiently flexible, finding instead that the continual changes to the City's Indigent Persons policy reflected the necessary level of flexibility, in that the City was 'continually reconsidering its policy and investigating ways to ensure that the poorest inhabitants of the City gained access ... to water'.[93]

The Constitutional Court further dismissed the applicants' equality-based claims (based on ss 9(1), 9(3) of the Constitution), pointing out that consumers with prepaid meters pay a lower tariff rate than those with credit meters, and they cannot incur arrears, which means they are protected from 'a range of severe consequences' such as having to pay interest or having their names listed with a credit bureau as a defaulter.[94] The Court concluded that 'correcting the deep inequality which characterises our society, as a consequence of apartheid policies, will often require differential treatment.'[95]

In relation to the question of whether prepaid meters result in an unauthorised discontinuation of water supply by denying consumers reasonable notice and an opportunity to be heard (as required by section 4(3) of the WSA), the Court found that imposing such a requirement on accounts with prepaid meters would 'have a result that borders on the absurd,'[96] and that notice was unnecessary, since '[a] customer in Johannesburg who has a pre-paid water meter understands that the water meter will provide a certain quantity of water which may be exhausted...'[97] The Court also held that a water service is merely suspended rather than discontinued by the operation of the meters and that consumers are not denied basic water services because their free water allocation (which constitutes their 'basic water services' as defined by Regulation 3(b)) will still be available the following month.[98]

Finally, the Constitutional Court dismissed the applicants' administrative justice-based arguments, finding that the decision to impose prepaid meters was an executive rather than an administrative action and thus did not need to comply with the PAJA.[99] Nonetheless, the Court went on to consider the characteristics of the implementation of Operation Gcin'amanzi and concluded that it had been procedurally fair.[100] In this regard, the Court diverged from Tsoka J's findings and accepted the evidence of the City that it had engaged in significant amounts of public participation and consultation throughout the implementation process.[101]

At the conclusion of the case, the applicants had argued that if their application were denied, it would make cases such as theirs pointless and render the guarantee of social rights under the constitution hollow. In response, O'Regan J suggested the case should actually be seen as a victory for community participation in the dialogue over social rights in South Africa.[102] The Court pointed out that, although they had been unsuccessful in their claims, the applicants had been able to force the City and DWAF to provide a detailed account of its policies, thus increasing the transparency and accountability of water governance in South Africa.[103] Furthermore, this process had led the City to reconsider some elements of its water services policies and to increase the amount of free water available to households on the indigent register as a result.[104] In relation to the applicants' claim that these changes were spurred by the litigation itself, the Court found that this could only be a positive development and that the 'litigation will in that event have attained at least some of what it sought to achieve.'[105]

Analysis

The Court's deferential approach to the City's budgetary constraints (or choices) and use of prepaid meters illustrates the way that legal frameworks can naturalise socio-spatial inequality through what Blomley terms 'legal violence' – the reproduction and legitimation of unjust geographies through seemingly neutral legal mechanisms.[106] By accepting differentiated service delivery as reasonable, the judgment sanctioned the entrenchment of Johannesburg's racialised patterns of spatial injustice, illustrating how legal frameworks and spatial relations continuously shape and reshape each other. Just as Chile's water markets and Manila's concession agreements (and regulatory decisions) produced differentiated water territories, the Court's emphasis on 'progressive realisation' and 'reasonableness' legitimised spatially uneven water access. While incurring interest or going into debt is far from ideal, being forced to go without water is clearly a more 'severe consequence' – and, of course, the decision to impose interest on unaffordable water bills was entirely optional.

The Court's emphasis on procedural reasonableness rather than substantive adequacy (or equality) echoes patterns seen in earlier cases, where technical and financial criteria were used to justify uneven water access. The particular focus on the City's budgetary choices rather than on the substantive outcomes for the community and lived experiences of the applicants reflects what Wendy Brown describes as neoliberalism's tendency to replace political judgement with technical criteria – shifting the space for democratic control in the process.[107] However, the South African context introduced distinct dynamics through its constitutional rights framework and historical legacy of spatial apartheid.

Boaventura de Sousa Santos has critiqued rights jurisprudence for systematically rendering alternative ways of knowing and organising social relations invisible in a process he describes as 'the sociology of absences.'[108] By adopting a highly deferential approach through the lens of 'reasonableness,' the Constitutional Court's judgment in Mazibuko transformed the community's radical critique of water commodification into a narrow question of administrative procedure, exemplifying what Pieterse terms the 'abstract and conceptually empty articulation of socioeconomic rights' that serves to contain and suppress social movements.[109] This process reflects Samuel Moyn's argument that rights frameworks are frequently mobilised to legitimate market-based solutions to fundamentally political problems of resource distribution.[110] This process of neutralisation and containment demonstrates precisely the risks that CLS scholars have identified – not just of the deradicalisation of specific claims, but the broader occupation of political imagination by market rationalities. [111] By refusing to specify a minimum water allocation and accepting prepaid meters as reasonable demand management tools, the judgment reveals how rights-based approaches can be coopted to naturalise rather than challenge neoliberal governance paradigms while marginalising community-based understandings of water.

The right to water at the United Nations

The Mazibuko judgment emerged within a broader context of evolving interpretations of the right to water across multiple scales of governance. While the Constitutional Court was grappling with the right's implications in post-apartheid South Africa, parallel debates were unfolding in international forums about the relationship between human rights and neoliberal water governance. And these parallel debates resulted in remarkably similar outcomes, revealing how rights frameworks operate differently across scales while often producing similar effects – the containment of more radical challenges to dominant political economic logic (in this case, water commodification). Just as South Africa's Constitutional Court adopted a highly deferential approach that legitimised market mechanisms, the UN system also developed interpretations that emphasised neutrality regarding service delivery models.

After General Comment No. 15 (discussed in Chapter 4), the next significant development at the United Nations level was a 2006 resolution of the UN Human Rights Council (HRC) to request that the Office of the UN High Commissioner on Human Rights (OHCHR) prepare a report on 'the scope and content of the human rights obligations related to the equitable access to safe drinking water and sanitation under human rights instruments' and to make conclusions and recommendations.[112] In preparing its report, OHCHR consulted widely with 'States, intergovernmental organizations, national human rights institutions, non-governmental organizations (NGOs), experts, and representatives of the private sector' and reviewed the existing international legal framework.[113] Reflecting on this wide consultation, OHCHR made a number of observations, including 'the growing importance of this issue to the international community' (evidenced by 'increasing references to safe drinking water in human rights instruments' and 'the inclusion of access to safe drinking water and sanitation amongst the Millennium Development Goals') and that 'an increasing number of States are recognizing safe drinking water as a human right in their constitutions, as well as national legislation, while national courts are enforcing it as a justiciable right.'[114] OHCHR also reached a number of conclusions around the scope and content of the right to water, including that there was 'a need for further elaboration of certain aspects of human rights obligations attached to access to safe drinking water and sanitation,' such as the regulation of the private sector in the context of private provision of safe drinking water and sanitation.[115]

Ultimately, the issue of private sector participation and the related issue of government responsibility continued to be the most contentious.[116] This was particularly apparent at the UN General Assembly (UNGA), where 41 countries abstained from voting on the 2010 resolution on the human right to water and sanitation,[117] while expressing concerns around the lack of clarity provided by the resolution over what responsibilities the right to water would impose on governments.[118] It was also apparent at the triennial World Water Forum, particularly the fourth in Mexico City (2006) and fifth in Istanbul (2009), where the corporate water lobby sought to promote the value of their role in delivering investment and increased efficiency, while civil society congregated outside to promote community-driven alternatives.[119]

OHCHR's report highlighted the lack of existing mechanisms to monitor the realisation of the right to water and sanitation,[120] which led the HRC to appoint an Independent Expert on the issue of human rights obligations relating to access to safe drinking water and sanitation. One of the Independent Expert's first tasks was to prepare a report on 'the human rights obligations and responsibilities which apply in cases of non-State service provision of water and sanitation.'[121] After consulting widely with civil society, states, and the private sector, the Independent Expert ultimately concluded that '[h]uman rights are neutral as to economic models in general, and models of service provision more specifically.'[122]

United Nations declarations

Although the Independent Expert's report did emphasise the ongoing obligations of states regardless of delegated service provision and the fundamental right of communities to participate in water governance, it had significant implications for both the development of the normative content of the right to water and the willingness of many states to recognise the right without reservation. Shortly after its publication, the HRC adopted a declaration recognising that a human right to water can be implied from articles 11 and 12 of the ICESCR.[123] By 2012, the tide of global opinion had completely shifted, and states made further declarations at the HRC,[124] the UN Conference on Sustainable Development,[125] and the Sixth World Water Forum[126]—all by consensus (meaning that, unlike previous declarations, no states abstained or made contrary statements in the debates). Following this, UNGA also adopted two further resolutions on the right to water.[127]

These international dynamics demonstrate how rights frameworks operate differently across scales of governance. While domestic courts tend to focus on questions of reasonableness and progressive realisation within specific constitutional contexts, international institutions must construct more flexible interpretative frameworks that can accommodate multiple legal systems while maintaining coherent normative content. This multi-scalar complexity helps explain both the apparent success in achieving international recognition of the right to water and the simultaneous difficulty in translating this recognition into transformative change.

The evolution of the right to water within the UN system also reflected patterns of institutional adaptation and containment unique to the international sphere. The Independent Expert's conclusion that human rights are neutral regarding service provision models exemplifies the particular way that international institutions process radical demands – not through outright rejection, but through a form of technocratic neutralisation that strips rights of their transformative potential while retaining their progressive rhetoric.

The tension between competing conceptualisations of water – as economic good versus commons, as commodity versus sacred kin – played out in distinct ways at the international level. A classic example of this was the spatial politics of the World Water Forum. Here, the physical separation between corporate water interests promoting investment and efficiency frameworks inside the forum and civil society activists articulating alternative community-based approaches outside spatially reflected the ontological divide in conceptions of water governance.

Discussion

South Africa's experience with the human right to water, particularly through the *Mazibuko* judgment, mirrors broader patterns of institutional adaptation and containment evident in the international sphere. In both contexts, rights frameworks demonstrated a remarkable capacity to absorb radical demands while preserving existing power relations – though they operated through distinct mechanisms. While the Constitutional Court employed the language of reasonableness and progressive realisation to legitimate neoliberal water governance, international institutions achieved similar ends through the construction of technical neutrality. These parallel processes operated at different scales but produced similarly depoliticised interpretations of the human right to water that privileged market rationalities while marginalising alternative conceptualisations of water's social and cultural significance.

Yet, as the following analysis demonstrates, these institutional interpretations represent only one dimension of rights discourse – one that has been continuously contested through community resistance and alternative articulations of water justice. This institutional containment of water rights claims operates within a broader matrix of power relations that requires deeper theoretical examination. While CLS scholars highlight the deradicalising tendencies of rights discourse, postcolonial theory reveals how these processes are embedded within deeper structures of epistemic violence and ontological erasure that characterise the project of modernity itself.

A key insight of this postcolonial critique is that the fundamental Eurocentricity of human rights frameworks – evident in both domestic constitutional interpretation and international law – reflects not just an individualistic bias,[128] but a particular way of knowing and categorising the world that systematically delegitimises and erases alternative conceptualisations of human–water relations. Here it is argued that the foundational texts of international human rights law, and particularly the Universal Declaration of Human Rights (UDHR), were drafted almost exclusively by White (mostly male) elites. It is further argued that when the UDHR was adopted by 48 of the 58 existing members of the United Nations, '[a]lmost two-thirds of world countries were still colonies and as a result without a voice.'[129] Consequently, the foundational legal texts that have shaped the international human rights regime (and the domestic regimes that have developed in its shadow) reflect a particularly Western (male, elite) worldview to the exclusion of all others. Relatedly, it is argued that this regime ignores the issue of colonialism and prioritises individualism over equality and solidarity. Underpinning this critique are two further interlinked arguments – first, there is something unique about this Eurocentric understanding of human rights (and wider worldview); and second, that part of this philosophical tradition is a drive to assert itself as universal by erasing other world(view)s – a drive to hegemony.

Reminiscent of CLS critiques, it is argued that Eurocentric conceptions of rights are based on an atomised understanding of humanity and idealised concept of individual freedom that sits at odds with alternative solidarity-based traditions. As Keba M'baye and Henri Collomb argue, this Eurocentric rights framework sits in tension with more relational understandings of both humanity and rights prevalent in many traditional African societies.[130] These alternative traditions conceptualise rights not as individual claims against the collective but as frameworks for maintaining harmony within human communities and with the broader environment. This ontological difference helps explain why the

Mazibuko applicants' arguments about water's cultural and social significance found little traction in a legal framework structured around individual entitlements and market efficiency.

This postcolonial critique also points out that human rights have been used to erase other ways of knowing and to assert and justify dominance and imperialism by asserting European (or Western) values and ideologies as universal. Here the language of human rights is used to frame Western culture (and its economic system) as superior and civilised and to frame other cultures as the opposite. The related civilising mission of the West – in which the adoption of Western values is automatically associated with progress – has been a key theme in justifying colonisation and military intervention (often motivated by the protection of access to key markets or resources – or, simply, land grabbing).[131] This weaponisation of human rights has been described as the *dark side* of human rights, and it ultimately leaves non-Western peoples outside the protection of human rights themselves (and Western powers – and their elite proxies – beyond challenge).[132]

Beyond its attempts to categorise people, societies, and nations, this worldview (or ontology) also seeks to categorise the more-than-human and humanity's relationship with it. As discussed in Chapter 1, within a Eurocentric or modernist ontology, there is a strict dichotomy (dualism) and indeed hierarchy between the human and the more-than-human, which is categorised as an object or resource for human exploitation. This has particular implications for the human right to water because a modernist approach to human rights can only understand water as a resource to be controlled and exploited for value. This understanding of water fundamentally shaped early debates around the human right to water and helps to explain the challenges faced by those seeking a more relational approach – one grounded in an ontology in which humanity is intimately entangled with the rest of the environment (including with each other). This ontological divide was vividly illustrated in the Phiri residents' articulation of water as life itself – 'if you haven't got water, you got nothing'[133] – which stands in stark contrast to its judicial construction as a quantifiable resource.

While a justifiable response to these multiple critiques would be to abandon human rights as a discourse and lens through which to engage with water justice concerns, others have argued for ongoing critical engagement. This process of critical engagement has (at least) two elements. The first is the strategic use of rights to achieve tangible and necessary short-term outcomes. The second is a long-term project to decolonise rights themselves.

In relation to the first strand of engagement, it can be argued that the recognition and implementation of the right to water is having a positive, albeit gradual, impact on water governance in South Africa. The adoption of FBW is one example of this impact. While the details of the policy require improvement, it has been a positive step in increasing access and equality, and by the time of the Mazibuko judgment, a growing number of municipalities had begun adopting more generous allocations and eligibility criteria.[134] Beyond the courtroom, the *Mazibuko* case itself also delivered positive results in both increasing equity and participation.[135] The applicants themselves reported finding the process empowering – seeing the case more as a platform for political intervention than as a legal verdict.[136]

These pragmatic, strategic uses of the human right to water also contribute to the second project of decolonisation. While the Constitutional Court of South Africa articulated a narrow conception of the human right to water, reflecting an individualistic and modernist understanding of both rights and water, and a similar interpretation was also embedded in the resolutions of the UN Human Rights Council, the applicants in *Mazibuko* and civil society movements campaigning within the UN system articulated a relational, solidarity-based interpretation. Court judgments and UN resolutions have both legal and political significance, but it is important not to exaggerate their significance or to accept their interpretations as permanent. Human rights, like all legal concepts, are continuously reshaped and redefined from below as well as from above.[137]

In the South African context, Tshepo Madlingozi argues that social movements have used the language of rights to legitimise their movements while maintaining an activist or political use of the discourse, rather than a legal one.[138] Even with the *Mazibuko* case, the APF sought to combine litigation with direct action – a legal win was never the sole focus. Litigation provided a powerful political platform, and this enabled the APF to reinvigorate their broader political struggle against capitalism. The politicising effect of this advocacy was such that the City of Johannesburg fundamentally reviewed its water policies, and civil society was able to change the national conversation around water governance and politics.[139]

These community responses to institutional containment demonstrate how prefigurative practices can reshape legal geographies through the performance of alternative spatial-legal relations. Rather than simply contesting specific policies, the combination of direct action and strategic litigation enacted new ways of knowing and governing water. Alongside the Mazibuko case, the protection of community water points and maintenance of reciprocal sharing practices performed legal relationships grounded in solidarity rather than commodification. This prefigurative dimension reveals how resistance operates through the active creation of alternative legal spaces that challenge both technical exclusion and ontological erasure. While the longer-term impact of community-level activism remains to be seen,[140] the resistance and community solidarity of these activists have embodied a relational and communal understanding of the human right to water that defies commodification and that has continued to resonate well beyond South Africa's borders.

At a broader level, many critical postcolonial scholars have argued that it is possible to (at least partly) redeem human rights if its universalist articulation and simultaneous Western exceptionalism are abandoned in favour of a pluralist approach informed by the lived experiences and expertise of those most affected by violations (sometimes described as the 'subaltern'). Makau Mutua, for example, argues for 'the human rights movement to rethink and reorient its hierarchised, binary view of the world in which the European West leads the way and the rest of the globe follows in a structure that resembles a child–parent relationship.'[141] This process of decolonisation would also involve dismantling the binary between humans and the rest of the environment.

This interplay between the institutional interpretation of the human right to water – and its legitimisation of neoliberal water governance – and an alternative community-driven framing of the right (and of water itself) that foregrounds solidarity and relationality has continued to play out both in local contexts and within ongoing debates within the UN human rights system. The following two chapters continue to track these developments, starting with an analysis of the water crisis in the US state of Michigan.

Notes

1 World Bank, *Guide to Ring-Fencing of Local Government-Run Water Utilities* (World Bank, 2010) 1.
2 World Bank, *Ring-Fencing* 1–2.
3 David Hemson et al, *Still Paying the Price: Revisiting the Cholera Epidemic of 2000–2001 in South Africa* (No Occasional Papers No. 10, Municipal Services Project, 2006); Hameda Deedat and Eddie Cottle, 'Cost Recovery and Pre-Paid Water Meters and the Cholera Outbreak in KwaZulu Natal: A Case Study in Madlebe' in David A. McDonald and John Pape (eds), *Cost Recovery and the Crisis of Service Delivery in South Africa* (Zed Books, 2002) 81.
4 City of Johannesburg, *Reflecting on a Solid Foundation: Building Development Local Government 2000-2005* (City of Johannesburg, 2006).
5 Coalition Against Water Privatisation (CAWP), Anti-Privatisation Forum (APF), and Public Citizen, *Nothing for Mahala: The Forced Installation of Prepaid Water Meters in Stretford, Extension 4, Orange Farm, Johannesburg, South Africa* (Centre for Civil Society, 2004).
6 City of Johannesburg, *Reflecting on a Solid Foundation* (n 4) 116.
7 City of Johannesburg, *Reflecting on a Solid Foundation* (n 4) 116.
8 *Mazibuko & Others v City of Johannesburg & Others* (06/13865) [2008] ZAGPHC 491; [2008] 4 All SA 471 (W) (30 April 2008) [106]–[108]; Patrick Bond and Jackie Dugard, 'The Case of Johannesburg Water: What Really Happened at the Pre-Paid Parish Pump' (2008) 12(1) *Law, Democracy and Development* 1, 9.
9 Interview with Gladys Mokolo, *Project Coordinator for the Orange Farm Water Crisis Committee Women's Empowerment Project* (Cristy Clark, Orange Farm, South Africa, 3 October 2006).
10 Interview with Gladys Mokolo, Project Coordinator for the Orange Farm Water Crisis Committee Women's Empowerment Project (n 9).

11 Interview with Silumko Radebe, 'National Organiser with Anti-Privatisation Forum (APF)' (Cristy Clark, Braamfontein, Johannesburg, South Africa, 4 October 2006).
12 Vusumuzi Paki, *Affidavit in Mazibuko & Others v City of Johannesburg & Others* (High Court of South Africa (Witwatersrand Local Division), 2007) <https://apf.org.za/spip.php?article155> (last accessed 27 March 2025).
13 Interview with Jennifer Makoatsane, 'Applicant in Mazibuko Water Rights Case' (Cristy Clark, Phiri, South Africa, 5 October 2006).
14 Interview with Jennifer Makoatsane, 'Applicant in Mazibuko Water Rights Case' (n 13).
15 Tshepo Madlingozi, 'Post-Apartheid Social Movements and Legal Mobilisation' in Malcolm Langford et al (eds), *Socio-Economic Rights in South Africa: Symbols or Substance?* (Cambridge University Press, 2013) 92 <https://www.cambridge.org/core/product/9C83665E3B5673F4BD037EA4C04EB972>; Patrick Bond, *Elite Transition: From Apartheid to Neoliberalism in South Africa* (Pluto Press, 2nd edition, 2000).
16 Interview with Tshepo Madlingozi, 'Lecturer in Law at the University of Pretoria, "Social Movements in South Africa"' (Cristy Clark, University of Pretoria, South Africa, 26 September 2006); Interview with Dale McKinley, 'Organiser with the Coalition against Water Privatisation and the Anti-Privatisation Forum' (Cristy Clark, Melville, South Africa, 30 September 2006).
17 Interview with Tshepo Madlingozi, 'Lecturer in Law at the University of Pretoria, "Social Movements in South Africa"' (n 16).
18 CAWP, APF, and Public Citizen, *Nothing for Mahala* (n 5) 25; Interview with Dale McKinley, 'Organiser with the Coalition against Water Privatisation and the Anti-Privatisation Forum' (n 16); Interview with Tshepo Madlingozi, 'Lecturer in Law at the University of Pretoria, "Social Movements in South Africa"' (n 16).
19 Interview with Palesa, 'Administrative Officer for Orange Farm Water Crisis Committee' (Cristy Clark, Orange Farm, South Africa, 3 October 2006).
20 CAWP, APF, and Public Citizen, *Nothing for Mahala* (n 5) 25.
21 Interview with Palesa, 'Administrative Officer for Orange Farm Water Crisis Committee' (n 19); Interview with Dale McKinley, 'Organiser with the Coalition against Water Privatisation and the Anti-Privatisation Forum' (n 16).
22 Interview with Silumko Radebe, 'National Organiser with Anti-Privatisation Forum (APF)' (n 11).
23 Interview with Sarrafina Morsopa, 'Resident of Phiri and Member of the Anti-Privatisation Forum (APF)' (Cristy Clark, Phiri, South Africa, 5 October 2006).
24 Interview with Sarrafina Morsopa, 'Resident of Phiri and Member of the Anti-Privatisation Forum (APF)' (n 23).
25 Interview with Sarrafina Morsopa, 'Resident of Phiri and Member of the Anti-Privatisation Forum (APF)' (n 23).
26 Interview with Sarrafina Morsopa, 'Resident of Phiri and Member of the Anti-Privatisation Forum (APF)' (n 23).
27 Interview with Jennifer Makoatsane, 'Applicant in Mazibuko Water Rights Case' (n 13).
28 Interview with Sarrafina Morsopa, 'Resident of Phiri and Member of the Anti-Privatisation Forum (APF)' (n 23).
29 Dale McKinley, 'Lessons in Community-Based Resistance? South Africa's Anti-Privatisation Forum' (2016) 34(2) *Journal of Contemporary African Studies* 268.
30 Carin Runciman, 'The Decline of the Anti-Privatisation Forum in the Midst of South Africa's "Rebellion of the Poor"' (2015) 63(7) *Current Sociology* 961, 965 citing APF Constitution 2007.

31 Runciman, 'The Decline of the Anti-Privatisation Forum in the Midst of South Africa's "Rebellion of the Poor"' (n 30).
32 Henri Lefebvre, *The Right to the City [Le Droit à La Ville, 1968]*, tr Eleonore Kofman and Elizabeth Lebas (The Anarchist Library, 1996). See also Chris Butler, *Henri Lefebvre, Spatial Politics, Everyday Life and the Right to the City* (Routledge, 2012); David Harvey, 'The Right to the City' (2008) 53 *New Left Review* 23.
33 See, e.g., Bond and Dugard, 'The Case of Johannesburg Water' (n 8) 9; Jackie Dugard, 'Rights, Regulation and Resistance: The Phiri Water Rights Campaign' (2009) 24(3) *South African Journal on Human Rights* 593, 602; Jackie Dugard, 'Civic Action and the Legal Mobilisation: The Phiri Water Meters Case' in Jeff Handmaker and Remko Berkhout (eds), *Mobilising Social Justice in South Africa: Perspectives from Researchers and Practitioners* (2010) 71, 88. Jennifer Makoatsane also described these activities in an interview with the author: Interview with Jennifer Makoatsane, 'Applicant in Mazibuko Water Rights Case' (n 13).
34 See Dugard, 'Civic Action and the Legal Mobilisation' (n 33) 88; CAWP, APF, and Public Citizen, *Nothing for Mahala* (n 5) 7.
35 Dugard, 'Civic Action and the Legal Mobilisation' (n 33) 88; CAWP, APF, and Public Citizen, *Nothing for Mahala* (n 5) 7.
36 *Mazibuko v City of Johannesburg* (n 8) [112]; Bond and Dugard, 'The Case of Johannesburg Water' (n 8) 9.
37 Bond and Dugard, 'The Case of Johannesburg Water' (n 8) 2.
38 Bond and Dugard, 'The Case of Johannesburg Water' (n 8) 2.
39 Bond and Dugard, 'The Case of Johannesburg Water' (n 8) 2.
40 David Kennedy, 'The International Human Rights Movement: Part of the Problem?' (2002) 15 *Harvard Human Rights Journal* 101.
41 Marius Pieterse, 'Eating Socioeconomic Rights: The Usefulness of Rights Talk in Alleviating Social Hardship Revisited' (2007) 29(3) *Human Rights Quarterly* 796, 797–799.
42 Jackie Dugard and Malcolm Langford, 'Art or Science? Synthesising Lessons from Public Interest Litigation and the Dangers of Legal Determinism' (2011) 27 *South African Journal on Human Rights* 39.
43 Yolandi Groenewald, 'Soweto Starts Its Water War', *Mail & Guardian* (24 July 2006). The residents were Lindiwe Mazibuko, Grace Munyai, Jennifer Makoatsane, Sophia Malekutu and Vusimuzi Paki.
44 'Applicants' Heads of Argument', *Mazibuko & Others v City of Johannesburg & Others* (High Court of South Africa (Witwatersrand Local Division), 2007) [5]. The applicants argued that the installation of the prepaid meters was not authorised by the City's by-laws, because they only provided for the installation of such meters a penalty for contravening the conditions for receiving water service level two, and the applicants had not so breached the conditions of their water service: *Mazibuko v City of Johannesburg* (n 8) [165]. They also argued that this forced installation of prepaid water meters was a violation of requirement to progressively realise the right to water under s 27(2) of the Constitution; and was an unconstitutional interference with their existing access to water, because it was a deliberately retrogressive measure: *Mazibuko v City of Johannesburg* (n 8) [161.1]–[161.3], [178].
45 *Mazibuko v City of Johannesburg* (n 8) [6].
46 *Mazibuko v City of Johannesburg* (n 8) [7].
47 *Mazibuko v City of Johannesburg* (n 8) [270].
48 *Mazibuko v City of Johannesburg* (n 8) [161.4], [161.5], [226]. The arguments around equality focused on s 9 of the Constitution.
49 *Mazibuko v City of Johannesburg* (n 8) [245]–[247].

50 *Mazibuko v City of Johannesburg* (n 8) [287] citing United Nations Committee on Economic, Social and Cultural Rights (CESCR), *General Comment No. 15: The Right to Water (Arts. 11 and 12 of the International Covenant on Economic, Social and Cultural Rights)*, 29th sess, UN Doc E/C.12/2002/11 (20 January 2003) [12(a)]; Guy Howard and Jamie Bartram, Domestic water quantity, service level and health, World Health Organisation, WHO/SDE/WSH/03.02 (2003); Peter Henry Gleick, *Supporting affidavit in Mazibuko & Others v City of Johanesburg & Others* (High Court of South Africa (Witwatersrand Local Division), 2005) <https://apf.org.za/spip.php?article160> (last accessed 27 March 2025).
51 *Mazibuko v City of Johannesburg* (n 8) [313] citing Schreiner Answering affidavit A11 4004 [116].
52 *Water Services Act 1997* (South Africa).
53 'Applicants' Heads of Argument' (n 44) [245]–[247]. The applicants also argued that such a disconnection was without authorisation from by-law 9C, which only authorises disconnection for non-payment of arrears.
54 *Constitution of the Republic of South Africa 1996* (South Africa) art 33(1).
55 *Promotion of Administrative Justice Act 2000* (South Africa) s 3.
56 City of Johannesburg, *Answering Affidavit in Mazibuko & Others v The City of Johannesburg & Others* (High Court of South Africa (Witwatersrand Local Division), 2007) [25.6]–[25.8]. In this regard, the City pointed out that in providing 6 kilolitres for free, it was doing more for its citizens than most countries around the world: ibid [13.1].
57 City of Johannesburg, 'Answering Affidavit' (n 56) [25.6]–[25.8].
58 Gerald Dumas, Answering Affidavit of Gerald Dumas (Managing Director of Johannesburg Water) in Mazibuko & Others v City of Johannesburg & Others (High Court of South Africa (Witwatersrand Local Division), 2007) [34].
59 City of Johannesburg, 'Answering Affidavit' (n 56) [28.10.16]–[28.10.19].
60 City of Johannesburg, 'Answering Affidavit' (n 56) [26.2].
61 City of Johannesburg, 'Answering Affidavit' (n 56) [30.55.4]; 'Applicants' Heads of Argument' (n 44) [345].
62 City of Johannesburg, 'Answering Affidavit" (n 56) [26.22.1]; 'Applicants' Heads of Argument' (n 44) [346].
63 'Applicants' Heads of Argument' (n 44) [348], [349.1], [349.2], [349.3] (citations omitted).
64 Randir Singh, *Singh Supplementary Affidavit in Mazibuko & Others v City of Johannesburg & Others* (High Court of South Africa (Witwatersrand Local Division), 2007) [9.2].
65 'Applicants' Heads of Argument' (n 44) [203.1], [344] citing Brits Answering affidavit A3 686 [30.75], 611 [25.10.1] (incorrectly numbered as [26.10.1]).
66 *Mazibuko v City of Johannesburg* (n 8) [183.5.1].
67 *Mazibuko v City of Johannesburg* (n 8) [183.5.2].
68 *Mazibuko v City of Johannesburg* (n 8) [184].
69 *Mazibuko v City of Johannesburg* [36], [40]–[42].
70 *Mazibuko v City of Johannesburg* (n 8) [169].
71 *Mazibuko v City of Johannesburg* (n 8) [181] (This took into account the need for waterborne sanitation, the high levels of poverty and unemployment, the high levels of HIV//AIDS and other illnesses, and the large household sizes in Phiri.).
72 *Mazibuko v City of Johannesburg* (n 8) [117].
73 *Mazibuko v City of Johannesburg* (n 8) [91].
74 *Mazibuko v City of Johannesburg* (n 8) [105]–[106].
75 *Mazibuko v City of Johannesburg* (n 8) [107].
76 *Mazibuko v City of Johannesburg* (n 8) [110].
77 *Mazibuko v City of Johannesburg* (n 8) [122].

78 *City of Johannesburg & Others v Mazibuko & Others* (2009) 20(3) ZASCA 592, [54]–[55] (Streicher JA found that the operation of the prepaid meters in 'limiting or discontinuing water services' in a manner that was not fair and equitable, and did not provide for reasonable notice and the opportunity to make representations, was a breach of s 4[3] of the *Water Services Act 1997* (South Africa).).
79 *City of Johannesburg v Mazibuko* (n 78) [21]–[24]. (This finding was based on allocating 15 litres to sanitation (or 1.5 flushes per person per day) rather than 20, and by deducting several litres from the allocations for bathing and drinking because Phiri was not a tropical or subtropical environment.).
80 *City of Johannesburg v Mazibuko* (n 78) [60].
81 See Dugard and Langford, 'Art or Science?' (n 42) 45. For a critique of the Supreme Court of Appeal's judgment, see Jackie Dugard and Sandra Liebenberg, 'Muddying the Waters: The Supreme Court of Appeal's Judgment in the Mazibuko Case' (2009) 10(2) *ESR Review* 11.
82 See Dugard and Liebenberg, 'Muddying the Waters' (n 81).
83 *Mazibuko & Others v City of Johannesburg* & Others (2009) 28 ZACC 28; 2010 4 SA 1, Constitutional Court of South Africa (8 October 2009).
84 *Mazibuko v City of Johannesburg* (n 83).
85 *Mazibuko v City of Johannesburg* (n 83) [106]–[112]. The Court held that this conclusion was supported by section 8(2) of the *Municipal Systems Act 2000* (South Africa), which gives local governments the right 'to do anything reasonably necessary for, or incidental to, the effective performance of its functions and the exercise of its powers.'
86 *Mazibuko v City of Johannesburg* (n 83) [9].
87 *Mazibuko v City of Johannesburg* (n 83) [85].
88 *Mazibuko v City of Johannesburg* (n 83) [68].
89 *Mazibuko v City of Johannesburg* (n 83) [50].
90 *Mazibuko v City of Johannesburg* (n 83) [57].
91 *Mazibuko v City of Johannesburg* (n 83) [61].
92 *Mazibuko v City of Johannesburg* (n 83) [60].
93 *Mazibuko v City of Johannesburg* (n 83) [94].
94 *Mazibuko v City of Johannesburg* (n 83) [152]–[153].
95 *Mazibuko v City of Johannesburg* (n 83) [156].
96 *Mazibuko v City of Johannesburg* (n 83) [122].
97 *Mazibuko v City of Johannesburg* (n 83) [123].
98 *Mazibuko v City of Johannesburg* (n 83) [120]–[122].
99 *Mazibuko v City of Johannesburg* (n 83) [127]–[131].
100 *Mazibuko v City of Johannesburg* (n 83) [132]–[138].
101 *Mazibuko v City of Johannesburg* (n 83) [133]. See also City of Johannesburg, 'Answering Affidavit' (n 56) [26.4], [30.49.5].
102 *Mazibuko v City of Johannesburg* (n 83) [161]–[163].
103 *Mazibuko v City of Johannesburg* (n 83) [163].
104 *Mazibuko v City of Johannesburg (n 83)* [163].
105 *Mazibuko v City of Johannesburg* (n 83) [97].
106 Nicholas Blomley, *Law, Space, and the Geographies of Power* (The Guildford Press, 1994).
107 Wendy Brown, *Undoing the Demos: Neoliberalism's Stealth Revolution* (Zone Books, 2015).
108 Boaventura de Sousa Santos, 'Épistémologies du Sud', tr Magali Watteaux (2011) 187 *Études rurales* 21.
109 Pieterse, 'Eating Socioeconomic Rights' (n 41) 797–799.
110 Samuel Moyn, 'A Powerless Companion: Human Rights in the Age of Neoliberalism' in Ben Golder and Daniel McLoughlin (eds), *The Politics of Legality in a Neoliberal Age* (Routledge, 2017) 147.

111 See, e.g., Joel Bakan, *Just Words: Constitutional Rights and Social Wrongs* (University of Toronto Press, 1997); Duncan Kennedy, 'The Critique of Rights in Critical Legal Studies' in Wendy Brown and Janet Halley (eds), *Left Legalism/Left Critique* (Duke University Press, 2002); Kennedy 'The International Human Rights Movement' (n 40); Danie Brand, 'The "Politics of Need Interpretation" and the Adjudication of Socio-Economic Rights Claims in South Africa' in A.J. van deer Wait (ed), *Theories of Social and Economic Justice* (Sun Press, 2005); Pieterse, 'Eating Socioeconomic Rights' (n 41).

112 United Nations Human Rights Council (HRC), *Human Rights and Access to Water,* 31st mtg, UN Doc A/HRC/Dec/2/104 (4 October 2006).

113 Office of the High Commissioner for Human Rights (OHCHR), *Report of the United Nations High Commissioner for Human Rights on the Scope and Content of the Relevant Human Rights Obligations Related to Equitable Access to Safe Drinking Water and Sanitation under International Human Rights Instruments,* 6th sess, UN Doc A/HRC/6/3 (17 August 2007) 2.

114 OHCHR, *Report on the Scope and Content* (n 113) [65].

115 OHCHR, *Report on the Scope and Content* (n 113) [67].

116 Oriol Mirosa and Leila M. Harris, 'Human Right to Water: Contemporary Challenges and Contours of a Global Debate' (2012) 44(3) *Antipode* 932; Cristy Clark, 'Of What Use Is a Deradicalized Human Right to Water?' (2017) 17(2) *Human Rights Law Review* 231.

117 United Nations General Assembly (UNGA), *The Human Right to Water and Sanitation,* GA Res 64/292, UN Doc A/RES/64/292 (28 July 2010).

118 United Nations, 'General Assembly Adopts Resolution Recognizing Access to Clean Water, Sanitation as Human Right, by Recorded Vote of 122 in Favour, None against, 41 Abstentions (Meetings Coverage)', *United Natios Meetings Coverage and Press Releases* (28 July 2010) <https://www.un.org/press/en/2010/ga10967.doc.htm>.

119 See, eg, Henri Smets, 'Diluted View of Water as a Right' (2006) 36(2) *Environ mental Policy and Law; Amsterdam* 88; Paul Van Hofwegen and Polioptro Martinez Austria (eds), *Synthesis of the Fourth World Water Forum* (World Water Council and the Secretariat of the 4th World Water Forum, 2006); Anita McNaught, 'World Water Forum Diary', *Al Jazeera* (online, 19 March 2009) <https://www.aljazeera.com/news/2009/3/19/world-water-forum-diary-2>; Claire Provost, 'World Water Forum Declaration Falls Short on Human Rights, Claim Experts', *The Guardian* (14 March 2012).

120 OHCHR, *Report on the Scope and Content* (n 113) [69].

121 Catarina de Albuquerque, *Report of the Independent Expert on the Issue of Human Rights Obligations Related to Access to Safe Drinking Water and Sanitation,* 15th sess, Agenda Item 3, UN Doc A/HRC/15/31 (29 June 2010).

122 de Albuquerque, *Report of the Independent Expert* (n 121) 15.

123 United Nations Human Rights Council (HRC), *Human Rights and Access to Safe Drinking Water and Sanitation,* 15th sess, UN Doc A/HRC/Res/15/9 (6 October 2010).

124 United Nations Human Rights Council (HRC), Resolution on the Human Right to Safe Drinking Water and Sanitation, 21st sess, UN Doc A/HRC/21/L.1 (20 September 2012).

125 United Nations, *The Future We Want: Report of the United Nations Conference on Sustainable Development (Rio+20),* UN Doc A/CONF.216/L.1 (19 June 2012) 121.

126 Sixth World Water Forum, *Ministerial Declaration* (13 March 2012) <http://6.worldwaterforum.org/fileadmin/user_upload/pdf/Ministerial_Declaration_Final_EN.pdf> (last accessed 27 March 2025) 8. It is worth noting that this declaration has been criticised for not going far enough in recognising water as

a human right and for promoting privatisation policies in relation to increasing access to water: Provost, 'World Water Forum Declaration Falls Short on Human Rights, Claim Experts' (n 119).

127 United Nations General Assembly (UNGA), *The Human Right to Water and Sanitation,* GA Res 68/157, UN Doc A/RES/68/157 (18 December 2013); United Nations General Assembly (UNGA), *The Human Right to Water and Sanitation,* GA Res 70/169, UN Doc A/RES/70/169 (17 December 2015).

128 Bobby S. Sayyid, *A Fundamental Fear: Eurocentrism and the Emergence of Islamism* (Zed Books, 2003) 285.

129 Hakimeh Saghaye-Biria, 'Decolonizing the "Universal" Human Rights Regime: Questioning American Exceptionalism and Orientalism' (2018) 4(1) *ReOrient* 59, 61.

130 Keba M'baye, Les dimensions internationales des droits de l'homme (Paris 1978) 602 and Henri Collomb, Quarantieme Congres Medical Francophone (Dakar) 1975, cited in B. Obinna Okere, 'The Protection of Human Rights in Africa and the African Charter on Human and Peoples' Rights: A Comparative Analysis with the European and American Systems' (1984) 6(2) *Human Rights Quarterly* 141, 148–149.

131 See, e.g., Ratna Kapur, 'Human Rights in the 21st Century: Take a Walk on the Dark Side' (2006) 28(4) *Sydney Law Review* 665; Saghaye-Biria, 'Decolonizing the "Universal" Human Rights Regime' (n 129) 68.

132 Kapur, 'Human Rights in the 21st Century' (n 131).

133 Interview with Sarrafina Morsopa, 'Resident of Phiri and Member of the Anti-Privatisation Forum (APF)' (n 23).

134 Kate Tissington et al, *Water Service Fault Lines: An Assessment of South Africa's Water and Sanitation Provision across 15 Municipalities* (Centre for Applied Legal Studies (CALS), Centre on House Rights and Evictions (COHRE), and Norwegian Centre for Human Rights (NCHR), 2008) 32; Andrea Szabo, 'The Value of Free Water – Analyzing South Africa's Free Basic Water Policy' (2015) 83(5) *Econometrica* 1913, 1917, 1925, 1938.

135 Dugard and Langford, 'Art or Science?' (n 42).

136 Jackie Dugard, 'Losing Mazibuko: (Re) Considering the Campaign Following Judicial Defeat' (Conference Paper, Law's Locations: Textures of Legality in Developing and Transitional Societies, University of Wisconsin Law School, 23 April 2010); Dugard and Langford, 'Art or Science?' (n 42).

137 John Griffiths, 'What Is Legal Pluralism?' (1986) 18(24) *The Journal of Legal Pluralism and Unofficial Law* 1; Margaret Davies, 'The Ethos of Pluralism' (2005) 27(1) Sydney Law Review 87.

138 Interview with Tshepo Madlingozi, 'Lecturer in Law at the University of Pretoria, "Social Movements in South Africa"' (n 16).

139 Dugard and Langford, 'Art or Science?' (n 42); Laila Smith, 'Conflict versus Cooperation between the State and Civil Society: A Water-Demand Management Comparison between Cape Town and Johannesburg, South Africa' in Bernard Barraque (ed), *Urban Water Conflicts* (Routledge, 2011) 147; Jackie Dugard, 'Urban Basic Services: Rights, Reality, and Resistance' in Malcolm Langford et al (eds), *Socio-Economic Rights in South Africa: Symbols or Substance?* (Cambridge University Press, 2013) 275 <https://www.cambridge.org/core/product/3084E35AB43FA404EBBCAE73497EF57A>.

140 Jackie Dugard, Malcolm Langford and Edward Anderson, 'Determining Progress on Access to Water and Sanitation' in Anna F.S. Russell and Malcolm Langford (eds), *The Human Right to Water: Theory, Practice and Prospects* (Cambridge University Press, 2017) 223.

141 Makau Mutua, *Human Rights: A Political and Cultural Critique* (University of Pennsylvania Press, 2002) 8–9.

References

Applicants' Heads of Argument in Mazibuko & Others v City of Johannesburg & Others (High Court of South Africa (Witwatersrand Local Division), 2007)

de Albuquerque, Catarina, *Report of the Independent Expert on the Issue of Human Rights Obligations Related to Access to Safe Drinking Water and Sanitation,* 15th sess, Agenda Item 3, UN Doc A/HRC/15/31 (29 June 2010)

Bakan, Joel, *Just Words: Constitutional Rights and Social Wrongs* (University of Toronto Press, 1997)

Blomley, Nicholas, *Law, Space, and the Geographies of Power* (The Guildford Press, 1994)

Bond, Patrick, *Elite Transition: From Apartheid to Neoliberalism in South Africa* (Pluto Press, 2nd edition, 2000)

Bond, Patrick and Jackie Dugard, 'The Case of Johannesburg Water: What Really Happened at the Pre-Paid Parish Pump' (2008) 12(1) *Law, Democracy and Development* 1

Brand, Danie, 'The "Politics of Need Interpretation" and the Adjudication of Socio-Economic Rights Claims in South Africa' in A.J. van deer Wait (ed), *Theories of Social and Economic Justice* (Sun Press, 2005) 17

Brown, Wendy, *Undoing the Demos: Neoliberalism's Stealth Revolution* (Zone Books, 2015)

Butler, Chris, Henri Lefebvre, *Spatial Politics, Everyday Life and the Right to the City* (Routledge, 2012)

City of Johannesburg, *Answering Affidavit in Mazibuko & Others v The City of Johannesburg & Others* (High Court of South Africa (Witwatersrand Local Division), 2007)

City of Johannesburg & Others v Mazibuko & Others (2009) 20(3) ZASCA 592

City of Johannesburg, *Reflecting on a Solid Foundation: Building Development Local Government 2000-2005* (City of Johannesburg, 2006)

Clark, Cristy, 'Of What Use Is a Deradicalized Human Right to Water?' (2017) 17(2) *Human Rights Law Review* 231

Coalition Against Water Privatisation (CAWP), Anti-Privatisation Forum (APF), and Public Citizen, *Nothing for Mahala: The Forced Installation of Prepaid Water Meters in Stretford, Extension 4, Orange Farm, Johannesburg, South Africa* (Centre for Civil Society, 2004)

Constitution of the Republic of South Africa 1996 (South Africa)

Davies, Margaret, 'The Ethos of Pluralism' (2005) 27(1) *Sydney Law Review* 87

Deedat, Hameda and Eddie Cottle, 'Cost Recovery and Pre-Paid Water Meters and the Cholera Outbreak in KwaZulu Natal: A Case Study in Madlebe' in David A. McDonald and John Pape (eds), *Cost Recovery and the Crisis of Service Delivery in South Africa* (Zed Books, 2002) 81

Dugard, Jackie, 'Civic Action and the Legal Mobilisation: The Phiri Water Meters Case' in Jeff Handmaker and Remko Berkhout (eds), *Mobilising Social Justice in South Africa: Perspectives from Researchers and Practitioners* (Pretoria University Law Press, 2010) 71

Dugard, Jackie, 'Losing Mazibuko: (Re) Considering the Campaign Following Judicial Defeat' (Conference Paper, Law's Locations: Textures of Legality in Developing and Transitional Societies, University of Wisconsin Law School, 23 April 2010)

Dugard, Jackie, 'Rights, Regulation and Resistance: The Phiri Water Rights Campaign' (2009) 24(3) *South African Journal on Human Rights* 593

Dugard, Jackie, 'Urban Basic Services: Rights, Reality, and Resistance' in Malcolm Langford et al (eds), *Socio-Economic Rights in South Africa: Symbols or Substance?* (Cambridge University Press, 2013) 275 <https://www.cambridge.org/core/product/3084E35AB43FA404EBBCAE73497EF57A>
Dugard, Jackie and Malcolm Langford, 'Art or Science? Synthesising Lessons from Public Interest Litigation and the Dangers of Legal Determinism' (2011) 27 *South African Journal on Human Rights* 39
Dugard, Jackie, Malcolm Langford and Edward Anderson, 'Determining Progress on Access to Water and Sanitation' in Anna F.S. Russell and Malcolm Langford (eds), *The Human Right to Water: Theory, Practice and Prospects* (Cambridge University Press, 2017) 223
Dugard, Jackie and Sandra Liebenberg, 'Muddying the Waters: The Supreme Court of Appeal's Judgment in the Mazibuko Case' (2009) 10(2) *ESR Review* 11
Dumas, Gerald, *Answering Affidavit of Gerald Dumas (Managing Director of Johannesburg Water) in Mazibuko & Others v City of Johannesburg & Others* (High Court of South Africa (Witwatersrand Local Division), 2007)
Gleick, Peter Henry, *Supporting affidavit in Mazibuko & Others v City of Johanesburg & Others* (High Court of South Africa (Witwatersrand Local Division), 2005) <https://apf.org.za/spip.php?article160> (last accessed 27 March 2025).
Griffiths, John, 'What Is Legal Pluralism?' (1986) 18(24) *The Journal of Legal Pluralism and Unofficial Law* 1
Groenewald, Yolandi, 'Soweto Starts Its Water War', *Mail & Guardian* (24 July 2006)
Harvey, David, 'The Right to the City' (2008) 53 *New Left Review* 23
Hemson, David et al, *Still Paying the Price: Revisiting the Cholera Epidemic of 2000–2001 in South Africa* (No Occasional Papers No. 10, Municipal Services Project, 2006)
Interview with Tshepo Madlingozi, 'Lecturer in Law at the University of Pretoria, "Social Movements in South Africa"' (Cristy Clark, University of Pretoria, South Africa, 26 September 2006)
Interview with Jennifer Makoatsane, 'Applicant in Mazibuko Water Rights Case' (Cristy Clark, Phiri, South Africa, 5 October 2006)
Interview with Dale McKinley, 'Organiser with the Coalition against Water Privatisation and the Anti-Privatisation Forum' (Cristy Clark, Melville, South Africa, 30 September 2006)
Interview with Gladys Mokolo, 'Project Coordinator for the Orange Farm Water Crisis Committee Women's Empowerment Project' (Cristy Clark, Orange Farm, South Africa, 3 October 2006)
Interview with Sarrafina Morsopa, 'Resident of Phiri and Member of the Anti-Privatisation Forum (APF)' (Cristy Clark, Phiri, South Africa, 5 October 2006)
Interview with Palesa, 'Administrative Officer for Orange Farm Water Crisis Committee' (Cristy Clark, Orange Farm, South Africa, 3 October 2006)
Interview with Silumko Radebe, 'National Organiser with Anti-Privatisation Forum (APF)' (Cristy Clark, Braamfontein, Johannesburg, South Africa, 4 October 2006)
Kapur, Ratna, 'Human Rights in the 21st Century: Take a Walk on the Dark Side' (2006) 28(4) *Sydney Law Review* 665
Kennedy, Duncan, 'The Critique of Rights in Critical Legal Studies' in Wendy Brown and Janet Halley (eds), *Left Legalism/Left Critique* (Duke University Press, 2002)
Kennedy, David, 'The International Human Rights Movement: Part of the Problem?' (2002) 15 *Harvard Human Rights Journal* 101

Lefebvre, Henri, *The Right to the City [Le Droit à La Ville, 1968*], tr Eleonore Kofman and Elizabeth Lebas (The Anarchist Library, 1996)

Madlingozi, Tshepo, 'Post-Apartheid Social Movements and Legal Mobilisation' in Malcolm Langford et al (eds), *Socio-Economic Rights in South Africa: Symbols or Substance?* (Cambridge University Press, 2013) 92 <https://www.cambridge.org/core/product/9C83665E3B5673F4BD037EA4C04EB972>

Mazibuko & Others v City of Johannesburg & Others (06/13865) [2008] ZAGPHC 491; [2008] 4 All SA 471 (W) (30 April 2008)

Mazibuko & Others v City of Johannesburg & Others (2009) 28 ZACC 28; 2010 4 SA 1, Constitutional Court of South Africa (8 October 2009)

McKinley, Dale, 'Lessons in Community-Based Resistance? South Africa's Anti-Privatisation Forum' (2016) 34(2) *Journal of Contemporary African Studies* 268

McNaught, Anita, 'World Water Forum Diary', *Al Jazeera* (online, 19 March 2009) <https://www.aljazeera.com/news/2009/3/19/world-water-forum-diary-2>

Mirosa, Oriol and Leila M. Harris, 'Human Right to Water: Contemporary Challenges and Contours of a Global Debate' (2012) 44(3) *Antipode* 932

Moyn, Samuel, 'A Powerless Companion: Human Rights in the Age of Neoliberalism' in Ben Golder and Daniel McLoughlin (eds), *The Politics of Legality in a Neoliberal Age* (Routledge, 2017) 147

Mutua, Makau, *Human Rights: A Political and Cultural Critique* (University of Pennsylvania Press, 2002)

Office of the High Commissioner for Human Rights (OHCHR), *Report of the United Nations High Commissioner for Human Rights on the Scope and Content of the Relevant Human Rights Obligations Related to Equitable Access to Safe Drinking Water and Sanitation under International Human Rights Instruments*, 6th sess, UN Doc A/HRC/6/3 (17 August 2007)

Okere, B. Obinna, 'The Protection of Human Rights in Africa and the African Charter on Human and Peoples' Rights: A Comparative Analysis with the European and American Systems' (1984) 6(2) *Human Rights Quarterly* 141

Paki, Vusumuzi, *Affidavit in Mazibuko & Others v City of Johannesburg & Others* (High Court of South Africa (Witwatersrand Local Division), 2007) <https://apf.org.za/spip.php?article155> (last accessed 27 March 2025)

Pieterse, Marius, 'Eating Socioeconomic Rights: The Usefulness of Rights Talk in Alleviating Social Hardship Revisited' (2007) 29(3) *Human Rights Quarterly* 796

Promotion of Administrative Justice Act 2000 (South Africa)

Provost, Claire, 'World Water Forum Declaration Falls Short on Human Rights, Claim Experts', *The Guardian* (14 March 2012)

Runciman, Carin, 'The Decline of the Anti-Privatisation Forum in the Midst of South Africa's "Rebellion of the Poor"' (2015) 63(7) *Current Sociology* 961

Saghaye-Biria, Hakimeh, 'Decolonizing the "Universal" Human Rights Regime: Questioning American Exceptionalism and Orientalism' (2018) 4(1) *ReOrient* 59

Sayyid, Bobby S., *A Fundamental Fear: Eurocentrism and the Emergence of Islamism* (Zed Books, 2003)

Singh, Randir, *Singh Supplementary Affidavit in Mazibuko & Others v City of Johannesburg & Others* (High Court of South Africa (Witwatersrand Local Division), 2007)

Sixth World Water Forum, *Ministerial Declaration* (13 March 2012) <http://6.worldwaterforum.org/fileadmin/user_upload/pdf/Ministerial_Declaration_Final_EN.pdf> (last accessed 27 March 2025)

Smets, Henri, 'Diluted View of Water as a Right' (2006) 36(2) *Environmental Policy and Law; Amsterdam* 88

Smith, Laila, 'Conflict versus Cooperation between the State and Civil Society: A Water- Demand Management Comparison between Cape Town and Johannesburg, South Africa' in Bernard Barraque (ed), *Urban Water Conflicts* (Routledge, 2011) 147

de Sousa Santos, Boaventura, 'Épistémologies du Sud', tr Magali Watteaux (2011) 187 *Études rurales* 21

Szabo, Andrea, 'The Value of Free Water – Analyzing South Africa's Free Basic Water Policy' (2015) 83(5) *Econometrica* 1913

Tissington, Kate et al, Water Service Fault Lines: An Assessment of South Africa's Water and Sanitation Provision across 15 Municipalities (Centre for Applied Legal Studies (CALS), Centre on House Rights and Evictions (COHRE), and Norwegian Centre for Human Rights (NCHR), 2008)

United Nations, 'General Assembly Adopts Resolution Recognizing Access to Clean Water, Sanitation as Human Right, by Recorded Vote of 122 in Favour, None against, 41 Abstentions (Meetings Coverage)', *United Natios Meetings Coverage and Press Releases* (28 July 2010) <https://www.un.org/press/en/2010/ga10967.doc.htm>

United Nations, *The Future We Want: Report of the United Nations Conference on Sustainable Development (Rio+20),* UN Doc A/CONF.216/L.1 (19 June 2012)

United Nations General Assembly (UNGA), *The Human Right to Water and Sanitation,* GA Res 68/157, UN Doc A/RES/68/157 (18 December 2013)

United Nations General Assembly (UNGA), *The Human Right to Water and Sanitation*, GA Res 70/169, UN Doc A/RES/70/169 (17 December 2015)

United Nations General Assembly (UNGA), *The Human Right to Water and Sanitation,* GA Res 64/292, UN Doc A/RES/64/292 (28 July 2010)

United NationsHuman Rights Council (HRC), *Human Rights and Access to Water*, 31st mtg, UN Doc A/HRC/Dec/2/104 (4 October 2006)

United Nations Human Rights Council (HRC), *Human Rights and Access to Safe Drinking Water and Sanitation,* HRC Res 15/9, UN Doc A/HRC/Res/15/9 (6 October 2010)

United Nations Human Rights Council (HRC), *Resolution on the Human Right to Safe Drinking Water and Sanitation*, 21st sess, Agenda Item 3, UN Doc A/HRC/21/L.1 (20 September 2012)

Van Hofwegen, Paul and Polioptro Martinez Austria (eds), *Synthesis of the Fourth World Water Forum* (World Water Council and the Secretariat of the 4th World Water Forum, 2006)

Water Services Act 1997 (South Africa)

World Bank, *Guide to Ring-Fencing of Local Government-Run Water Utilities* (World Bank, 2010)

6

THE FINANCIALISATION OF WATER

Introduction

The corporatisation of Johannesburg Water illustrates one mechanism through which water supply and sanitation (WSS) services can be subjected to neoliberal reforms regardless of whether they technically remain in public hands. Another similarly flexible mechanism for shaping water governance on private sector terms is financialisation – a process that also serves to transform water into a tradeable commodity and financial asset.[1]

This chapter examines the influence of financialisation on the legal geography of water governance and its role in producing new spatial configurations of power, access, and exclusion. Building on the analysis of neoliberal water reforms in earlier chapters, this chapter argues that financialisation is both a continuation and evolution of these processes, operating to transform water from a public service into an abstract financial asset while reconfiguring institutional power structures and community relationships with water. Through the case studies of Detroit and Flint, Michigan, the chapter demonstrates how financialised governance intersects with existing patterns of racial and economic inequality to produce new forms of spatial injustice. These cases highlight the scalar politics of water governance, as global and national financial imperatives override local democratic control through mechanisms like emergency management. Yet they also illustrate how water's material and relational properties conflict with neoliberal logic, producing new forms of resistance that prefigure alternative governance models. This analysis advances the book's central argument about the way that legal frameworks, social relations, and water's materiality and agency operate to co-constitute water governance, while highlighting how financialisation builds on and

DOI: 10.4324/9781003273219-6

intensifies the democratic deficits and ontological tensions examined in previous chapters.

The concept of financialisation has been critiqued for lacking a coherent definition, but there are consistent themes in its application. Kate Bayliss describes it as referring to 'the increasing importance of financial markets, financial motives, financial institutions, and financial elites in the operation of the economy and its governing institutions.'[2] While noting the conceptual slipperiness of the term, Alex Loftus and others identify two main features of financialisation – first, the growing power of new financial actors, and second, a shift in the locus of profit-making from the 'real economy' to the financial economy.[3] Under this process, the provision of actual infrastructure needs (or, indeed, WSS services) becomes secondary to extracting 'value from illiquid assets by turning them into liquid forms.'[4] This process supports speculative debt-driven investment underpinned by the absorption of risk by the public sector (much as we saw in the privatisation of Manila's WSS sector in Chapter 3).[5]

This chapter explores the financialisation of water and considers whether it is simply a continuation (or variation) of other forms of neoliberal water governance, bringing with it a similar commodification of water, or whether it can be better understood as a distinct shift in water governance with distinct effects on community relationships with water. Following this discussion, these somewhat abstract questions will be explored through the case studies of Detroit and Flint, Michigan, along with a brief foray into Dublin, Ireland – a discussion that will particularly focus on how financialisation affects communities and how communities respond, including by using the human right to water as a key framing device and rallying call.

Financialisation

While building on the neoliberal reforms examined in previous chapters, financialisation involves the intensification of many of its features, including abstraction and the tendency to create and entrench unjust spatial relations of power and access. As Bayliss notes in her 2014 analysis of the financialisation of water,

> [t]he delivery of water is becoming increasingly 'financialized' which is to say that the financial, economic, and institutional architecture on which service delivery is based has become skewed to support the interests of private financial capital. As private sector interests have gained momentum in the sector, increasingly complex water-related financial products have been created which are traded speculatively, creating wealth for a tiny minority.[6]

In a later paper, Bayliss turns her attention specifically to the situation in England and Wales, where (as we saw in Chapter 2) the WSS sector was privatised in 1989.[7] Here she notes that while the original ten companies that purchased the water utilities across England and Wales were listed on the London Stock Exchange, over time many were instead owned by unlisted financial equity investors.[8] An almost inevitable result of these changes has been the dramatic increase in water bills.[9] In 2013, John Allen and Michael Pryke argued this model 'has engineered benefits more towards investors than customers,'[10] with Thames Water's debt doubling while shareholder funds remained static, suggesting financial gains were extracted rather than reinvested in infrastructure.[11] Similarly, in 2017, Bayliss noted, '[a]verage household bills [for Thames Water customers] have increased by 40 percent in real terms since privatisation.'[12] Notably, over a quarter of average household bill was dedicated to covering 'return on capital,'[13] confirming Allen and Pryke's hypothesis that these high levels of debt financing have been used to increase financial returns for investors through special dividends rather than fund infrastructure.[14]

Despite the promise of private finance delivering increased access to water by helping to upgrade and expand cash-strapped public water systems, Bayliss notes that financialisation creates 'assets for the financial sector in rich countries while...failing to make a dent in the under-resourced infrastructure in developing countries'[15] or, indeed, in the under-resourced water infrastructure across the global north. Despite being used as a justification for private sector involvement, water scarcity in this context has ultimately been treated as a financial opportunity. As Bayliss argues, '[t]he reason that some finance companies are investing in water is not so much because it is a steady long-term investment as envisaged by OECD but rather because anticipated scarcity will put a price premium on water providers.'[16]

Transforming water into a financial asset

Similarly to the commodification process we saw under privatisation (and corporatisation), financialisation operates to transform water from a public service into a tradeable commodity, but it also appears to go one step further by transforming water (or, at least, household water bills) into an abstract financial asset, forcing 'households around the world [to become] engaged in the trickle-up of wealth to the richest through the consumption of water.'[17] According to this analysis, the financialisation of water goes further than privatisation by transforming water (or people's need for water) into a financial asset through increasingly complex instruments and ownership structures underpinned by speculative, debt-driven investment. Allen and Pryke argue that this model of financialised infrastructure transforms 'households themselves [into] the financial asset, a "human revenue stream."'[18]

Loftus and others situate financialisation within a broader historical trajectory of water infrastructure ownership and management, from early private provision to municipal ownership, nationalisation, privatisation, and current financialisation.[19] While acknowledging it as a continuation of past neoliberal water governance reforms, Loftus and others argue that financialisation represents a fundamental shift in how water infrastructure functions in society.[20] Under a financialised model, predicted household water bill payments are securitised, packaged, and sold to global investors through financial mechanisms.[21] Through this process, water infrastructure is being radically reconfigured into 'wealth extraction mechanisms'.[22] As a result, '[t]he private sector is now deeply involved in water delivery in numerous guises from service provision to investment finance in complex layers of global ownership and contractual relationships.'[23] As we have already seen, this has implications for social equity and for the democratic control of water governance.

This transformation of water into a financial asset fundamentally reshapes the legal landscape of water governance, producing new spatial configurations of power that operate across multiple scales. While previous chapters examined how privatisation and corporatisation commodified water through direct ownership and market mechanisms, financialisation introduces more abstract forms of control through complex financial instruments. This scalar shift enables distant financial actors to exercise power over local water resources while obscuring lines of accountability. The concept of 'bio-financialization'[24] helps illuminate how this process interacts with water's material properties and ecological dimensions. In relation to water, Patrick Bresnihan argues that this description focuses on 'the convergence of two dynamics that are rarely analyzed together in the literature: financialization and ecological modernization.'[25] Here, in addition to emphasising the transformation of water infrastructure into financial assets through new measurement and valuation techniques that make water systems legible to financial markets and investors, Bresnihan highlights the interconnected implementation of highly technical environmental metrics and monitoring systems that aim to demonstrate regulatory compliance and resource efficiency. His argument here is that it is this second ecological dimension that creates an imperative to modernise infrastructure and, thus, to access significant amounts of additional finance.[26] This also exposes the active role of the state in the financialisation process, in contrast to narratives of neoliberal governance that depict the state in retreat.

A feature of the literature on the financialisation of water is the emphasis on the complexity and sophistication of the financial instruments involved, including water-targeted investment funds, exchange-traded funds, and structured water products. Nadine Reis and others, for example, document the increasing importance of complex financial instruments that enable profit extraction without direct ownership.[27] This complexity, which is particularly prominent in the WSS sector, means that financialisation often operates via indirect mechanisms such as blended finance, securitisation, and even public debt (rather than only direct private investment).[28]

A key focus of Loftus, March, and Purcell's analysis of financialisation (and one that the authors expand on in a later paper) is the role of rent extraction, and the clarification that profits in financialised water utilities come from 'the capture of different forms of rent through the monopoly ownership of water infrastructure.'[29] In a subsequent paper, the same authors develop a 'value-rent-finance triad' to explain how financialisation operates through the extraction of rents and that financialisation must be understood through its internal relations with value and rent rather than as an independent process.[30] Purcell and others note that financialisation operates to extract 'absolute rents' as part of this process.[31] However, the focus here is on monopoly rents, 'according to which the owners of special and limited resources can charge a monopoly price formed "independently of the price of the product as determined by prices of production and value."'[32] While monopoly rents are often understood as relating to 'the unique qualities of land,' here they are enabled by the non-substitutable character of water.[33]

Allen and Pryke similarly note that the captive nature of household water customers, who cannot switch providers or opt out of payments, makes this revenue stream particularly attractive for investors.[34] As they put it, '[t]he ultimate clients – households – underwrite the profitability of the asset.'[35]

In terms of the specific steps involved, Purcell and others note that financialisation involves the commodification of infrastructure, the creation of revenue streams, the establishment (or transfer) of monopoly rights, and the extraction of rents from households and communities.[36] Here it is worth noting the role of the state in facilitating these steps, as it is regulatory frameworks that enable water companies to charge monopoly prices – extracting rent from households and communities with very little choice to opt out.[37]

Bayliss is also critical of the variety of ways that the state has enabled and supported private sector involvement in the WSS sector, despite the growing evidence of negative impacts on the community and sustainability, particularly as public resources are increasingly used to make water infrastructure attractive to private investors.[38] Bayliss argues that this privatisation of profits coupled with the socialisation of risks (and the associated losses) represents a 'rentiers' delight' where public investment generates private profit.[39]

Material resistance to financial abstraction

While financialisation attempts to transform water into an abstract financial asset, water's materiality continues to assert itself in ways that complicate and resist this process. As examined throughout this book, water's material characteristics – its essential role in sustaining life, fluidity, and physical embeddedness – fundamentally resist abstraction, whether through commodification or financialisation. As we will see in the case studies below, the Detroit water shutoffs and the dramatic health consequences from water contamination in Flint both demonstrate the way that attempts to treat water purely as a financial asset collide with its material necessity for human survival. This material (and biological) resistance to financialisation emerged through public health crises and community mobilisation around water as a fundamental human right. A further feature of this materiality is the physical embeddedness of water infrastructure in specific geographical contexts, which limits the mobility of capital, constraining financial abstraction. The Flint crisis illustrates this tension: while financial logic demanded cost-cutting measures, the material reality of corroding pipes ultimately undermined this abstract calculus.

Paradoxically, these material limitations can also drive further rounds of financialisation, as capital seeks what David Harvey calls the 'spatial fix' – new geographic areas for accumulation and profit-making.[40] As we will see, this helps explain the push for parallel infrastructure development seen in the Karegnondi Water Authority (KWA) project, where capital's need for expansion led to the construction of redundant infrastructure despite the existence of functioning systems.

Anti-democratic effects

These analyses expose how financialisation processes are attempting to transform water from a public good into an asset class and the various ways that this affects social equity, environmental sustainability, and people's relationships with water. Perhaps most significantly for this chapter, a particularly problematic feature of financialisation is the way it enables financial actors to gain increasing influence over water policy and governance both domestically and internationally, producing a democratic deficit in water governance.[41] Bayliss documents corporate interests dominating water policy through vehicles like the Water Resources Group.[42] Here she cautions,

> The international financial elite has bought its way into the heart of policy design and this has been facilitated by state organizations as well as international financial institutions... The development apparatus has become hijacked by the private sector agenda. The ethos of 'efficiency,' and the notion that this will emerge from the operations of the private sector, is deeply embedded in the policy mindset. State solutions are rejected and equity and social justice have slipped from the radar.[43]

Purcell and others emphasise that understanding financialisation requires examining how it restructures social relations and enables new forms of value extraction from communities.[44] As they argue in their earlier paper, '[i]n many instances financialisation favors a process of accumulation by dispossession in which ecologies are produced out of an increasingly risky, heavily leveraged, and fundamentally undemocratic financial model.'[45]

This political impact of financialisation is further explored by Allen and Pryke, noting that the financial aspects of this process have been effectively 'ring-fenced' politically and removed from public scrutiny and debate. They argue that this represents a 'postpolitical' condition in which any scrutiny or critique of financial engineering is rendered illegitimate and displaced by discussions of sustainability, efficiency, and consumer protection.[46] Like Bayliss,[47] Allen and Pryke note the reluctance of the UK water regulator, OFWAT, to scrutinise the financial arrangements of water companies, despite the evident impact of these arrangements on consumers.[48]

The broader, anti-democratic effects of financialisation (and its precursors) have also been examined in relation to city governance. For example, in the late 1980s, Harvey critiqued the impact of 'urban entrepreneurialism' – a style of governance characterised by inter-urban competition exerting an 'external coercive power over individual cities to bring them closer into line with the discipline and logic of capitalist development.'[49] Harvey notes the results of this shift have included increased financial instability, indebtedness, polarisation of wealth, and the impoverishment and disempowerment of an expanded urban underclass.[50] This financial instability and polarisation has only increased under financialisation and the related growth of the municipal bond market, leading to predictable financial crises and structural adjustment by financial means.[51] A further significant consequence of this process has been described as 'a drift towards postdemocratic technocratic management.'[52]

This trend has serious, wide-ranging implications for democracy, community well-being, and human rights, as well as specific implications for water governance, as we will see in our analysis below of how financialisation – accelerated by the 'Emergency Management' arrangements mandated for Michigan cities that experience financial distress – resulted in water crises in Detroit and Flint, Michigan. In both cities, the financialisation of urban water governance meant that decisions were determined almost exclusively through the lens of financial sustainability and efficiency. It also served to comprehensively alienate the community from the management of their water – and, in the case of Flint, from water itself – and to shrink the available avenues for challenging water management decisions despite their serious public health effects, including fatalities.

Emergency management uses a financial crisis to justify the differential application of democratic rights across urban space. This spatial distribution of democratic deficits maps directly onto existing geographies of racial capitalism, with predominantly Black cities like Detroit and Flint experiencing the wholesale suspension of local governance in contrast to the wealthier, whiter suburbs that surround them. These democratic deficits produced by financialisation reflect broader patterns in the spatial politics of water governance examined throughout this book. Just as previous chapters highlighted the way that neoliberal reforms concentrated control in technical experts and private corporations, financialisation further removes water governance from local democratic oversight through new scalar arrangements. The case studies that follow demonstrate how these abstract financial imperatives result in concrete spatial inequalities, particularly affecting marginalised communities whose relationships with water are already constrained by existing patterns of racial and economic discrimination.

Community response

Some have argued that financialisation is becoming the most significant transformation to water governance of our times. However, Reis and others argue that it remains limited, despite occurring across multiple water sectors and locations.[53] Although not explored by Reis and others, part of the picture of this partial implementation (detailed further below) is that the changes associated with the financialisation of water are often highly contested, and community resistance has operated to limit its scope.

Bayliss argues that financialisation has largely occurred by stealth, and the community is often unaware of it and its implications – in part due to the complexity of the financial instruments involved – and that this explains the limited community backlash. While it may be true that the community lacks a detailed understanding of the investment arrangements underpinning financialised systems, they do experience the flow-on effects such as high tariffs, water disconnections (as occurred – and are still occurring – in Detroit, Michigan), and the increasingly evident impacts of minimal infrastructure investment (leading, for example, to the sewerage contamination of rivers and streams across England and to the lead contamination of tap water in Flint, Michigan). As we will explore below, it is these direct impacts that are contested by communities.

A notable feature of the water crises in Detroit and Flint was the way the community responded through solidarity and mutual aid – a response that bears strikingly similarities to the community responses in Phiri and Orange Farm, South Africa, after the forced installation of prepaid water meters. These communities also shared a common focus of using both the language and legal power of the human right to water to support their struggles – again illustrating that the community's interpretation and strategic engagement with this right goes well beyond individual (market-friendly) rights to water to include community rights to manage (and, indeed, control) water resources for the common good.

As we will examine below, the water justice movements in Detroit and Flint (and Dublin) engaged with multiple scales of governance, strategically leveraging different political spaces to advance their claims. In Detroit, activists moved between local direct action (blocking water shutoffs), national litigation (bankruptcy proceedings), and international advocacy (UN Special Rapporteurs), reflecting how resistance necessarily operates across multiple scales to match financialisation's own scalar mobility. Similarly, Flint residents combined local mutual aid and protest with state-level accountability demands and litigation. Finally, as we will explore, a Detroit-Dublin solidarity network further illustrates how communities are developing transnational resistance networks to match global financial flows. This multi-scalar approach seems to reflect a growing understanding of how financialised governance operates through nested scales of power, requiring correspondingly layered resistance strategies. It is to these case studies that we will now turn our attention.

The water crises in Flint and Detroit

The water crises in Detroit and Flint illustrate the material consequences of allowing financial imperatives to override both democratic governance and water's essential role in sustaining life and community. They also demonstrate how this financialisation process conflicts not only with water's materiality but also with community conceptions of water and its relational values.

When residents in Flint, Michigan, turned on their taps in April 2014, the water that came out smelt foul and had changed colour. For some, it was brown; others reported shades of beige, green, and yellow.[54] In the same month, in the nearby state capital of Detroit, tens of thousands of households had their water supply disconnected for non-payment.[55] These interconnected water crises were both the result of financialisation, which operated to entrench and further exacerbate existing structural, racialised discrimination and disadvantage and to largely extinguish democratic rights. As we will explore below, communities in both cities responded to these impacts by campaigning for the human right to water, despite its apparent track record of legitimising neoliberal water governance. They also supported each other through mutual aid and engaged in direct action and sustained community resistance.

Background to the crises

Like much of the US and, indeed, the world,[56] the cities of Flint and Detroit, Michigan, have deep pockets of poverty and disadvantage. Between 31 and 41 percent of the population of both cities live below the poverty line, and, relatedly, 57–78 percent are Black.[57] This economic polarisation and spatial inequality are both racialised and systemic and have historical roots in US policy, including colonisation, slavery, lynchings, criminalisation, and segregation.

A central pillar of segregation was the discriminatory housing policies given force through a combination of state-sanctioned private power (including racist private restrictive covenants and significant racial disparities in rental and sales prices) and the effects of the *Home Owners' Loan Act of 1933*.[58] The *Home Owners' Loan Act* provided heavily subsidised federal housing loans to households purchasing houses in neighbourhoods with certain ratings, which were coded on detailed maps. 'D rated' neighbourhoods were coded red due to their poor rating and ineligibility for the loans – the origin of the term 'redlining.'[59] A core criterion for a D rating was the presence of non-white households.[60]

These discriminatory housing (and related educational) policies had 'cumulative and compounding effects' by seriously limiting opportunities for investment, security, and career choice.[61] The net result was to consolidate White wealth and privilege through 'state-subsidized housing equity, which in turn translated into larger inheritances and better educational opportunities for the next generation.'[62] Despite the passage of formal equality laws over time, they have regularly failed to deliver substantive equality,[63] and the long-term implications of this history of structural discrimination continue to reverberate today, resulting in ongoing spatial segregation and racialised injustice.

By the 1960s, frustration with this entrenched injustice spilt over into race rebellions that erupted across US cities.[64] They arrived in Detroit and Flint in July 1967 with participants sharing similar motivations to those across the country: deep frustration with entrenched structural inequality compounded by the Johnson administration's 'war on crime' that had resulted in a new wave of the over-policing, criminalisation, and mass incarceration of Black communities.[65] As Heather Ann Thompson argues in relation to Detroit, '[i]t happened because access to everything from good housing stock to strong schools remained elusive for black Detroiters while, for white city residents, such access was a given.'[66] Detroit's rebellion and the police response played out in the streets over five nights, leaving an estimated 43 people dead and 696 wounded.[67]

'White flight' from the city to the suburbs was the next wave that deepened segregation and poverty in both cities. In just four decades, from 1970, the populations (and tax base) of both cities more than halved (shrinking from 1,514,063 to 713,777 in Detroit and from more than 200,000 to below 100,000 in Flint).[68] Discriminatory housing policies and poverty trapped Black people in the cities, even as de-industrialisation reduced the employment and economic opportunities historically provided by the automobile industry. The cities themselves were further stripped of finances through new policies that led to dramatic reductions in state revenue sharing.[69] By November 2011, the City of Flint had declared a State of Financial Emergency, leading Michigan Governor Snyder to appoint an Emergency Manager.[70] Detroit's Emergency Manager was appointed in March 2013, and on 18 July, with an estimated debt of USD20 billion, the City of Detroit filed for Chapter 9 bankruptcy.[71]

Michigan's emergency manager laws have been described as 'the nation's strictest' and as a mechanism for installing 'preemptive, unitary, and close-to unilateral forms of financial control, overriding the powers of elected officials and circumventing local democratic channels.'[72] Under Emergency Management, community well-being, including basic health and safety, effectively ceased to be a priority, and local democratic rights of participation and procedural justice were suspended.[73] Jamie Peck and Heather Whiteside liken emergency management measures to the 'structural-adjustment approaches pioneered by multilateral lending institutions like the World Bank, not least in their apparently wilful contempt for local democracy.'[74] A further similarity is the imposition of 'dramatic austerity measures' and the racial disparities in their impacts.[75] Just as we saw in South Africa, it was these austerity measures that had the most significant impact on water services in both cities.

Interlinked water crises

In April 2014, the City of Detroit began disconnecting the water supply of tens of thousands of households who were behind on their bills.[76] Simultaneously, tap water in Flint became toxic.[77] These separate water crises were linked by more than history and Emergency Management. Until April 2014, both cities (and their surrounding counties) drew water from Lake Huron, which was then treated by the Detroit Water and Sewerage Department (DWSD). In early 2013, Flint's emergency manager decided to sign the City up for the KWA, a new private water venture planning to construct a brand-new pipeline that would run parallel to DWSD's existing pipeline and transport untreated Lake Huron water into Genesee County.[78] In response, 'DWSD notified [Flint] of the termination of its then-current water supply contract terms, effective April 2014.'[79]

Demand for this project had originated in the county's (largely White) suburbs and the business and agricultural sectors. It was unclear what value it offered to Flint residents, who were now shouldering a new debt despite their existing financial woes and also placed in the position of needing to find a new water supply for the two-year construction period scheduled for the new pipeline.[80]

Before 1967, Flint had operated its own water service, drawing water from the now-heavily polluted Flint River. The Flint water treatment plant was still standing and had been used for emergency backup purposes over the years.[81] In preparation for the switch, scoping work was carried out to determine the upgrade works that would be necessary to enable the treatment plant to make Flint River water safe for community consumption. The cost was estimated to be USD61 million.[82] In the end, the City spent just USD8 million on upgrades before the switch.[83] It also followed (incorrect) advice from the Michigan Department of Environmental Quality (MDEQ) not to immediately include corrosion control in the new water treatment regime, instead choosing to wait for the results of two six-month monitoring periods.[84]

With the loss of Genesee County's contract and USD22 million in revenue, DWSD was placed under financial strain and pressure to extract more revenue from its remaining customer base, leading directly to tariff increases and mass disconnections for non-payment.[85]

Material and social effects

The communities of Detroit and Flint were affected in multiple ways by these water crises. In Detroit, the households whose water service was terminated for nonpayment were forced to go without water until they could afford to reconnect to the system. Without water, you cannot flush a toilet, wash yourself, cook food, or drink. The health implications can be swift and serious. Researchers found that 'residents who lived on blocks that had experienced water shutoffs were 60% more likely to have experienced water-associated illness than those that lived on blocks with no shutoffs.'[86] There was an added element for households with children, with the absence of running water being considered 'as grounds to remove children from the home' by the Michigan Department of Child Protective Services.[87] Finally, water arrears are added to the property tax bill, and property tax arrears lead to foreclosure – meaning that households risk losing their homes. In the year following the water shutoffs, 'in March 2015, the county sent tax foreclosure notices to 62,000 households in Detroit,' and at least 18,000 of these were still occupied. [88]

In a public relations move to soften its image and reduce community resistance, the City of Detroit introduced payment plans as a 'social affordability measure' to enable households to remain connected to the system.[89] The problem was, just as we saw in South Africa, unaffordable tariffs do not become magically more affordable when a poor household is given more time to pay.[90] Instead, under the best-case scenario, these financial disciplinary measures simply trap households in increasing debt.[91] A more common scenario is that they also operate to slightly delay disconnection – by April 2015, 'fewer than 300 households, less than 2%, had actually managed to remain on the payment plans.'[92]

Instead of having their water disconnected (although that happened too), Flint residents had their water poisoned and then had their concerns dismissed. Despite immediate, widespread complaints from residents about the appearance, smell, and taste, the City's first response was to deny there were any issues with Flint water.[93] Fairly soon, residents began experiencing painful skin rashes, respiratory problems, and hair loss.[94] In time, the evidence mounted that Flint tap water was causing acute and long-term health impacts – lead poisoning and a deadly outbreak of Legionnaires' disease – but even then officials dismissed test results and refused to acknowledge the seriousness of the situation or to address it.[95]

This situation continued until 16 October 2015, when Flint finally switched back to DWSD water.[96] By this time, long-term damage had been done to the city's water pipes, the community's health, the brain development of Flint's children, and the relationship between the community and government – and with water.[97] During this 18-month period, government officials repeatedly dismissed community concerns and even worked to discredit or bury alarming test results.[98] Two emergency managers responded to community concerns and mounting evidence of serious water quality issues by concluding that 'switching back to DWSD would be too costly.'[99] Understandably, these actions seriously eroded community trust in both government and their water.

The Flint water crisis did not, however, end with the switch back to DWSD. In early 2017, the City issued 8,000 disconnection notices to residents who were behind on their water bills – and residents believed these were tied to plans to evict them from their homes to make way for developers.[100] Residents were particularly outraged because their water was still not safe to drink. The lead water service lines that provided the City's water had been so badly damaged by the poorly treated Flint River water that they continued to leach into household water even after the switch back to DWSD.[101] To compound the situation, there were no reliable records of which pipes were lead and which were the newer copper variety.[102] In 2016, the City commenced a long, costly operation to dig up and check every water service pipe in Flint and replace all of the lead and galvanised steel pipes.[103] This process was not fully completed even by March 2023, in contempt of an earlier (very generous) court-ordered deadline.[104] When the City announced in 2019 that it had largely completed the project and that there were a raft of positive water test results, many residents were still unwilling to drink their tap water.[105] They had been lied to too many times.

Community resistance

In both Detroit and Flint, the community responded by organising and engaging in everything from protest to direct action, mutual aid, litigation, and appeals to the Special Procedures of the UN Human Rights Council (HRC) – often explicitly employing the language of the human right to water. This focus on the human right to water has been a strong theme running through campaign slogans and mission statements in both Detroit and Flint, with activists frequently foregrounding the right in their street protests, media, and political communications.[106] While it is true that the institutional articulation of human rights standards has been largely reform oriented, failing to fundamentally challenge the financialisation of water or to champion community control over water governance (as discussed below and in earlier chapters), the same cannot be said for the community's interpretation of rights. As with the Mazibuko case (discussed in Chapter 5), construing the community's legal, rights-based strategies as a capitulation to a (neo)liberal individualist and state-centric interpretation of the human right to water – or to the consumer relationship to a commodified water that is implied under this model – would be to ignore their context.[107] Not only were these strategic actions of last resort, but they also took place against a backdrop of ongoing community building, radical direct action, and the articulation of a highly relational understanding of water (and rights).[108]

The Detroit community responded to the disconnections through an (ultimately unsuccessful) adversary complaint in the Detroit bankruptcy proceedings, seeking a stay on the cutoffs and a declaration that the City had breached their rights to both due process and equal protection.[109] Despite the historically hostile approach of the US to socioeconomic rights, the litigants emphasised the human right to water in their complaint.

Detroit civil society organisations also engaged the Special Procedures of the HRC by inviting the UN Special Rapporteurs on the human right to water and the right to adequate housing to visit Detroit, to meet with households affected by the water disconnections, and to examine the impacts on their human rights to water, sanitation, and housing according to international standards.[110] In their joint statement following the visit, the Special Rapporteurs noted the unaffordability of Detroit's high water tariffs for many households, noting that over 40 percent live below the poverty line and that 20 percent live on '800 USD or less per month, while the average monthly water bill is currently 70.67 USD.'[111] In keeping with their mandates, the Special Rapporteurs emphasised the impact of water disconnections on 'the rights to adequate housing, life, health, adequate food, integrity of the family,' in addition to the way disconnections exacerbate inequalities, stigmatise people, and threaten public health.[112] In relation to these unequal effects, they also highlighted the racialised impacts of the disconnections, with 99 percent of Detroit's poor being African American.[113]

The Special Rapporteurs made pragmatic suggestions for addressing these issues, including restoring water services to 'residents unable to pay and vulnerable groups of people,' the adoption of an effective Water Affordability Plan, the provision of financial assistance and 'a specially low tariff or subsidies' to those in need, an investigation into the discriminatory impact of disconnections, and the guarantee of due process and access to justice for households facing disconnection.[114] However, these recommendations did not address the underlying financial drivers behind Detroit's financial woes or its decision to impose mass disconnections, nor did they emphasise community control over water governance. The technical application of human rights standards appeared to render these financial and governance arrangements beyond the scope of legitimate inquiry.

The community's application of the human right to water was notably more radical. Shortly after the water shutoffs started in Detroit, several activists, including Danny McGlashing (founder of Occupy Sandy) and Justin Wedes (founder of the Paul Robeson Freedom School), formed the Detroit Water Brigade (DWB).[115] Since being founded, the DWB and other organisations, like the People's Water Board (PWB), have engaged in direct action by coordinating physical blockades of city disconnections and the provision of water to disconnected households.[116] Their broader agenda is to fight for water justice, including affordability and community control.[117] In emphasising community control over water, these organisations not only oppose private sector involvement but also seek to challenge the control of the neoliberal state through plans to build self-sufficiency (rainwater) systems.[118]

Members of the DWB and the PWB express a highly relational understanding of the human right to water – one that prioritises and nurtures community relations of solidarity and human relationships with water.[119] The 2018 PWB mission statement, for example, read,

> Water is life. The People's Water Board advocates for access, protection, and conservation of water. We believe water is a human right and all people should have access to clean and affordable water. Water is a commons that should be held in the public trust free of privatisation. The People's Water Board promotes awareness of the interconnectedness of all people and resources.[120]

While the human relationship with water was fundamentally damaged in Flint due to industrial contamination of the Flint River and the poisoning of the city's tap water, solidarity also remained at the forefront of the community's response to the crisis. The community organised and mobilised, primarily through Facebook groups,[121] to both fight for change and to support each other – running help centres and community water drops, gathering to protest in town hall meetings and on the streets, and lobbying local politicians.[122] Outsiders were also moved to solidarity, with a small group of 'Water Protectors' coming to Flint in April 2017, many directly from the protest camp at Standing Rock (where they had been fighting to stop the proposed construction of an oil pipeline partly crossing under Lake Oahe, near the Standing Rock Reservation in North Dakota)[123] to establish 'Camp Promise' in the run-down Kearsley Park near downtown Flint.[124] Their goal was to raise outside awareness of the ongoing crisis in Flint (in 2017 many of Flint's pipes were still corroded and leaching lead into the water)[125] and to provide support to the community.[126]

Having lost faith in the state, the community turned to each other while also seeking to hold the state to account. In Flint, there have been multiple class actions to force the State of Michigan to pay for a lead pipe replacement program and for the provision of bottled water to residents, in addition to substantial compensation payments.[127] There have also been criminal charges, but ultimately most were dropped.[128] Perhaps the most significant accountability mechanisms in Flint have been the inquiries and reports of the Flint Water Advisory Task Force and the Michigan Civil Rights Commission.[129]

The Final Report of the Task Force (provided to the Governor in 2016) was significant for setting the record straight and clearly assigning accountability to the organisations and individuals responsible for the Flint water crisis. The Task Force pulled no punches, describing the crisis as 'a story of government failure, intransigence, unpreparedness, delay, inaction, and environmental injustice.'[130] While it assigned particular blame to the MDEQ for failing to effectively enforce drinking water regulations, it identified serious failures across the board, including by the Michigan Department of Health and Human Services (MDHHS), the Flint Water Department, the United States Environmental Protection Agency (EPA), the Governor and the Governor's office, and the city's Emergency Managers.[131] In its cover letter to the Governor, the Task Force concluded, '[t]he causes of the crisis lie primarily at the feet of the state by virtue of its agencies' failures and its appointed emergency managers' misjudgements.'[132]

The Michigan Civil Rights Commission adopted a slightly different approach, choosing not to replicate existing investigations into 'the decisions made and actions taken' between 2013 and 2016.[133] Instead, the Commission focused on unpacking 'the role decades of structural and institutional discrimination and racism played in quieting [the]… voices [of the Flint community] and enabling the poisoning of [its] public water supply.'[134] Through this approach, the Commission was able to critically analyse the role of 'structural and systemic discrimination and racism'[135] and to clearly articulate the crisis as an issue of environmental racism.

Importantly, both reports explicitly critiqued the role of Emergency Management in causing and exacerbating the crisis. Rather than placing these financial issues outside the lens of legitimate political debate, these enquiries attempted to bring them front and centre. The Task Force, for example, emphasised,

> The Flint water crisis occurred when state-appointed emergency managers replaced local representative decision-making in Flint, removing the checks and balances and public accountability that come with public decision-making. Emergency managers made key decisions that contributed to the crisis, from the use of the Flint River to delays in reconnecting to DWSD once water quality problems were encountered. Given the demographics of Flint, the implications for environmental injustice cannot be ignored or dismissed.[136]

Despite this, the Task Force's recommendations were more reform oriented than radical, including a review of 'Michigan's Emergency Manager Law (PA 436) and its implementation, and identify measures to compensate for the loss of the checks and balances that are provided by representative government.'[137] It then proposed a number of such checks and balances, including,

> a structured way to engage locally elected officials on key decisions; an Ombudsman function in state government to ensure that local concerns are a factor in decisions made by the emergency manager; and/or a means of appealing emergency manager decisions to another body,[138]

in addition to ensuring that the '[d]ecisions on matters potentially affecting public health and safety, for example, should be informed by subject matter experts identified and/or provided by the state.'[139]

The recommendations of the Michigan Civil Rights Commission go a little further. In addition to recommending the amendment of 'the emergency manager law to provide for local representation and the ability to appeal an adverse decision,' the Commission recommends replacing or restructuring the law altogether.[140] Nonetheless, although the detailed recommendations to focus on the underlying causes of any 'fiscal emergency' and ensuring accountability for emergency managers would be an improvement, even these recommendations still appear to accept the premise of emergency management itself and the logic of financialisation that underpins it.

Finally, it is worth noting that the Task Force made special mention of the crucial role of the community in responding to the crisis and ensuring that something was (eventually) done to properly address it, noting,

> the critical role played by engaged Flint citizens, by individuals both inside and outside of government who had the expertise and willingness to question and challenge government leadership, and by members of a free press who used the tools that enable investigative journalism.[141]

Global solidarity – from Detroit to Dublin

As discussed in Chapter 5, the 'ground-up' conception of the human right to water developed through water justice campaigns (in places like Johannesburg, Flint, and Detroit) has also developed through global networks of solidarity. In December 2014, for example, activists from the DWB flew to Dublin, Ireland, to support the Irish Right2Water campaign in its 'water charges' protests against the ongoing imposition of neoliberal water governance reforms,[142] including the introduction of water charges (which had previously been funded through general taxation), the installation of household water meters, and the corporatisation of Irish Water ('reforms' that were widely understood to be preparations for privatisation).[143] In addition to providing solidarity, their goal was to share lessons learned in Detroit about the risks of these kinds of reforms and the damage they can do to community well-being and human rights.[144]

The early seeds of this Irish Right2Water campaign also highlight another theme that can be observed running through these water justice campaigns – the distinctive significance of water in activating community resistance to broad-reaching neoliberal austerity policies. Similarly to Flint, much of this Irish movement was self-organised by community members using Facebook groups.[145] As Dave Gibney, a union organiser working on the Right2Water campaign, reported,

> no one would ever have expected in Ireland that street meetings would work. It was October – it's raining all the time, you know? But it was hard-pressed, working-class communities organising in kind of a low entry way for people to come to a meeting. [...W]e didn't really appreciate just how naturally people would organise – They'd set up a Facebook group first, then they'd have a street meeting, and they'd keep the Facebook group going, and they'd have more street meetings. And this flowered across the country.[146]

This wave of self-organised political mobilisation was unexpected because the Irish people had previously appeared to simply accept the inevitability of the harsh austerity policies being imposed in the wake of the 2008 financial crisis – even if they did not believe they were just.[147] Paul Murphy, a Teachta Dála (member of the lower house of the Irish legislature) for the far-left Solidarity party, reported that, early in 2014, he had the impression that there was 'a general mood in society of relatively deep powerlessness – a sense that there is nothing that we can do.'[148] But, under the surface, anger was accumulating over the impact of austerity measures and evidence that the wealthy were continuing to prosper.[149] Murphy believes the water charges were a catalyst for popular mobilisation both 'because of the issue in and of itself – people know that you need water to live' and because they were the final straw that released a wave of accumulated resentment.[150] Bresnihan described this emerging Right2Water movement as 'by far the largest and most significant mobilization of people since the economic crisis of 2008 and the austerity policies implemented after 2010.'[151] This was reflected in the results of a 2015 survey in which 54.4 percent of respondents involved in the Right2Water campaign reported having never participated in a previous protest movement.[152]

The Irish Right2Water campaign demonstrated interesting parallels with water justice movements in Flint, Detroit, and Johannesburg, particularly in how it catalysed broader resistance to neoliberal governance and austerity – and demands to deepen democracy across the board. Like these other movements, the Irish campaign was fundamentally grassroots-driven, with working-class communities playing a foundational role in organising resistance through street protests. This reflected a pattern seen across these movements, where water commodification sparked community solidarity and political mobilisation that extends well beyond water issues. In mid-October 2014, over 100,000 people took to Dublin's streets in a water charges protest. This was followed by around 100 protests across Ireland and a wave of water charge boycotts by households who refused to register or to pay the new tariffs.[153]

The community response resulted in almost immediate practical wins, with the government announcing in November that it would cap water charges and provide an environmental consideration grant of €100 per year.[154] The opposition also managed to pass a motion that prevented Irish Water from being privatised without a plebiscite.[155] These concessions mirror similar, if more limited, policy reforms won by water justice movements in Michigan and South Africa.

The public response to the water charges in Ireland had flow-on effects in Irish politics. In October 2014 (as the first significant wave of protests was marching through Dublin), Murphy had an unprecedented win in a by-election in his home area of South-West Dublin as a far-left candidate. He believed 'the two things were absolutely connected.'[156] Following this, an unprecedented number of Independents were elected in the 2016 Irish General Election, resulting in the three main parties (Fianna Fáil, Fine Gael, and Labour) holding the lowest share of TDs in the new Dáil they had ever had – upsetting the longstanding 'stranglehold' these main parties traditionally held.[157] In the aftermath, many ascribed this dramatic shift in Irish politics to the water charges protests and the political awakening they had created.[158] It is worth noting that this link is disputed, with only 8 percent of voters citing 'water charges as the most important issue influencing their choice of first preference candidates' in exit polls – 'even amongst those voting for parties and candidates active in the anti-water charges campaign.'[159] Nonetheless, the election resulted in an immediate suspension of the water charges,[160] and they were ultimately abolished in 2017 – with refunds being issued to those households who had already paid since charges were introduced.[161]

In addition to these tangible outcomes, there is evidence that the Irish Right2Water campaign played a key role in political consciousness-raising and community empowerment, with community members who became involved in the campaign reporting feeling newly empowered to demand broader economic justice and democratic reform.[162] Laurence Cox also argues that this mass political mobilisation was experienced as emancipatory by working-class communities who became aware of their collective political agency through the campaign.[163] This transformative effect on political engagement echoes experiences in Michigan and Johannesburg, where water activism similarly led communities to develop more radical critiques of existing power structures and governance models. In each case, the tangible, daily impact of water commodification served to activate deeper community resistance to financialised governance and demands for democratic control. This trajectory demonstrates how water justice campaigns can serve as powerful vehicles for broader resistance to neoliberal reforms – a pattern seen across all these case studies where struggles over water became focal points for challenging the democratic deficits created by both financialisation and austerity.

Discussion

The water crises examined in this chapter share striking continuities with previous struggles while highlighting new dimensions of contestation under financialisation. As in earlier chapters, spatial justice remains central, and we can observe that financialised governance both reproduces and intensifies historical patterns of racial and economic segregation. The targeting of Detroit's predominantly Black neighbourhoods for water shutoffs and Flint's subordination to emergency management echo the spatial inequality produced through prepaid meters in South African townships.

The spatial politics of financialisation in Michigan operated through multiple, interconnected mechanisms. Emergency management created differentiated zones of democratic rights, while water shutoffs and infrastructure decisions produced new geographies of access and exclusion. These spatial arrangements overlaid historical patterns of racial segregation while introducing new forms of regulatory control through cost recovery mechanisms. The KWA pipeline project (with its focus on providing water for agricultural and suburban customers at the expense of Flint residents) exemplifies how financialisation drives infrastructure development that reinforces rather than remedies spatial inequality. This layering of financial and racial discrimination demonstrates once again how seemingly technical decisions about bonds and water infrastructure actively produce and legitimate spatial injustice.

The place-based, relational understanding of water reflected in the response of communities in Flint, Detroit, and Dublin also remains a powerful counter-narrative to financialisation's attempts at abstraction. Just as Phiri residents challenged the commodification of their water relationships through prepaid meters, Detroit and Flint residents insisted on water's fundamental role in sustaining life and community. The PWB's emphasis on water as a interconnected commons directly contradicts financialisation's attempts to reduce water to a financial asset.

The democratic deficits produced by financialisation mirror patterns seen in previous chapters, where technical expertise and private contracts excluded community participation. However, emergency management represents an intensification of this anti-democratic tendency, using financial crisis as a narrative to justify the wholesale suspension of local democracy. This evolution demonstrates that financialisation can operate as an even more extreme form of the democratic constraints seen under privatisation and corporatisation. Paradoxically, this intensification of democratic deficits created new openings for resistance.

Within this resistance, activists navigated the contradictions of rights-based approaches in a sophisticated manner, reminiscent of the approaches seen in South Africa by the Anti-Privatisation Forum and others. In this approach, rights are employed as tactical tools alongside (and in service of) the broader pursuit of broader transformative agendas centred on democratic control and counter-hegemonic water relationships. When embedded within broader struggles for democratic control and economic justice, the human right to water can support radical transformative demands well beyond the reforms offered within a liberal rights framework.

Alongside their use of human rights discourse, community responses in Detroit, Flint, and Dublin also used mutual aid networks, direct action, and the promotion of alternative governance models to perform and enact new spatial-legal relationships grounded in solidarity rather than financial abstraction. The DWB's combination of practical support and political mobilisation exemplifies how prefigurative politics can challenge both the material effects of financialisation and its anti-democratic logic.

Finally, these movements illustrate how water's essential nature – as a source of life, identity, and community – makes it a powerful frontier for resistance to accumulation by dispossession. The visceral public response to water commodification has proven particularly effective at mobilising broader opposition to austerity and neoliberal governance, as seen in Ireland, where water charges became the catalyst for the country's largest post-2008 social movement. The persistence of relational water ontologies in these struggles challenges assumptions about both neoliberalism and modernism's totalising effects – a theme that will be further developed in the following chapter's examination of living water.

Notes

1. Kate Bayliss, 'The Financialization of Water' (2014) 46(3) *Review of Radical Political Economics* 292, 305.
2. Bayliss, 'The Financialization of Water' 293.
3. Alex Loftus, Hug March and Thomas F. Purcell, 'The Political Economy of Water Infrastructure: An Introduction to Financialization' (2019) 6(1) *WIREs Water* e1326, 2.
4. Loftus, March and Purcell, 'The Political Economy of Water Infrastructure' 1–2.
5. David Harvey, 'From Managerialism to Entrepreneuralism: The Transformation in Urban Governance in Late Capitalism' (1989) 71(1) *Geografiska Annaler B* 3, 10–12.
6. Bayliss, 'The Financialization of Water' (n 1) 293.
7. Kate Bayliss, 'Material Cultures of Water Financialisation in England and Wales' (2017) 22(4) *New Political Economy* 383.
8. Bayliss, 'Material Cultures of Water Financialisation in England and Wales' n (7) 383.
9. Bayliss, 'Material Cultures of Water Financialisation in England and Wales' n (7) 388.
10. John Allen and Michael Pryke, 'Financialising Household Water: Thames Water, MEIF, and "Ring-Fenced" Politics' (2013) 6 *Cambridge Journal of Regions, Economy and Society* 419, 419.

11 Allen and Pryke, 'Financialising Household Water' (n 10) 431–432.
12 Bayliss, 'Material Cultures of Water Financialisation in England and Wales' (n 7) 388.
13 Bayliss, 'Material Cultures of Water Financialisation in England and Wales' (n 7) 388.
14 Bayliss, 'Material Cultures of Water Financialisation in England and Wales' n (7) 387–388.
15 Bayliss, 'The Financialization of Water' (n 1) 300.
16 Bayliss, 'The Financialization of Water' (n 1) 301; citing OECD, *Innovative Financing Mechanisms for the Water Sector: Working Party on Global and Structural Policies* (Organisation for Economic Co-operation and Development, 2010).
17 Bayliss, 'The Financialization of Water' (n 1) 305.
18 Allen and Pryke, 'Financialising Household Water' (n 10) 419.
19 Loftus, March and Purcell, 'The Political Economy of Water Infrastructure' (n 3) 2–4.
20 Loftus, March and Purcell, 'The Political Economy of Water Infrastructure' (n 3).
21 Allen and Pryke, 'Financialising Household Water' (n 10).
22 Loftus, March and Purcell, 'The Political Economy of Water Infrastructure' (n 3) 1.
23 Bayliss, 'The Financialization of Water' (n 1) 293.
24 Patrick Bresnihan, 'The Bio-Financialization of Irish Water: New Advances in the Neoliberalization of Vital Services' (2016) 40 *Utilities Policy* 115; Paul Langley, 'The Financialization of Life' in Philip Mader, Daniel Mertens, and Natascha van der Zwan (eds), *The Routledge International Handbook of Financialization* (Routledge, Taylor & Francis Group, 2020) 68.
25 Bresnihan, 'The Bio-Financialization of Irish Water' (n 24) 116.
26 Bresnihan, 'The Bio-Financialization of Irish Water' (n 24) 122.
27 Nadine Reis, Germán Vargas Magaña and Santiago Vélez Villegas, 'Water, Finance and Financialisation: A Review' (2024) 17(2) *Water Alternatives* 266, 284.
28 Reis, Vargas Magaña and Vélez Villegas, 'Water, Finance and Financialisation' (n 27).
29 Loftus, March and Purcell, 'The Political Economy of Water Infrastructure' (n 3) 5.
30 Thomas F. Purcell, Alex Loftus and Hug March, 'Value–Rent–Finance' (2020) 44(3) *Progress in Human Geography* 437, 437–438.
31 Purcell, Loftus and March, 'Value–Rent–Finance' (n 30) 437.
32 Purcell, Loftus and March, 'Value–Rent–Finance' (n 30) 441; citing Karl Marx, *Capital, Volume III* (Penguin, 1991) 910.
33 Purcell, Loftus and March, 'Value–Rent–Finance' (n 30) 441.
34 Allen and Pryke, 'Financialising Household Water' (n 10).
35 Purcell, Loftus and March, 'Value–Rent–Finance' (n 30) 448.
36 Purcell, Loftus and March, 'Value–Rent–Finance' (n 30) 443–444.
37 Purcell, Loftus and March, 'Value–Rent–Finance' (n 30) 447–449.
38 Bayliss, 'The Financialization of Water' (n 1) 297.
39 Bayliss, 'The Financialization of Water' (n 1).
40 David Harvey, 'Globalization and the "Spatial Fix"' (2008) 3(2) *Geographische Revue: Zeitschrift für Literatur und Diskussion* 23.
41 Bayliss, 'The Financialization of Water' (n 1) 305.
42 Bayliss, 'The Financialization of Water' (n 1) 303.
43 Bayliss, 'The Financialization of Water' (n 1) 305.
44 Purcell, Loftus and March, 'Value–Rent–Finance' (n 30).
45 Loftus, March and Purcell, 'The Political Economy of Water Infrastructure' (n 3) 6.
46 Allen and Pryke, 'Financialising Household Water' (n 10) 432–436.
47 Bayliss, 'Material Cultures of Water Financialisation in England and Wales' (n 7) 390–391.
48 Allen and Pryke, 'Financialising Household Water' (n 10) 433.
49 Harvey, 'From Managerialism to Entrepreneuralism' (n 5) 10–12.
50 Harvey, 'From Managerialism to Entrepreneuralism' (n 5) 12.

51 Jamie Peck and Heather Whiteside, 'Financializing Detroit' (2015) 92(3) *Economic Geography* 235, 238.
52 Peck and Whiteside, 'Financializing Detroit' (n 51).
53 Reis, Vargas Magaña and Vélez Villegas, 'Water, Finance and Financialisation' (n 27).
54 Josh Sanburn, 'The Poisoning of an American City [First Published as 'The Toxic Tap']', *Time Magazine* (21 February 2016) <https://time.com/4188328/the-poisoning-of-an-american-city/>.
55 Sharmila L. Murthy, 'A New Constitutive Commitment to Water' (2016) 36(2) *Boston College Journal of Law and Social Justice* 159, 220–224.
56 United Nations Human Settlements Programme (UN-Habitat), *World Cities Report: Urbanization and Development - Emerging Futures* (UN-Habitat, 2016) 262, 69–84 <https://unhabitat.org/world-cities-report-2016>.
57 Matthew M. Davis et al, *Final Report* (Flint Water Advisory Task Force, 21 March 2016) 15 <https://flintwaterstudy.org/2016/03/flint-water-advisory-task-force-final-report/>; United States Census Bureau, 'Quick Facts - Detroit, Michigan' (1 April 2020) <https://www.census.gov/quickfacts/fact/table/detroitcitymichigan,US/POP010220>; UN-Habitat, *World Cities Report* (n 56).
58 Michigan Civil Rights Commission, *The Flint Water Crisis: Systematic Racism Through the Lens of Flint* (Michigan Civil Rights Commission, 17 February 2017) 30–40 <http://www.michigan.gov/documents/mdcr/VFlintCrisisRep-F-Edited3-13-17_554317_7.pdf>; Prottoy A. Akbar et al, *Racial Segregation in Housing Markets and the Erosion of Black Wealth* (No Working Paper 25805, National Bureau of Economic Research (NBER), May 2019) <http://www.nber.org/papers/w25805>.
59 Michigan Civil Rights Commission, *The Flint Water Crisis* (n 58) 33–40.
60 Michigan Civil Rights Commission, *The Flint Water Crisis* (n 58) 33–40.
61 Michigan Civil Rights Commission, *The Flint Water Crisis* (n 58) 42; Akbar et al, *Racial Segregation in Housing Markets and the Erosion of Black Wealth* (n 58).
62 Malini Ranganathan, 'Thinking with Flint: Racial Liberalism and the Roots of an American Water Tragedy' (2016) 27(3) *Capitalism Nature Socialism* 17, 25.
63 Kimberlé W. Crenshaw, 'Race, Reform, and Retrenchment: Transformation and Legitimation in Antidiscrimination Law' (1988) 101(7) *Harvard Law Review* 1331.
64 Malcolm McLaughlin, *The Long, Hot Summer of 1967* (Palgrave Macmillan US, 2014) <http://link.springer.com/10.1057/9781137269638>; Joseph Boskin, 'The Revolt of the Urban Ghettos, 1964-1967' (1969) 382(1) *The ANNALS of the American Academy of Political and Social Science* 1.
65 Michigan Civil Rights Commission, *The Flint Water Crisis* (n 58) 65–67; Heather Ann Thompson, *Whose Detroit?: Politics, Labor, and Race in a Modern American City* (Cornell University Press, 2nd edition, 2017) ix, xi–xv.
66 Thompson, *Whose Detroit?* (n 65) ix.
67 Thompson, *Whose Detroit?* (n 65) ix.
68 Thompson, *Whose Detroit?* (n 65) xv; Davis et al, *Final Report* (n 57) 15.
69 Mathieu Hikaru Desan, 'Bankrupted Detroit' (2014) 12(1) *Thesis Eleven* 122.
70 Kristin Longley, 'Former Acting Mayor Michael Brown Named Flint's Emergency Manager', *MLive* (Flint, Michigan, 29 November 2011).
71 *In re City of Detroit, 504 BR 97* (United States Bankruptcy Court, E.D. Michigan, Southern Division, 2013) 128.
72 Peck and Whiteside, 'Financializing Detroit' (n 51) 254.
73 Michigan Civil Rights Commission, *The Flint Water Crisis* (n 58) 113.
74 Peck and Whiteside, 'Financializing Detroit' (n 51) 255.
75 Michigan Civil Rights Commission, *The Flint Water Crisis* (n 58) 109, 122.
76 *Lyda v City of Detroit* (2016) 6th Circuit Court 15-2236.

77 Michigan Civil Rights Commission, *The Flint Water Crisis* (n 58) 12; Sanburn, 'The Poisoning of an American City [First Published as 'The Toxic Tap']' (n 54) 34; Anna Clark, *The Poisoned City: Flint's Water and the American Urban Tragedy* (Metropolitan Books, 2018) 79–80.
78 Davis et al, *Final Report* (n 57); Peter J. Hammer, 'The Flint Water Crisis, KWA and Strategic-Structural Racism: Written Testimony Submitted to the Michigan Civil Rights Commission Hearings on the Flint Water Crisis' <ttps://papers.ssrn.com/sol3/papers.cfm?abstract_id=2812171>.
79 Davis et al, *Final Report* (n 57) 16.
80 Hammer, 'KWA and Strategic-Structural Racism' (n 78) 16.
81 Hammer, 'KWA and Strategic-Structural Racism' (n 78) 16.
82 Hammer, 'KWA and Strategic-Structural Racism' (n 78) 16.
83 Hammer, 'KWA and Strategic-Structural Racism' (n 78) 33.
84 Davis et al, *Final Report* (n 57) 16.
85 Caitlin Devitt, 'Flint Departure A Blow to Detroit Water System', *The Bond Buyer* (18 April 2013).
86 Jessi Quizar, 'A Bucket in the River: Race and Public Discourse on Water Shut-offs in Detroit' (2020) 26(4) *Social Identities* 429, 431 citing Alexander Plum, Kyle Moxley and Marcus Zervos, *The Impact of Geographical Water Shutoffs on the Diagnosis of Potentially Water-Associated Illness, with the Role of Social Vulnerability Examined* (Henry Ford Health System, 2017).
87 Quizar, 'A Bucket in the River' (n 86) 431.
88 Quizar, 'A Bucket in the River' (n 86) 432 citing; Quinn Klinefelter, 'Mass Tax Foreclosure Threatens Detroit Homeowners', *NPR - All Things Considered* (online, 30 March 2015) <http://www.npr.org/2015/03/30/396317153/mass-tax-foreclosure-threatens-detroithomeowners>.
89 Murthy, 'A New Constitutive Commitment to Water' (n 55) 220–224.
90 Murthy, 'A New Constitutive Commitment to Water' (n 55) 167–170; Michigan Civil Rights Commission, *The Flint Water Crisis* (n 58) 54.
91 Murthy, 'A New Constitutive Commitment to Water' (n 55) 220–224.
92 Quizar, 'A Bucket in the River' (n 86) 432.
93 Michigan Civil Rights Commission, *The Flint Water Crisis* (n 58) 12.
94 Michigan Civil Rights Commission, *The Flint Water Crisis* (n 58) 12; Sanburn, 'The Poisoning of an American City [First Published as 'The Toxic Tap']' (n 54) 34; Clark, *The Poisoned City* (n 77) 79–80.
95 Davis et al, *Final Report* (n 57) 6, 16.
96 Davis et al, *Final Report* (n 57) 21.
97 Davis et al, *Final Report*; Michigan Civil Rights Commission, *The Flint Water Crisis* (n 58).
98 Davis et al, *Final Report* (n 57).
99 Davis et al, *Final Report* (n 57) 41.
100 Oona Goodin-Smith, 'Flint Residents Warned They Could Lose Their Homes for Unpaid Water Bills', *mlive.com* (Flint, Michigan, online, 5 May 2017) <https://web.archive.org/web/20200612165810/https://www.mlive.com/news/flint/2017/05/theyre_threatening_to_kick_us.html>; Interview with Teresa Farley and Nancy Burgher, 'Residents of Flint - The Flint Water Crisis' (Cristy Clark, 'Camp Promise', Kearsley Park, Flint, Michigan, 23 May 2017).
101 City of Flint, Michigan, 'Fast Start Initiative' (Archive, 29 July 2017) <https://web.archive.org/web/20170729011920/https://www.cityofflint.com/fast-start/>.
102 Leonard N. Fleming, 'Flint: Water Line Replacement Won't Be Done till 2019', *The Detroit News* (online, 4 December 2018) <https://web.archive.org/web/20201124131741/https://www.detroitnews.com/story/news/michigan/flint-water-crisis/2018/12/04/state-shrugs-flint-pipe-replacement-work-ahead/2204132002/>.

103 City of Flint, Michigan, 'Get the Lead Out - Service Line Replacement Program' (Archive 15 September 2022, 16 July 2021) <https://web.archive.org/web/20220915034217/https://www.cityofflint.com/get-the-lead-out/>.

104 *Concerned Pastors for Social Action, et al vs Khouri et al* (2024) United States District Court, ED Michigan, Southern Division No. 16-10277 (12 March 2024).

105 Derek Robertson, 'Flint Has Clean Water Now: Why Won't People Drink It? -', *Politico* (Flint, Michigan, online, 23 December 2020) <https://web.archive.org/web/20210117104737/https://www.politico.com/news/magazine/2020/12/23/flint-water-crisis-2020-post-coronavirus-america-445459>.

106 People's Water Board (PWB), 'Mission' (2018) <https://peopleswaterboard.org>; Sabrina Kozikis and Inga T. Winkler, 'The Paradox of Framing Water as a Human Right in the United States: An Analysis of Power and Resistance' (2020) 19(4) *Journal of Human Rights* 464; Sabrina Kozikis and Inga T. Winkler, 'Between Confrontation and Cooperation: Right to Water Advocacy in the Courts, on the Streets, and at the Capitols in the United States' (2021) 13(24) *Water* 3541; Jackie Dugard, 'Water Rights Struggles in Johannesburg and Detroit Revisited: Looking Beyond Courts at the Politics and Power of Rights-Based Legal Mobilization in a Neoliberal Global Order: A "Powerpack" Analysis' (2022) 15(1) *Journal of Human Rights Practice* 46.

107 Cristy Clark, 'Of What Use Is a Deradicalized Human Right to Water?' (2017) 17(2) *Human Rights Law Review* 231; Cristy Clark, 'Race, Austerity and Water Justice in the US: Fighting for the Human Right to Water in Detroit and Flint, Michigan' in Farhana Sultana and Alex Loftus (eds), *Water Politics: Governance, Justice, and the Right to Water* (Routledge, 2020).

108 Cristy Clark, 'Water Justice Struggles as a Process of Commoning' (2019) 54(1) *Community Development Journal* 80; Dugard, 'Water Rights Struggles in Johannesburg and Detroit Revisited' (n 106).

109 *Lyda v City of Detroit (In re City of Detroit)* (2014) United States Bankruptcy Court Eastern District of Michigan Southern Division 13-53846.

110 Office of the High Commissioner for Human Rights (OHCHR), 'Joint Press Statement by Special Rapporteur on Adequate Housing as a Component of the Right to an Adequate Standard of Living and the Right to Non-Discrimination in This Context, and Special Rapporteur on the Human Right to Safe Drinking Water and Sanitation Visit to City of Detroit (United States of America) 18-20 October 2014', *OHCHR* (20 October 2014) <www.ohchr.org/EN/NewsEvents/Pages/DisplayNews.aspx?NewsID=15188#sthash.qn8zdOlz.dpuf>.

111 OHCHR, 'Joint Press Statement' (n 110).

112 OHCHR, 'Joint Press Statement' (n 110).

113 OHCHR, 'Joint Press Statement' (n 110).

114 OHCHR, 'Joint Press Statement' (n 110).

115 Jan Lee, 'Detroit Water Shutoff Crisis: Public Water Brigade Grows, Triple Pundit' (online, 26 February 2015) <https://www.triplepundit.com/2015/02/detroit-water-shutoff-crisis-public-water-brigade-grows/>.

116 Lee, 'Detroit Water Shutoff Crisis' (n 115).

117 Detroit Water Brigade (DWB), 'About – Mission Statement' (2016) http://detroitwaterbrigade.org/mission-statement/ (last accessed 24 September 2018); Interview with Meeko Williams and Makita Taylor, 'Organisers with The Detroit Water Brigade' (Cristy Clark, Avalon Bakery, Midtown Detroit, USA, 22 May 2017).

118 DWB 'Mission Statement' (n 117); Interview with Meeko Williams and Makita Taylor, 'Organisers with The Detroit Water Brigade' (n 117).

119 Interview with Meeko Williams and Makita Taylor, 'Organisers with The Detroit Water Brigade' (n 117); Clark, 'Water Justice Struggles as a Process of Commoning' (n 108).

120 PWB, 'Mission' (n 106).
121 In 2018 there were around 100 groups, the largest (with 6,000 members) was the 'Flint Water Class Action Group' <https://www.facebook.com/groups/379333262224146/>. See Clark, 'Water Justice Struggles as a Process of Commoning' (n 108).
122 'Flint Residents Protest amid Water Crisis', *CBS News* (Directed by Adriana Diaz, 20 January 2016) <https://www.cbsnews.com/video/flint-residents-protest-amid-water-crisis/>; Flint Water Recovery Group, 'Flint Cares' (25 June 2018) <https://flintcares.com/>; Ray Sanchez, 'Flint Residents Rally in Michigan's Capital against End of Bottled Water Program', *CNN Online* (online, 11 April 2018) <https://edition.cnn.com/2018/04/11/us/flint-michigan-water-rally/index.html>; Interview with Teresa Farley and Nancy Burgher, 'Residents of Flint - The Flint Water Crisis' (n 100); Joe DePaolo, 'Police Arrest Six at Flint Water Crisis Town Hall' (Flint, Michigan, online, 21 April 2017) <https://web.archive.org/web/20170425000635/http://www.mediaite.com/online/police-arrest-six-at-flint-water-crisis-town-hall/>.
123 Nick Estes, *Our History Is the Future: Standing Rock versus the Dakota Access Pipeline, and the Long Tradition of Indigenous Resistance* (Verso, 2019).
124 Clark, 'Water Justice Struggles as a Process of Commoning' (n 108); Camp Promise of Flint, 'About' (Facebook page, 2017) https://www.facebook.com/CampPromiseFlint (last accessed 27 March 2025).
125 City of Flint, Michigan, 'Get the Lead Out - Service Line Replacement Program' (n 103).
126 Camp Promise of Flint, 'About' (n 124). Personal communication with organisers on 23 May 2017 at 'Camp Promise', Kearsley Park, Flint, Michigan.
127 *Beatrice Boler, et al v Darnell Earley, et al* (2017) United States Court of Appeals for the Sixth Circuit Case nos. 16-1684/17-1144; *Concerned Pastors for Social Action, et. al vs. Khouri et. Al.* (n 104); *Concerned Pastors for Social Action, et al v Khouri, et al* (2016) US District Court for the Eastern District of Michigan Case No. 2:16-cv-10277 (10 November 2016); 'Concerned Pastors for Social Action v. Khouri - Settlement Agreement' (23 March 2017) <https://www.michigan.gov/-/media/Project/Websites/flintwater/documents/2017/Settlement_Agreement_dated_032717.pdf?rev=9e1974374edf4cb68fc46d348d823d0a>.
128 Richard Gonzales, 'Mich. Prosecutors Drop Charges in Flint Water Investigation, But Promise New Probe', *NPR* (online, 13 June 2019) <https://www.npr.org/2019/06/13/732540100/mich-prosecutors-drop-charges-in-flintwater-investigation-but-promise-new-probe>; Brakkton Booker, 'Former Michigan Gov. Rick Snyder Charged In Flint Water Crisis', *NPR* (online, 13 January 2021) <https://www.npr.org/2021/01/13/956592508/new-charges-in-flint-water-crisis-including-former-michigan-gov-rick-snyder>.
129 Davis et al, *Final Report* (n 57); Michigan Civil Rights Commission, *The Flint Water Crisis* (n 58).
130 Davis et al, *Final Report* (n 57) 1.
131 Davis et al, *Final Report* 1 (n 57).
132 Davis et al, *Final Report* (n 57) 1 cover letter.
133 Michigan Civil Rights Commission, *The Flint Water Crisis* (n 58) 2.
134 Michigan Civil Rights Commission, *The Flint Water Crisis* (n 58) iv.
135 Michigan Civil Rights Commission, *The Flint Water Crisis* (n 58) v.
136 Davis et al, *Final Report* (n 57) 1.
137 Davis et al, *Final Report* (n 57) 11.
138 Davis et al, *Final Report* (n 57) 11.
139 Davis et al, *Final Report* (n 57) 12.
140 Michigan Civil Rights Commission, *The Flint Water Crisis* (n 58) 5.
141 Davis et al, *Final Report* (n 57) v.

142 Holly Fournier, 'Detroit Water Brigade to Protest in Ireland', *The Detroit News* (4 December 2014) <http://www.detroitnews.com/story/news/local/wayne-county/2014/12/04/detroit-water-brigade-ireland/19892561/>.
143 Bresnihan, 'The Bio-Financialization of Irish Water' (n 24); Martin Power, Amanda Haynes and Eoin Devereux, *Reasonable People v The Sinister Fringe: Interrogating the Framing of Ireland's Water Charge Protestors through the Media Politics of Dissent* (University of Limerick Report, 2015) <https://hdl.handle.net/10344/4481> (last accessed 27 March 2025).
144 Brian Fitzpatrick and Foreign Policy in Focus, 'From Detroit to Dublin, a Fight for the Right to Water', *The Nation* (29 January 2015) <https://www.thenation.com/article/archive/detroit-dublin-fight-right-water/>; Interview with David Gibney, 'Communications Officer for Mandate Trade Union' (Cristy Clark, 9 Cavendish Row, Dublin, Ireland, 6 September 2017); Interview with Meeko Williams and Makita Taylor, 'Organisers with The Detroit Water Brigade' (n 117).
145 Laurence Cox, 'The Irish Water Charges Movement: Theorising "the Social Movement in General"' (2017) 9(1) *Interface: A Journal for and about Social Movements* 161.
146 Interview with David Gibney, 'Communications Officer for Mandate Trade Union' (n 144).
147 Kieran Allen and Brian O'Boyle, 'Why Don't the Irish Protest?' in *Austerity Ireland: The Failure of Irish Capitalism* (Pluto Press/JSTOR, 2013) 126.
148 Interview with Paul Murphy, 'Teachta Dála for the Solidarity Party and Right-2Water Campaign Organiser' (Cristy Clark, Agriculture House, Dublin, Ireland, 7 September 2017).
149 Conor McCabe, 'The Radical Left in Ireland' (2015) 29(3) *Socialism and Democracy* 158.
150 Interview with Paul Murphy, 'Teachta Dála for the Solidarity Party and Right2 Water Campaign Organiser' (n 148).
151 Bresnihan, 'The Bio-Financialization of Irish Water' (n 24).
152 Rory Hearne, 'Irish Water War' (2015) 7(1) *Interface: A Journal for and about Social Movements* 309.
153 Cox, 'The Irish Water Charges Movement' (n 145) 162, 182.
154 Hearne, 'Irish Water War' (n 152); Power, Haynes and Devereux, *Reasonable People v The Sinister Fringe* (n 143).
155 Power, Haynes and Devereux, *Reasonable People v The Sinister Fringe* (n 143).
156 Interview with Paul Murphy, 'Teachta Dála for the Solidarity Party and Right-2Water Campaign Organiser' (n 148).
157 Dan MacGuill, 'How the Three Main Parties Lost Their Stranglehold on Irish Politics - in Just a Decade', *TheJournal.ie* (online, 3 March 2016) <https://www.thejournal.ie/three-main-parties-rise-of-independents-sinn-fein-election-2016-2629283-Mar2016/>.
158 Henry McDonald, 'Ireland to Have Minority Fine Gael Government after Deal Agreed', *The Guardian* (Ireland, online, 3 May 2016) <https://www.theguardian.com/world/2016/may/03/ireland-to-have-minority-fine-gael-government-after-deal-agreed>; Interview with David Gibney, 'Communications Officer for Mandate Trade Union' (n 144); Interview with Paul Murphy, 'Teachta Dála for the Solidarity Party and Right2Water Campaign Organiser' (n 148).
159 J. Peter Clinch and Anne Pender, '"You Don't Miss the Water 'til the Well Runs Dry': Factors Influencing the Failure of Domestic Water Charges in Ireland' (2019) 50(2) *The Economic and Social Review* 369, 371.
160 McDonald, 'Ireland to Have Minority Fine Gael Government after Deal Agreed' (n 158).

161 'Universal Water Charges in Ireland to Come to an End', *BBC News* (online, 13 April 2017) <https://www.bbc.com/news/world-europe-39594886>; Clinch and Pender, 'You Don't Miss the Water 'til the Well Runs Dry' (n 159).
162 Hearne, 'Irish Water War' (n 152).
163 Cox, 'The Irish Water Charges Movement' (n 145) 187.

References

Akbar, Prottoy A. et al, *Racial Segregation in Housing Markets and the Erosion of Black Wealth* (No Working Paper 25805, National Bureau of Economic Research (NBER), May 2019) <https://www.nber.org/papers/w25805>

Allen, Kieran and Brian O'Boyle, 'Why Don't the Irish Protest?' in *Austerity Ireland: The Failure of Irish Capitalism* (Pluto Press/JSTOR, 2013) 126

Allen, John and Michael Pryke, 'Financialising Household Water: Thames Water, MEIF, and "Ring-Fenced" Politics' (2013) 6 *Cambridge Journal of Regions, Economy and Society* 419

Bayliss, Kate, 'Material Cultures of Water Financialisation in England and Wales' (2017) 22(4) *New Political Economy* 383

Bayliss, Kate, 'The Financialization of Water' (2014) 46(3) *Review of Radical Political Economics* 292

Beatrice Boler, et al v Darnell Earley, et al (2017) United States Court of Appeals for the Sixth Circuit Case nos. 16-1684/17-1144

Booker, Brakkton, 'Former Michigan Gov. Rick Snyder Charged in Flint Water Crisis', *NPR* (online, 13 January 2021) <https://www.npr.org/2021/01/13/956592508/new-charges-in-flint-water-crisis-including-former-michigan-gov-rick-snyder>

Boskin, Joseph, 'The Revolt of the Urban Ghettos, 1964-1967' (1969) 382(1) *The ANNALS of the American Academy of Political and Social Science* 1

Bresnihan, Patrick, 'The Bio-Financialization of Irish Water: New Advances in the Neoliberalization of Vital Services' (2016) 40 *Utilities Policy* 115

Camp Promise of Flint, 'About' (Facebook page, 2017) https://www.facebook.com/CampPromiseFlint (last accessed 27 March 2025)

City of Flint, Michigan, 'Fast Start Initiative' (Archive, 29 July 2017) <https://web.archive.org/web/20170729011920/https://www.cityofflint.com/fast-start/>

City of Flint, Michigan, 'Get the Lead Out - Service Line Replacement Program' (Archive 15 September 2022, 16 July 2021) <https://web.archive.org/web/20220915034217/https://www.cityofflint.com/get-the-lead-out/>

Clark, Anna., *The Poisoned City: Flint's Water and the American Urban Tragedy* (Metropolitan Books, 2018)

Clark, Cristy, 'Of What Use Is a Deradicalized Human Right to Water?' (2017) 17(2) *Human Rights Law Review* 231

Clark, Cristy, 'Race, Austerity and Water Justice in the US: Fighting for the Human Right to Water in Detroit and Flint, Michigan' in Farhana Sultana and Alex Loftus (eds), *Water Politics: Governance, Justice, and the Right to Water* (Routledge, 2020)

Clark, Cristy, 'Water Justice Struggles as a Process of Commoning' (2019) 54(1) *Community Development Journal* 80

Clinch, J. Peter and Anne Pender, '"You Don't Miss the Water 'til the Well Runs Dry': Factors Influencing the Failure of Domestic Water Charges in Ireland' (2019) 50(2) *The Economic and Social Review* 369

Concerned Pastors for Social Action, et al v Khouri, et al (2016) US District Court for the Eastern District of Michigan Case No. 2:16-cv-10277 (10 November 2016)

Concerned Pastors for Social Action, et al vs Khouri et al (2024) United States District Court, ED Michigan, Southern Division No. 16-10277 (12 March 2024)

'Concerned Pastors for Social Action v. Khouri - Settlement Agreement' (23 March 2017) <https://www.michigan.gov/-/media/Project/Websites/flintwater/documents/2017/Settlement_Agreement_dated_032717.pdf?rev=9e1974374edf4cb68fc46d348d823d0a>

Cox, Laurence., 'The Irish Water Charges Movement: Theorising "the Social Movement in General"' (2017) 9(1) *Interface: A Journal for and about Aocial Movements* 161

Crenshaw, Kimberlé W., 'Race, Reform, and Retrenchment: Transformation and Legitimation in Antidiscrimination Law' (1988) 101(7) *Harvard Law Review* 1331

Davis, Matthew M. et al, *Final Report* (Flint Water Advisory Task Force, 21 March 2016) <https://flintwaterstudy.org/2016/03/flint-water-advisory-task-force-final-report/>

DePaolo, Joe, 'Police Arrest Six at Flint Water Crisis Town Hall' (Flint, Michigan, online, 21 April 2017) https://web.archive.org/web/20170425000635/https://www.mediaite.com/online/police-arrest-six-at-flint-water-crisis-town-hall/ (last accssed 24 September 2018)

Desan, Mathieu Hikaru, 'Bankrupted Detroit' (2014) 12(1) *Thesis Eleven* 122

Detroit Water Brigade (DWB), 'About – Mission Statement', (2016) https://detroitwaterbrigade.org/mission-statement/ (last accessed 24 September 2018)

Devitt, Caitlin., 'Flint Departure A Blow to Detroit Water System', *The Bond Buyer* (18 April 2013)

Dugard, Jackie, 'Water Rights Struggles in Johannesburg and Detroit Revisited: Looking Beyond Courts at the Politics and Power of Rights-Based Legal Mobilization in a Neoliberal Global Order: A "Powerpack" Analysis' (2022) 15(1) *Journal of Human Rights Practice* 46

Estes, Nick, *Our History Is the Future: Standing Rock versus the Dakota Access Pipeline, and the Long Tradition of Indigenous Resistance* (Verso, 2019)

Fitzpatrick, Brian and Foreign Policy in Focus, 'From Detroit to Dublin, a Fight for the Right to Water', *The Nation* (29 January 2015) <https://www.thenation.com/article/archive/detroit-dublin-fight-right-water/>

Fleming, Leonard N., 'Flint: Water Line Replacement Won't Be Done till 2019', *The Detroit News* (online, 4 December 2018) <https://web.archive.org/web/20201124131741/https://www.detroitnews.com/story/news/michigan/flint-water-crisis/2018/12/04/state-shrugs-flint-pipe-replacement-work-ahead/2204132002/>

'Flint Residents Protest amid Water Crisis', *CBS News* (Directed by Adriana Diaz, 20 January 2016) <https://www.cbsnews.com/video/flint-residents-protest-amid-water-crisis/>

'Flint Water Class Action Group' <https://www.facebook.com/groups/379333262224146/>

Flint Water Recovery Group, 'Flint Cares' (25 June 2018) <https://flintcares.com/>

Fournier, Holly, 'Detroit Water Brigade to Protest in Ireland', *The Detroit News* (4 December 2014) <https://www.detroitnews.com/story/news/local/wayne-county/2014/12/04/detroit-water-brigade-ireland/19892561/>

Gonzales, Richard, 'Mich. Prosecutors Drop Charges in Flint Water Investigation, But Promise New Probe', *NPR* (online, 13 June 2019) <https://www.npr.org/2019/

06/13/732540100/mich-prosecutors-drop-charges-in-flint-water-investigation-but-promise-new-probe>

Goodin-Smith, Oona, 'Flint Residents Warned They Could Lose Their Homes for Unpaid Water Bills', *mlive.com* (Flint, Michigan, online, 5 May 2017) <https://web.archive.org/web/20200612165810/https://www.mlive.com/news/flint/2017/05/theyre_threatening_to_kick_us.html>

Hammer, Peter J., 'The Flint Water Crisis, KWA and Strategic-Structural Racism: Written Testimony Submitted to the Michigan Civil Rights Commission Hearings on the Flint Water Crisis' <ttps://papers.ssrn.com/sol3/papers.cfm?abstract_id=2812171>

Harvey, David, 'From Managerialism to Entrepreneuralism: The Transformation in Urban Governance in Late Capitalism' (1989) 71(1) *Geografiska Annaler B* 3

Harvey, David, 'Globalization and the "Spatial Fix"' (2008) 3(2) *Geographische Revue: Zeitschrift für Literatur und Diskussion* 23

Hearne, Rory, 'Irish Water War' (2015) 7(1) *Interface: A Journal for and about Social Movements* 309

In re City of Detroit, 504 BR 97 (United States Bankruptcy Court, E. D. Michigan, Southern Division, 2013)

Interview with Teresa Farley and Nancy Burgher, 'Residents of Flint - The Flint Water Crisis' (Cristy Clark, 'Camp Promise', Kearsley Park, Flint, Michigan, 23 May 2017)

Interview with David Gibney, 'Communications Officer for Mandate Trade Union' (Cristy Clark, 9 Cavendish Row, Dublin, Ireland, 6 September 2017)

Interview with Paul Murphy, 'Teachta Dála for the Solidarity Party and Right2Water Campaign Organiser' (Cristy Clark, Agriculture House, Dublin, Ireland, 7 September 2017)

Interview with Meeko Williams and Makita Taylor, 'Organisers with The Detroit Water Brigade' (Cristy Clark, Avalon Bakery, Midtown Detroit, USA, 22 May 2017)

Klinefelter, Quinn, 'Mass Tax Foreclosure Threatens Detroit Homeowners', *NPR - All Things Considered* (online, 30 March 2015) <https://www.npr.org/2015/03/30/396317153/mass-tax-foreclosure-threatens-detroithomeowners>

Kozikis, Sabrina and Inga T. Winkler, 'Between Confrontation and Cooperation: Right to Water Advocacy in the Courts, on the Streets, and at the Capitols in the United States' (2021) 13(24) *Water* 3541

Kozikis, Sabrina and Inga T. Winkler, 'The Paradox of Framing Water as a Human Right in the United States: An Analysis of Power and Resistance' (2020) 19(4) *Journal of Human Rights* 464

Langley, Paul, 'The Financialization of Life' in Philip Mader, Daniel Mertens, and Natascha van der Zwan (eds), *The Routledge International Handbook of Financialization* (Routledge, Taylor & Francis Group, 2020) 68

Lee, Jan, 'Detroit Water Shutoff Crisis: Public Water Brigade Grows, Triple Pundit' (online, 26 February 2015) <https://www.triplepundit.com/2015/02/detroit-water-shutoff-crisis-public-water-brigade-grows/>

Loftus, Alex, Hug March and Thomas F. Purcell, 'The Political Economy of Water Infrastructure: An Introduction to Financialization' (2019) 6(1) *WIREs Water* e1326

Longley, Kristin, 'Former Acting Mayor Michael Brown Named Flint's Emergency Manager', *MLive* (Flint, Michigan, 29 November 2011)

Lyda v City of Detroit (2016) 6th Circuit Court 15-2236

Lyda v City of Detroit (In re City of Detroit) (2014) United States Bankruptcy Court Eastern District of Michigan Southern Division 13–53846

MacGuill, Dan, 'How the Three Main Parties Lost Their Stranglehold on Irish Politics - in Just a Decade', *TheJournal.ie* (online, 3 March 2016) <https://www.thejournal.ie/three-main-parties-rise-of-independents-sinn-fein-election-2016-2629283-Mar2016/>

Marx, Karl, *Capital, Volume III* (Penguin, 1991)

McCabe, Conor, 'The Radical Left in Ireland' (2015) 29(3) *Socialism and Democracy* 158

McDonald, Henry, 'Ireland to Have Minority Fine Gael Government after Deal Agreed', *The Guardian* (Ireland, online, 3 May 2016) <https://www.theguardian.com/world/2016/may/03/ireland-to-have-minority-fine-gael-government-after-deal-agreed>

McLaughlin, Malcolm, *The Long, Hot Summer of 1967* (Palgrave Macmillan US, 2014) <https://link.springer.com/10.1057/9781137269638>

Michigan Civil Rights Commission, *The Flint Water Crisis: Systematic Racism Through the Lens of Flint* (Michigan Civil Rights Commission, 17 February 2017) <https://www.michigan.gov/documents/mdcr/VFlintCrisisRep-F-Edited3-13-17_554317_7.pdf>

Murthy, Sharmila L., 'A New Constitutive Commitment to Water' (2016) 36(2) *Boston College Journal of Law and Social Justice* 159

OECD, *Innovative Financing Mechanisms for the Water Sector: Working Party on Global and Structural Policies* (Organisation for Economic Co-operation and Development, 2010)

Office of the High Commissioner for Human Rights (OHCHR), 'Joint Press Statement by Special Rapporteur on Adequate Housing as a Component of the Right to an Adequate Standard of Living and the Right to Non-Discrimination in This Context, and Special Rapporteur on the Human Right to Safe Drinking Water and Sanitation Visit to City of Detroit (United States of America) 18-20 October 2014', *OHCHR* (20 October 2014) <www.ohchr.org/EN/NewsEvents/Pages/DisplayNews.aspx?NewsID=15188#sthash.qn8zdOlz.dpuf>

Peck, Jamie and Heather Whiteside, 'Financializing Detroit' (2015) 92(3) *Economic Geography* 235

People's Water Board (PWB), 'Mission' (2018) https://peopleswaterboard.org (last accessed 25 September 2018)

Plum, Alexander., Kyle Moxley and Marcus Zervos, *The Impact of Geographical Water Shutoffs on the Diagnosis of Potentially Water-Associated Illness, with the Role of Social Vulnerability Examined* (Henry Ford Health System, 2017)

Power, Martin, Amanda Haynes and Eoin Devereux, *Reasonable People v The Sinister Fringe: Interrogating the Framing of Ireland's Water Charge Protestors through the Media Politics of Dissent* (University of Limerick Report, 2015) <https://hdl.handle.net/10344/4481> (last accessed 27 March 2025)

Purcell, Thomas F., Alex Loftus and Hug March, 'Value–Rent–Finance' (2020) 44(3) *Progress in Human Geography* 437

Quizar, Jessi, 'A Bucket in the River: Race and Public Discourse on Water Shutoffs in Detroit' (2020) 26(4) *Social Identities* 429

Ranganathan, Malini., 'Thinking with Flint: Racial Liberalism and the Roots of an American Water Tragedy' (2016) 27(3) *Capitalism Nature Socialism* 17

Reis, Nadine, Germán Vargas Magaña and Santiago Vélez Villegas, 'Water, Finance and Financialisation: A Review' (2024) 17(2) *Water Alternatives* 266

Robertson, Derek, 'Flint Has Clean Water Now: Why Won't People Drink It?', *Politico* (Flint, Michigan, online, 23 December 2020) https://www.politico.com/news/magazine/2020/12/23/flint-water-crisis-2020-post-coronavirus-america-445459 (last accessed 27 March 2025)

Sanchez, Ray, 'Flint Residents Rally in Michigan's Capital against End of Bottled Water Program', *CNN Online* (online, 11 April 2018) https://edition.cnn.com/2018/04/11/us/flint-michigan-water-rally/index.html (last accessed 26 September 2018)

Sanburn, Josh, 'The Poisoning of an American City [First Published as 'The Toxic Tap']', *Time Magazine* (21 February 2016) https://time.com/4188328/the-poisoning-of-an-american-city/ (last accssed 27 March 2025)

Thompson, Heather Ann, *Whose Detroit?: Politics, Labor, and Race in a Modern American City* (Cornell University Press, 2nd edition, 2017)

United Nations Human Settlements Programme (UN-Habitat), *World Cities Report: Urbanization and Development - Emerging Futures* (UN-Habitat, 2016) 262 <https://unhabitat.org/world-cities-report-2016> (last accssed 27 March 2025)

United States Census Bureau, 'Quick Facts - Detroit, Michigan' (1 April 2020) <https://www.census.gov/quickfacts/fact/table/detroitcitymichigan,US/POP010220>

'Universal Water Charges in Ireland to Come to an End', *BBC News* (online, 13 April 2017) <https://www.bbc.com/news/world-europe-39594886> (last accssed 27 March 2025)

7

ONTOLOGIES OF LIVING WATERS

Introduction

The neoliberal water governance reforms that we have explored in the preceding chapters, including Chile's water markets, the privatised water supply and sanitation (WSS) systems in England, Wales, and Manila, Johannesburg's corporatised WSS utility with its prepaid water meters, and the financialised systems in Detroit, Flint, and Dublin, all operated in various ways to (attempt to) transform water into a commodity (and, in the case of financialisation, a financial asset). This approach only makes sense in a world that understands water to be an inert (economic) resource, separable from humans and land, and available for exploitation. Such a world can be described as belonging to a Western or modernist ontology. This chapter argues that, despite its dominance, such an ontology is not universally shared – particularly in its extreme neoliberal form. Time and time again, communities appear to reject the idea that water is a detached, economic resource that ought to be governed through the logic of the market.

While some of this pushback is tied to the essential nature of water to individual and community health and well-being (and, indeed, survival), another theme that comes up is the sacred and/or spiritual nature of water. Veronica Strang has documented the persistence of these ontologies of *living water*, noting that most of the world's spiritual traditions understand water as both a source of life and a 'primal creative force,' and, from this understanding, 'cosmologies around the world draw ideas about "living water": the water that flows through the world enabling life.'[1] She observes here that this agentic understanding of water tends to transcend the dualism embedded

DOI: 10.4324/9781003273219-7

in conventional 'Western' conceptual boundaries between nature and culture, material and spiritual domains.[2]

Through the case studies considered in the previous chapters, we have analysed the co-constitutive nature of people's relationships with water and water governance regimes (including the legal regulation of water that underpins them). In this analysis, the role of water itself in this co-constitutive process has been largely implicit. In this chapter, water's agency will be explicitly considered through an exploration of *living water* and of the emerging legal and governance frameworks that are beginning to recognise this ontology.

Over the last decade, there has been a marked increase in the institutional recognition of this concept of living water, including through the growing number of constitutions, laws, and judicial decisions that have recognised watery entities (such as rivers) as single living entities, sometimes also granting them legal personhood and/or rights. These legal developments include the constitutional recognition of rivers (as a component of 'Nature') in Ecuador,[3] river personhood judgments in Colombia,[4] India,[5] and Bangladesh,[6] and treaty-based legislative recognition of some rivers (amongst other natural entities) in Aotearoa New Zealand,[7] to name a few of the most prominent. As with the human right to water, these so-called rights of nature (RoN) legal developments represent the institutionalisation of a far larger groundswell of community activism and theorising. And, like the human right to water, the underlying meanings of these institutionalised legal concepts and community legal theories (which are often flattened into a singular movement or theory) are highly diverse, place based, and pluralist – even as global networks of solidarity and inspiration operate to facilitate the exchange of concepts and approaches.

This chapter starts by exploring ontologies of living water, including by closely analysing what we mean by 'ontology' in this context. It will then examine some of the theories and social movements that have been described as forming part of the so-called 'new ontological turn' – including those working to promote RoN legal developments (described below as 'instrumental RoN discourse') – and consider some of the fault lines that exist within these theories and social movements, particularly in relation to ontology. Finally, this chapter will critically review instrumental RoN discourse against the specific place-based context and detail of recent legislation that established new governance frameworks and guiding principles for the Whanganui River in Aotearoa New Zealand. This chapter concludes by considering lessons for how legal and ontological pluralism might be promoted in water governance frameworks elsewhere.

Living water

As we have seen through the case studies explored in earlier chapters, a modernist ontology dominates institutional approaches to water governance and the legal regulation of water – both at the international and domestic levels.[8] Within this ontology, water is an inert, economic resource, available for human exploitation. The reduction of water to an inert economic resource through modernist ontology laid crucial groundwork for the neoliberal reforms examined throughout this book. While Chapter 6 analysed how financialisation represents the ultimate abstraction of water's value, this ontological analysis reveals the deeper conceptual foundations enabling such abstraction. The erasure of water's agency and spiritual significance through modernist ontology created the conditions for increasingly sophisticated forms of commodification – from Chile's water markets to England's securitisation schemes. However, as demonstrated repeatedly, water's ontological complexity continues to resist such reduction, manifesting through both material 'uncooperativeness' and persistent community relationships with living waters. These community relationships with living water reflect the widely documented reality of many communities around the world (and most religions) – that water is a living entity with agency and deeply entangled, interdependent relationships with humans (and the rest of the environment).

A prominent manifestation of this material and spiritual agency of water is *water beings*, which Strang describes as being ubiquitous in early human history and as resurfacing persistently over time.[9] 'Wherever they went, water serpent beings embodied ideas about non-human powers and water's elemental capacities to shape human lives. Celebrated, worshipped and propitiated, they expressed respectful relationships with water and people's appreciation of its essentiality to all living organisms.'[10] In her recent study of these water beings, Strang asks how 'humankind move[d] from worshipping water to wreaking havoc upon it, and upon the ecosystems through which it flows?'[11] The central hypothesis that she then explores is that in addition to being reflected in their socio-political arrangements, '[p]eople's beliefs and values are co-constituted by how they engage materially with their environments, and by the extent to which human agency supercedes that of the non-human domain.'[12]

The persistent recognition of water beings across cultures and time provides crucial theoretical context for understanding water's broader resistance to commodification – a theme that has emerged repeatedly throughout this book. While water's material resistance to commodification has led to its description as an 'uncooperative commodity,' this ontological analysis reveals a deeper dimension of this resistance. The sacred and relational qualities of water that manifest through water beings help explain why attempts to reduce water to an economic resource consistently encounter material *and* social obstacles. From Yorkshire's drought-stricken communities to Detroit's resistance to financialisation, we see how water's ontological complexity fundamentally challenges modernist attempts at reduction and abstraction.

While personified water serpent beings are a widespread (even ubiquitous) expression of people's understanding of water's agency and power, these understandings are also reflected 'in more abstract ideas about spiritually infused "living water"'[13] – and evidence of these ideas is often hidden in plain sight. One such example of spiritual (or sacred) water is holy water, which often takes the form of holy wells across Europe and the UK.[14] Terje Oestigaard, for example, has documented the enduring popular belief in holy or sacred water in England, despite Protestant reforms attempting to eliminate 'magical' (or 'superstitious') Catholic practices.[15] His analysis challenges Max Weber's thesis about Protestantism's role in disenchanting nature and demonstrates how beliefs in holy water's protective and healing powers proved remarkably durable within what he calls 'lay Christianity.'[16] Oestigaard documents that holy wells remained important ritual sites, despite official condemnation, with around 8,000 sites enduring across Great Britain and Ireland, and at least 2,000 just in England.[17] He describes these beliefs as 'the water cult' and argues that it 'was so strong that it persisted alongside Protestantism and capitalism, and, furthermore, one may argue that it defined lay Christianity.'[18]

While I would not use the word 'cult' to describe this phenomenon, Oestigaard's research is significant for demonstrating how communities maintained integrated spiritual-material understandings of water well into the modern period notwithstanding censure from authorities and powerful institutions.[19] Despite Protestant theological attempts to reduce water to mere matter, communities continued to understand water as an active, spiritually potent entity.[20] These same beliefs have been documented by Strang, who observed that even the non-Christian inhabitants of Dorset (in the UK) attributed spiritual significance to holy water, using words like 'aura' and 'mystical power' to describe it.[21]

The persistence of these beliefs in holy or sacred water has been widely documented[22] and is a further indication that modernist conceptualisations of water as an inert resource have never fully supplanted more complex community understandings of water as living, relational, and sacred. This persistence, even in contexts of aggressive modernist reform, provides a valuable theoretical context for understanding the forms of resistance documented throughout this book. This historical continuity provides important context for understanding contemporary resistance to the technical, market-based approaches to water governance demanded by neoliberal reforms and why these reforms so often encounter both material and social obstacles to implementation.

Despite this ongoing resistance, modernist ontology still dominates the academy and the water scholarship that takes place within its auspices (although notably this dominance appears to be waning). This dominance of modernism has created a tension between the relational reality of water that many communities live with, and many scholars have empirically observed (and, indeed, lived), and the asserted 'universal truth' that water is an inert economic resource. Academia's loyalty to a modernist ontology of water can be partly attributed to its related commitment to rationalism's belief in a universal and objectively deducible reality, which serves to render alternative realities not just suspect but invalid or fanciful. This is well illustrated by Vernon Scarborough's observation that he does 'not see water as having a mind of its own or any sentience to deliberately work for or against human interests. *Water simply is,* and humans have directed its course with all the unintended consequences of their efforts.'[23] His position here appears to stem from a rationalist commitment to a singular understanding of the world and of the nature of knowledge production. Indeed, this commitment is further underscored in Scarborough's closing paragraph,

> It is true that non-Western societies have given ideological agency to both non-human life and the inorganic world that has surrounded them, but to do so sacrifices notions of evolutionary theory and frequently conflates historical time depth. The Water People or the Bird People of indigenous groups are highly significant metaphors and concepts that have unified and worshipfully affected the fundamental fabric of many societies. However, they need separation from our science and aspects of our scholarship. We need both, but like church–state separations they require some distance from one another if we are to most effectively address our societal human futures and project a world where myths and metaphors of non-Western ways can be thoughtfully contextualized.[24]

Strang's scholarship on water carefully navigates this tension. In relation to holy water, for example, she emphasises the importance of this interaction between the materiality of water and the cultural or spiritual frameworks of humans.[25] Strang is careful to clarify that this recognition of water's material agency does not require 'proposing or implying a form of faux animism.'[26] Rather, it enables recognition of how water's physical properties interact with cultural and spiritual frameworks. Strang argues that acknowledging the 'agentive capacities of things' does not require attributing intentionality or consciousness to them.[27] Instead she reasons that agency can be understood as 'capacity to act (upon)' – a framing that allows for material agency without implying animism or sentience.[28]

Ontology

I have used the term 'modernist' ontology above (in preference to Western), precisely because despite its dominance within so much of present-day law, politics, and economics, this ontology is relatively new, particularly in its application to water. It is a product of the European Enlightenment and has been used in a political way to promote capitalism, colonialism, and a hierarchical understanding of human development that assumes a progression from living with to ordering, conquering, and exploiting 'nature' through agricultural, industrial, and post-industrial production (and scientific categorisation).[29] As already noted, despite this long-running campaign of naturalisation, this modernist ontology does not reflect past documented understandings of water in (even) the West nor the relational approach to water that is still modelled and enacted by communities globally – including by water justice campaigners in places such as Johannesburg, Flint, Detroit, and Dublin.

Before exploring this ontological diversity any further, it is necessary to dwell briefly on the concept of ontology itself. This is because ontology is a word with contested meanings and deeply political connotations.[30] While it is widely agreed that ontology is the lens through which we understand what is real, the meaning of the 'lens' here is slippery. One interpretation that has been adopted – and that I implicitly use throughout this book – is that the gap between this lens and reality is largely irrelevant, meaning that ontology is virtually synonymous with 'world' or 'what is real.' Within this interpretation, the concept of ontology acknowledges the existence of multiple worlds,[31] resulting in a 'pluriverse.'[32] As Mihnea Tănăsescu explains, 'there are fundamentally different worlds that are being perceived, and not just views on the same world.'[33]

John Laws contrasts this pluriverse (or 'fractiverse' as he calls it) with the 'one-world world' (and a 'one-nature metaphysics') of a modernist ontology due to modernism's hegemonic insistence on erasing the existence (or validity) of other ontologies.[34] Indeed, 'this erasure is a key component of the colonial project.'[35] A key mechanism for this erasure is modernism's resort to rationalism, an epistemology that sees knowledge as the product of deductive reasoning and believes that nature can be scientifically understood and categorised or ordered. This epistemology leads to what Donna Haraway calls the 'god-trick' or 'the view from nowhere.'[36]

Laws points out that the 'one-world world' of modernism is not just 'monstrous and utterly painful in a colonial or post-colonial context,' but does not even hold true in the 'North.'[37] As we have already noted, there are multiple ontologies in the North (or 'West'), and these are being enacted and lived 'alongside one-world imaginaries.'[38] Laws argues, therefore, that,

> though the one-world metaphysics of the North are powerful, they are not as powerful as they imagine themselves to be. They rest on a raggedy set of strategies that are also in the business of (partially) repressing difference. The hope is that if we can detect those strategies at work then we can try to unstitch them. We can create imaginaries within the North that include difference.[39]

The new ontological turn

The scholarly work associated with detecting and unstitching those strategies that seek to maintain modernism's dominance – particularly in relation to human-(rest of) nature relations and the concomitant erasure of alternative ontologies – has been described as 'the new ontological turn.' As noted above, despite being lumped together (and certainly sharing some important aims), this scholarship is diverse. Very broadly speaking, it ranges from addressing the limits of environmental law through the promotion of rights or legal personhood for Nature or specific natural entities,[40] sometimes for purely instrumental reasons of environmental protection,[41] to 'posthuman legal theory,'[42] to 'decolonial'[43] approaches that include the promotion of Indigenous rights and legal and ontological pluralism.[44] While all of these approaches seek to increase the legal visibility and protection of natural entities or 'Nature' (and, of course, there are interrelationships and blurred lines between them), there are significant fault lines, particularly in their engagement with ontology (and related epistemological issues) and the politics of (de)colonisation.

Instrumental RoN scholarship

Early RoN scholarship, which came to define the early terms of the field, includes Christopher Stone's well-known article, 'Should trees have standing?,' which contained a pragmatic (and largely instrumental) proposal for granting legal standing to natural entities in order to get around the limitations of US environmental law.[45] Stone's scholarship is particularly well known, in good part because he is American and wrote in English, but he had a contemporary working in Chile by the name of Godofredo Stutzin, who was also promoting the recognition of rights for nature – although Stutzin's work was less pragmatic, as his end goal was to realise a complete 'ecocentric turn.'[46] These early scholars were then followed by Thomas Berry's 'ecotheological'[47] promotion of natural rights for nature in the late 1990s,[48] and Cormac Cullinan's 2003 'Wild Law,' which refined Berry's work for a legal context.[49] Since this time, the field has significantly expanded and become increasingly diverse. In addition to work that picks up these early calls for an ecocentric turn in the law and the promotion of nature's rights to address the ecological crisis,[50] the field now includes a wide range of critical scholarship that is more focused on understanding the (broadly described) RoN legal developments and theories that are emerging around the world than on promoting ecocentrism – work that has been described as 'critical ecological jurisprudence.'[51]

One of the key critiques that has been made of the more instrumental RoN scholarship (and its associated movements) is that it seeks to promote universalist 'truths,' including what Tănăsescu calls an 'ecotheological' concept of 'Nature.'[52] Related to this critique is that this naturalisation of a singular concept of 'Nature' inadvertently re-enacts the human-nature dualism of modernist ontology, particularly when coupled with calls to decentre the human by swapping 'anthropocentrism' with 'eco-centrism.'[53] It makes little sense to (de) centre either humans or nature unless you believe they are separate categories in the first place. A further concern is that such eco-centrism can all too easily slip into protecting Nature from humans – an approach known as 'environmental colonialism' due to its history of forcing Indigenous peoples off their lands and waters to create zones of 'wilderness.'[20]

Posthuman legal theory

Posthuman legal theory,[54] which sometimes overlaps with and sometimes sits alongside a diverse range of theoretical interventions, including 'new materialism'[55] and 'eco-legality,'[56] goes beyond decentring the human by seeking to deconstruct its very meaning.[57] Importantly, a key part of this deconstruction is achieved by challenging modernist ontology and dualism. To counter this dualism, these theoretical interventions focus on healing 'eco-social fragmentation and rift,'[58] and paying far closer attention to relationality. New materialism, for example, emphasises 'the relation of all entities, the entanglements between and among human and non-human, and the vibrancy of matter.'[59]

Decolonial legal ontological work

I have termed the final strand of these approaches 'decolonial,' and here I note that many of the above theoretical interventions also involve decolonial agendas. Angela Harris has described these interventions as 'legal-ontological work'[60] and argues that this work requires simultaneously 'rethinking the legal subjecthood of nonhuman entities, and rethinking the legal subjecthood of human collectivities.'[61] She describes this as the construction of new legal subjects and the deconstruction of old ones.[62] In colonial contexts, such a decolonial approach will also require engaging with Indigenous law and knowledge systems and directly confronting the politics of colonialism.[63] As Kirsten Anker argues, 'ecological lawyers must recognize that traditional ecological knowledge is rooted in legal orders, making the desired shift not just cognitive but political.'[64] Val Napoleon and Hadley Friedland explain that this includes 'creating space for Indigenous legal traditions.'[65] To achieve this, it will be necessary to unsettle the dominance of modernist ontology over many legal systems.

The question of how this unsettling, or 'unstitching,' is achieved remains contested – which brings us back again to the definition of ontology. You will recall that ontology is the lens through which we understand what is real – and that one interpretation of this definition is that ontology is virtually synonymous with 'what is real' or 'reality.' From here we reach the claim that ontological pluralism implies the existence of multiple worlds – a pluriverse. For others, the *lens* is foregrounded, and ontology becomes more synonymous with *worldview* – a concept that is at least somewhat distinct from *reality* itself.

Rutgerd Boelens and others, for example, define ontologies as 'modes of conceptualising and ordering the world, providing a means by which we can imagine, explain, live with, and act upon "the world we are and live in."'[66] You'll note here the slipperiness of the lens, particularly within a constructivist perspective that understands reality as co-constituted by the interrelationships between the material and the imaginary. Here they expand,

> Ontologies allow us to make sense of socio-ecological entities' nature and properties, their interrelated constituent parts, and the relationships that give them substance and meaning. Therefore, ontological constitution and practices include the process of material-political translation from the imaginary to material becoming.[67]

Nonetheless, Boelens and others take issue with the absolute or universal truth claims that have emerged from a particular strand of new ontological turn scholarship, particularly the 'the popularising activist and policy-oriented versions of' it.[68] Here they point out the dangers of adopting the 'god trick' or 'view from nowhere' in making truth claims about, for example, the very existence of a pluriverse – a danger, for example, of falling into the very same traps as modernism itself. For Boelens and others, a key value of 'new ontological turn' scholarship (and related legal developments) comes from its capacity to unsettle the naturalisation of a universalist modernist worldview by highlighting that proponents of this ontology have no greater claim to objective truth than anyone else. Nonetheless, this also means that proponents of a pluriverse also have no right to make universal truth claims.

While I agree with the central concerns raised about scholarship that promotes a universalist concept of Nature or flattens Indigenous peoples, cultures, and ontologies into a singular category, I'd like to pause here to highlight a few issues with this apparent conflation between a modernist ontology and the pluriverse. The great danger of modernism's one-world world and its totalising logic is that it operates, deliberately, to erase other worlds and to assert itself as a singular reality. As mentioned above, this process of erasure is central to colonisation and to the hegemonic politics that seek to present extractive capitalism as the only rational political economy. While superficially similar, a claim that there are actually multiple worlds results in the opposite outcome – it opens up the space for everyone's reality to be recognised and for people to begin to build ontological bridges between worlds. One seeks to dominate and erase, the other to acknowledge, include, and decolonise. These are not the same outcomes.

Nonetheless, this critique of universal truth claims does highlight a risk of circularity that does need to be carefully navigated in so-called 'new ontological turn' scholarship. If we accept the limitations of situated knowledge, then it is not possible to stand outside this proposed 'pluriverse' (one made up of multiple worlds/ontologies) to verify its existence – and to claim to do so would be to adopt the same 'god trick' that rationalist epistemologies are critiqued for. Mario Blaser describes this as 'the claim of multiple ontologies ... [turning] into a sort of meta-ontology, the statement of a fact... [with the result that] the crucial problem of the one-reality world remains unshaken.'[69] To counter this problem, Blaser suggests 'treating ontology as a way of worlding' and that it be used 'as a heuristic device, a tool to force our attention on how we deploy our own ontological assumptions in the analysis and how they might differ from those of our interlocutors.'[70] Worlding here 'assumes an entangled, non-lineal, and indeterminable world, where being is co-constituted and cannot be reduced to knowing.'[71]

Isabelle Stengers takes a slightly different approach by connecting ontological politics 'with the old art of diplomacy' and by arguing that it demands more than tolerance.[72] In contrasting 'the Zapatista call for "a world where many worlds fit"' with the ontological politics of 'the global West', she also notes that,

> The global West is not a "world" and recognizes no world. Referring to Deleuze and Guattari, I would rather characterize it as a "machine," destroying both politics and ontologies. ... A world-destroying machine cannot fit with other worlds. Whatever its meaning, ontological politics is thus connected with the possibility of resisting our worlds' ongoing destruction.[73]

What are the implications of these framings? Boelens and others argue that 'these new and alternative ontological understandings of the world – and their related initiatives – are politically produced, culturally enacted, and strategically mobilised. In effect, they contribute to the constitution (or contestation) of particular power relations.'[74] It is certainly true that using ontology to contest the universalist ontological claim of a modernist 'one-world' order is inherently political,[75] and the way this process often involves strategic engagement with power deserves further attention (which we will come to below). Nonetheless, the claim of multiple ontologies is not *just* political – it cannot be reduced to a political strategy. While the ontologies foregrounded in ontological turn scholarship are (largely) place-based, meaning that universal claims to truth make little sense, this does not mean that they are not real in place nor that they are only relevant to (re)ordering power relations. As Blaser notes, the concept of ontology is also employed to encourage a deeper level of self-reflection amongst scholars and other 'experts' about the ontological assumptions we bring to our work. It also highlights that, since we do not all live in the same world, far more attention needs to be spent on building ontological bridges than we may have realised.[76] I would also argue that inviting others in and having one's ontology recognised and understood has an intrinsic value that extends well beyond power relations (again, an issue explored below).

To consider how some of these issues play out in practice, the next section will explore a case study from Aotearoa New Zealand – the *Te Awa Tupua (Whanganui River Claims Settlement) Act 2017* (NZ), which was passed, after an extended period of conflict, protest, litigation, and negotiation,[77] to settle Māori claims under the 1840 *Te Tiriti*/ o Waitangi Treaty of Waitangi.[78] This legislation/treaty settlement is focused on the Whanganui River – or *Te Awa Tupua* in *te reo Māori* (the indigenous language of Aotearoa, New Zealand) – and is best known for granting the River legal personhood. As we will explore in the following section, the attention given to this particular legal innovation has, perhaps, led many to overlook some of the more significant innovations, including the challenge it presents to modernist water ontology by explicitly embedding ontological pluralism within the new governance framework for the River.

Te Awa Tupua

Flowing from Mount Tongariro to the mouth at the port of Whanganui, where it discharges into the Tasman Sea, the Whanganui River is the third longest river (and longest navigable river) in Aotearoa.[79] It runs for 290 kilometers, and its catchment covers 7,380 square kilometers of land.[80] To quote *Ngā Tāngata Tiaki o Whanganui* (the post-settlement *Iwi* (local Māori tribe) governance entity established by trust),[81]

> The Whanganui River is central to the existence of Whanganui Iwi and their health and wellbeing. The River has provided both physical and spiritual sustenance to Whanganui Iwi and its hapū from time immemorial. The Whanganui River has acted from early times as an artery for Māori inhabiting its forests and fertile river terraces and travelling to and from the central North Island.[82]

Today, land in the Whanganui catchment includes native cover (particularly in the Whanganui National Park, located in the River's upper reaches), pastoral agriculture (predominantly sheep and beef farming), and forestry. As a result of colonial development activities, the ecosystem health of the River is rated 'poor' along its full length, and there is a significant presence of suspended fine sediment and other contaminants from agricultural runoff and other pollutants.[83]

Although settler law, at the time of the 1840 Treaty of Waitangi, recognised Iwi ownership and control of the River (or *Awa*), the settler government began to breach these rights almost immediately through a series of actions to occupy and 'develop' the River and its catchment without Iwi consent or consultation.[84] The first of these breaches occurred in the early 1840s, when the Crown essentially rubber stamped a dubious and contested claim by Colonel Wakefield of the New Zealand Company to have purchased an extensive tract of land along (and across) the River.[85] Following this, the settler population on the coast expanded significantly, and the settler government began 'developing' the River and its surrounding catchment.

In the 1880s, in order to facilitate inland development, the settler government decided to make the River navigable by steamer. This channel clearance work involved the destruction of *pā tuna* (eel weirs) and *utu piharau* (lamprey weirs) and damage to the River's bed, banks, rapids, and fisheries.[86] Other interventions included the extraction of sand and gravel for road and rail construction and the introduction of trout, killing off native fish. A further significant development occurred in 1964, when the headwaters of the River were diverted into Lake Rotoaira, then on into Lake Taupo, and the nearby Waikato River catchment for hydroelectric power generation as part of the Tongariro Power Scheme.[87] Although many of these actions were illegal, even under settler law, the government repeatedly passed legislation to retrospectively 'authorise' their ongoing breaches of Iwi treaty rights.[88]

These actions were consistently resisted by Iwi, who never stopped asserting their sovereignty over the River or their customary rights. Iwi resistance was sustained and included everything from parliamentary petitions in 1873 and 1978;[89] direct action to object the channel clearance work;[90] a petition to the Queen in 1977; a stream of litigation to protect fishing rights, claim compensation for the taking of sand and gravel, and for the loss of native rights, to challenge the ownership of the River, and to object to the diversion of the headwaters; negotiations with the Crown; an 80-day protest occupation at Pākaitore (on the banks of the River) in 1995; proceedings in the Waitangi Tribunal, resulting in the Whanganui River Report in 1999; and, finally, Treaty Settlement negotiations beginning in the early 2000s.[91]

The end result of these Treaty Settlement negotiations was the *Te Awa Tupua (Whanganui River Claims Settlement) Act 2017* (NZ), which establishes a variety of new water governance mechanisms and guiding principles for the River as a compromised result of this drawn-out period of conflict and negotiation between the Whanganui Iwi and the New Zealand Crown (essentially the settler-state government). As we have seen, this conflict was fundamentally about the power to exercise Māori sovereignty to govern and exercise jurisdiction over the River and its community according to Māori law, traditional knowledge, and values (known locally as *kawa*). This law, knowledge, and values reflect a living water ontology that, unlike modernism, dictated against much of the destructive development carried out by the Crown without Iwi consent since the mid-1800s.

Given this background, the most significant outcome of the legislation is that it recognises four *kawa* in section 13 as the 'intrinsic values that represent the essence of Te Awa Tupua,'[92] and that it empowers Whanganui Iwi and *hapū* (sub-tribes or place-based kinship groups) to play a central role in the governance of the River. Despite this, it is section 14, which declares that 'Te Awa Tupua is a legal person and has all the rights, powers, duties, and liabilities of a legal person,'[93] that has received the most attention from international media and researchers.[94] The juxtaposition between this emphasis on legal personhood and the background context and detail of the legislation illustrates some of the most important ways that it, and the water governance framework it establishes, performs legal ontology work in the decolonial sense discussed above – with important implications for human-river relations in place.

The reasons for this disproportionate focus on legal personhood are diverse and complex, and I will not pretend that I can know or summarise them all accurately. Part of the story is that legal personhood has been used as a hook in the title or lede of an article or bulletin but is not actually the sole (or even primary) focus of the publication itself. Nonetheless, it is still the case that the device of 'legal personhood' does appear to have captured global attention, and there are a range of likely contributing reasons for this phenomenon.

One of these reasons can be traced back to Stone's 1972 article, entitled 'Should Trees Have Standing?'.[95] Stone's article was a response to a pending legal matter – a case brought by the Sierra Club in 1969 against Rogers Clark Ballard Morton, Secretary of the Interior, and others, for declaratory relief and an injunction to restrain the approval of ski resort development by the Walt Disney Company to accommodate 1.7 million annual visitors and 20,000 skiers at 'Mineral King' in the Sequoia National Forest.[96] As the Sierra Club was not a local property owner, it had been forced to focus on the adverse impacts on the area's aesthetics and ecology in order to rely (unsuccessfully, as it turns out) on s 10 of the *Administrative Procedure Act*, which accorded judicial review to a 'person suffering legal wrong because of agency action, or [who is] adversely affected or aggrieved by agency action within the meaning of a relevant statute.'

Reflecting on this situation, Stone's article sketches out an argument for why trees (and other natural objects) should be granted rights, including legal personhood, so that they (or their guardians) would have standing in court to protect their substantive rights. While Stone's argument is a largely pragmatic response to the limited standing rights for environmental organisations in the US, he also focuses on the importance of shifting social and legal consciousness to create '[a] radical new conception of man's relationship to the rest of nature' and of moving away from the 'view that nature exists *for men*.'[97] Stone claims, 'until the rightless thing receives its rights, we cannot see it as anything but a thing for the use of "us" —those who are holding rights at the time.'[98]

Stone acknowledges that many of the changes that he is proposing (improved legal visibility and protection of the rest of the environment) could be achieved without granting rights to natural entities, but he argues that the language of rights is important, in part because the 'vocabulary and expressions that are available to us influence and even steer our thought.'[99] Relevantly to this chapter, he expands,

> [i]f my sense of these influences is correct, then a society in which it is stated, however vaguely, that "rivers have legal rights" would evolve a different legal system than one which did not employ that expression, even if the two of them had, at the start, the very same "legal rules" in other respects.[100]

Here Stone is noting the co-constitutive relationship between law and our understanding of the world – including of water – but, at this stage, water (and indeed the rest of nature) appears to play no role in this relationship.

While the article is squarely focused on extending rights to non-human (or more-than-human) natural entities, Stone acknowledges the interdependence of interests at play, noting,

> [b]ecause the health and well-being of mankind depend upon the health of the environment, these goals will often be so mutually supportive that one can avoid deciding whether our rationale is to advance "us" or a new "us" that includes the environment.[101]

Here Stone does appear to be recognising a degree of relationality between humans and the rest of the environment, and he is certainly challenging the extractive mindset that treats 'nature' as an economic resource, but only humans appear to have agency in this dynamic. Finally, Stone digresses into a discussion of the looming planetary crisis (one that we in the 21st century are all too familiar with) and engages in a revealing attempt to defend 'western environmental consciousness' from its primary responsibility for causing the crisis.[102]

While there have been other prominent scholars in the development of RoN theory (as discussed above),[103] Stone's article has been particularly influential, especially in North America and other English-speaking countries.[104] It is this influence that perhaps helps to explain the disproportionate emphasis on the granting of legal personhood by the Te Awa Tupua legislation and some of the interpretations that have been made of the governance arrangements it establishes.

Leaving aside the fact that legal standing limitations for public interest environmental litigation are far less common outside the USA, Stone's insistence that our then-looming, now present, planetary crisis has been a shared endeavour, rather than the result of 'western environmental consciousness,' operates to absolve that particular consciousness, and the colonialism that it drove, from its central role in creating and sustaining environmental destruction. In Stone's argument, a global 'we' are responsible for the crisis and must change 'our' consciousness and laws to remedy this situation. Our brief tour of the history of the colonisation of the Whanganui River is a clear illustration of the flaws in this argument.

Scholars, especially Indigenous scholars, have been sharply critical of approaches that seek to implicate all humans equally in the creation of our present-day ecological crisis. Heather Davis and Zoe Todd, for example, argue that the start of the 'Anthropocene' should be accepted as 1610 – the beginning of the colonial period – due to the central role that colonisation has played in its genesis.[105] Davis and Todd explain that it is only by 'making the relations between the Anthropocene and colonialism explicit, [that we will be] ... in a position to understand our current ecological crisis and to take the steps needed to move away from this ecocidal path.'[106] Naomi Klein is similarly critical of blaming a universal concept of humanity for the ecological crisis while letting off the hook 'the systems that certain humans created and other humans powerfully resisted' – 'capitalism, colonialism, patriarchy.'[107] She points out that in erasing the central contribution of these ideologies and the elites that drove them, we risk simultaneously erasing 'the very existence of human systems that organized life differently: systems that insist that humans ... must be not only good citizens but also good ancestors.'[108]

Te Pā Auroa nā Te Awa Tupua – *a new water governance framework*

It is one such system that the Te Awa Tupua legislation recognises and empowers – that of the Whanganui Iwi. The legislation establishes a new governance framework, *Te Pā Auroa nā Te Awa Tupua*, and core to this framework are the four *Tupua te Kawa* recognised in section 13.[109] These *kawa* (a concept that simultaneously encapsulates law, traditional knowledge, and intrinsic values) reflect a deeply relational approach to river governance, emphasising the inseparable reciprocal relationship between iwi and hapū of the Whanganui River and their ancestral river; the fact that the River is a living and indivisible whole that provides both spiritual and physical sustenance; and a commitment to collaborative governance:

> *Ko te Awa te mātāpuna o te ora*: the River is the source of spiritual and physical sustenance: Te Awa Tupua is a spiritual and physical entity that supports and sustains both the life and natural resources within the Whanganui River and the health and well-being of the iwi, hapū, and other communities of the River.
>
> *E rere kau mai i te Awa nui mai i te Kahui Maunga ki Tangaroa*: the great River flows from the mountains to the sea: Te Awa Tupua is an indivisible and living whole from the mountains to the sea, incorporating the Whanganui River and all of its physical and metaphysical elements.

> *Ko au te Awa, ko te Awa ko au*: I am the River and the River is me: The iwi and hapū of the Whanganui River have an inalienable connection with, and responsibility to, Te Awa Tupua and its health and well-being.
>
> *Ngā manga iti, ngā manga nui e honohono kau ana, ka tupu hei Awa Tupua*: the small and large streams that flow into one another form one River: Te Awa Tupua is a singular entity comprised of many elements and communities, working collaboratively for the common purpose of the health and well-being of Te Awa Tupua.

The careful embedding of Tupua te Kawa within state legal frameworks while preserving their ontological integrity represents a sophisticated intervention in scalar politics. Unlike the 'glocalisation' processes examined in earlier chapters,[110] where local water governance was subordinated to global financial logics, this framework demonstrates how scalar relationships can be reconfigured to protect place-based ontologies. The legislation's strategic combination of rights-based mechanisms with relational governance principles illustrates how different scalar interventions can work together to create space for ontological pluralism. This approach offers important theoretical insights for decolonial water governance beyond the specific context of Aotearoa New Zealand.

These elements of the legislation extend well beyond Stone's proposal to grant legal rights and standing to natural entities such as rivers. While Stone recognised the interdependence of humanity with the rest of the environment, he did not emphasise the spiritual sustenance provided by specific natural entities to the communities that belong to them – nor the depth of connection that this reflects. He also did not appear to view natural entities as living – at least not in a metaphysical sense. Nor did he emphasise collaboration. Most significantly, despite writing in a colonial context, where the Indigenous populations have longstanding reciprocal relationships with natural entities, Stone suggested that essentially anyone ought to be able to ask to be made the guardian of an 'endangered natural entity' by a court[111] and that this role would be particularly suited to environmental NGOs.[112]

In contrast to Stone's guardianship concept, section 13 recognises the distinct *whakapapa* (ancestral kin-based) relationship of Whanganui Iwi and Hapū with the River, and sections 18 and 19 of the legislation also establish the office of *Te Pou Tupua*, the human face of Te Awa Tupua with all the powers reasonably necessary to act and speak for and on behalf of Te Awa Tupua, and to perform a range of functions under the *Te Pā Auroa* (Te Awa Tupua framework) – a model that is distinct from guardianship. These differences are legal, ontological, and highly political. The political nature of these differences goes back to the context of the legislation itself: it was the result of a longstanding conflict over the recognition of Māori sovereignty and jurisdiction over the River, and it operates to embed a degree of recognition of this sovereignty and jurisdiction in settler-state law – it is explicitly decolonial.[113]

While there are clear limitations to this recognition – particularly that it stops well short of full sovereignty and explicitly excludes any limitations on 'existing private property rights in the Whanganui River; or … any rights to, or interests in, water'[114] – the legislation is a political intervention (strategically negotiated by Iwi leaders) that is squarely focused on redressing some of the impacts of colonisation and Crown breaches of the Treaty of Waitangi.[115] Part of this redress includes the explicit recognition of legal and ontological pluralism through the recognition of Tupua te Kawa.[116] The potential impact of this recognition of kawa may somewhat reflect Stone's vision of working to shift social and legal consciousness, at least for Pākehā (New Zealanders of European descent). However, the necessary shift goes deeper than Stone seemed to anticipate.

Ontological implications

Miriama Cribb, Jason Paul Mika, and Sarah Leberman, for example, argue that meaningfully implementing Te Pā Auroa requires non-Indigenous organisations to undergo a deep ontological shift rather than simply engaging in legal or technical compliance with the legislation.[117] Here they emphasise the need to develop a new consciousness that recognises Indigenous ways of relating to the River.[118] Importantly, Cribb and others note that from a Whanganui Iwi perspective, this 'consciousness' (or ontology) and the knowledge and relationships it encompasses are not new – they have existed 'since time immemorial … [and are] embedded in *pepeha,*[119] *whakapapa, whakataukī,*[120] *and tikanga.*'[121] What is new is the framework for translating this into settler state legal and governance systems (with related management systems being the focus for Cribb and others). Here they emphasise the focus on pluralism through decolonisation rather than 'substituting one—non-Indigenous—model of knowledge production with control by another—Indigenous.'[122]

Inviting people in

Cribb, Elizabeth Macpherson, and Axel Borchgrevink expand on this discussion further by emphasising the significance of the collaborative approach embedded in the Whanganui governance model and the way that this operates to invite people into the process.[123] Here they note that it is 'an Indigenous sharing model by virtue of the fact that through relationality, abundance, working together, putting the river first, and bringing a whole community in conversation with the river, the Whanganui model benefits us all.'[124] Cribb, Macpherson, and Borchgrevink examine the implementation of this model in relation to two case studies, *Te Pūwaha* (the Whanganui Port Revitalisation Project) and *Te Kōpuka nā Te Awa Tupua* (the permanent joint committee or 'Strategy Group').

The governance structure for the Whanganui port revitalisation initiative (Te Pūwaha) centres hapū authority through *Te Mata Pūau*, 'a hapū-led collective overseeing the application of Te Awa Tupua together with key partners at both the governance and operational levels.'[125] This approach operates to position river wellbeing as the overarching objective; implement collaborative decision-making processes; integrate kawa through inductions for all project participants; and enable meaningful community participation and consultation.[126] The Strategy Group, Te Kōpuka nā Te Awa Tupua, has been established as a permanent joint committee under the Act, and Cribb, Macpherson, and Borchgrevink describe it as embodying a sophisticated approach to pluralistic river governance.[127] With representation from Iwi, local authorities, and diverse stakeholders, it is tasked with developing *Te Heke Ngahuru* (the river strategy) and 'act[ing] collaboratively to advance the health and well-being of Te Awa Tupua.'[128] With a maximum of 17 members representing diverse interests, Te Kōpuka is led by Iwi representatives whose key focus is on building shared understanding through deliberative processes, with an emphasis on relationship and consensus-building.[129]

Cribb, Macpherson, and Borchgrevink note that the significance of these institutions is the way they operationalise the Act's theoretical innovations in practice, demonstrating concrete manifestations of relational legal pluralism and illustrating a successful pathway for Indigenous legal principles to be meaningfully integrated into governance structures while maintaining their ontological integrity.[130] They acknowledge ongoing challenges, including the reliance on voluntary participation and the time required for genuine paradigm shifts in governance approaches, but their analysis reveals how these institutions move beyond consultation toward genuine power-sharing and ontological transformation. Here the authors note,

> [t]he centring of *Tupua te Kawa* in both *Te Pūwaha* and *Te Kōpuka*, not only elevates human to non-human relationships, but is holistic and collaborative in its approach, devolving decision-making to allow more equitable participation by communities including hapū and iwi – all with a common purpose of ensuring the health and well-being of *Te Awa Tupua*.[131]

Discussion

From this analysis – and the juxtaposition with Stone's more instrumental legal personhood proposals – we can observe that the *Te Awa Tupua Act* represents a sophisticated intervention in legal theory and practice, one that strategically deploys legal mechanisms to enable Indigenous ontologies and authority while fostering new forms of relational governance. It has been observed that when Indigenous communities are forced to have their laws (and ontologies) 'recognised' in settler-state systems, it reinforces,

> a political bias in which 'what matters', including procedures and institutions, are decided by "the recogniser", who in most cases is the state. In many countries, technocratic procedures define how such recognition and representation will take place. So if they are legally recognised, local rights frameworks and related socio-natural relationships may face expert-dominated re-definition, assimilation, or subordination.[132]

Here it is worth noting the strategic wisdom observed by Cribb, Macpherson, and Borchgrevink of embedding Tupua te Kawa in the legislation because, unlike *tikanga* (the more commonly embedded Māori law), 'no national court or Parliament has the authority to determine what it means or how it should be applied without the people that hold the appropriate knowledge about these kawa.'[133]

To return to the discussion above, embedding ontological (and legal) pluralism in settler-state law through the treaty settlement legislation was certainly a political strategy, and it has important implications for power relations in the governance of Te Awa Tupua – particularly within the resulting governance arrangements. Nonetheless, it cannot be reduced to a political strategy. It is clear from the terms of the legislation and the governance of its implementation that there is a genuine commitment to 'inviting people in' and enabling them to enact their own relationships with the Whanganui River – by experiencing an ontology/world in which this living River has agency. While the changes to settler law created by the legislation are important in creating the enforcement mechanisms necessary to drive these governance and ontological changes – and the decolonisation process that they enable – these downstream changes offer further transformative potential. Of particular relevance to this chapter is the capacity of these changes to protect and foster reciprocal place-based human-river relationships that can support the long-term health of the entire community.

While earlier chapters explored how neoliberal water governance produced and entrenched spatial inequalities in water access and control – from Manila's informal settlements to Soweto's prepaid meters and Michigan's majority Black cities – this case study reveals how the recognition of Indigenous laws and ontologies can begin to unwind these colonial and neoliberal spatial (and racial) hierarchies. Similarly, while the scalar dynamics examined in Manila (in Chapter 3), where 'glocalisation' processes subordinated local water relationships to global financial imperatives and ideology, this framework illustrates how scalar relationships can be reconfigured to protect and enable place-based ontologies. The way that Tupua te Kawa operates simultaneously at the local hapū level, the river-basin scale, and within national legislation models one (place-based) pathway to navigating decolonial approaches to multi-scalar water governance. The framework's protection of place-based relationships with water demonstrates how legal and ontological pluralism can reshape water governance spaces. This spatial reconfiguration occurs not just through formal legal recognition but also through the transformation of governance processes themselves – as illustrated by Te Pūwaha's centring of hapū authority and Te Kōpuka's collaborative approach to strategy development.

This chapter has examined how a modernist ontology that understands water as an inert resource faces persistent challenges from alternative understandings of 'living water,' resulting (in some contexts) in innovative legal frameworks that recognise rivers as living entities. While much scholarly attention has focused on the legal personhood provisions of the Te Awa Tupua legislation, this analysis emphasises that its most transformative aspects lie in the sophisticated recognition of Tupua te Kawa and the establishment of collaborative governance structures. These mechanisms operate simultaneously to centre iwi relationships while 'inviting people in' to develop their own meaningful connections with the River. The framework's strategic combination of rights-based mechanisms with relational governance principles demonstrates how different interventions can work together to create space for ontological pluralism while protecting both human and riverine rights.

The chapter's opening discussion of the persistence of living water ontologies, even in contexts of aggressive modernist reform, also provides a new lens for understanding the forms of resistance documented throughout this book. While earlier case studies – from Phiri to Flint – demonstrated communities contesting neoliberal water governance through rights-based frameworks, this ontological analysis reveals deeper dimensions of such resistance, suggesting that the global water justice movement represents not just political resistance but ontological persistence. Although global water governance continues to be dominated by a modernist ontology that enables water's commodification, this analysis demonstrates that such reduction has never fully succeeded in erasing community understandings of water as living and sacred. The endurance of these diverse, place-based ontologies of 'living water' suggests alternative pathways toward more sustainable water relationships. While the specific water ontology of the Whanganui Iwi cannot be transplanted to other locations, the framework's sophisticated approach to decolonising governance systems while building ontological bridges through pluralism and collaboration offers important theoretical and practical insights for water governance reform. In their analysis of the globally relevant lessons that can be drawn from the Te Awa Act as a mechanism for 'enabling Indigenous water jurisdiction', Macpherson and Hayden Turoa note the importance of 'inclusive, collaborative governance arrangements and power-sharing, legal dispute resolution processes utilising place-based Indigenous expertise, and adequate funding to make it all work.'[134]

They also emphasis the need to decentre 'Western law and a commitment from governments and communities to work together to uphold the values and principles of a legal system that is grounded in a distinct, relational worldview from the current Western law approach.'[135]

This case study thus advances the book's broader argument about the co-constitution of water governance through the interaction between people's relationships with water, legal frameworks, and water's own agency. By demonstrating how recognition of ontological pluralism can reshape water governance spaces, it reveals pathways beyond both market mechanisms and individual rights toward more sustainable and just water futures – pathways that we will explore further in the next and final chapter of this book.

Notes

1 Veronica Strang, *Water: Nature and Culture* (Reaktion Books, 2015) 41.
2 Veronica Strang, 'Fluid Consistencies: Material Relationality in Human Engagements with Water' (2014) 21(2) *Archaeological Dialogues* 133.
3 See, e.g., *Wheeler v Director de la Procuraduria General de Estado de Loja* (2011) Corte Provincial de Justicia de Loja 11121-2011-0010 (*Vilcabamba Case*). In addition to the Preamble, the Ecuadorian Constitution of 2008 recognises the rights of Nature, or *Pacha Mama*, in articles 71 through to 74.
4 *Center for Social Justice Studies v. Presidency of the Republic et al. Decision T-622/16* (Atrato River Case), Corte Constitucional (10 November 2016) (Colombia).
5 *Mohd Salim v State of Uttarakhand & Others* (2017) 126 (*Ganges and Yamuna Case*); *Lalit Miglani v State of Uttarakhand & Others* (2017) 139 (*Glaciers Case*). Note, these judgments have been appealed to the Indian Supreme Court and are currently stayed.
6 *Human Rights and Peace for Bangladesh v Government of Bangladesh and others* (2019) High Court Division of the Supreme Court of Bangladesh (HCD) Writ Petition No. 13989 of 2016 (*Bangladesh Rivers Case*); Mohammad Sohidul Islam and Erin O'Donnell, 'Legal Rights for the Turag: Rivers as Living Entities in Bangladesh' (2020) 23(2) *Asia Pacific Journal of Environmental Law* 160.
7 *Te Awa Tupua (Whanganui River Claims Settlement) Act 2017* (NZ); *Waikato-Tainui Raupatu Claims (Waikato River) Settlement Act 2010* (NZ); *Ngati Tuwharetoa, Raukawa, and Te Arawa River Iwi Waikato River Act 2010* (NZ); *Te Arawa River Iwi Waikato River Act (NZ)* (2010); *Nga Wai o Maniapoto (Waipa River) Act 2012* (NZ).
8 Julian S. Yates, Leila M. Harris and Nicole J. Wilson, 'Multiple Ontologies of Water: Politics, Conflict and Implications for Governance' (2017) 35(5) *Environment and Planning D: Society and Space* 797; Sarah Laborde and Sue Jackson, 'Living Waters or Resource? Ontological Differences and the Governance of Waters and Rivers' (2022) 27(3) *Local Environment* 357; Cristy Clark and Anne Poelina, 'Indigenous Ontology and International Law' in Mattias Åhrén et al (eds), *Oxford Handbook of Indigenous Peoples and International Law* (Oxford University Press, 2025).
9 Veronica Strang, *Water Beings: From Nature Worship to the Environmental Crisis* (Reaktion Books, 2023) 13.
10 Strang, *Water Beings* (n 9) 7–8.
11 Strang, *Water Beings* (n 9) 8.

12 Strang, *Water Beings* (n 9) 10.
13 Strang, *Water Beings* (n 9) 22.
14 Terje Oestigaard, 'The Topography of Holy Water in England after the Reformation' in K.V. Lykke Syse and Terje Oestigaard (eds), *Perceptions of Water in Britain from Early Modern Times to the Present: An Introduction* (BRIC Press, 2010) 15.
15 Oestigaard, 'The Topography of Holy Water in England after the Reformation' (n 14) 15.
16 Oestigaard, 'The Topography of Holy Water in England after the Reformation' (n 14) 21.
17 Oestigaard, 'The Topography of Holy Water in England after the Reformation' (n 14) 21.
18 Oestigaard, 'The Topography of Holy Water in England after the Reformation' (n 14) 31.
19 Oestigaard, 'The Topography of Holy Water in England after the Reformation' (n 14) 23.
20 Oestigaard, 'The Topography of Holy Water in England after the Reformation'.
21 Veronica Strang, *The Meaning of Water* (Berg, 2004) 93.
22 Strang, *Water: Nature and Culture* (n 1); Wendy Jepson et al, 'Advancing Human Capabilities for Water Security: A Relational Approach' (2017) 1 *Water Security* 46; Terje Oestigaard, 'Holy Water: The Works of Water in Defining and Understanding Holiness' (2017) 4(3) *WIREs Water* e1205; Yates, Harris and Wilson, 'Multiple Ontologies of Water' (n 8); Christiana Zenner, 'Turning to Traditions: Three Cultural-Religious Articulations of Fresh Waters' Value(s) in Contemporary Governance Frameworks' in Farhana Sultana and Alex Loftus (eds), *Water Politics: Governance, Justice and the Right to Water* (Routledge, 2020) 42; Strang, *Water Beings* (n 9).
23 Vernon L. Scarborough, 'Does Water Have Agency? Does It Need To?' (2014) 21(2) *Archaeological Dialogues* 150, 152 (emphasis added).
24 Scarborough, 'Does Water Have Agency? Does It Need To?' (n 23) 152.
25 Strang, 'Fluid Consistencies' (n 2).
26 Strang, 'Fluid Consistencies' (n 2) 167.
27 Strang, 'Fluid Consistencies' (n 2) 165.
28 Strang, 'Fluid Consistencies' (n 2) 165.
29 Bill Gammage, *The Biggest Estate on Earth: How Aborigines Made Australia* (Allen and Unwin 2011); Usha Natarajan, 'TWAIL and the Environment: The State of Nature, the Nature of the State and the Arab Spring' (2012) 14 *Oregon Review of International Law* 177.
30 For a debate on this issue, see Michael Carrithers et al, 'Ontology Is Just Another Word for Culture: Motion Tabled at the 2008 Meeting of the Group for Debates in Anthropological Theory, University of Manchester' (2010) 30(2) *Critique of Anthropology* 152.
31 See, e.g., Laborde and Jackson, 'Living Waters or Resource?' (n 8).
32 Marisol de la Cadena and Mario Blaser (eds) *A World of Many Worlds* (Duke University Press, 2018).
33 Mihnea Tănăsescu, *Understanding the Rights of Nature: A Critical Introduction* (Transcript Publishing, 2022) 62.
34 See, e.g., Laborde and Jackson, 'Living Waters or Resource?' (n 8).
35 Clark and Poelina, 'Indigenous Ontology and International Law' (n 8).
36 Donna Haraway, 'Situated Knowledges: The Science Question in Feminism and the Privilege of Partial Perspective' (1988) 14(3) *Feminist Studies* 575, 589.
37 John Law, 'What's Wrong with a One-World World?' (2015) 16(1) *Distinktion: Journal of Social Theory* 126, 135.

38 Law, 'What's Wrong with a One-World World?' (n 37).
39 Law, 'What's Wrong with a One-World World?' (n 37).
40 Roderick Frazier Nash, *The Rights of Nature: History of Environmental Ethics* (The University of Wisconsin Press, 1989); David Boyd, *The Rights of Nature: A Legal Revolution That Could Save the World* (ECW Press, 2017); Craig M. Kauffman and Pamela L. Martin, *The Politics of Rights of Nature: Strategies for Building a More Sustainable Future* (The MIT Press, 2021) <https://doi.org/10.7551/mitpress/13855.001.0001>.
41 Christopher Stone, 'Should Trees Have Standing? Towards Legal Rights for Natural Objects' (1972) 45 *Southern California Law Review* 450.
42 See, e.g., Donna Haraway, *Staying with the Trouble* (Duke University Press, 2016); Anna Grear, 'Introduction: "Staying with the Trouble"*—Environmental Justice for the Anthropocene–Capitalocene' in *Environmental Justice* (Edward Elgar Publishing, 2020) <http://orca.cf.ac.uk/126039/>; Emily Jones, 'Posthuman International Law and the Rights of Nature' (2021) 12(Special Issue) *Journal of Human Rights and The Environment* 82; Jana Norman, *Posthuman Legal Subjectivity: Reimagining the Human in the Anthropocene* (Routledge, 2022).
43 Angela P. Harris, 'Decolonizing Legal Subjects in Climate Chaos' (2022) 121(2) *The South Atlantic Quarterly* 359, 359.
44 Kirsten Anker, 'Ecological Jurisprudence and Indigenous Relational Ontologies beyond the "Ecological Indian"?' in Kirsten Anker et al (eds), *From Environmental to Ecological Law* (Routledge, 2020) 104; Martuwarra RiverOfLife, Katherine S. Taylor and Anne Poelina, 'Living Waters, Law First: Nyikina and Mangala Water Governance in the Kimberley, Western Australia' (2021) 25(1) *Australasian Journal of Water Resources* 40; Lieselotte Viaene, 'Indigenous Water Ontologies, Hydro-Development and the Human/More-Than-Human Right to Water: A Call for Critical Engagement with Plurilegal Water Realities' (2021) 13(12) *Water* 1660; Miriama Cribb, Jason Paul Mika and Sarah Leberman, 'Te Pā Auroa Nā Te Awa Tupua: The New (but Old) Consciousness Needed to Implement Indigenous Frameworks in Non-Indigenous Organisations' (2022) 18(4) *AlterNative: An International Journal of Indigenous Peoples* 566; Cristy Clark, Karen Fisher and Elizabeth Macpherson, 'Indigenous Rights and Ontological Plurality in the Institutional Arrangements for the Waikato and Waipā Rivers in Aotearoa' (2024) *The International Journal of Human Rights* 1.
45 Stone, 'Should Trees Have Standing?' (n 41).
46 Godofredo Stutzin, 'Un Imperativo Ecológico: Reconocer Los Derechos de La Naturaleza' (1984) 1(1) *Ambiente y Desarrollo* 97. See Tănăsescu, *Understanding the Rights of Nature* (n 33) 24–26 for further discussion of Stutzin's work and ongoing influence over today's RoN scholarship and movement.
47 Tănăsescu, *Understanding the Rights of Nature* (n 33) 26.
48 Thomas Berry, *The Great Work: Our Way into the Future* (Three Rivers Press, 1999).
49 Cormac Cullinan, *Wild Law: A Manifesto for Earth Justice* (Green Books, 1st edition, 2003).
50 Boyd, *The Rights of Nature* (n 40).
51 Emille Boulot and Joshua Sterlin, 'Steps Towards a Legal Ontological Turn: Proposals for Law's Place beyond the Human' (2022) 11(1) *Transnational Environmental Law* 13, 31.
52 Tănăsescu, *Understanding the Rights of Nature* (n 33) 63.
53 See, e.g., Norman, *Posthuman Legal Subjectivity* (n 42) 46; Tănăsescu, *Understanding the Rights of Nature* (n 33); Rutgerd Boelens, Lena Hommes and Jaime Hoogesteger, 'Ontological Politics in River Defence Debates: Unpacking Fields

of Contention in Eco-Centric and Non-Human Turns' (2024) 17(3) *Water Alternatives* 649.
54 See, e.g., Haraway, *Staying with the Trouble* (n 42); Grear, 'Introduction' (n 42); Jones, 'Posthuman International Law and the Rights of Nature' (n 42); Norman, *Posthuman Legal Subjectivity* (n 42).
55 See, e.g., Diana Coole and Samantha Frost, 'Introducing the New Materialisms' in Diana Coole and Samantha Frost (eds), *New Materialisms: Ontology, Agency, and Politics* (Duke University Press, 2010) 1; Anna Grear, '"Anthropocene, Capitalocene, Chthulucene": Re-Encountering Environmental Law and Its "Subject" with Haraway and New Materialism' in *Environmental Law and Governance for the Anthropocene* (Hart Publishing, 2017) 77; Anna Grear, 'Resisting Anthropocene Neoliberalism: Towards New Materialist Commoning?' in Anna Grear and David Bollier (eds), *The Great Awakening: New Modes of Life Amidst Capitalist Ruins* (Punctum Press, 2019) <http://orca.cf.ac.uk/122785/>; Grear, 'Introduction' (n 42).
56 Margaret Davies, 'Re-Forming Property to Address Eco-Social Fragmentation and Rift' (2021) 12(Special Issue) *Journal of Human Rights and the Environment* 13, 14.
57 Emille Boulot, Anna Grear and Iván D. Vargas-Roncancio (eds), *Posthuman Legalities: New Materialism and Law Beyond the Human* (Edward Elgar Publishing, 2021) 4.
58 Davies, 'Re-Forming Property to Address Eco-Social Fragmentation and Rift' (n 56).
59 Jessie Hohmann, 'Diffuse Subjects and Dispersed Power: New Materialist Insights and Cautionary Lessons for International Law' (2021) 34(3) *Leiden Journal of International Law* 585, 587.
60 Boulot and Sterlin, 'Steps Towards a Legal Ontological Turn' (n 51) 32; Harris, 'Decolonizing Legal Subjects in Climate Chaos' (n 43).
61 Harris, 'Decolonizing Legal Subjects in Climate Chaos' (n 43) 359.
62 Harris, 'Decolonizing Legal Subjects in Climate Chaos' (n 43) 371.
63 Zoe Todd, 'An Indigenous Feminist's Take on the Ontological Turn: "Ontology" Is Just Another Word for Colonialism' (2016) 29(1) *Journal of Historical Sociology* 4.
64 Anker, 'Ecological Jurisprudence and Indigenous Relational Ontologies Beyond the "Ecological Indian"?' (n 44).
65 Val Napoleon and Hadley Friedland, 'An inside Job: Engaging with Indigenous Legal Traditions through Stories' (2016) 61(4) *McGill Law Journal* 725–754.
66 Boelens, Hommes and Hoogesteger, 'Ontological Politics in River Defence Debates' (n 53) 651.
67 Boelens, Hommes and Hoogesteger, 'Ontological Politics in River Defence Debates' (n 53) 651.
68 Boelens, Hommes and Hoogesteger, 'Ontological Politics in River Defence Debates' (n 53) 653–655.
69 Mario Blaser, 'Ontology and Indigeneity: On the Political Ontology of Heterogeneous Assemblages' (2014) 21 *Cultural Geographies* 49, 52–53.
70 Blaser, 'Ontology and Indigeneity' 53.
71 Clark and Poelina, 'Indigenous Ontology and International Law' (n 8) citing Carl Mika et al, 'The Ontological Differences Between Wording and Worlding the World' (2020) 8(1) *Language, Discourse & Society* 15.
72 Isabelle Stengers, 'The Challenge of Ontological Politics' in Marisol de la Cadena and Mario Blaser (eds) A World of Many Worlds (Duke University Press, 2018) 83, 83-84.

73 Stengers, 'The Challenge of Ontological Politics' (n 72) 83, 86.
74 Boelens, Hommes and Hoogesteger, 'Ontological Politics in River Defence Debates' (n 53) 655–657.
75 Clark and Poelina, 'Indigenous Ontology and International Law' (n 8).
76 See, e.g., Laborde and Jackson, 'Living Waters or Resource?' (n 8).
77 Ngā Tāngata Tiaki o Whanganui, *Historical Journey - The Whanganui River* (Ngā Tāngata Tiaki o Whanganui, 2023) <https://www.ngatangatatiaki.co.nz/our-story/historical-journey/>.
78 Note, while *Te Tiriti* is the *te reo Māori* term for the 'Treaty of Waitangi', they are often considered to refer to two different treaties – one written in *te reo Māori* and the other written in English – which were not faithful translations of each other, particularly when it comes to the matter of sovereignty.
79 Gerard Albert, *Te Awa Tupua* (PowerPoint at the He Waka Pakoko, 2023) <https://www.ngatangatatiaki.co.nz/important-documents/>.
80 Albert, *Te Awa Tupua* (n 79).
81 Ngā Tāngata Tiaki o Whanganui, *Deed of Trust* <https://www.ngatangatatiaki.co.nz/assets/6.-Nga-Tangata-Tiaki-o-Whanganui-Trust-Deed.pdf>.
82 Ngā Tāngata Tiaki o Whanganui, *Historical Journey - The Whanganui River* (n 77).
83 Horizons Regional Council, *Whanganui Freshwater Management Unit* (Whanganui Freshwater Management Unit, 22 May 2023) <https://storymaps.arcgis.com/stories/02871c92a1044f0bb2414b3154b06bd8>.
84 Waitangi Tribunal, *The Whanganui River Report* (1999) xiv, 165 <https://forms.justice.govt.nz/search/Documents/WT/wt_DOC_68450539/Whanganui%20River%20Report%201999.pdf>.
85 Waitangi Tribunal, *The Whanganui River Report* (n 84) 130–141.
86 Waitangi Tribunal, *The Whanganui River Report* (n 84).
87 Ngā Tāngata Tiaki o Whanganui, *Historical Journey - The Whanganui River* (n 77).
88 Waitangi Tribunal, *The Whanganui River Report* (n 84).
89 Waitangi Tribunal, *The Whanganui River Report* (n 84) 4.
90 Waitangi Tribunal, *The Whanganui River Report* (n 84) 4.
91 Ngā Tāngata Tiaki o Whanganui, *Historical Journey - The Whanganui River* (n 77).
92 *Te Awa Tupua (Whanganui River Claims Settlement) Act (NZ)* (n 7) s 13.
93 *Te Awa Tupua (Whanganui River Claims Settlement) Act (NZ)* s 14.
94 Meg Good, 'The River as a Legal Person: Evaluating Nature Rights-Based Approaches to Environmental Protection in Australia' (2013) *National Environmental Law Review* <https://www.austlii.edu.au/cgi-bin/viewdoc/au/journals/NatEnvLawRw/2013/15.html>; Abigail Hutchison, 'The Whanganui River as a Legal Person' (2014) 39(3) *Alternative Law Journal* 179; Eleanor Ainge Roy and Eleanor de Jong, 'New Zealand River Granted Same Legal Rights as Human Being', *The Guardian* (online, 16 March 2017) <https://www.theguardian.com/world/2017/mar/16/new-zealand-river-granted-same-legal-rights-as-human-being>; Jeremy Lurgio, 'Saving the Whanganui: Can Personhood Rescue a River?', *The Guardian* (Whanganui, New Zealand, online, 29 November 2019) <https://www.theguardian.com/world/2019/nov/30/saving-the-whanganui-can-personhood-rescue-a-river>; Kennedy Warne, 'This River in New Zealand Is a Legal Person: How Will It Use Its Voice?' (*National Geographic,* 24 April 2019) <https://www.nationalgeographic.com/culture/graphics/maori-river-in-new-zealand-is-a-legal-person>; *The New Zealand River That Became a Legal Person* (Directed by Kate Evans, 20 March 2020) <https://www.bbc.com/travel/article/20200319-the-new-zealand-river-that-became-a-legal-person>; Julia Hollingsworth, 'This

River in New Zealand Is Legally a Person: Here's How It Happened', *CNN* (Whanganui, New Zealand, online, 11 December 2020) <https://www.cnn.com/2020/12/11/asia/whanganui-river-new-zealand-intl-hnk-dst/index.html>; Matthias Kramm, 'When a River Becomes a Person' (2020) 21(4) *Journal of Human Development and Capabilities* 307.

95 Stone, 'Should Trees Have Standing?' (n 41).

96 *Sierra Club v Morton* (1972) 405 US Supreme Court No. 70-34, 727.

97 Stone, 'Should Trees Have Standing?' (n 41) 38, 33 (emphasis in the original).

98 Stone, 'Should Trees Have Standing?' (n 41) 5.

99 Stone, 'Should Trees Have Standing?' (n 41) 33.

100 Stone, 'Should Trees Have Standing?' (n 41) 33.

101 Stone, 'Should Trees Have Standing?' (n 41) 33.

102 Stone, 'Should Trees Have Standing?' (n 41) 34–37.

103 See nn 45–49, and accompanying text, above.

104 For a detailed discussion of the background to the rights of nature movement, see Tănăsescu, *Understanding the Rights of Nature* (n 33).

105 Heather Davis and Zoe Todd, 'On the Importance of a Date, or, Decolonizing the Anthropocene' (2017) 16(4) *ACME: An International Journal for Critical Geographies* 761, 763.

106 Davis and Todd, 'On the Importance of a Date, or, Decolonizing the Anthropocene' (n 105).

107 Naomi Klein, 'Let Them Drown: The Violence of Othering in a Warming World' (2016) 38(11) *London Review of Books* <https://www.lrb.co.uk/the-paper/v38/n11/naomi-klein/let-them-drown>.

108 Klein, 'Let Them Drown' (n 107).

109 Albert, *Te Awa Tupua* (n 79).

110 Erik Swyngedouw, 'Globalisation or "Glocalisation"? Networks, Territories and Rescaling' (2004) 17(1) *Cambridge Review of International Affairs* 25.

111 Stone, 'Should Trees Have Standing?' (n 41) 13.

112 Stone, 'Should Trees Have Standing?' (n 41) 14.

113 Ngā Tāngata Tiaki o Whanganui, Our Story (Ngā Tāngata Tiaki o Whanganui, 2023) <https://www.ngatangatatiaki.co.nz/our-story/>.

114 *Te Awa Tupua (Whanganui River Claims Settlement) Act (NZ)* (n 7) ss 16, 46. Here it is important to note that Iwi also own property rights in the Whanganui catchment and so the preservation of 'existing private property rights, including customary rights and title' also protects Iwi rights.

115 Ngā Tāngata Tiaki o Whanganui, *Our Story* (n 113).

116 Cribb, Mika and Leberman, 'Te Pā Auroa Nā Te Awa Tupua' (n 44); Miriama Cribb, Elizabeth Macpherson and Axel Borchgrevink, 'Beyond Legal Personhood for the Whanganui River: Collaboration and Pluralism in Implementing the Te Awa Tupua Act' (2024) *The International Journal of Human Rights* 1.

117 Cribb, Mika and Leberman, 'Te Pā Auroa Nā Te Awa Tupua' (n 44) 570.

118 Cribb, Mika and Leberman, 'Te Pā Auroa Nā Te Awa Tupua' (n 44) 570.

119 'A statement by which a Māori group or tribe declares its identity and association with a particular place and ancestral people. Now also: such a statement used to introduce oneself, typically including one's name, place of origin, and tribal connections.' Oxford English Dictionary, *S.v. "Pepeha (n.)"* (July 2023) <https://doi.org/10.1093/OED/9536027635>.

120 Māori proverb.

121 Cribb, Mika and Leberman, 'Te Pā Auroa Nā Te Awa Tupua' (n 44) 571.

122 Cribb, Mika and Leberman, 'Te Pā Auroa Nā Te Awa Tupua' (n 44) 571.

123 Cribb, Macpherson and Borchgrevink, 'Beyond Legal Personhood for the Whanganui River' (n 116).

124 Cribb, Macpherson and Borchgrevink, 'Beyond Legal Personhood for the Whanganui River' (n 116) 16.
125 Cribb, Macpherson and Borchgrevink, 'Beyond Legal Personhood for the Whanganui River' (n 116) 9.
126 Cribb, Macpherson and Borchgrevink, 'Beyond Legal Personhood for the Whanganui River' (n 116).
127 Cribb, Macpherson and Borchgrevink, 'Beyond Legal Personhood for the Whanganui River' (n 116).
128 Cribb, Macpherson and Borchgrevink, 'Beyond Legal Personhood for the Whanganui River' (n 116) 12.
129 Cribb, Macpherson and Borchgrevink, 'Beyond Legal Personhood for the Whanganui River' (n 116).
130 Cribb, Macpherson and Borchgrevink, 'Beyond Legal Personhood for the Whanganui River' (n 116).
131 Cribb, Macpherson and Borchgrevink, 'Beyond Legal Personhood for the Whanganui River' (n 116) 15.
132 Boelens, Hommes and Hoogesteger, 'Ontological Politics in River Defence Debates' (n 53) 660 citing Erin O'Donnell, *Legal Rights for Rivers: Competition, Collaboration and Water Governance* (Routledge, 2018); Carolina Valladares and Rutgerd Boelens, 'Mining for Mother Earth. Governmentalities, Sacred Waters and Nature's Rights in Ecuador' (2019) 100 *Geoforum* 68; Rachel Sieder, 'The Juridification of Politics' in Marie-Claire Foblets et al (eds), *The Oxford Handbook of Law and Anthropology* (Oxford University Press, 2020) 701.
133 Cribb, Macpherson and Borchgrevink, 'Beyond Legal Personhood for the Whanganui River' (n 116) 7.
134 Elizabeth Macpherson and Hayden Turoa, 'Untapping the potential of Indigenous water jurisdiction: perspectives from Whanganui and Aotearoa New Zealand' (2025) 12(86) *Humanities & Social Science Communications* 1, 6.
135 Macpherson and Turoa, 'Untapping the potential of Indigenous water jurisdiction' (n 134) 6.

References

Albert, Gerard, 'Te Awa Tupua' (PowerPoint at the He Waka Pakoko, 2023) <https://www.ngatangatatiaki.co.nz/important-documents/>

Anker, Kirsten, 'Ecological Jurisprudence and Indigenous Relational Ontologies beyond the "Ecological Indian"?' in Kirsten Anker et al (eds), *From Environmental to Ecological Law* (Routledge, 2020) 104

Berry, Thomas, *The Great Work: Our Way into the Future* (Three Rivers Press, 1999)

Blaser, Mario, 'Ontology and Indigeneity: On the Political Ontology of Heterogeneous Assemblages' (2014) 21(1) *Cultural Geographies* 49

Boelens, Rutgerd, Lena Hommes and Jaime Hoogesteger, 'Ontological Politics in River Defence Debates: Unpacking Fields of Contention in Eco-Centric and Non-Human Turns' (2024) 17(3) *Water Alternatives* 649

Boulot, Emille, Anna Grear and Iván D. Vargas-Roncancio (eds), *Posthuman Legalities: New Materialism and Law Beyond the Human* (Edward Elgar Publishing, 2021)

Boulot, Emille and Joshua Sterlin, 'Steps Towards a Legal Ontological Turn: Proposals for Law's Place beyond the Human' (2022) 11(1) *Transnational Environmental Law* 13

Boyd, David, *The Rights of Nature: A Legal Revolution That Could Save the World* (ECW Press, 2017)

Carrithers, Michael et al, 'Ontology Is Just Another Word for Culture: Motion Tabled at the 2008 Meeting of the Group for Debates in Anthropological Theory, University of Manchester' (2010) 30(2) *Critique of Anthropology* 152

Center for Social Justice Studies v. Presidency of the Republic et al. Decision T-622/16 (Atrato River Case), Corte Constitucional (10 November 2016) (Colombia)

Clark, Cristy, Karen Fisher and Elizabeth Macpherson, 'Indigenous Rights and Ontological Plurality in the Institutional Arrangements for the Waikato and Waipā Rivers in Aotearoa' (2024) *The International Journal of Human Rights* 1 <https://doi.org/10.1080/13642987.2024.2361650>

Clark, Cristy and Anne Poelina, 'Indigenous Ontology and International Law' in Mattias Åhrén et al (eds), *Oxford Handbook of Indigenous Peoples and International Law* (Oxford University Press, 2025)

Coole, Diana and Samantha Frost, 'Introducing the New Materialisms' in Diana Coole and Samantha Frost (eds), *New Materialisms: Ontology, Agency, and Politics* (Duke University Press, 2010) 1

Cribb, Miriama, Elizabeth Macpherson and Axel Borchgrevink, 'Beyond Legal Personhood for the Whanganui River: Collaboration and Pluralism in Implementing the Te Awa Tupua Act' (2024) *The International Journal of Human Rights* 1 <https://doi.org/10.1080/13642987.2024.2314532>

Cribb, Miriama, Jason Paul Mika and Sarah Leberman, 'Te Pā Auroa Nā Te Awa Tupua: The New (but Old) Consciousness Needed to Implement Indigenous Frameworks in Non-Indigenous Organisations' (2022) 18(4) *AlterNative: An International Journal of Indigenous Peoples* 566

Cullinan, Cormac, *Wild Law: A Manifesto for Earth Justice* (Green Books, 1st edition, 2003)

Davies, Margaret, 'Re-Forming Property to Address Eco-Social Fragmentation and Rift' (2021) 12(Special Issue) *Journal of Human Rights and the Environment* 13

Davis, Heather and Zoe Todd, 'On the Importance of a Date, or, Decolonizing the Anthropocene' (2017) 16(4) *ACME: An International Journal for Critical Geographies* 761

de la Cadena, Marisol, and Mario Blaser (eds) *A World of Many Worlds* (Duke University Press, 2018)

Gammage, Bill, *The Biggest Estate on Earth: How Aborigines Made Australia (Allen and Unwin 2011)* (Allen and Unwin, 2011)

Good, Meg, 'The River as a Legal Person: Evaluating Nature Rights-Based Approaches to Environmental Protection in Australia' (2013) *National Environmental Law Review* <https://www.austlii.edu.au/cgi-bin/viewdoc/au/journals/NatEnvLawRw/2013/15.html>

Grear, Anna, '"Anthropocene, Capitalocene, Chthulucene": Re-Encountering Environmental Law and Its "Subject" with Haraway and New Materialism' in *Environmental Law and Governance for the Anthropocene* (Hart Publishing, 2017) 77

Grear, Anna, 'Introduction: "Staying with the Trouble"*—Environmental Justice for the Anthropocene–Capitalocene' in *Environmental Justice* (Edward Elgar Publishing, 2020) <https://orca.cf.ac.uk/126039/>

Grear, Anna, 'Resisting Anthropocene Neoliberalism: Towards New Materialist Commoning?' in Anna Grear and David Bollier (eds), *The Great Awakening: New Modes of Life Amidst Capitalist Ruins* (Punctum Press, 2019) <https://orca.cf.ac.uk/122785/>

Haraway, Donna, 'Situated Knowledges: The Science Question in Feminism and the Privilege of Partial Perspective' (1988) 14(3) *Feminist Studies* 575

Haraway, Donna, *Staying with the Trouble* (Duke University Press, 2016)
Harris, Angela P., 'Decolonizing Legal Subjects in Climate Chaos' (2022) 121(2) *The South Atlantic Quarterly* 359
Hohmann, Jessie, 'Diffuse Subjects and Dispersed Power: New Materialist Insights and Cautionary Lessons for International Law' (2021) 34(3) *Leiden Journal of International Law* 585
Hollingsworth, Julia, 'This River in New Zealand Is Legally a Person: Here's How It Happened', *CNN* (Whanganui, New Zealand, online, 11 December 2020) <https://www.cnn.com/2020/12/11/asia/whanganui-river-new-zealand-intl-hnk-dst/index.html>
Horizons Regional Council, *Whanganui Freshwater Management Unit* (Whanganui Freshwater Management Unit, 22 May 2023) <https://storymaps.arcgis.com/stories/02871c92a1044f0bb2414b3154b06bd8>
Human Rights and Peace for Bangladesh v Government of Bangladesh and others (2019) High Court Division of the Supreme Court of Bangladesh (HCD) Writ Petition No. 13989 of 2016
Hutchison, Abigail, 'The Whanganui River as a Legal Person' (2014) 39(3) *Alternative Law Journal* 179
Islam, Mohammad Sohidul and Erin O'Donnell, 'Legal Rights for the Turag: Rivers as Living Entities in Bangladesh' (2020) 23(2) *Asia Pacific Journal of Environmental Law* 160
Jepson, Wendy et al, 'Advancing Human Capabilities for Water Security: A Relational Approach' (2017) 1 *Water Security* 46
Jones, Emily, 'Posthuman International Law and the Rights of Nature' (2021) 12(Special Issue) *Journal of Human Rights and The Environment* 82
Kauffman, Craig M. and Pamela L. Martin, *The Politics of Rights of Nature: Strategies for Building a More Sustainable Future* (The MIT Press, 2021) <https://doi.org/10.7551/mitpress/13855.001.0001>
Klein, Naomi, 'Let Them Drown: The Violence of Othering in a Warming World' (2016) 38(11) *London Review of Books* <https://www.lrb.co.uk/the-paper/v38/n11/naomi-klein/let-them-drown>
Kramm, Matthias, 'When a River Becomes a Person' (2020) 21(4) *Journal of Human Development and Capabilities* 307
Laborde, Sarah and Sue Jackson, 'Living Waters or Resource? Ontological Differences and the Governance of Waters and Rivers' (2022) 27(3) *Local Environment* 357
Lalit Miglani v State of Uttarakhand & Others (30 March 2017) 139 (Uttarakhand High Court)
Law, John, 'What's Wrong with a One-World World?' (2015) 16(1) *Distinktion: Journal of Social Theory* 126
Lurgio, Jeremy, 'Saving the Whanganui: Can Personhood Rescue a River?', *The Guardian* (Whanganui, New Zealand, online, 29 November 2019) <https://www.theguardian.com/world/2019/nov/30/saving-the-whanganui-can-personhood-rescue-a-river>
Elizabeth Macpherson and Hayden Turoa, 'Untapping the potential of Indigenous water jurisdiction: perspectives from Whanganui and Aotearoa New Zealand' (2025) 12(86) *Humanities & Social Science Communications* 1
Mika, Carl et al, 'The Ontological Differences between Wording and Worlding the World' (2020) 8(1) *Language, Discourse & Society* 15
Mohd Salim v State of Uttarakhand & Others (20 March 2017) 126 (Uttarakhand High Court)

Napoleon, Val and Hadley Friedland, 'An inside Job: Engaging with Indigenous Legal Traditions through Stories' (2016) 61(4) *McGill Law Journal* 725–754

Nash, Roderick Frazier, *The Rights of Nature: History of Environmental Ethics* (The University of Wisconsin Press, 1989)

Natarajan, Usha, 'TWAIL and the Environment: The State of Nature, the Nature of the State and the Arab Spring' (2012) 14 *Oregon Review of International Law* 177

Ngā Tāngata Tiaki o Whanganui, *Deed of Trust* (4 August 2014) <https://www.ngatangatatiaki.co.nz/assets/6.-Nga-Tangata-Tiaki-o-Whanganui-Trust-Deed.pdf> (last accessed 27 March 2025)

Ngā Tāngata Tiaki o Whanganui, *Historical Journey - The Whanganui River* (Ngā Tāngata Tiaki o Whanganui, 2023) <https://www.ngatangatatiaki.co.nz/our-story/historical-journey/>

Ngā Tāngata Tiaki o Whanganui, *Our Story* (Ngā Tāngata Tiaki o Whanganui, 2023) <https://www.ngatangatatiaki.co.nz/our-story/> (last accessed 27 March 2025)

Nga Wai o Maniapoto (Waipa River) Act 2012 (NZ)

Ngati Tuwharetoa, Raukawa, and Te Arawa River Iwi Waikato River Act 2010 (NZ)

Norman, Jana, *Posthuman Legal Subjectivity: Reimagining the Human in the Anthropocene* (Routledge, 2022)

O'Donnell, Erin, *Legal Rights for Rivers: Competition, Collaboration and Water Governance* (Routledge, 2018)

Oestigaard, Terje, 'Holy Water: The Works of Water in Defining and Understanding Holiness' (2017) 4(3) *WIREs Water* e1205

Oestigaard, Terje, 'The Topography of Holy Water in England after the Reformation' in K.V. Lykke Syse and Terje Oestigaard (eds), *Perceptions of Water in Britain from Early Modern Times to the Present: An Introduction* (BRIC Press, 2010) 15

Oxford English Dictionary, *S.v. "Pepeha (n.)"* (July 2023) <https://doi.org/10.1093/OED/9536027635>

RiverOfLife, Martuwarra, Katherine S. Taylor and Anne Poelina, 'Living Waters, Law First: Nyikina and Mangala Water Governance in the Kimberley, Western Australia' (2021) 25(1) *Australasian Journal of Water Resources* 40

Roy, Eleanor Ainge and Eleanor de Jong, 'New Zealand River Granted Same Legal Rights as Human Being', *The Guardian* (online, 16 March 2017) <https://www.theguardian.com/world/2017/mar/16/new-zealand-river-granted-same-legal-rights-as-human-being>

Scarborough, Vernon L., 'Does Water Have Agency? Does It Need To?' (2014) 21(2) *Archaeological Dialogues* 150

Sieder, Rachel, 'The Juridification of Politics' in Marie-Claire Foblets et al (eds), *The Oxford Handbook of Law and Anthropology* (Oxford University Press, 2020) 701

Sierra Club v Morton (1972) 405 US Supreme Court No. 70-34, 727

Stengers, Isabelle, 'The Challenge of Ontological Politics' in Marisol de la Cadena and Mario Blaser (eds) A World of Many Worlds (Duke University Press, 2018) 83

Stone, Christopher, 'Should Trees Have Standing? Towards Legal Rights for Natural Objects' (1972) 45 *Southern California Law Review* 450

Strang, Veronica, 'Fluid Consistencies: Material Relationality in Human Engagements with Water' (2014) 21(2) *Archaeological Dialogues* 133

Strang, Veronica, *The Meaning of Water* (Berg, 2004)

Strang, Veronica, *Water Beings: From Nature Worship to the Environmental Crisis* (Reaktion Books, 2023)

Strang, Veronica, *Water: Nature and Culture* (Reaktion Books, 2015)

Stutzin, Godofredo, 'Un Imperativo Ecológico: Reconocer Los Derechos de La Naturaleza' (1984) 1(1) *Ambiente y Desarrollo* 97
Swyngedouw, Erik, 'Globalisation or "Glocalisation"? Networks, Territories and Rescaling' (2004) 17(1) *Cambridge Review of International Affairs* 25
Tănăsescu, Mihnea, *Understanding the Rights of Nature: A Critical Introduction* (Transcript Publishing, 2022)
Te Arawa River Iwi Waikato River Act 2010 (NZ)
Te Awa Tupua (Whanganui River Claims Settlement) Act 2017 (NZ)
The New Zealand River That Became a Legal Person (Directed by Kate Evans, 20 March 2020) <https://www.bbc.com/travel/article/20200319-the-new-zealand-river-that-became-a-legal-person>
Todd, Zoe, 'An Indigenous Feminist's Take on the Ontological Turn: "Ontology" Is Just Another Word for Colonialism' (2016) 29(1) *Journal of Historical Sociology* 4
Valladares, Carolina and Rutgerd Boelens, 'Mining for Mother Earth: Governmentalities, Sacred Waters and Nature's Rights in Ecuador' (2019) 100 *Geoforum* 68
Viaene, Lieselotte, 'Indigenous Water Ontologies, Hydro-Development and the Human/More-Than-Human Right to Water: A Call for Critical Engagement with Plurilegal Water Realities' (2021) 13(12) *Water* 1660
Waikato-Tainui Raupatu Claims (Waikato River) Settlement Act 2010 (NZ)
Waitangi Tribunal, *The Whanganui River Report* (1999) <https://forms.justice.govt.nz/search/Documents/WT/wt_DOC_68450539/Whanganui%20River%20Report%201999.pdf>
Warne, Kennedy, 'This River in New Zealand Is a Legal Person: How Will It Use Its Voice?' *National Geographic* (24 April 2019) <https://www.nationalgeographic.com/culture/graphics/maori-river-in-new-zealand-is-a-legal-person>
Wheeler v Director de la Procuraduria General de Estado de Loja (2011) Corte Provincial de Justicia de Loja 11121-2011-0010
Yates, Julian S., Leila M. Harris and Nicole J. Wilson, 'Multiple Ontologies of Water: Politics, Conflict and Implications for Governance' (2017) 35(5) *Environment and Planning D: Society and Space* 797
Zenner, Christiana, 'Turning to Traditions: Three Cultural-Religious Articulations of Fresh Waters' Value(s) in Contemporary Governance Frameworks' in Farhana Sultana and Alex Loftus (eds), *Water Politics: Governance, Justice and the Right to Water* (Routledge, 2020) 42

8

TOWARDS RELATIONAL WATER GOVERNANCE

Introduction

The preceding chapters have explored how legal frameworks fundamentally reshape human relationships with water while simultaneously encountering resistance from communities and water's material, relational, and agentic values. Through examining the last four decades of water governance transformations, this book has demonstrated the co-constitutive relationship between legal regulation, human-water relations, and water itself. This analysis reveals both the limitations of conventional regulatory approaches and emerging possibilities for more relational frameworks that recognise water's multiple values and ontologies.

Drawing from this examination, this book makes several main conclusions about the spaces, places, and narratives of human-water relations. First, market-based water governance inevitably reflects and reinforces existing power relations, producing highly unequal socio-spatial distributions of access and control. Second, its attempts to abstract water through legal mechanisms inevitably confront the reality that water is simultaneously embedded in place (materially and socially) while also resistant to human control due to its fluid, unreliable nature. Third, human rights narratives can be used to contain and neutralise radical resistance to neoliberalism – and to naturalise neoliberal logic – but they can also be used strategically by communities to legitimise their own agendas and to create openings for transformation. Finally, long-standing, reciprocal community relations with water (often, but not always or exclusively, found in Indigenous communities) can provide prefigurative guideposts for alternative water governance models that can support sustainable well-being for humans and more-than-humans.

DOI: 10.4324/9781003273219-8

These insights could help us to confront the intensifying water challenges facing the planet. Climate change, growing inequality, and the continued dominance of extractive development models create mounting pressure towards further commodification and financialisation of water – and the degradation of water systems that this inevitably brings. Yet it is possible to find hope in the emergence (and continued existence) of innovative legal frameworks that attempt to recognise water's living nature and protect communities' reciprocal relations with water and each other. This tension between competing governance paradigms shapes contemporary struggles over water and humanity's future.

After reflecting on the theoretical lessons of earlier chapters and on the last four decades of water governance explored in their pages, this concluding chapter examines several promising developments that suggest pathways towards more pluralistic and relational approaches to water governance. These pathways have been charted by communities and, in two instances, legally embedded in the state legal system (and its institutions). These include new ecological protections for several rivers in Chile; a declaration of Ancestral Personhood for the Martuwarra Fitzroy River in Western Australia; recent legislation in Victoria, Australia, that embeds Indigenous water ontologies and influence within state legal frameworks; and a growing right to swim movement in the UK that reveals how embodied relationships with water can generate momentum for change. These initiatives illustrate both the possibilities and challenges of developing legal mechanisms that recognise water's multiple values while protecting community relationships.

Through analysing these emerging frameworks alongside the lessons of previous chapters, this chapter considers how legal geography can inform the development of more equitable and sustainable approaches to water governance. Rather than presenting a singular solution, it considers how different communities strategically engage with existing frameworks and place-based context to prefigure alternative water relationships. This attention to multiple pathways reflects the need for governance approaches that recognise the plurality of human-water relations and the ongoing significance of place in their development and implementation.

Theoretical reflections

The theoretical insights developed throughout this book suggest both the limitations of conventional regulatory approaches and possibilities for more transformative change. Legal geography's emphasis on the co-constitution of law and space reveals how different legal frameworks actively produce distinct configurations of water access and control rather than simply managing existing arrangements. This lesson challenges technocratic approaches that treat water governance as merely administrative while helping to chart potential pathways for reimagining water governance.

Let's start first with space. In noting that the seemingly neutral legal mechanisms of market-based water governance reproduce spatial inequalities, we observe the way that the law operates to legitimate injustice through its material impacts on space.[1] From Chile's uneven water markets to Phiri's prepaid water meters to Michigan's emergency management, technical regulations, and administrative procedures often entrench existing patterns of advantage along lines of race, class, and colonial relations. The Manila case study examined in Chapter 3 illustrates these spatial dynamics, demonstrating how regulatory frameworks are used to legitimate spatial inequality through seemingly technical decisions about contract amendments and related infrastructure investment and service delivery models. The emergence of 'micro-networks' in informal settlements reveals how market mechanisms necessarily generate differentiated service territories while the narrative of 'community participation' was used to both legitimise this differentiation and romanticise the requirement that communities shoulder the financial risks and the manual labour of connecting households to the bulk water mains. A key lesson here is the central importance of addressing spatial inequalities through water governance frameworks that actively redistribute power and resources.

In paying attention to place, the case studies also demonstrate how attempts to impose universal governance frameworks and to transform water into an abstract commodity (or even a financial asset) inevitably encounter resistance from water's material properties and place-based relationships with communities. As a result of this resistance, the implementation of neoliberal water governance remains incomplete and contested, as communities maintain alternative water relationships and continue to demand water justice, despite institutional pressure. Rather than viewing such resistance as implementation failure, it signals the need for governance approaches that recognise water's embedded, relational nature.

Place also highlights the scalar politics of water governance. The case studies explored in this book have been deliberately situated in their international policy context to explore the politics and challenges of scale in water governance. In earlier chapters, neoliberal reforms were often driven by global financial ideologies (and imperatives) that failed to account for place-based relations and material context – a dynamic that Erik Swyngedouw terms 'glocalisation.'[2] In response, across various case studies, we observed communities successfully navigating these scalar politics to pursue transformation by strategically deploying rights discourse, building global alliances alongside local systems of mutual aid, and engaging in prefigurative actions towards radical transformation.

On the subject of scale, we also saw in Chapter 4 how the devolution of power to South African municipal governments without sufficient resources or capacity for water service delivery operated to disempower local communities, contradicting theories that decentralisation will increase democratic control – an assumption that has been labelled the 'local trap.'[3] On the other hand, in Chapter 7, we also noted that the Te Awa Tupua framework demonstrates how local governance can protect place-based ontologies by shifting power and financial resources down the governance scale. This suggests possibilities for the decolonisation of water governance to enhance rather than undermine local water relationships and raises the related place-based issue of pluralism.

The similarities and contrasts between the Te Awa Tapua Act and the Victorian experience (considered below) also highlight how institutional legal frameworks can create space for Indigenous leadership while maintaining the integrity of Indigenous legal orders. Here it is essential to ensure the recognition of Indigenous water ontologies and legal frameworks and to embed mechanisms for meaningful Indigenous authority in decision-making. Once again, this highlights the need to provide sufficient resources, in this case to support Indigenous governance capacity and provide strong protections for Indigenous water rights and relationships. Above all, this requires moving beyond consultation towards genuine power-sharing while respecting Indigenous sovereignty and jurisdiction.

Here we can observe the role of contingency in this co-constitutive process. As David Delaney argues, 'any chain of human events involving numerous actors, divergent institutional settings, competing ideologies, interests, motivations, and capacities unfolding over time and implicating multiple scales of action will include slippages, mistakes, mis-transmissions from rule to implementation.'[4] Contingency is evident in the uneven implementation of neoliberal water governance reforms and reflected in the need for the neoliberal state to engage in increasingly more interventionist regulation to attempt to institutionalise market logic while managing social and ecological consequences.

Contingency – and the inherent messiness of the complex implementation process that it explains – is also relevant to the realisation of the human right to water and the significance of narrative in this process. Since its recognition in international law, the right to water has been variously demonised, treated as a panacea, or cynically repurposed for political ends (an approach best exemplified by Nestle's sudden acceptance of the right and declaration that it was supporting this right by helping to place an economic value on this 'precious resource').[5] South Africa's experience implementing both a constitutional human right to water and neoliberal reforms, examined in Chapters 4 and 5, provides useful insights into these dynamics. This simultaneous implementation created hybrid legal spaces where rights discourse and market logic coexist in dynamic tension. This dynamic tension played out in the Mazibuko judgment, which further illustrated how legal interpretations of the right to water can reflect and reinforce existing patterns of spatial inequality rather than promoting transformative justice. Nonetheless, insights from both legal pluralism and legal geography help us to look beyond the state and its institutions to understand that law is also shaped and enacted from below. When we turn our gaze towards these community engagements, we can see that the strategic and radical use of the human right to water operated to challenge the status quo and to prefigure alternative socio-legal relations on the ground.

Beyond its material resistance to abstraction, water's capacity to inspire these reciprocal and sustainable relations is perhaps the most significant force for change. As examined in Chapter 7, modernist ontology's reduction of water to an economic resource laid crucial groundwork for the neoliberal reforms examined throughout this book. However, water's ontological complexity continues to resist such reduction, including through the persistence of community relationships with living waters. This resistance helps explain patterns documented throughout the case studies – from the low levels of water trading in Chile's 'free water markets' to the contestation of financialisation in Detroit.

These insights have implications for both scholarship and practice. They suggest the need to focus less on analysing governance 'models' and more on how different legal mechanisms interact with specific spatial, material, and metaphysical contexts. This approach emphasises the limitations of universal solutions and the importance of supporting place-based governance innovations. For policymakers, these insights highlight the importance of developing legal frameworks that can recognise and protect multiple water values while enabling community relationships to flourish. Rather than attempting to resolve tensions between different approaches, this may require courageous acts of prefiguration and frameworks that create space for alternative water futures to emerge. In the following section, we will explore four examples of what these prefigurative acts and frameworks might look like.

Emerging frameworks for relational water governance

As examined in Chapter 7, the Te Awa Tupua framework represents a sophisticated approach to embedding ontological pluralism in water governance. While scholarly attention has often focused on its legal personhood provisions, arguably its most transformative aspects lie in the recognition of Indigenous law and values (Tupua te Kawa) and the establishment of collaborative governance structures. Perhaps more prosaically, the careful attention to institutionality in the Act may also help to explain why this framework appears more effective at enabling genuine legal and ontological pluralism than broader constitutional provisions or isolated judicial decisions.

Recent developments in Chile, Australia, and the UK further illustrate both the possibilities and challenges of developing more relational approaches to water governance. While operating in distinct contexts and through different mechanisms, these initiatives share important commonalities in their attempts to protect and nurture reciprocal human-water relationships while engaging strategically with existing institutions. The emerging frameworks examined here demonstrate different approaches to reconciling the theoretical tensions identified in this book – between abstract legal mechanisms and place-based relationships, between state authority and legal pluralism, and between institutional change and prefigurative action.

Chile

Returning full circle to this book's opening case study, the first development explored here relates to the 2022 Water Code reforms in Chile that were discussed in Chapter 2. Under these reforms, the President was granted the power to 'establish reserves of available surface water or groundwater, and actively reserve water in those watersheds where there is water available for the purpose of ecosystem preservation.'[6] In contrast to the water-as-economic-good paradigm promoted by Chile's early adoption of market-based reforms, a recent broad survey, with 1,612 respondents, revealed strong public support for river protection in Chile, with respondents identifying 'environmental values as the highest priority (95%), followed by cultural (65%), recreational or touristic (56%) and scenic landscapes (52%).'[7]

This growing public support for river protection has begun to yield results. In 2023, two Patagonian rivers, the Futaleufú and Puelo Rivers, were granted the status of protected areas for ecosystem conservation, preserving their free flow.[8] Community engagement was a significant factor in achieving this outcome, with Pia Weber Salazar and others noting the existence of strong grassroots campaigns to protect the Futaleufú and Puelo Rivers, involving 'community members, local, national and international actors [and] reflecting strong societal concern for the protection of Chile's still free-flowing and healthy southern rivers.'[9] Other rivers, including the Serrano in Southern Patagonia, are now the focus of ongoing campaigns, drawing from the early precedent of the Futaleufú and Puelo.[10]

In late 2024, a different approach was taken in relation to the Biobío River, with a coalition of local communities, including Indigenous peoples and civil society organisations, launching a 'Declaration of the Rights of the Biobío River' and calling for endorsements from the public and international organisations.[11] Here they note, '[t]his historic declaration seeks to rekindle the bond between communities and their river while safeguarding the rights of Chile's Biobío River against mounting environmental threats.'[12] The Declaration emerged 'in the context of the "Somos Cuenca" festival, held in November 2023 in the towns of Concepción and Talcahuano, Chile.'[13] (*Cuenca* is Spanish for 'basin,' so the festival roughly translates as 'We are the basin'). During a series of participatory workshops, attendees discussed the ecological and social challenges facing the River and 'testified to the importance of the link between the community and the river.'[14]

Unlike the protected status granted to the Futaleufú and Puelo Rivers, this Declaration of the Rights of the Biobío River is not recognised under the law of the Chilean state. Instead, the community is performing the Biobío River's rights into existence, engaging in an act of what Amy Cohen and Bronwen Morgan call 'prefigurative legality' – 'efforts to use the language, form, and legitimacy of law to imagine law otherwise ... through various kinds of direct actions.'[15] Though partial and even fragile in status, both initiatives offer a glimmer of hope by appearing to reflect the beginnings of a shift in Chile in relation to community expectations around the status of rivers and how the law ought to protect their ecological and relational values.

These developments illustrate the complex politics of water governance transformation. While the protection of the Futaleufú and Puelo Rivers is provided through state legal mechanisms, the Declaration of Rights for the Biobío River exemplifies the performative and prefigurative dimension of legal relations. Just as Blomley argues that legal relations are 'performed into being through arrangement of fences, pronouncements of judges...and practices of ordinary people,'[16] these community initiatives demonstrate how alternative water relationships can be enacted through prefigurative actions. The Declaration of Rights for the Biobío River represents more than symbolism – it actively performs new legal relationships into being.

Martuwarra Fitzroy River

The prefigurative action of the Declaration of the Rights of the Biobío River has many global precedents, as communities take matters into their own hands and claim the ecological protections that their governments have (thus far) failed to deliver.[17] Another example is the (Martuwarra) Fitzroy River Declaration drafted at a 2016 meeting of Martuwarra Nations (Traditional Owners) to declare, 'The Fitzroy River is a living ancestral being and has a right to life. It must be protected for current and future generations and managed jointly by the Traditional Owners of the river.'[18] To facilitate this joint management, the Martuwarra Fitzroy River Council was established in 2018.[19] The promotion of legal and ontological pluralism is a key goal of the Council, which asserts the continuing authority of Indigenous law, or 'First Law,' including in relation to the River.[20] Reflecting the commonality of personified water serpent beings introduced in Chapter 7, the Martuwarra is an ancestral Serpent, called *Yoongoorrookoo* in the Nyikina language, and it is a key source of First Law for his peoples.[21]

The Council and Traditional Owners of the Martuwarra have been inspired by the legal developments in Aotearoa New Zealand, like the Te Awa Tapua Act explored in Chapter 7, and other legal developments that extend legal rights to rivers.[22] However, they have avoided the language of 'legal personhood' and instead developed the concept of an 'ancestral person' to better reflect their ontological conception of the Martuwarra.[23] In addition to the Declaration itself, Council members have engaged in a range of prefigurative acts to raise awareness about both the Martuwarra and the living, agentic nature of rivers globally – acts that have included political theatre, film-making, song, dance, and story festivals.[24] More recently, Council Chair Professor Anne Poelina has made a 'Declaration of Peace with Martuwarra Indigenous Peoples our Lands and Living Waters'[25] calling on all people to commit to a reciprocal relationship with the river, and to share the Martuwarra as an 'asset in the commons.'[26]

Again, while these prefigurative actions have yet to be formally acknowledged by either the state or national governments, it would be a mistake to ignore their significant power in shaping global conversations about river futures and water governance. There are multiple publications referencing these developments in relation to the Martuwarra Fitzroy River, including in the mainstream press.[27] Many more scholarly outputs have been authored by Poelina and the Martuwarra itself,[28] with others coming from scholars from around the world.[29] Beyond this conceptual influence, the Council also appears to be influencing the Western Australian state government, with a new national park being declared to protect part of the River in August 2023,[30] and the government committing to protect the entire River from large-scale irrigation in a policy position paper in October of the same year.[31]

The Council's use of 'ancestral person' rather than 'legal personhood' demonstrates a sophisticated engagement with questions of ontological pluralism raised in the introduction and in Chapter 7. Rather than adopting existing frameworks, this approach maintains the integrity of First Law while strategically engaging with state institutions and law. The Council's diverse prefigurative actions – from political theatre to storytelling – exemplify how narrative practices can reshape water relationships while building momentum for institutional change.[32]

Yarra Birrarung

Moving to another corner of the Country, the state of Victoria in Australia's southeast has emerged as a significant site of innovation in relational water governance through state legal frameworks that recognise local Indigenous (*Wurundjeri Woi Wurrung* and *Bunurong*) relationships with water while enabling broader community connections. In 2017, the *Yarra River Protection (Wilip-gin Birrarung murron) Act 2017* (Vic) (Yarra Birrarung Act) recognised the Birrarung (Yarra River), which flows through the capital city of Melbourne, as a single living and integrated entity and established mechanisms for Traditional Owner guidance in its governance.

One such governance mechanism is the independent Birrarung Council, established under Part 5 of the Act and mandated to act as a voice for the

River through its advisory and advocacy functions.[33] Under the Act, the minister can appoint up to 12 members of the Birrarung Council, at least two of whom must be nominated by the Wurundjeri Council.[34] The current membership includes three Wurundjeri Woi Wurrung Elders and one Bunurong Elder.[35] The proceedings and work of the Birrarung Council have been guided by Traditional Owners, including in its use of yarning circles and the Walking Together Action Plan.[36]

The Preamble of the Act includes a statement from Wurundjeri Woi Wurrung Traditional Owners, in both Woi-wurrung language and English, that includes the following text,

> We, the Woi-wurrung, the First People, and the Birrarung, belong to this Country. This Country, and the Birrarung are part of us.
>
> The Birrarung is alive, has a heart, a spirit and is part of our Dreaming. We have lived with and known the Birrarung since the beginning. We will always know the Birrarung. …
>
> Since our beginning it has been known that we have an obligation to keep the Birrarung alive and healthy—for all generations to come.

The inclusion of this statement along with the Act's bilingual title signals an emerging opening for legal pluralism, while its recognition of the River as a living and indivisible entity challenges modernist ontology. Indeed, Erin O'Donnell argues,

> The preamble is essential foregrounding for legal interpretation of the rest of the legislation, so it plays an important role. The Birrarung Council, for instance, has been guided by the preamble in developing its policies for understanding what the interests of the river are. To do so, it relies on both the 50 year community vision as well as the 'Ancient Spirit and Lore of the Yarra,' a water policy vision developed by Wurundjeri Woi Wurrung.[37]

Through these innovations, the Act lays the foundations for a new approach to water governance. Like Aotearoa New Zealand's Te Awa Tupua Act, the Yarra Birrarung Act draws inspiration from Indigenous legal relations while elevating the role of Traditional Owners in governance. However, the power dynamics differ. While the Te Awa Tupua Act emerged from treaty settlement and has involved a genuine devolution of power and resources, the Yarra framework must operate within – while attempting to transform – existing institutional constraints. Early implementation, particularly of the 'Burndap Birrarung burndap umarkoo: Yarra Strategic Plan,'[38] has revealed challenges around resources and structural barriers to meaningful participation.[39]

Yet, despite these institutional challenges, evidence suggests the framework is still successfully creating space for multiple ways of understanding and relating to rivers. The governance model is being adapted for other Victorian waterways, including through the creation of new action plans for the Rivers of the Barwon-*Barre Warre Yulluk*,[40] and for the Waterways of the West, including the Maribyrnong-*Mirrangbamurn* River.[41] More broadly, the state government has committed to including Traditional Owners in managing all of Victoria's waterways, including through handing back water rights.[42] While inadequate to date, particularly given Australia's colonial history and ongoing reality of what Virginia Marshall has called 'aqua nullius,'[43] these are positive steps towards the decolonisation of Victorian water governance.

Perhaps most significantly, the community has responded enthusiastically through initiatives that enact new relationships with the Birrarung. These include a major exhibition at the National Gallery of Victoria featuring speculative visions of the River's future that invite people to reimagine human-river relations.[44] The exhibition features creative use of film and cartography to illustrate colonisation's impacts,[45] alongside speculative representations of both utopic and dystopic possibilities for the future – depending on the choices made in the present.[46] Material objects like felted models of river sediment layers[47] and visualisations of the Birrarung as an autonomous territory[48] carry prefigurative power to shape community values and governance choices. As the exhibit states, 'Reimagining Birrarung invites us to free our minds from the constraints and assumptions of today and to consider, together, the future of the Birrarung, but also what the river might want for itself.'[49]

A second example is an annual river festival that combines cultural education, restoration activities, and direct engagement through 'love stories' and letters to the river.[50] This practice builds on a touching precedent where Melbourne residents responded to a new interactive map of the City's 70,000 trees by writing personal emails to individual trees,[51] sharing stories, and expressing deep connection.[52] One wrote to a Moreton Bay Fig,

> You are beautiful. Sometimes I sit or walk under you and feel happier. I love the way the light looks through your leaves and how your branches come down so low and wide it is almost as if you are trying to hug me. … You are my favourite tree because you are a native, standing proud in a cultivated English garden of colonising trees, imported to remind settlers of a home they may never return to.[53]

To a golden elm, another correspondent wrote: 'Dear 1037148, … You deserve to be known by more than a number. I love you. Always and forever.'[54] Such expressions reflect the reality that human relationships with the rest of nature persist despite – and perhaps in resistance to – modernist frameworks that treat natural entities as mere resources.

The community's commitment to deepening its relationship with the River is further exemplified through ambitious infrastructure projects. For example, a community-led initiative is creating a 220 kilometer continuous 'Birrarung Valley Walk' linking existing tracks from the River's mouth to its source.[55] Beyond physical access, the project aims to enhance understanding of the River's cultural and ecological values through a digital platform and educational programs.[56] The vision that Victorian schoolchildren might one day include multi-day sections of this river walk in their curriculum reflects the kind of long-term, intergenerational thinking needed for the genuine transformation of human-water relations.[57]

Finally, the 'Swimmable Birrarung' initiative is a collaborative project that is working towards making the River 'healthy, thriving and swimmable again, from source to sea' through seven key steps, from water quality improvement to governance reform.[58] The emphasis on connecting 'hands, hearts & stories' and on getting people back into the water reflects a growing global movement that recognises how direct physical engagement builds understanding of water's living nature and creates constituencies for protection. While institutional change may proceed slowly, these cultural and ontological shifts occurring on the ground suggest promising pathways towards sustainable transformation. The Victorian experience thus reveals both the challenges and possibilities of embedding relational water governance within existing legal frameworks.

UK right to swim movement

As with the 'Swimmable Birrarung' project, the growing right to swim movement in the UK exemplifies how embodied relationships with water can generate momentum for governance transformation while revealing deeper tensions around access, commodification, and spatial justice. The right to swim movement emerged in the UK against the backdrop of customary access rights and contemporary exclusions from watery spaces. Building on Roger Deakin's influential 2000 work *Waterlog: A Swimmer's Journey Throughout Britain*,[59] the movement gained momentum through organisations like the Outdoor Swimming Society (founded in 2006) that began documenting and advocating for public access to inland waters.[60] While estimates vary (and are even contentious), some research suggests that up to 97 percent of England's rivers and waterways remain inaccessible to the public,[61] with access constrained by the privatisation of reservoirs during the 1980s–1990s and growing restrictions at traditional swimming spots. The movement encompasses both organised advocacy – including campaigns for legislative reform and strategic litigation – and direct action, exemplified by mass 'swim-trespass' events that deliberately echo the historic 1932 Kinder Scout protests.[62] These actions take place within a broader cultural renaissance of outdoor swimming, where growing public interest in 'wild swimming' intersects with questions of spatial justice, public health, and climate resilience.

This convergence of recreational practice and prefigurative politics reveals how seemingly leisure-focused activities can challenge dominant property paradigms while prefiguring alternative human-water relationships. The movement confronts multiple mechanisms of exclusion, including the direct privatisation of water bodies, obstruction of access ways by riparian landowners, and more subtle forms of enclosure through prohibitive fees and risk-based restrictions. As Imogen Radford (an organiser with the Outdoor Swimming Society) observed, commercial swimming venues are 'utterly inadequate' substitutes because they exclude 'ordinary families and young people' through requirements around timing, equipment, and payment.[63]

The movement exhibits a sophisticated engagement with questions of lawfulness and legitimacy. Rather than focusing solely on formal legal reform, campaigners strategically combine direct action, community education, and careful legal analysis.[64] This includes challenging overly restrictive interpretations of liability and risk while building public understanding of existing access rights.[65] In common with other case studies in this book, the movement thus demonstrates how communities maintain and enact alternative spatial relationships despite institutional constraints.

Particularly instructive is how the movement connects contemporary struggles to historical precedent, as exemplified by protests at Kinder Reservoir that deliberately reference the 1932 mass trespass.[66] This temporal linking helps 'make it feel unarguable' that change is possible, as Kate Rew (Founder of the Outdoor Swimming Society) explains,[67] while positioning current exclusions as historically contingent rather than inevitable. The movement thus demonstrates a sophisticated understanding of how property relations are performed and contested over time.

These insights suggest important lessons and inspiration for governance transformation. The movement reveals how the embodied experience of direct engagement with water can build understanding of its living nature, deepening human-water relations in a way that creates constituencies for protection. It also demonstrates the importance of frameworks that enable rather than restrict community relationships with water.

While emerging in different contexts, at different scales, and from different sites of power, these diverse examples reveal the importance of prefigurative practice in creating space for alternative water futures while engaging strategically with existing institutions. They suggest a range of hopeful pathways for legal frameworks that can better recognise water's multiple values while enabling community relationships to flourish.

Persistent challenges and creative tensions

While the emerging initiatives identified in this book (and elsewhere) suggest pathways towards more relational water governance, they operate within a context of intensifying pressure towards commodification and financialisation. These countervailing forces create persistent challenges while also generating productive tensions that may enable transformation. The ongoing dominance of neoliberal water governance frameworks poses significant challenges for implementing more relational approaches. As demonstrated in earlier chapters, the logic of financialisation continues to (re)shape water governance, including through attempts to transform water into increasingly abstract financial assets. This process operates through sophisticated financial instruments and arrangements that are difficult to engage with due to their complexity and deliberate opacity. Within such a context, even seemingly progressive frameworks risk reinforcing market logic without careful attention to implementation.

The Manila case study provides instructive baackground context for these contemporary challenges. As examined in Chapter 3, regulatory frameworks, while theoretically designed to ensure public benefit, often operate to institutionalise service differentiation and protect corporate interests. Yet Manila's experience also revealed how privatisation's transformation of citizens into consumers generated new forms of resistance and political mobilisation – dynamics that continue to shape contemporary struggles.

These pressures manifest differently across contexts. In Detroit and Flint, for example, financialisation entrenched existing racial and economic inequalities with significant long-term consequences for the health and well-being of both communities. Financialisation also generated new forms of resistance that connect water justice to fundamental critiques of the political economy of (neoliberal) capitalism and its impact on democracy. In Dublin, attempts to financialise water triggered mass protests from a population that seemingly had become resigned to the politics of austerity – ultimately leading to political change and the protection of public water. Finally, while Kate Bayliss argued in 2017 that the UK public was largely unaware of the extent of the financialisation of the water sector,[68] they have certainly become aware of its effects, as evidenced by mounting public outrage over untreated sewage discharge,[69] rising tariffs,[70] and evidence of financial mismanagement.[71]

As we have seen throughout this book, questions of scale present challenges for water governance and, perhaps, particularly for relational approaches. Place-based frameworks that work well for specific rivers or communities may prove difficult to replicate or scale up. The Whanganui experience suggests the importance of allowing governance arrangements to emerge from particular contexts while developing mechanisms for coordination across scale. While this lesson is reflected in Victoria's experiences, implementation challenges have also emerged around resources and capacity. Meaningful participation in collaborative governance requires significant investment in both time and money. Without adequate support, new frameworks risk reproducing existing power imbalances or becoming merely symbolic. Yet creative tensions emerge here too, as community initiatives adopt nimble, flexible approaches that can allude institutions.

Perhaps the most fundamental challenge involves maintaining genuine plurality while addressing power inequities. Legal frameworks must create space for multiple water values and relationships while protecting community and Indigenous authority and addressing historical injustices. This requires careful attention to how different governance mechanisms interact and whose values (and ontologies) they privilege. This challenge plays out differently across contexts. The Whanganui context provides an instructive example of the sophisticated navigation of scalar politics in the way that the *Tupua te Kawa* (iwi law and values about the River) were embedded into state legislation while preserving their ontological integrity – including through the well-resourced and legislatively empowered *Ngā Tangata Tiaki o Whanganui* (the post-settlement governance entity for Whanganui Iwi for the purpose of the Whanganui River Settlement) and *Te Pou Tupua* (human face of Te Awa Tupua).

The accelerating impacts of climate change create additional urgency and complexity. Changing rainfall patterns, more frequent extreme events, and growing water scarcity pose fundamental challenges for all governance approaches. These pressures may intensify calls for technocratic solutions while also revealing the limitations of market-based frameworks. Yet climate impacts reinforce the importance of relational approaches that can recognise and respond to water's agency. Indigenous knowledge systems and place-based governance arrangements often prove more adaptive than centralised management frameworks. This suggests that engaging with plurality will enhance effective responses to environmental change – even if this requires slowing down and resisting short-term 'emergency' thinking.

Future research directions

The analysis in this book suggests several areas requiring further theoretical development and empirical investigation – although I note that this research is already ongoing, and I do not mean to imply otherwise. Rather than attempting to catalogue all possible research directions, this section identifies key priorities organised around the book's core theoretical framework.

In terms of space and spatial justice, more research is needed on how the impacts of climate change intersect with and potentially exacerbate existing spatial inequalities in water access and control. This requires examining how different governance frameworks can dynamically respond to changing environmental conditions and whether this will end up challenging or reinforcing patterns of (dis)advantage.

The book's analysis of place also highlights several critical areas that merit deeper theoretical work. Starting with relationality, more research is needed on mechanisms for protecting place-based relationships while enabling coordination across scales – a particular challenge for governance frameworks that attempt to recognise multiple values and authorities. The Te Awa Tupua framework, discussed in Chapter 7, suggests possibilities for reconfiguring scalar relationships to protect place-based ontologies, but further research is needed on how such approaches might be adapted across different contexts while maintaining their transformative potential.

If we turn to materiality, more research could help us to understand how to translate relational governance approaches to urban contexts, where the materiality of water supply and sanitation infrastructure creates distinct challenges for both connecting to water and participating in its governance. Finally, in responding to pluralism, including the recognition of water's agency, further research could continue to consider how this agency operates across different scales and contexts. Legal geography's attention to co-constitution provides a useful starting point here, but (in addition to learning from Indigenous experts) further insights could also be drawn from post-humanism, political ecology, and the biological sciences.

Within the book's emphasis on narrative and performance, there are several potential directions for future research. The wild swimming movement, for example, suggests how direct embodied engagement with water generates momentum for change, but more research could help us to understand these connections. A burgeoning movement in prefigurative theory (discussed in Chapter 1) provides a promising framework for this investigation and may also help to further examine the performative dimensions of emerging legal frameworks, especially how they might enable or constrain alternative water relationships.

Conclusion

Water governance stands at a crucial juncture. The intensifying global water crisis, accelerating climate impacts, and persistent spatial inequalities in access and control demand a fundamental transformation of global water governance and reorientation of its role in shaping human-water relationships. Yet the analysis in this book suggests reasons for both concern and hope. While pressure towards commodification and financialisation continues, we can draw inspiration from the emergence of sophisticated governance innovations that recognise water's agency and protect community relationships. Shifting our gaze from state-sanctioned institutional arrangements, this book also documents the deep commitment from communities across the globe to fight for these relational water values and to enact them into being through prefigurative actions such as declarations, mutual aid, care work, swimming, and love letters to rivers. These actions have power, regardless of whether governments are currently listening.

Legal geography reveals how legal frameworks actively shape human-water relationships, but it also emphasises that the reverse is true. While infrastructure networks materialise power relations in urban space, and regulatory frameworks legitimate spatial inequalities through technical language and market rationality, the persistence of alternative water relationships and emerging governance innovations create countervailing pressures and suggest possibilities for transforming these material and institutional arrangements.

This book has demonstrated the need for governance frameworks that recognise the fundamentally relational nature of both place and water itself. In response, water governance must move beyond treating water as an abstract resource to recognise its relational values, both in terms of the reciprocal relationships between water, peoples, and places and in supporting healthy relationships between multiple legal systems and ontologies – by building relational bridges.[72] The emerging frameworks examined in this chapter suggest pathways towards such relational approaches and how legal frameworks might better align with water's fundamental nature. Water flows, connects, and sustains life. It resists attempts at reduction to either commodity or abstract right. Governance approaches that recognise these qualities, by working with rather than against water's agency, prove more equitable and effective. This suggests the importance of flexible (or even fluid) frameworks that maintain structure while enabling adaptation and transformation. The path forward involves supporting multiple governance innovations from below (as well as above) while maintaining pressure for systemic change. This requires sophisticated engagement across scales, from place-based initiatives to international movements. It demands careful attention to power relations while creating space for alternative water futures to emerge. And it requires remaining open to water's own agency in shaping these transformations.

As communities across the globe confront intensifying water challenges, the importance of developing more relational governance approaches becomes increasingly clear. The theoretical insights and practical innovations examined in this book suggest pathways forward while highlighting the challenging nature of this work. Water's essential role in sustaining life, its tendency to flow and connect, and its capacity to inspire deep, reciprocal relationships ensure it will continue to shape governance transformations. Our task is to develop frameworks that can better recognise and work with these qualities while protecting the plurality of human-water relations.

In closing, this book represents both an engagement with scholarly debates about water governance and a contribution to practical efforts at transformation. By revealing how legal frameworks shape human-water relationships while encountering both material and social resistance, it demonstrates both the limitations of conventional approaches and the possibilities for change. The future of water governance remains uncertain, but the innovations examined in this book suggest hope for more equitable and sustainable approaches that recognise water's living nature and multiple values.

Notes

1 Nicholas Blomley, *Law, Space, and the Geographies of Power* (The Guildford Press, 1994).
2 Erik Swyngedouw, 'Globalisation or "Glocalisation"? Networks, Territories and Rescaling' (2004) 17(1) *Cambridge Review of International Affairs* 25.
3 J. Christopher Brown and Mark Purcell, 'There's Nothing Inherent about Scale: Political Ecology, the Local Trap, and the Politics of Development in the Brazilian Amazon' (2005) 36(5) *Geoforum* 607.
4 David Delaney, 'Legal Geography I: Constitutivities, Complexities, and Contingencies' (2015) 39(1) *Progress in Human Geography* 96, 101.
5 *Nestlé's Peter Brabeck: Water Is a Human Right* (Directed by Nestlé, 27 August 2013) <https://www.youtube.com/watch?v=-dMA0_cLdeE>.
6 *Law No. 21.435 (Water Code Amendments)* 2022 (Chile).
7 Pía Weber Salazar, Elizabeth Macpherson and Barbara A. Willaarts, 'Towards Durable Legal Protections for Rivers in Chile' (2024) 49(6) *Water International* 792, 805.
8 Interview with Pia Weber Salazar, 'Freshwater Officer, Chilean Patagonia Project, The Pew Charitable Trust, Futaleufú, Chile' (Cristy Clark, Santiago, Chile, 9 November 2023).
9 Weber Salazar, Macpherson and Willaarts, 'Towards Durable Legal Protections for Rivers in Chile' (n 7) 801.
10 The Pew Charitable Trusts, 'Why Protecting Chilean Patagonia's Freshwater Is Crucial', *Pew* (9 January 2023) <https://pew.org/3Gc93Ik>.
11 International Rivers and Defensa Ambiental, 'Breaking News: The Biobío River Becomes the First Ecosystem in Chile to Have a Declaration of Rights', *International Rivers* (Press Release, 25 September 2024) <https://www.internationalrivers.org/news/press-release-breaking-news-the-biobio-river-becomes-the-first-ecosystem-in-chile-to-have-a-declaration-of-rights/>.
12 International Rivers and Defensa Ambiental, 'Breaking News: The Biobío River Becomes the First Ecosystem in Chile to Have a Declaration of Rights' (n 11).
13 Defensa Ambiental, 'Declaración de Derechos Del Río Biobío (Declaration of the Rights of the Biobío River)' (5 September 2024) <https://www.ongdefensaambiental.cl/derechosdelriobiobio/>.
14 Defensa Ambiental, 'Declaración de Derechos Del Río Biobío (Declaration of the Rights of the Biobío River) (n 11)'.
15 Amy J. Cohen and Bronwen Morgan, 'Prefigurative Legality' (2023) 48(3) *Law & Social Inquiry* 1053, 1053.
16 Nicholas Blomley, 'The Boundaries of Property: Complexity, Relationality, and Spatiality' (2016) 50(1) *Law & Society Review* 224, 250.
17 See, e.g., *Universal Declaration of the Rights of Mother Earth* (World People's Conference on Climate Change and the Rights of Mother Earth, 22 April 2010).
18 Kimberely Land Council, 'Kimberley Traditional Owners Unite for the Fitzroy River' (15 November 2016) <https://www.klc.org.au/kimberley-traditional-owners-unite-for-the-fitzroy-river>.
19 See, e.g., Martuwarra RiverOfLife et al, 'Yoongoorrookoo: The Emergence of Ancestral Personhood' (2021) 30(3) *Griffith Law Review* 505.
20 RiverOfLife et al, 'Yoongoorrookoo' (n 19).
21 RiverOfLife et al, 'Yoongoorrookoo' (n 19). Here I note that Yoongoorrookoo is not gendered male as the use of the pronoun 'he' would appear to indicate. This simply reflects Aboriginal English.
22 See, e.g., *Wheeler v Director de la Procuraduria General de Estado de Loja* (2011) Corte Provincial de Justicia de Loja 11121-2011-0010 ('*Vilcabamba Case*');

Center for Social Justice Studies et al. v. Presidency of the Republic et al. Judgment T-622/16, Constitutional Court of Colombia (10 November 2016) ('The Atrato River Case'); Mohammad Sohidul Islam and Erin O'Donnell, 'Legal Rights for the Turag: Rivers as Living Entities in Bangladesh' (2020) 23(2) *Asia Pacific Journal of Environmental Law* 160.

23 RiverOfLife et al, 'Yoongoorrookoo' (n 19).

24 Interview with Anne Poelina, 'Chair of the Martuwarra Fitzroy Council, "Sharing First Law and Wake Up the Snake (2.0)"' (Cristy Clark, Microsoft Teams, 30 May 2022) <https://doi.org/10.5281/zenodo.6592374>.

25 Anne Poelina, 'Declaration of Peace with Martuwarra Indigenous Peoples Our Lands and Living Waters' <https://www.search.org.au/declaration_of_peace_with_martuwarra_indigenous_peoples_our_lands_and_living_waters>.

26 Interview with Anne Poelina, 'Chair of the Martuwarra Fitzroy Council, "Sharing First Law and Wake Up the Snake (2.0)"' (n 24).

27 ABC Radio National, 'Martuwarra Fitzroy River: First They Came for the Land' <https://www.abc.net.au/listen/programs/earshot/martuwarra-fitzroy-river/13419878>; Lorena Allam and Carly Earl, 'A Journey Down WA's Mighty Martuwarra, Raging River and Sacred Ancestor', *The Guardian* (online, 5 June 2021) <https://www.theguardian.com/australia-news/2021/jun/05/a-journey-down-was-mighty-martuwarra-raging-river-and-sacred-ancestor>; Alys Marshall, 'Surface Water, Groundwater or No Water at All? The Mission to Avoid a Murray-Darling Basin-Style Debacle in WA', *ABC News* (online, 9 December 2023) <https://www.abc.net.au/news/2023-12-10/fitzroy-river-water-licensing-debate-kimberley/103146542>; Giovanni Torre, 'Docuseries Tells Powerful Stories of Martuwarra/Fitzroy River', *National Indigenous Times* (online, 30 July 2021) <https://nit.com.au/30-07-2021/2200/docuseries-tells-powerful-stories-of-martuwarra-fitzroy-river>; Calla Wahlquist, 'Fitzroy River: The Push to Prevent a Repeat of the Murray-Darling Basin "Disaster"', *The Guardian* (online, 5 September 2020) <https://www.theguardian.com/australia-news/2020/sep/06/fitzroy-river-the-push-to-prevent-a-repeat-of-the-murray-darling-basin-disaster>; Western Australian Museum, 'The Martuwarra Fitzroy River: Lifeblood of the Kimberley' (24 September 2022) <https://visit.museum.wa.gov.au/maritime/the-fitzroy-river>; 'Serpent's Tale Backs Fitzroy River Conservation', *Broome Advertiser* (25 March 2021) <https://www.broomead.com.au/news/broome-advertiser/new-kimberley-short-film-serpents-tale-hopes-to-inspire-fitzroy-river-conservation-push-ng-b881819458z>.

28 See, e.g., RiverOfLife et al, 'Yoongoorrookoo' (n 19); Martuwarra RiverOfLife, Katherine S. Taylor and Anne Poelina, 'Living Waters, Law First: Nyikina and Mangala Water Governance in the Kimberley, Western Australia' (2021) 25(1) *Australasian Journal of Water Resources* 40; Anne Poelina, Donna Bagnall and Michelle Lim, '"Recognizing the Martuwarra's First Law Right to Life as a Living Ancestral Being"' (2020) 9(3) *Transnational Environmental Law* 541; Martuwarra RiverOfLife et al, 'Recognizing the Martuwarra's First Law Right to Life as a Living Ancestral Being' (2020) 9(3) *Transnational Environmental Law* 541; Erin O'Donnell et al, 'Stop Burying the Lede: The Essential Role of Indigenous Law(s) in Creating Rights of Nature' (2020) 9(3) *Transnational Environmental Law* 403.

29 See, e.g., Mihnea Tănăsescu, *Understanding the Rights of Nature: A Critical Introduction* (Transcript Publishing, 2022) 145–150; Cristy Clark and Beth Goldblatt, 'Prefiguring Legal Alternatives in Environmental and Climate Justice Struggles in Australia' (2024) 15(2) *Journal of Human Rights and the Environment* 214-236; Rosemary Hill et al, 'Learning Together for and with the Martuwarra Fitzroy River' (2022) 17(2) *Sustainability Science* 351; Sarah Laborde

and Sue Jackson, 'New River Council Will Give Traditional Owners in the Kimberley a Unified Voice', *The Conversation* (20 June 2018) <http://theconversation.com/new-river-council-will-give-traditional-owners-in-the-kimberley-a-unified-voice-98390>; Sarah Laborde and Sue Jackson, 'Living Waters or Resource? Ontological Differences and the Governance of Waters and Rivers' (2022) 27(3) *Local Environment* 357; Elizabeth Macpherson, 'Indigenous Water Rights in Comparative Law' (2020) 9(3) *Transnational Environmental Law* 393; Nadeem Samnakay, 'The Multiple Values of the Martuwarra – Fitzroy River (Australia) – New Governance Required to Protect Free-Flowing Rivers', *Global Water Forum* (27 September 2020) <https://www.globalwaterforum.org/2020/09/27/the-multiple-values-of-the-martuwarra-fitzroy-river-australia-new-governance-required-to-protect-free-flowing-rivers/>; Cornelia Tscheppe, 'River of Life: A Case Study' (2023) 7(1) *University of Vienna Law Review* 1.

30 Giovanni Torre, 'Bunuba National Park Creation a Key Step in Protecting Martuwarra Fitzroy River', *National Indigenous Times* (online, 23 August 2023) <https://nit.com.au/23-08-2023/7336/bunuba-national-park-creation-a-key-step-in-protecting-martuwarra-fitzroy-river>.

31 Giovanni Torre, 'Traditional Owners Welcome Commitment to Protect Martuwarra Fitzroy River from Large-Scale Irrigation', *National Indigenous Times* (online, 24 October 2023) <https://nit.com.au/24-10-2023/8300/traditional-owners-welcome-wa-governments-commitment-to-protect-martuwarra-fitzroy-river-from-large-scale-irrigation>.

32 For a more detailed discussion of this argument, see Clark and Goldblatt, 'Prefiguring Legal Alternatives in Environmental and Climate Justice Struggles in Australia' (n 29).

33 *Yarra River Protection (Wilip-Gin Birrarung Murron) Act 2017* (Vic) ss 46–48; Katie O'Bryan, 'The Changing Face of River Management in Victoria: The Yarra River Protection (Wilip-Gin Birrarung Murron) Act 2017 (Vic)' (2019) 44(6–7) *Water International* 769, 775.

34 Yarra Birrarung Act (n 33) s 49.

35 Birrarung Council, 'Who We Are', *Birrarung Council* (4 June 2024) <https://birrarung-council.vic.gov.au/about-us/who-we-are>. Another member of the Birrarung Council, Zena Cumpston, is a Barkandji woman, bringing the number of Indigenous members of Council to 5 out of 12– although her river, the Barka, lies 800 kilometer to the north of the Birrarung – see 'Barka: The Forgotten River', *The Australian Museum* <https://australian.museum/about/organisation/media-centre/barka/>.

36 RM Consulting Group Pty Ltd, *Birrarung Council Review* (Department of Energy, Environment and Climate Action, September 2023) 11.

37 Erin O'Donnell, 'Repairing Our Relationship with Rivers: Water Law and Legal Personhood' in Rhett Larson and Vanessa Casado Perez (eds), *Research Agenda for Water Law* (Edward Elgar, 2023) 334.

38 Victorian State Government, 'Burndap Birrarung Burndap Umarkoo: Yarra Strategic Plan 2022-32' (Melbourne Water Corporation, February 2022).

39 Yarra Riverkeeper Association, *Burndap Birrarung Burndap Umarkoo: A Review of the First Year of Implementation of the Yarra Strategic Plan* (Yarra Riverkeeper, 18 September 2023) <https://yarrariver.org.au/reports/>.

40 Victorian State Government, 'Rivers of the Barwon / Barre Warre Yulluk Action Plan', *Water and catchments* (16 February 2024) <https://www.water.vic.gov.au/waterways/rivers-of-the-barwon-barre-warre-yulluk-action-plan>.

41 Victorian State Government, 'Waterways of the West', *Planning* (9 June 2023) <https://www.planning.vic.gov.au/guides-and-resources/strategies-and-initiatives/waterways-planning/waterways-of-the-west>.

42 Victorian State Government, 'Aboriginal Water Program', *Water and catchments* (22 November 2024) <https://www.water.vic.gov.au/our-programs/aboriginal-water-program>; Erin O'Donnell and Troy McDonald, 'Victoria Just Gave 2 Billion Litres of Water Back to Indigenous People. Here's What That Means for the Rest of Australia', *The Conversation* (29 November 2020) <http://theconversation.com/victoria-just-gave-2-billion-litres-of-water-back-to-indigenous-people-heres-what-that-means-for-the-rest-of-australia-150674>.
43 Virginia Marshall, *Overturning Aqua Nullius: Securing Aboriginal Water Rights* (Aboriginal Studies Press, 2017).
44 National Gallery of Victoria (NGV), 'Reimagining Birrarung: Design Concepts for 2070' (2024) <https://www.ngv.vic.gov.au/exhibition/reimagining-birrarung/>.
45 Office, 'Kew / Ivanhoe', *Reimagining Birrarung: Design Concepts for 2070* (2024) <https://www.ngv.vic.gov.au/reimagining-birrarung-office/>; Aspect Studios, 'Cremorne / Burnley', *Reimagining Birrarung: Design Concepts for 2070* (2024) <https://www.ngv.vic.gov.au/reimagining-birrarung-aspect-studios/>.
46 For example, SBLA, 'Yarra Valley / Launching Place', *Reimagining Birrarung: Design Concepts for 2070* (2024) <https://www.ngv.vic.gov.au/reimagining-birrarung-sbla/>; REALMstudios, 'Abbotsford / Clifton Hill', *Reimagining Birra rung: Design Concepts for 2070* (2025) <https://www.ngv.vic.gov.au/reimagining-birrarung-realmstudios/>; Office, 'Kew / Ivanhoe' (n 45); McGregor Coxall, 'The Birrarung Catchment', *Reimagining Birrarung: Design Concepts for 2070* (2024) <https://www.ngv.vic.gov.au/reimagining-birrarung-mcgregor-coxall/>.
47 TLC, 'Yering / Yarra Glen', *Reimagining Birrarung: Design Concepts for 2070* (2024) <https://www.ngv.vic.gov.au/reimagining-birrarung-tcl/>.
48 Openwork, 'Heidelberg / Templestowe', *Reimagining Birrarung: Design Concepts for 2070* (2024) <https://www.ngv.vic.gov.au/reimagining-birrarung-openwork/>.
49 National Gallery of Victoria (NGV) (n 44).
50 Yarra Riverkeeper Association, 'Birrarung Riverfest 2024', *Birrarung Riverfest* (2024) <https://riverfest.com.au>.
51 City of Melbourne, 'Urban Forest Visual', *Melbourne Urban Forest Visual* (2020) <http://melbourneurbanforestvisual.com.au/>.
52 Cited in Oliver Milman, 'Melbourne's Trees Bombarded with Emailed Love Letters', *The Guardian* (online, 29 January 2015) <https://www.theguardian.com/environment/2015/jan/29/city-of-melbourne-prepares-to-see-some-emails-lovely-as-its-trees>.
53 Cited in Margaret Burin, 'People from All over the World Are Sending Emails to Melbourne's Trees', *ABC News* (online, 11 December 2018) <https://www.abc.net.au/news/2018-12-12/people-are-emailing-trees/10468964>.
54 Cited in Adrienne LaFrance, 'People Are Writing Thousands of Emails to Trees', *The Atlantic* (10 July 2015) <https://www.theatlantic.com/technology/archive/2015/07/when-you-give-a-tree-an-email-address/398210/>.
55 Interview with Nichola Lefroy, 'Executive Director of Birrarung Valley Walk Inc' (Cristy Clark, Melbourne, Australia, 26 August 2024); See also Birrarung Valley Walk Inc., 'Birrarung Valley Walk Memorandum of Understanding' <https://nillumbik.infocouncil.biz/Open/2024/06/CM_25062024_ATT_1380.PDF>; Jin Hui, 'Council Supports Birrarung Valley Walk Project', *Upper Yarra Star Mail* (13 July 2024) <https://upperyarra.mailcommunity.com.au/news/2024-07-13/council-supports-birrarung-valley-walk-project/>.
56 Birrarung Valley Walk Inc., 'Birrarung Valley Walk Memorandum of Understanding' (n 55).
57 Interview with Nichola Lefroy, 'Executive Director of Birrarung Valley Walk Inc' (n 55).

58 Regen Melbourne, 'Swimmable Birrarung' (28 July 2024) <https://www.regen.melbourne/swimmable-birrarung>.

59 Roger Deakin, *Waterlog: The Book That Inspired the Wild Swimming Movement* (Vintage, Reprint edition, 2000).

60 Outdoor Swimming Society, 'Right to Swim', *Outdoor Swimming Society* (2025) <https://www.outdoorswimmingsociety.com/category/right-to-swim/>.

61 The figure of 97 percent comes from Guy Shrubsole, *Who Owns England? How We Lost Our Land, and How to Take It Back* (Harper Collins, 2020); but it is disputed by Rew and Willmott: Interview with Kate Rew, 'Founder of the Outdoor Swimming Society' (Cristy Clark and John Page, Microsoft Teams, 21 March 2024); Interview with Nathan Willmott, 'Pro Bono Lawyer for the Outdoor Swimming Society' (Cristy Clark, Microsoft Teams, 22 March 2024).

62 Outdoor Swimming Society, 'Right to Swim' (n 60); Interview with Pam Bell, 'Member of the Outdoor Swimming Society and Welsh Canoeing Association' (Cristy Clark and John Page, Microsoft Teams, 25 March 2024); Interview with Imogen Radford, 'Inland Access Team Lead for Outdoor Swimming Society' (Cristy Clark and John Page, Microsoft Teams, 12 March 2024); Interview with Kate Rew, 'Founder of the Outdoor Swimming Society' (n 61); Interview with Nathan Willmott, 'Pro Bono Lawyer for the Outdoor Swimming Society' (n 61).

63 Interview with Imogen Radford, 'Inland Access Team Lead for Outdoor Swimming Society' (n 62).

64 Interview with Imogen Radford, 'Inland Access Team Lead for Outdoor Swimming Society' (n 62); Interview with Kate Rew, 'Founder of the Outdoor Swimming Society' (n 61); Interview with Nathan Willmott, 'Pro Bono Lawyer for the Outdoor Swimming Society' (n 61).

65 Interview with Imogen Radford, 'Inland Access Team Lead for Outdoor Swimming Society' (n 62); Interview with Kate Rew, 'Founder of the Outdoor Swimming Society' (n 61); Interview with Nathan Willmott, 'Pro Bono Lawyer for the Outdoor Swimming Society' (n 61).

66 Jessica Murray, 'Swimmers Poised for Biggest Mass Trespass so far at Kinder Reservoir', *The Guardian* (online, 22 April 2023) <https://www.theguardian.com/environment/2023/apr/22/swimmers-poised-for-biggest-mass-trespass-so-far-at-kinder-reservoir>; Helen Pidd, 'The Right to Swim: Mass Trespass of Kinder Reservoir Planned', *The Guardian* (online, 23 April 2022) <https://www.theguardian.com/lifeandstyle/2022/apr/23/kinder-reservoir-mass-trespass-swimpass-peak-district-wild-swimmers>.

67 Interview with Kate Rew, 'Founder of the Outdoor Swimming Society' (n 61).

68 Kate Bayliss, 'Material Cultures of Water Financialisation in England and Wales' (2017) 22(4) *New Political Economy* 383.

69 Sandra Laville et al, 'Water Companies in England Face Outrage over Record Sewage Discharges', *The Guardian* (online, 27 March 2024) <https://www.theguardian.com/environment/2024/mar/27/water-companies-in-england-face-outrage-over-record-sewage-discharges>; Nicola Newson, *River Pollution and the Regulation of Private Water Companies* (House of Lords Library, 19 February 2024) <https://lordslibrary.parliament.uk/river-pollution-and-the-regulation-of-private-water-companies/>; Rachel Salvidge and Leana Hosea, '"Dirty Secret": Insiders Say UK Water Firms Knowingly Break Sewage Laws', *The Guardian* (online, 20 April 2024) <https://www.theguardian.com/environment/2024/apr/20/dirty-secret-insiders-say-uk-water-firms-knowingly-breaking-sewage-laws>; Esme Stallard, 'Government Has Broken the Law on Sewage, Says Watchdog', *BBC News* (17 December 2024) <https://www.bbc.com/news/articles/c4g38drwmrlo>; The Rivers

Trust, 'Raw Sewage in Our Rivers', *The Rivers Trust* (2025) <https://theriverstrust.org/key-issues/sewage-in-rivers>.

70 Guy Taylor, 'Thames Water Allowed 35 per Cent Bill Hike but Faces £18m Fine over Dividend Payouts', *City AM* (19 December 2024) <https://www.cityam.com/thames-water-allowed-35-per-cent-bill-hike-but-faces-18m-fine-over-dividend-payouts/>; Lars Mucklejohn, 'Water Bills Set to Rise by a Fifth as Government Calls for "complete Reset" of Sector', *City AM* (15 December 2024) <https://www.cityam.com/water-bills-set-to-rise-by-a-fifth-as-government-calls-for-complete-reset-of-sector/>.

71 Taylor, 'Thames Water Allowed 35 per Cent Bill Hike but Faces £18m Fine over Dividend Payouts' (n 70); Mucklejohn, 'Water Bills Set to Rise by a Fifth as Government Calls for "complete Reset" of Sector' (n 70); Maria Ward-Brennan, 'Thames Water Creditors in Talks with Ofwat for Debt Rescue Plan', *City AM* (9 October 2024) <https://www.cityam.com/thames-water-creditors-in-talks-with-ofwat-for-debt-rescue-plan/>.

72 Elizabeth Macpherson, 'Can Western Water Law Become More "Relational"? A Survey of Comparative Laws Affecting Water across Australasia and the Americas' (2022) 53(3) *Journal of the Royal Society of New Zealand* 395, 399.

References

ABC Radio National, 'Martuwarra Fitzroy River: First They Came for the Land' <https://www.abc.net.au/listen/programs/earshot/martuwarra-fitzroy-river/13419878>

Allam, Lorena and Carly Earl, 'A Journey Down WA's Mighty Martuwarra, Raging River and Sacred Ancestor', *The Guardian* (online, 5 June 2021) <https://www.theguardian.com/australia-news/2021/jun/05/a-journey-down-was-mighty-martuwarra-raging-river-and-sacred-ancestor>

Aspect Studios, 'Cremorne / Burnley', *Reimagining Birrarung: Design Concepts for 2070* (2024) <https://www.ngv.vic.gov.au/reimagining-birrarung-aspect-studios/>

'Barka: The Forgotten River', *The Australian Museum* <https://australian.museum/about/organisation/media-centre/barka/>

Bayliss, Kate, 'Material Cultures of Water Financialisation in England and Wales' (2017) 22(4) *New Political Economy* 383

Birrarung Valley Walk Inc., 'Birrarung Valley Walk Memorandum of Understanding' <https://nillumbik.infocouncil.biz/Open/2024/06/CM_25062024_ATT_1380.PDF>

Birrarung Council, 'Who We Are', *Birrarung Council* (4 June 2024) <https://birrarungcouncil.vic.gov.au/about-us/who-we-are>

Blomley, Nicholas, *Law, Space, and the Geographies of Power* (The Guildford Press, 1994)

Blomley, Nicholas, 'The Boundaries of Property: Complexity, Relationality, and Spatiality' (2016) 50(1) *Law & Society Review* 224

Brown, J. Christopher, and Mark Purcell, 'There's Nothing Inherent about Scale: Political Ecology, the Local Trap, and the Politics of Development in the Brazilian Amazon' (2005) 36(5) *Geoforum* 607

Burin, Margaret, 'People from All over the World Are Sending Emails to Melbourne's Trees', *ABC News* (online, 11 December 2018) <https://www.abc.net.au/news/2018-12-12/people-are-emailing-trees/10468964>

Center for Social Justice Studies et al. v. Presidency of the Republic etal. Judgment T-622/16, Constitutional Court of Colombia (10 November 2016) ('The Atrato River Case')

City of Melbourne, 'Urban Forest Visual', *Melbourne Urban Forest Visual* (2020) <https://melbourneurbanforestvisual.com.au/>
Clark, Cristy and Beth Goldblatt, 'Prefiguring Legal Alternatives in Environmental and Climate Justice Struggles in Australia' (2024) 15(2) *Journal of Human Rights and the Environment* 214–236
Cohen, Amy J. and Bronwen Morgan, 'Prefigurative Legality' (2023) 48(3) *Law & Social Inquiry* 1053
Deakin, Roger, *Waterlog: The Book That Inspired the Wild Swimming Movement* (Vintage, Reprint edition, 2000)
Defensa Ambiental, 'Declaración de Derechos Del Río Biobío (Declaration of the Rights of the Biobío River)' (5 September 2024) <https://www.ongdefensaambiental.cl/derechosdelriobiobio/>
Delaney, David, 'Legal Geography I: Constitutivities, Complexities, and Contingencies' (2015) 39(1) *Progress in Human Geography* 96
Hill, Rosemary et al, 'Learning Together for and with the Martuwarra Fitzroy River' (2022) 17(2) *Sustainability Science* 351
Hui, Jin, 'Council Supports Birrarung Valley Walk Project', *Upper Yarra Star Mail* (13 July 2024) <https://upperyarra.mailcommunity.com.au/news/2024-07-13/council-supports-birrarung-valley-walk-project/>
International Rivers and Defensa Ambiental, 'Breaking News: The Biobío River Becomes the First Ecosystem in Chile to Have a Declaration of Rights', *International Rivers* (Press Release, 25 September 2024) <https://www.internationalrivers.org/news/press-release-breaking-news-the-biobio-river-becomes-the-first-ecosystem-in-chile-to-have-a-declaration-of-rights/>
Interview with Pam Bell, 'Member of the Outdoor Swimming Society and Welsh Canoeing Association' (Cristy Clark and John Page, Microsoft Teams, 25 March 2024)
Interview with Nichola Lefroy, 'Executive Director of Birrarung Valley Walk Inc' (Cristy Clark, Melbourne, Australia, 26 August 2024)
Interview with Anne Poelina, 'Chair of the Martuwarra Fitzroy Council, "Sharing First Law and Wake Up the Snake (2.0)"' (Cristy Clark, Microsoft Teams, 30 May 2022) <https://doi.org/10.5281/zenodo.6592374>
Interview with Imogen Radford, 'Inland Access Team Lead for Outdoor Swimming Society' (Cristy Clark and John Page, Microsoft Teams, 12 March 2024)
Interview with Kate Rew, 'Founder of the Outdoor Swimming Society' (Cristy Clark and John Page, Microsoft Teams, 21 March 2024)
Interview with Pia Weber Salazar, 'Freshwater Officer, Chilean Patagonia Project, The Pew Charitable Trust, Futaleufú, Chile' (Cristy Clark, Santiago, Chile, 9 November 2023)
Interview with Nathan Willmott, 'Pro Bono Lawyer for the Outdoor Swimming Society' (Cristy Clark, Microsoft Teams, 22 March 2024)
Islam, Mohammad Sohidul and Erin O'Donnell, 'Legal Rights for the Turag: Rivers as Living Entities in Bangladesh' (2020) 23(2) *Asia Pacific Journal of Environmental Law* 160
Kimberely Land Council, 'Kimberley Traditional Owners Unite for the Fitzroy River' (15 November 2016) <https://www.klc.org.au/kimberley-traditional-owners-unite-for-the-fitzroy-river>
Laborde, Sarah and Sue Jackson, 'Living Waters or Resource? Ontological Differences and the Governance of Waters and Rivers' (2022) 27(3) *Local Environment* 357

Laborde, Sarah and Sue Jackson, 'New River Council Will Give Traditional Owners in the Kimberley a Unified Voice', *The Conversation* (20 June 2018) <https://theconversation.com/new-river-council-will-give-traditional-owners-in-the-kimberley-a-unified-voice-98390>

LaFrance, Adrienne, 'People Are Writing Thousands of Emails to Trees', *The Atlantic* (10 July 2015) <https://www.theatlantic.com/technology/archive/2015/07/when-you-give-a-tree-an-email-address/398210/>

Laville, Sandra et al, 'Water Companies in England Face Outrage over Record Sewage Discharges', *The Guardian* (online, 27 March 2024) <https://www.theguardian.com/environment/2024/mar/27/water-companies-in-england-face-outrage-over-record-sewage-discharges>

Law No. 21.435 (Water Code Amendments) 2022 (Chile)

Macpherson, Elizabeth, 'Can Western Water Law Become More "Relational"? A Survey of Comparative Laws Affecting Water across Australasia and the Americas' (2022) 53(3), *Journal of the Royal Society of New Zealand* 395

Macpherson, Elizabeth, 'Indigenous Water Rights in Comparative Law' (2020) 9(3) *Transnational Environmental Law* 393

Marshall, Virginia, *Overturning Aqua Nullius: Securing Aboriginal Water Rights* (Aboriginal Studies Press, 2017)

Marshall, Alys, 'Surface Water, Groundwater or No Water at All? The Mission to Avoid a Murray-Darling Basin-Style Debacle in WA', *ABC News* (online, 9 December 2023) <https://www.abc.net.au/news/2023-12-10/fitzroy-river-water-licensing-debate-kimberley/103146542>

McGregor Coxall, 'The Birrarung Catchment', *Reimagining Birrarung: Design Concepts for 2070* (2024) <https://www.ngv.vic.gov.au/reimagining-birrarung-mcgregor-coxall/>

Milman, Oliver, 'Melbourne's Trees Bombarded with Emailed Love Letters', *The Guardian* (online, 29 January 2015) <https://www.theguardian.com/environment/2015/jan/29/city-of-melbourne-prepares-to-see-some-emails-lovely-as-its-trees>

Mucklejohn, Lars, 'Water Bills Set to Rise by a Fifth as Government Calls for "complete Reset" of Sector', *CityAM* (15 December 2024) <https://www.cityam.com/water-bills-set-to-rise-by-a-fifth-as-government-calls-for-complete-reset-of-sector/>

Murray, Jessica, 'Swimmers Poised for Biggest Mass Trespass so far at Kinder Reservoir', *The Guardian* (online, 22 April 2023) <https://www.theguardian.com/environment/2023/apr/22/swimmers-poised-for-biggest-mass-trespass-so-far-at-kinder-reservoir>

Nadeem Samnakay, 'The Multiple Values of the Martuwarra – Fitzroy River (Australia) – New Governance Required to Protect Free-Flowing Rivers', *Global Water Forum* (27 September 2020) <https://www.globalwaterforum.org/2020/09/27/the-multiple-values-of-the-martuwarra-fitzroy-river-australia-new-governance-required-to-protect-free-flowing-rivers/>

National Gallery of Victoria (NGV), 'Reimagining Birrarung: Design Concepts for 2070' (2024) <https://www.ngv.vic.gov.au/exhibition/reimagining-birrarung/>

Nestlé's Peter Brabeck: Water Is a Human Right (Directed by Nestlé, 27 August 2013) <https://www.youtube.com/watch?v=-dMA0_cLdeE>

Newson, Nicola, *River Pollution and the Regulation of Private Water Companies* (House of Lords Library, 19 February 2024) <https://lordslibrary.parliament.uk/river-pollution-and-the-regulation-of-private-water-companies/>

O'Bryan, Katie, 'The Changing Face of River Management in Victoria: The Yarra River Protection (Wilip-Gin Birrarung Murron) Act 2017 (Vic)' (2019) 44(6–7) *Water International* 769

O'Donnell, Erin, 'Repairing Our Relationship with Rivers: Water Law and Legal Personhood' in Rhett Larson and Vanessa Casado Perez (eds), *Research Agenda for Water Law* (Edward Elgar, 2023)

O'Donnell, Erin et al, 'Stop Burying the Lede: The Essential Role of Indigenous Law(s) in Creating Rights of Nature' (2020) 9(3) *Transnational Environmental Law* 403

O'Donnell, Erin and Troy McDonald, 'Victoria Just Gave 2 Billion Litres of Water Back to Indigenous People: Here's What That Means for the Rest of Australia', *The Conversation* (29 November 2020) <https://theconversation.com/victoria-just-gave-2-billion-litres-of-water-back-to-indigenous-people-heres-what-that-means-for-the-rest-of-australia-150674>

Office, 'Kew / Ivanhoe', *Reimagining Birrarung: Design Concepts for 2070* (2024) <https://www.ngv.vic.gov.au/reimagining-birrarung-office/>

Openwork, 'Heidelberg / Templestowe', *Reimagining Birrarung: Design Concepts for 2070* (2024) <https://www.ngv.vic.gov.au/reimagining-birrarung-openwork/>

Outdoor Swimming Society, 'Right to Swim', *Outdoor Swimming Society* (2025) <https://www.outdoorswimmingsociety.com/category/right-to-swim/>

Pidd, Helen, 'The Right to Swim: Mass Trespass of Kinder Reservoir Planned', *The Guardian* (online, 23 April 2022) <https://www.theguardian.com/lifeandstyle/2022/apr/23/kinder-reservoir-mass-trespass-swimpass-peak-district-wild-swimmers>

Poelina, Anne, 'Declaration of Peace with Martuwarra Indigenous Peoples Our Lands and Living Waters' <https://www.search.org.au/declaration_of_peace_with_martuwarra_indigenous_peoples_our_lands_and_living_waters>

Poelina, Anne, Donna Bagnall and Michelle Lim, 'Recognizing the Martuwarra's First Law Right to Life as a Living Ancestral Being' (2020) 9(3) *Transnational Environmental Law* 541

REALMstudios, 'Abbotsford / Clifton Hill', *Reimagining Birrarung: Design Concepts for 2070* (2025) <https://www.ngv.vic.gov.au/reimagining-birrarung-realmstudios/>

Regen Melbourne, 'Swimmable Birrarung' (28 July 2024) <https://www.regen.melbourne/swimmable-birrarung>

RiverOfLife, Martuwarra et al, 'Recognizing the Martuwarra's First Law Right to Life as a Living Ancestral Being' (2020) 9(3) *Transnational Environmental Law* 541

RiverOfLife, Martuwarra et al, 'Yoongoorrookoo: The Emergence of Ancestral Personhood' (2021) 30(3) *Griffith Law Review* 505

RiverOfLife, Martuwarra, Katherine S. Taylor and Anne Poelina, 'Living Waters, Law First: Nyikina and Mangala Water Governance in the Kimberley, Western Australia' (2021) 25(1) *Australasian Journal of Water Resources* 40

RM Consulting Group Pty Ltd, *Birrarung Council Review* (Department of Energy, Environment and Climate Action, September 2023)

Salvidge, Rachel and Leana Hosea, '"Dirty Secret": Insiders Say UK Water Firms Knowingly Break Sewage Laws', *The Guardian* (online, 20 April 2024) <https://www.theguardian.com/environment/2024/apr/20/dirty-secret-insiders-say-uk-water-firms-knowingly-breaking-sewage-laws>

Shrubsole, Guy, *Who Owns England? How We Lost Our Land, and How to Take It Back* (Harper Collins, 2020)

SBLA, 'Yarra Valley / Launching Place', *Reimagining Birrarung: Design Concepts for 2070* (2024) <https://www.ngv.vic.gov.au/reimagining-birrarung-sbla/>

'Serpent's Tale Backs Fitzroy River Conservation', *Broome Advertiser* (25 March 2021) <https://www.broomead.com.au/news/broome-advertiser/new-kimberley-short-film-serpents-tale-hopes-to-inspire-fitzroy-river-conservation-push-ng-b881819458z>

Stallard, Esme, 'Government Has Broken the Law on Sewage, Says Watchdog', *BBC News* (17 December 2024) <https://www.bbc.com/news/articles/c4g38drwmrlo>

Swyngedouw, Erik, 'Globalisation or "Glocalisation"? Networks, Territories and Rescaling' (2004) 17(1) *Cambridge Review of International Affairs* 25

Tănăsescu, Mihnea, *Understanding the Rights of Nature: A Critical Introduction* (Transcript Publishing, 2022)

Taylor, Guy, 'Thames Water Allowed 35 per Cent Bill Hike but Faces £18m Fine over Dividend Payouts', *City AM* (19 December 2024) <https://www.cityam.com/thames-water-allowed-35-per-cent-bill-hike-but-faces-18m-fine-over-dividend-payouts/>

Tscheppe, Cornelia, 'River of Life: A Case Study' (2023) 7(1) *University of Vienna Law Review* 1

The Pew Charitable Trusts, 'Why Protecting Chilean Patagonia's Freshwater Is Crucial', *Pew* (9 January 2023) <https://pew.org/3Gc93Ik>

The Rivers Trust, 'Raw Sewage in Our Rivers', *The Rivers Trust* (2025) <https://theriverstrust.org/key-issues/sewage-in-rivers>

TLC, 'Yering / Yarra Glen', *Reimagining Birrarung: Design Concepts for 2070* (2024) <https://www.ngv.vic.gov.au/reimagining-birrarung-tcl/>

Torre, Giovanni, 'Bunuba National Park Creation a Key Step in Protecting Martuwarra Fitzroy River', *National Indigenous Times* (online, 23 August 2023) <https://nit.com.au/23-08-2023/7336/bunuba-national-park-creation-a-key-step-in-protecting-martuwarra-fitzroy-river>

Torre, Giovanni, 'Docuseries Tells Powerful Stories of Martuwarra/Fitzroy River', *National Indigenous Times* (online, 30 July 2021) <https://nit.com.au/30-07-2021/2200/docuseries-tells-powerful-stories-of-martuwarra-fitzroy-river>

Torre, Giovanni, 'Traditional Owners Welcome Commitment to Protect Martuwarra Fitzroy River from Large-Scale Irrigation', *National Indigenous Times* (online, 24 October 2023) <https://nit.com.au/24-10-2023/8300/traditional-owners-welcome-wa-governments-commitment-to-protect-martuwarra-fitzroy-river-from-large-scale-irrigation>

Universal Declaration of the Rights of Mother Earth (World People's Conference on Climate Change and the Rights of Mother Earth, 22 April 2010)

Victorian State Government, 'Aboriginal Water Program', *Water and Catchments* (22 November 2024) <https://www.water.vic.gov.au/our-programs/aboriginal-water-program>

Victorian State Government, 'Burndap Birrarung Burndap Umarkoo: Yarra Strategic Plan 2022-32' (Melbourne Water Corporation, February 2022)

Victorian State Government, 'Rivers of the Barwon / Barre Warre Yulluk Action Plan', *Water and Catchments* (16 February 2024) <https://www.water.vic.gov.au/waterways/rivers-of-the-barwon-barre-warre-yulluk-action-plan>

Victorian State Government, 'Waterways of the West', *Planning* (9 June 2023) <https://www.planning.vic.gov.au/guides-and-resources/strategies-and-initiatives/waterways-planning/waterways-of-the-west>

Wahlquist, Calla, 'Fitzroy River: The Push to Prevent a Repeat of the Murray-Darling Basin "Disaster"', *The Guardian* (online, 5 September 2020) <https://www.theguardian.com/australia-news/2020/sep/06/fitzroy-river-the-push-to-prevent-a-repeat-of-the-murray-darling-basin-disaster>

Ward-Brennan, Maria, 'Thames Water Creditors in Talks with Ofwat for Debt Rescue Plan', *City AM* (9 October 2024) <https://www.cityam.com/thames-water-creditors-in-talks-with-ofwat-for-debt-rescue-plan/>

Weber Salazar, Pía, Elizabeth Macpherson and Barbara A. Willaarts, 'Towards Durable Legal Protections for Rivers in Chile' (2024) 49(6) *Water International* 792

Western Australian Museum, 'The Martuwarra Fitzroy River: Lifeblood of the Kimberley' (24 September 2022) <https://visit.museum.wa.gov.au/maritime/the-fitzroy-river>

Wheeler v Director de la Procuraduria General de Estado de Loja (2011) Corte Provincial de Justicia de Loja 11121-2011-0010

Yarra River Protection (Wilip-Gin Birrarung Murron) Act 2017 (Vic)

Yarra Riverkeeper Association, 'Birrarung Riverfest 2024', *Birrarung Riverfest* (2024) <https://riverfest.com.au>

Yarra Riverkeeper Association, *Burndap Birrarung Burndap Umarkoo: A Review of the First Year of Implementation of the Yarra Strategic Plan* (Yarra Riverkeeper, 18 September 2023) <https://yarrariver.org.au/reports/>

INDEX

Note: Page numbers followed by "n" denote endnotes.

FSC
www.fsc.org
MIX
Papier | Fördert gute Waldnutzung
FSC® C083411

Kolibri 360 GmbH
Ferdinand-Jühlke-Straße 7
99095 Erfurt, Deutschland
produktsicherheit@kolibri360.de